ISBN: 978-1-7773486-1-8

Cover by Elderlemon Designs.

Artwork by Kirk Shannon.

THE MIRACLE SIN

MARCUS HAWKE

hawkehaus
BOOKS

For Suzanne, Mugsy, Pearl,
and Carol.

The Miracle Sin

Act I:
In Heaven and Earth

ONE

FATHER ABBOTT WAS A MAN OF GOD.

His earliest memory was of seeing the crucifix above the altar during First Communion when he was seven years old. He knew even then that he wanted to be ordained. To serve the Lord. When the priest placed the wafer on his tongue and said the blessing, he felt an overwhelming calm. Peace. He knew in his heart that his life belonged to Him.

But now, more than sixty years later, as precious drops of his blood dripped away on the filthy floor, Father Abbott desperately wondered where He was.

Bitter pain coursed through his whole body. His wavy gray hair clung to the sides of his unshaven face with sweat. Several of his teeth were loose and where others had been were now raw, bloody gaps. Though his hands were bound behind the back of his chair so tight that they had lost feeling, he was sure a finger was missing. Perhaps two. With each labored breath his broken ribs stung; with each breath he silently prayed for death. The flesh around his left eye had swollen to the size of a fist. All he could see through it was a narrow slit of light.

1

Through that narrow slit, a silhouette appeared.

"Do you think me evil?" Even with his shallow pulse thundering in his ears, the serpentine tickle of the words sickened him.

"Yes," Abbott said weakly.

The creature smiled. "Good."

"You didn't have to do all this."

A shrug. "Where's the fun in that?"

The muted creak of a door as it opened, then a slam as it shut. Beyond the flickering halo of light cast by the lone brown bulb dangling from the ceiling, another figure entered the room. He could make out only the faintest of details—a woman, no doubt, judging by the clicking of high heels; long, frizzed hair nearly white around a blanched face with large, dark-purple shades obscuring the eyes.

"Has he said anything?" she asked, and took a seat in the corner, crossing one stockinged leg over the other. She giggled wickedly to herself.

The slightest of nods. "He has said *everything*."

"Are you going to kill me now?" Father Abbott half asked, half pleaded.

The fiend considered him a moment, moved in close so that the shadows became a face. Skin bone-tight against the cheeks, wild hair the color of rust, and eyes that glinted like those of an animal in the night.

"I am."

"Thank you," Abbott choked with what he could muster of his voice.

"But before I do," he said, and crouched down near the priest, "let me tell you two things. Thing the First: tonight you've provided us with information most valuable. So thanks all around are in order."

Father Abbott spat blood in his face.

His captor didn't seem to mind. Just the opposite. Smearing it down the slope of his nose until the tips of his fingers reached the end, dangling a drop of brilliant red for a moment before it fell and touched his tongue.

The creature got nearer to him, face to face, and smiled. The breath emanating from behind his pointed teeth, hot and foul as the depths of Hell, made Father Abbott's stomach turn. And the eyes, those horrible hollow eyes . . . no soul shone behind them.

"And Thing the Second, believe it or not, is good news for you, holy man." He licked the priest's forehead, lapping up the thick drops of sweat that gathered there, and looked him in the eyes again. "If you really are a man of faith, if you truly believe in a just and merciful god"—the creature took three slow steps back from the chair—"you are about to meet him."

Father Abbott's face sank. His impending demise was so real he could taste it. And with his last ounce of breath, he whispered, "Forgive me."

A colorless hand curled into a hook directed at Father Abbott's chest. An unbelievable bloom of heat swelled beneath the ribs until his heart itself burned with the intensity of a hot coal.

A quick twist and the priest's chest burst open with a spray of blood and bone. He didn't even have time to scream before seeing his own heart practically leap from his torso.

His head dropped forward, dead as Bela Lugosi.

"Mmm . . ." The only sound as the red-haired one towered over his corpse and fed on his heart.

TWO

Mason Cole couldn't sleep.

There was a dream, the same one he always had—the earth erupts and he falls into a bottomless pit with nothing but frightened screams for company. For more than an hour after he lay staring at the fading shadows on his ceiling, reading by the light of the single lamp he kept on at night. It did no good. He left his bed to wander.

It was a small house on Mill Creek Road, the only one on top of the hill overlooking the town. Decorated with doilies and Royal Doulton figurines gracing the shelves of the living room along with an old Stack-O-Matic record player, a vintage sewing machine, and a few other antiques. If one were to look closer, however, they'd see that the figurines had been broken and glued back together many times. Instead of the big band music of Glenn Miller or Benny Goodman one might expect a little old lady to have, the records were those of Led Zeppelin, Pink Floyd, and Bob Marley. By the sewing machine sat a wicker bowl of what looked like finger puppets but were really a collection of tiny yarn penises, all with different faces.

The house was full of cats, only one of which, a white Persian named Bossy, was actually alive. All the rest sat stuffed and mounted in various poses on the windowsills and bookshelves; in the one and only bathroom a cute little Calico guarded the toilet brush.

From the patterned wallpaper to the Formica countertops, everything about the kitchen looked like a time capsule of the 1960s. The mismatched chairs placed around the kitchen table, however, did not fit with the room, nor with each other. The only television set, a Montgomery Ward monolith of wood and glass, sat next to the record player. Seldom used, though its picture came through nice and clear with eleven channels of static and one for reruns of *M*A*S*H* and *The Golden Girls* on the oldies station.

Unusual by most standards, but to Mason it was home.

A modest-looking boy of eighteen, his shaggy brown hair hung at the sides of his face. Narrow chin. Blue eyes. Slight of build, except for just a touch of extra stuffing around the midsection from a steady diet of slurpies and burritos. A "fish belly," Rose called it, though he didn't understand why. Most people acquire a tan in the summer months, but he remained fair, almost pasty. He looked at everything with an undercurrent of curiosity, some observation or another poised on the tip of his tongue . . . and then it was gone. And so was he, lost to wistful thoughts.

The sun had not yet broken the horizon, but its pink pre-glow peeked through the leaves of a nearby maple tree in the backyard like a puzzle missing pieces. He loved the way the sky looked at first light. Cresting the canopy of darkened trees, a lone ember appeared in the bed of soft ashes that were the clouds, giving birth to a new day. From the hills at the east corner of town it was particularly amazing to see life breathed back into the world again. Heavenly rays of golden orange shot across the sky and for one moment everything was pure. Every beam of warm sun, every breath of freshly cut grass, a godsend in these last few days of summer.

Mason stood on the back porch, looking to the east, thinking about how different this year had been. True that each one came and went with a certain finality to it, but while his peers would be going off to college or university, he would remain. Like the certificate he had received in freshman year for making the Honor Roll, still stuck to the fridge door, he wasn't going anywhere.

Everyone else had a plan but him. Dale had a plan, even if it was a simple one. Julie had a plan, and at the thought of this a knot tied itself in his stomach. He didn't want to think about that, though, not now in these last few precious moments.

He went to the liquor cabinet above the kitchen stove to sneak a swig of gin. It heated him up from lungs to loins.

He took another swig.

And then another.

And another.

The first of September was this coming Tuesday, which meant just one more weekend and a day until the new school year began. The last one. Already autumn was daring to show its face. Evening shadows appeared earlier and earlier. Soon it would all be a memory, another summer gone before a long winter. Sprinklers taken off the lawns, chalk drawings on the sidewalks wiped away and covered by snow.

The time on the clock above the kitchen doorway said it was nearly 5:30, meaning Rose would be up soon. He had work in a few hours, and while looking like a zombie probably wouldn't matter much at his job, he figured it best to at least try and get back to sleep.

What a funny saying, he thought to himself, tip-toeing as quietly as possible down the basement's darkened stairs to his room. *"Back to sleep." As if it were the starting point. I suppose, in many ways, it is.*

The house was old and often whined like a rusty fence, but he knew every creak and groan in the place. Every loose step, every squeaky floorboard.

Flopping into bed, he took a swig of mouthwash from a bottle he kept beneath just in case. He grabbed a book, slid a bookmark from between its pages, and was instantly wandering the torchlit corridors of Elsinore Castle. But not for long. Only a few minutes passed before his eyelids grew heavy. His book fell open onto his chest, and when his head yielded to the pillow, he was welcomed instantly by a thankfully dreamless sleep.

When Mason awoke next, it was to the smell of breakfast and the sound of Rose singing to her flowers. The single window in his bedroom was open just enough for him to hear her humming some nameless tune to the bed of daffodils next to it. She must have been blocking the sun because, with a single movement, a blinding blade of light cut through his room, falling upon his lonely guitar that leaned in one corner, gathering dust.

Mason groaned and pulled the covers over his face. But it wasn't enough to block the savory scent of bacon wafting down from the kitchen.

He rolled out of bed wearing only a pair of flannel pajama pants, threw on whichever T-shirt he happened to gather up from the floor, and grabbed his book from beneath the still-lit lamp, which he turned off before leaving his room.

As he climbed the stairs, the sharp guitar notes and soft choral backing of The Beatles' "Across the Universe" reached him, coming from the record player in the den.

Upon entering the kitchen, Mason found a small feast prepared on the table. Scrambled eggs, bacon, grits, brown toast, a glass of orange juice, and a cup of coffee still steaming as if it had been poured moments ago. Milk and sugar in the center. Quite the spread considering he had done nothing to deserve it. At least he didn't think so. Clearly Rose disagreed.

Around the table were the four mismatched chairs: a lawn chair close to the counter, a large beanbag chair by the window, a tattered Barcalounger clockwise from the window, and a rocking chair where Mason's meal had been set.

He was just sitting down at the table, placing his book in front of him, when the back door opened and shut with a loud clatter. With his first sip of juice, Rose appeared in the kitchen.

Despite her seventy years, wrinkles were remiss to show themselves on a face as cheery as hers. Mouth, cheeks, and bright green
eyes—she smiled with all of it. Her silver hair hung in loose curls
down her shoulders and draped over a flowery wool shawl to fend off
the morning chill. She brought with her the fresh scent of morning
dew. In one hand, a tin watering can; in the other, a wicker basket of
various herbs and leaves, a pair of pinking shears resting gently
on top.

"Good morning, starshine." Her soft crooning of lyrics from *Hair*
synced up surprisingly well with John Lennon's voice considering he
sung different words.

"Morning, Rose," Mason answered with a yawn, and started
to eat.

As she entered the kitchen, Mason saw that her feet were caked
in a thick layer of rich, damp soil, as they usually were when tending
to her garden. Every step left black footprints behind her on her way
to the sink.

"Look! I made your favorite," said Rose, pointing at the table as if
he had missed it somehow.

"I see that," said Mason appreciatively. "Thanks."

She winked and carefully poured what little water was left in her
watering can into the pot of her prized African violet on the window
sill.

"Oh and look, I found a daffodil that looks like Abraham
Lincoln."

Mason's fork dangled in front of his mouth as she stuck the
yellow flower in front of his face, clasped between her thumb and
forefinger.

"Oh . . . yeah," he said without a clue in world what she was
talking about. "Totally Lincoln."

Rose's expression changed to one of quiet skepticism. "What's
wrong, sugar?" A slight Southern bend in her words.

"Nothing," Mason said as he stuffed half a sausage in his mouth.

She narrowed her eyes at him.

"What?"

Rose left the watering can in the sink and sat down in the lawn chair next to Mason. She thrust out her left hand, the earthy smell of freshly cut sage and St. John's wort along with it. "Gimme."

"Aw, c'mon," he said with his mouth full, "I'm eating."

"Choose it or lose it, boy," she said, making a chopping motion with her hand.

Mason sighed and let go of his fork so that it hit the plate with a clang. Reluctantly he held his hand out, palm up.

Rose caressed it gently with her fingertips, then gazed deeply into the intricate contours and crevasses of his inner hand as if she were looking through a kaleidoscope. "Hmm . . . I see a trip . . . a guest . . . and a—"

The phone rang.

"Saved by the bell." Rose got up from the table and disappeared down the hall.

As he resumed eating his breakfast, Mason suddenly became aware of the fact that he was being watched. Two wide blue eyes hovered just above the tabletop. Bossy arched, put one paw up on the table, then the other.

"Nope," he scolded, pointing at her. "Don't even think about it. If she finds you on the table . . ."

"Mrrrow?" She inched closer, twitching her pink little nose toward his plate.

Mason took a quick peek down the hall before breaking off the smallest corner from a strip of bacon. Bossy licked it up the moment it was placed in front of her before she could be discovered.

Too late.

"Aha, busted!" said Rose, returning to the kitchen.

Bossy immediately sprang down to the floor.

"Dammit!" Mason groaned.

"For that you have to mow the lawn when you get home."

"I'm going out with Julie and Dale later."

"When?"

"Five."

"That's plenty of time."

"Fine," Mason conceded. "Who was it?"

"Oh, just Missus Papanikolas confirming her appointment for this afternoon. She's such a worrywart."

He finished and took his plate to the sink.

Bossy was licking the last remaining taste off her whiskers.

He smirked. "Hope you enjoyed that."

After a quick shower and a proper change of clothes, Mason left for work.

It was a beautiful day. The sun shone bright and brilliant. As soon as he stepped outside, the air was fresh with the smell of wild-flowers from the garden and leaves from the tall maple in the back-yard. Birds chirped a melodious tune to each other from tree to tree. A light gloss of dew remained on the grass and pavement, telling him that there must have been a drizzle while he slept. Now there wasn't a cloud in the sky.

Tossing his book into the passenger's seat, Mason got in his truck, a cankerous rust-bucket the color of phlegm, and twisted the key in the ignition. The engine awoke with a loud snore. The muffler coughed black smoke as the truck pulled out of the driveway and gunned down the hill toward town.

On a nice day like this, Mason expected the town to be bustling with people. As bustling as it got in Stonehill, Ohio, anyway. At first glance, it was like any other small town. And it would have remained so after a second, third, and fourth glance as well. Some might even have called it quaint, without feeling remote or cut off from the rest of the world. Small farms surrounded the town—corn mostly, with a few cattle farms to the east. There were church bake sales in the spring, water balloon fights in the summer, food drives in the fall for Thanks-giving, and carolers at Christmas. It was the type of place where people sat on their front porches in the late evening sun sipping iced tea and said hello to familiar faces as they passed by.

He passed the high school and turned onto Main Street. Cars and minivans drove up and down the town's main artery. Parents walked along the sidewalk carrying plastic bags of last-minute school supplies, their children in tow behind them as they lapped up the melting sides of their ice cream cones.

The light turned red at the intersection in the center of town. Most people seemed to be congregating in Town Square between the sheriff's office and St. John Lutheran Church. A few had their noses stuck in either books or cell phones (more the latter than the former). On the grass near the creek couples walked their dogs, throwing balls or sticks for them to blissfully chase after. Others simply sat on the benches around the stone fountain, sunglasses shading their eyes as they enjoyed the day.

The light turned green and Mason moved his foot from the brake pedal to the gas.

Only it didn't move. Its sputtering ceased and the boisterous engine fell silent.

"Oh, *come on*," said Mason. "Not again!"

He turned the key.

"Come on, don't do this now."

The car behind him honked.

"Great." It wouldn't be long before every other asshole started.

He turned the key again, squeezing a shrill wheeze from the ignition.

Sure enough, the car behind him was joined by every other, each one sounding their horns in a cacophony all around him. Heads turned his way from passersby on the sidewalks and from the shop windows.

Mason reached his left hand out the window, wanting so badly to throw a middle finger up into the air for all to see, but instead waving them forward to go around before the light turned red again.

"Get that thing out of the road, Jew Boy!" shouted the driver of a much newer truck as he passed.

Mason knew exactly who it was, even before he saw the plate which read E-ROCK as it sped away. His grip tightened on the wheel until his knuckles turned white.

With little choice, he let go of the key and sat back in his seat. What he wouldn't have given right then to be anywhere else. Anywhere at all, as long as it wasn't here.

"Come on, you piece of junk," said Mason, turning the key gingerly this time. It coughed back to life with a burst of thick smoke in his rearview. "Finally!"

When the light turned green again, Mason steered the truck up Main Street and down the main drag of downtown Stonehill. It consisted of about twenty storefronts on either side, topped with the single tall white spire of the church. Mason thought it looked like a dunce cap over a strip mall.

Gus's Gas & Garage was at the southern end of town near Route 422. Mason saw the red-and-white lettering on the sign out front as he pulled up and parked near the gas pumps. The sound of a radio came from the garage, and Mason spied legs stuck under the front of an old Dodge.

"Hey, Gus," Mason called out.

A man slid out from under the bottom of the car. Grease stains all over his face and coveralls and a faded red cap plastered to his balding head. A pair of eyes distorted by glasses as thick as ashtrays peeked out at him. "Oh hi, Mason."

"How's it going?"

"Can't complain."

"Is Dale here yet?"

"Nope, Dale's off today," said Gus, wiping the sweat from his forehead with a rag. "Didn't he tell you?"

"Oh . . . yeah, he did, actually. Sorry, I must've forgot." *Damn!* he thought. *I wanted to talk to him about tonight.* "Well, I'll be inside if you need me."

"Sounds good. Say, how's the truck running?"

"Oh, just great. Thanks again for fixing her."

"I still say you should have waited to buy my old truck. She's got a good two hundred thou' left in her."

"Next time."

"I'll hold you to that," said Gus, and slid back under the car. Mason was walking away when he heard the board roll back out. "Oh, would you mind giving the back room a sweep when you have a minute?"

"Sure thing."

"You know where the broom is, right?"

"Sure do."

"Thanks." And he disappeared under the car again.

Mason entered the store and made his way down the aisle of pop and snacks, past the magazines, and sat himself behind the counter. The old familiar sound of Country 104.5 played on the radio. One time he tried switching the dial to ROCK-FM, but that didn't fly with Gus. He replaced it with the opening lyrics of Metallica's "Welcome Home (Sanitarium)" for this truly was where time stood still.

Within minutes Mason's gaze became glued to the road outside— a road which led far away from here for everyone but him—broken only by the occasional fleeting glimpse of a passing car.

There were no customers this early in the day and the back room could wait. His gaze wandered to the rack of magazines, drifting higher until it landed on the brightly colored plastic packaging of the top shelf. The hot pink lettering of the triple Xs across the likes of *Hustler, Escort,* and *Juggs* caught his eye. He could just see the tops of dolled-up faces, sultry eyes beckoning him closer.

Hey, big boy, come on over and pick me up . . . if you can.

"Tempting, but better not. Knowing my luck, that's just when a customer will walk in."

If you say so. I got all day and nowhere to be.

"Yeah, that makes two of us."

At this point, anything that shook things up a little would be a welcome break from the norm, but he didn't need any trouble. Not today.

Mason took out his phone, clicked on Julie's number, and tapped away at the letters beneath his thumbs.

Hey. Are we still on for tonight?

He knew the answer perfectly well but asked anyway. *Come on, baby, show me those dancing dots. Just once, just this once, let her respond right away instead of an hour later.*

Ten minutes passed. Ten became thirty, and thirty became forty-five. Still no response.

Fifty-nine minutes later, his phone pinged. Mason drew it from his pocket with the speed and dexterity of a veteran gunslinger.

Yup!

Not quite the lengthy response he had hoped for—it never was—but there was enough in that single word to breathe relief into him.

He typed back without a second thought.

Cool.

Is that all? Should I say something else? I should say something else . . . shouldn't I?

But before he could think of what that might be, those three little dots began to dance again.

· · ·

What R U up to?

Yes! Okay, what do I write back? How about the truth, that you're at work? His thumbs hit the *W, O,* and *R* keys and then stopped. *Nah, too boring. Something clever and a little funny. Not side-splitting, just enough to make her smile.*

Drooling on myself.

Okay . . . okay, it's the truth but with a spin.

WUT??

Oh god, she didn't get it. Of course she didn't get it.
    The woman from the magazine piped up. *And do you really want to put that image in her head, big boy? Just keep it simple.*

Working.

Yeah, that's better. I hope.

Oh gotcha! LOL :D

There we go. And with a smiley, too. Nice. Okay, that's the high note, just sign off and leave it.

. . .

Anyway. Better get back to it. See you tonight @ 5.

He hit the Send key with satisfaction.

K bye.

Hmm . . . a bit chilly. Was it because I reminded her of the time? Will she think that I think she's always late? I mean, she is always late, but I didn't mean it that way. Or does that mean she wanted to talk more? When he read what he wrote, it did kind of sound like he was blowing her off. *But that's not what I meant! She's got to know that, right? Oh god . . . or could it just mean "K bye"? It's possible that you could be reading too much into things.*

The bell above the door chimed.

Marcy Burgess, the pastor's wife. One of the many faithful in town who were not big fans of Rose or her "heathen fortune-telling." Nor of Mason, for that matter, just for being who he was. Blessedly thin, she moved like a gazelle on a mission, her hairdo bobbing just above the shoulders as she neared. Too many teeth filled her mouth, so much that even her pursed lips could not hide them. Her eyes hid behind a pair of dark sunglasses. Despite the heat, she wore a wool cardigan and a string of pearls that peeked from beneath the collar of her starched shirt. One arm crooked out in front of her, letting her handbag dangle. She slung it forward, placed it down on the counter.

"Pack of Virginia Slims."

Odd. She didn't smoke. At least, he didn't think so. Mason found her brand below the counter while she rummaged through her bag.

"That'll be nine-fifty."

Marcy took a ten-dollar bill from her wallet and held it out, head down, gingerly adjusting her sunglasses. She normally didn't pay him much mind, but when she did it was with an air of righteous superiority behind the wheel of her Lexus, talking loudly on her phone about some country club function or Senator Whoever-the-Hell visiting the church while he pumped her gas. Today she was quiet, almost diminished.

Mason took the money from her and she took the cigarettes from the counter. And without even waiting for her change, she left. Leaving Mason to wonder just what he might see behind the lenses of those sunglasses.

Still here, stud, said the blonde cover girl after thirty minutes of watching the road. *I've got four and a half minutes to spare if you do.*

His mind wandered, and whenever his mind wandered, instead of being blissfully lost in a tranquil sea of nothingness, it stumbled upon buried thoughts that had drifted to the surface.

Tonight was kind of a big deal. A last kick at the can before the school year started, and then Julie went away to college and he went . . . well . . . nowhere. Dale wasn't leaving either, but at least he was moving up.

Mason thought about what he had to do and lead butterflies began ceaselessly fluttering around his chest.

He started working at Gus's Gas & Garage at the beginning of the summer. Dale had got him the job after he started working in the garage for his old man. It was okay. Mason wasn't crazy about waiting on people, but Gus pretty much left him alone unless he needed the floor swept or the garbage taken out. Plus, it gave him time to read, so how bad could it be?

Could be worse.

Mason got A's in pretty much everything except gym, which he hated thanks largely to the jocks and their insistence on making him feel as awkward as possible. Here were a group of guys who greeted each other with a slap on the ass and waved their peckers at each other in the showers, but still called him a fag and said he looked like a girl because of his long hair.

Sure. Whatever.

His truck had to have been twenty years old, probably more. If kept in good shape, a vehicle's age shouldn't matter. This was not the case with Patches, so named by Dale due to the body so badly rusted it looked like lesions on a plague victim. The gearshift stuck, the transmission was ancient, and every time he started it up it coughed a hideous black cloud that would rob the breath from a chain-smoker. Though none of that bothered him as much as why he bought it in the first place; the very thought of it caused him to shake his head in disbelief.

He had been saving since he started working his sophomore year, the idea being to put enough aside for college. Then Julie got accepted to the University of Ohio. And that's when it struck him— sooner or later, she would be gone. Actually gone. Of course, they would still see each other. At first. Then it would just be at holidays. She would make new friends at school, and sooner or later there would be a boyfriend in the picture, and he would become some guy she knew back home and she'd be "too busy" to return his calls.

"So I panicked," said Mason to the empty store.

Rose had homeschooled him before finally enrolling him in regular classes after it became clear that she couldn't teach both him and the kids she tutored if they wanted to make ends meet. As a result, Mason was a full year older than Julie; she'd often bugged him about not having a car.

Easy to do when your parents buy you one.

Just a little harmless ribbing between friends. But to him it meant so much more.

A momentary lapse in judgment that led to a bad choice. A stupid choice! A choice that left me $1,500 in the hole, got Rose pissed at me, and delayed going to college by at least another year.

And how did Julie respond? She laughed. She actually laughed.

And I thought it would impress her.

"Idiot," he said.

I mean, it's not like nothing *has ever happened between us. There must have been some reason for it. So what if we were drunk? So what if we haven't talked about it since? So what if there were rumors about her giving head to Eric Riley in the boy's locker room that make me sick just to think about? Ridiculous . . . right?*

All he knew for sure was that one way or another, it was time to tell her how he felt. Now or never. Until then, he was confined to his role at Gus's Gas & Garage among the rest of the corn-fed, cow-tipping population of this town-sized rest stop for people just passing through on their way to somewhere bigger and better.

But again, it could have been worse.

Way worse.

THREE

WAS THAT GOOD FOR YOU?

"You know it," said Mason, washing his hands before emerging from the staff washroom at the back just under four minutes after he went in. A new record. He discreetly returned the copy of *Busty Blondes* to its place on the top rack.

It had been nearly impossible to focus on his book with the radio playing right next to him. Most of the time he could tune it out, but somewhere between "It's Alright to Be a Redneck" and news of the Massachusetts Mangler being moved to St. Jude's Hospital for the Criminally Insane, he wound up reading the same page over and over. Something had to give.

"Same time tomorrow?"

It's a date.

He had just started to read again when Mason spotted a car pulling up to the pumps. He rose from behind the cash register, using his finger as a bookmark, and went out to take care of the customer.

The air hit him like a blast of heat from an oven. It had grown even warmer since he'd arrived. As he approached the car, a clean, almost-polished Buick, he saw the man sitting behind the wheel. Dressed in an ash-gray suit over a black turtleneck, his face was strong and clever as he read from a map, tracing a path with his finger through the network of interstates. A thin pair of square spectacles sat atop his wide nose. Skin a rich brown, graying hair neatly cropped. A goatee and mustache salt-and-peppered his chin and upper lip.

He rolled down his window as Mason came around the front of the car.

"Fill 'er up?" Mason asked.

"Please," the man replied in a deep, pleasant British voice.

Clearly not from around here—but neither were most people who stopped in Stonehill. Mason unhooked the gas nozzle and stuck it in the tank.

"What are you reading?" he asked, pointing at the book Mason still held in his hand.

He turned it over, displaying the cover.

"Ah. 'To be, or not to be,' " the man recited.

Mason nodded and punctuated the air with his index finger. " 'That *is* the question.' "

"Do you like it so far?"

"Oh, I've read it before. So I guess I must."

"You don't say," said the man, his face brightening. "I don't see many young people reading Shakespeare nowadays."

"A shame. I can't get enough."

"That's brilliant."

How civilized. Most people in town didn't usually like to talk about anything other than the Browns game or whatever rumors and rumblings were going around like a bad cold. Even his friends didn't appreciate the written word like he did.

"Like to read, do you?"

Mason nodded. "Very much."

The man leaned over and reached into the glove compartment.

"Have you ever read this?" he asked as he held up a book bound in black leather with a silver cross etched into the middle of the cover, its arms flared out and pointed at each end.

Oh, brother.

"I'm familiar with it," said Mason dryly, and went back to his book, willing the gas tank to hurry up and fill. The tips of his fingers reached up and briefly touched the little weight against his sternum.

"Marvelous, isn't it?"

"Oh yeah . . . it's great." His eyes didn't leave the page. *Man, and this started out so well. Just play nice for now.*

"Have you accepted Christ as your Lord and Savior?"

Mason sighed. "What do you want to hear?"

"I'm sure the truth will suffice."

"The truth is that I don't need a savior, thank you very much."

"Maybe not now, but one day you may change your mind."

"Doubtful."

"And why's that?"

So it's a tug of wits you want? Alrighty then. Mason placed his bookmark between the pages, closed it, and faced him. "Because I don't see what good a collection of old myths and legends could make in my life."

"I find that hard to believe coming from an admirer of the Bard."

"I find it hard to believe that grown adults can be so convinced that their imaginary friend is real and wants them to tell everyone else how great he is, but here we are."

"Oh, but there is more to it than that."

He scoffed. "Like?"

"Knowledge."

"You're kidding, right?"

"Not at all. About life, the world . . . yourself."

"Why is it that every Bible-thumper I've ever met thinks I need to learn something about myself?"

"That's a good question. Do you?"

The gas nozzle clicked. Mason silently shook his head and went to hang it back on the pump. "That's twenty-five even." He spoke calmly now. The man kept his gaze fixed on Mason a moment before producing two crisp, barely folded bills from his wallet. Mason took the cash and issued a cheery "Have a nice day."

The man held the book out the window at him. "Consider it a gift."

Figuring it was the quickest way to end this, Mason took the book from him.

"True knowledge is to know the extent of one's ignorance," the man said serenely.

"Big words coming from a Bible salesman."

"They are those of a shepherd who became a teacher, to cast light through the darkness for all mankind."

"And, let's see, what comes next? The Lord works in mysterious ways?" Mason said with a feigned smile.

The man smiled back. "Amen to that."

The car rolled away from the gas station, brake lights flaring red as it slowed at the intersection and then disappeared down the road toward Route 422.

So much for playing nice.

Mason tucked his book under his arm and stared at the cover of the Bible, tracing the silver lines in the soft leather with his thumb. His fingers dipped beneath the collar of his shirt and found another one just like it, dangling from a thin chain around his neck. It even had the same hole in the middle. Only his was old and tarnished.

He swooned. For a moment his stomach churned as if the ground had dropped beneath him, could almost hear terrified prayers, the earth roaring, and screams as people ran for their lives.

He shook it off and tossed the Bible in the garbage before heading back inside.

FOUR

THE AFTERNOON WENT PRETTY MUCH AS EXPECTED. PEOPLE came in, people left; he pumped their gas and swept the back room. It was twenty to four when Gus asked what Mason would say to closing early. He agreed and left so fast that he almost left a cloud of dust in his wake.

The house was empty when he arrived home. It would still be a little while before his friends were due, so he went to the refrigerator, grabbed a Dr Pepper, and cracked it open, letting the cold fizz slip down his throat. It didn't quite hit the spot like a cold beer, but it did the trick.

Through the kitchen window he saw Rose digging away in the garden, happily plucking weeds, a straw sunhat keeping the sun off her face. She stood and turned around, a dirty spade in one gloved hand, and jumped when she saw him.

"Didn't hear you come in," said Rose as she glanced at her wristwatch. "You're home early."

"That's because I left early. Gus's idea."

"Great. You've got time to mow the lawn then."

Mason palmed his face. He came around to the back door and poked his head out. "Can I do it tomorrow?"

"Nuh-uh," said Rose, brandishing the spade. "You've been putting it off all week and it's starting to look like the Amazon out here."

"Exaggerating much? Besides, Julie and Dale will be here soon."

"Then you'd better hurry."

"Bah!"

" 'Bah' nothin', boy. Get to it."

Bossy sat by her dish, staring at him with round, sapphire eyes. If she were capable of it, he would have thought she was grinning like the Cheshire Cat.

"Smart-ass." He drained the rest of his soda and made for the shed.

Once he had finished both the front and back yards, Mason put the mower back in the shed and found Rose resting at the picnic table under the maple tree. Eyes shut, feet up, a glass of chardonnay by her hand, and a cigarette dangling from her lips—or what he thought was a cigarette at first, but smelled like that of the greener variety.

He still hadn't heard a word from his friends. They definitely should have arrived by now. Knowing Rose how he did, a fingernail of wine left in the sweating glass and spliff nearly gone, she would be feeling good and silly by now.

Right on cue, she began to sing: "Ground control to Major Tom . . ."

Mason whipped out his phone and began rapidly pressing the buttons as he walked around the house. The message was one simple word: HELP!

No sooner had he pressed the Send button, than the sound of a car could be heard coming up the road. A red Corolla that Mason instantly recognized pulled into the driveway, tires scraping the pavement as it came to a halt.

The driver's-side door opened and out came Mason's best friend, Julie Walsh.

A pretty young thing with a round, almost cherubic face. The sun danced across her ponytail, making it look more blond than brown as it bounced with each step. She wore a simple tank top, jeans, and a new pair of flip-flops. Each purple fingernail glistened in the sunlight beneath a silver charm bracelet as she approached, nervously jingling her keys as she tried to look cute and innocent.

She was followed closely by their friend Dale. A chubby fellow who, despite the heat, wore a black shirt patterned with skulls, a trucker cap, and his usual thick-rimmed glasses.

"Have trouble finding the place?" Mason asked with a sarcastic smile.

"Sorry," said Julie. "We had a little delay."

The three of them began walking toward the backyard.

"A delay?"

Dale snorted. "She took half an hour to get ready, then forgot her purse, then her makeup, then her tamp—"

"*Aaanyway,*" Julie interrupted before he could finish the thought. "On the way here I was going just a little too fast and got a ticket."

"Another one?" said Mason.

"It's nothing."

"That's three this month."

"Shut up."

"Better than your two last month, but still . . ."

"I said *shut up.*"

"Daddy's going to be mad."

"Zip it."

"Mad, mad, mad."

"Shush!" Julie shot a finger up like a purple-tipped dagger.

It was enough to rouse Rose from her stupor with a start. She straightened up and opened her eyes wide. "Well, if it isn't Thing One and Thing Two."

"Would that make Mason the Cat in the Hat?" asked Dale.

Rose shook her head. "Haw! If anyone's the Cat, it's me. Mason's the goldfish."

Mason put on his best Southern drawl to match hers, which showed more when she was like this. "I ain't no goldfish, woman."

"Who're you callin' 'woman,' *boy*?" Rose stood from the picnic table. "I'll slap the taste outta yer mouth."

Mason smirked. "How would I taste *yer* cookin'?"

"Last thing ya need to worry about when yer eatin' through a straw."

"I love you, Rose," said Julie, who put her arm around the older woman and gave her a peck on the cheek.

"Can I interest anyone in some homemade lemonade? Ooh, that rhymes. Sorta."

Mason was about to protest, but it was too late.

"Hell yeah," spoke Dale first, thin beads of sweat forming on his brow. "I mean, yes please."

"And I think I'll just use the bathroom before we get on the road," said Julie.

"On the road?" asked Rose, the slightest catch in her throat.

"Yeah. I mean, no. We're not running for the border, or anything."

"Course not," said Rose. "You'd never leave li'l ol' me, wouldja?"

Mason smirked. "Pretty sure you'd find me somehow."

"Dang right I would."

Mason led the way inside, followed by Rose, for whom he opened and held the door. Upon entering the kitchen, they were met by Bossy waiting for someone to fill up her bowl.

"I'll just be a minute," said Julie, and headed toward the bathroom.

"Yeah, right," Mason sniggered in a stage whisper.

"What was that?" said Julie from down the hall.

"Nothing," the two boys answered in unison, holding back full-blown laughter until they heard the bathroom door close.

"How's it going, dude?" said Dale with a slap on the back.

"Not bad. You?"

"Not bad. How was work?"

"Eh. You know. Same shit, different day."

"Yup."

They sat down at the table. Dale removed his hat to dab away the sweat as Rose set his drink down on the table in front of him.

"Thankya kindly."

"Don't mention it."

Rose set the pitcher in the center of the table, along with half of a pound cake on a platter, and took a seat in the lawn chair. "So, Mister Dale, how's work at the garage?"

Dale was in mid-gulp and drained his glass to the last drop. "So far, so good. Technically I'm just an apprentice for now. It'll be a while before I'm doing work on my own."

"Sounds tough."

"Oh, I love working on cars. I'll take tune-ups over my *brother's* career path any day."

"Which is?"

"The army."

"I see . . . said the blind man."

"Yeah, something about waking up at the ass-crack of dawn to be yelled at by a drill sergeant just doesn't appeal to me."

"Nor should it." Rose leaned back in her chair, sagely stroking her chin.

Julie returned from the bathroom, stuffing an assortment of things back into her purse. She flicked at something on the back of Mason's shirt. "You're wearing your shirt inside out."

Mason pulled the back of his collar to his shoulder, where he could just make it out, and sure enough, what she had flicked was the tag. "Oh, for god's sake."

"That wasn't on purpose?" Rose asked.

"You saw it? Why didn't you say anything?"

"I thought you meant to."

"Why on earth would I mean to?"

"I dunno what you kids do nowadays."

Mason felt an expression that could only be described as a squint of bewilderment overtake his face.

Rose continued. "And what about you, toots? Ready for college?"

"Oh, well . . ." Julie gave a coy bat of her eyelashes as she cut herself a modest sliver of pound cake. "It'll take some getting used to, but I'm sure I'll manage."

"Must've cost your folks a pretty penny."

"Actually, I wound up getting a scholarship."

"Well, I'll be a frog's fat ass. Bravo!" Rose congratulated her.

"Thank you," Julie said proudly.

Mason shot a narrow look at her. No one seemed to notice, not even Dale, who was refilling his glass.

"What are you studying?"

"Physical ther—" She stalled with a half-chewed mouthful of cake. "—apy." She finally caught Mason's confused glance. "What?"

"You didn't tell me you got a scholarship."

"Yes, I did."

"Nope."

"I must have"

"'Fraid not."

"Oh," she said, brushing a strand of hair from her face and tucking it behind her ear. "Oops!"

Awkwardness hung in the air like a bad smell. Mason remained silent, all but sure he knew why this little tidbit had slipped her mind. And he sure as hell wasn't going to bring it up in front of Rose.

There was a knock at the door.

"That'll be Missus Papanikolas," said Rose, hauling herself out of her seat and heading for the door.

"What's Missus Papanikolas doing here?" asked Julie curiously.

"Rose reads Tarot for her. Anyway, you guys ready to go?" said Mason, nodding insistently.

Dale had polished off the last of his drink, and said, "Ready, Eddie."

The three of them said their farewells to both Rose and Mrs. Papanikolas, who had brought her Pomeranian, Peanut, with her.

"Shouldn't you take a jacket?" said Rose.

"It's August, Rose," Mason answered.

"Eh, just take it anyway."

"I'm fine."

"Hi, Fine, I'm your grandma. Take your jacket."

Mason sighed and reluctantly took his jacket from the front hall closet.

"Love you, sugarplum."

"You too," he said without looking back.

"Shotgun!" Dale called before Mason could. "You snooze, you lose." He turned and puckered his lips. "Sugarplum."

"Drop dead," said Mason flatly.

"Have fun, kiddies," Rose called from the porch, and blew a kiss. "Be safe."

Mason waved back.

Julie's car was hot and awfully stuffy from sitting in the sun, yet Mason breathed a sigh of cool relief as soon as his door shut. They drove away just in time to hear Peanut burst into a fit of yips, no doubt at his first sight of Bossy.

"You friggin' guys!"

"What?" said Julie, looking at him in her rearview mirror.

Mason rolled his eyes. "You were supposed to be here over an hour ago."

"Hey, don't look at me," said Dale.

"I said I was sorry," she whined cutely, all but begging to be let off the hook.

"All right," said Mason. "Any longer, though, and she would have had me cleaning the rain gutters while she sang 'I Shot the Sheriff.'"

Dale craned his chubby head toward him. "At least you don't have to rub her bunions every time you see her. Thank god my family only visits Florida once a year."

"Gross," said Julie. Her phone began to vibrate in the cup holder next to her. "Hello?" she answered, and didn't say anything for a few moments. "Yeah, okay, see you in a bit." She hung up and placed her phone back in the cup holder, then met Mason's eyes in the rearview again. "I just have to pick up my mom's prescription. Is that okay?"

"Yeah, I guess so," said Mason.

The car came to a stop at the intersection at the bottom of the hill. Mason looked to his left, toward Chagrin Falls, but the car continued forward toward town.

FIVE

"Why don't you park at Town Hall?" Mason suggested as they passed it.

"No way," said Julie, pointing at the last view of the parking lot. "See? It's always busy."

As they reached the church parking lot, they found a variety of available parking spots. Some even in the shade.

"See?" said Julie as she exited the car, stretching her arms and basking in the cool shadow of the church. "Isn't this better?"

"Well, you know, maybe if we got here sooner . . ." Mason said with a smug grin.

Dale shook his head. "You two sound like an old married couple."

"Hey, keep it up and I won't share my toys." She fished through her back pocket and held up a thin piece of plastic.

"Sweet, you got it!" Mason said, and took the card in his hand. The license looked just like her real one, except that the birthdate had been adjusted to make Julie a full and legal twenty-one years of age.

Julie snatched it back from him and tapped him a few times on the forehead with it. "Not such a smart-ass now, are you?"

"Better a smart-ass than a dumb-ass."

Julie rolled her eyes. "That's one of Rose's, isn't it?"

"That obvious, huh?" he answered with a smile.

"Speaking of dumb-asses," Dale chimed in. "Maybe we should get a move on instead of standing in the church parking lot waving around a fake ID."

"Good thinking," Mason replied.

Julie stuck the card back in her pocket and clicked the button on her keychain until the car beeped, signaling that it was locked. "Shall we?"

"Actually," said Dale, drumming his fingers against the sides of his legs, "that's still another two blocks and I gotta take care of some business, if you know what I mean."

Julie shook her head. "Ugh! That's what you get for drinking so much lemonade."

"Yeah, well, now I have to make some 'lemonade' of my own."

Mason laughed and gave him some skin.

"Boys," Julie muttered. She looked across the road to the Star-bucks. "Well, go in—"

"I'll be back in a jiffy."

Dale was off before she could finish, leaving Mason and Julie alone.

He looked at her.

She looked back.

"Actually, I'm surprised he didn't have to go sooner," said Mason after an awkward pause.

"Yeah, like . . . in my car," she said, then another pause. Mason could see she was going to say something, so he shut up. "Listen, about the scholarship . . . I got the letter the day I left for Cleveland, but my mom held on to the mail she'd brought without telling me." She scoffed, annoyed. "Said she 'forgot'—even though she *knew* I was expecting a letter . . ."

"It's okay."

"Really?"

"Of course. I'm happy for you."

Julie relaxed, and secretly, so did Mason.

"What?" she asked, regarding his smirk of relief. Maybe not so secretly, then.

"Nothing. I thought that maybe it was because of . . . you know . . . what we did the night before you left."

"Oh . . . yeah."

"I thought maybe . . . I dunno."

"I was weirded out?" Julie said, finishing the thought for him.

"Something like that."

"No, no, we're cool."

"Good," said Mason awkwardly, expecting more. "Good."

"So we fooled around a bit. No big deal."

"Exactly."

Any cooler and there would be a chill in the air. Mason noticed her cheeks turning the color of ripened strawberries.

"Wannadoitagain?" said Mason, all in one quick breath.

Her mouth hung open. "You don't ask a girl that," she said, giving him a strong but friendly smack on the arm.

"How come?"

"Because—because . . ." she stammered, trying, god love her, to seem genuine while clearly grasping at straws. "Because."

"Uh-huh. Nice try."

"Well," she said, moving in closer. "Let's just see what happens."

"Okay." *Good enough for now,* he thought, and changed the subject. "That ID will come in handy around my birthday."

"Oh yeah, I almost forgot." Coy—a little *too* coy.

"You don't fool me," he said, and looked at the time on his cell phone. "What the hell's taking him so long?"

A minute later, Dale came trotting across the street, avoiding passing traffic.

"Ah, much better," said Dale "My back teeth were a-floatin'."

"Charming," said Julie, pointing yonder with both hands. "Let's go."

34

The trio headed off in the direction of Town Hall. Down Main Street they walked, past the sheriff's office and Calamus Books, until they came to a place called Halton's Drugstore.

Aside from the small line at the pharmacy and Penny, the clerk who sat at the cash register fending off boredom with a book of Sudoku puzzles, the place was empty. Speakers overhead played some Top 40 music station at a low volume, meant to blend into the background but instead seemed amplified in the still quiet of the store.

Julie vanished down the aisle of magazines and paperbacks. Mason and Dale stopped and glanced at the various covers while she continued to the back. Dale disappeared to the register with one of the magazines in hand, leaving Mason alone with his realization.

There had always been a twinge of guilt at harboring secret thoughts about Julie. But there was something else now . . . a stray spike of heat at the thought of her receiving a scholarship without telling him. Not that she needed to divulge every detail of her life to him the moment it happened, but considering the inescapable fact that this could only have been achieved thanks to his help—and, in some cases, flat-out doing homework *for* her—it was more than a slight bother. Was it envy? Perhaps, but . . . surely not *anger*? If not at her then at himself for unintentionally helping to ensure her ticket out of here?

You're smart, Mason. But sometimes, you're pretty dumb.

He felt Dale jab him in the ribs. "Hey," he said out of the corner of his mouth, his purchased magazine in one hand. "There's Miss Emily." And he gave a little nod in the direction of the pick-up counter where Julie was waiting patiently in line. Several people ahead of her, an attractive young woman with short brown hair was blowing on a cup of green tea. Miss Emily, the warm, honey-haired kindergarten teacher, passed by with a whiff of her perfume. There was some quality he couldn't explain. Something hidden. A veiled elegance about her, like champagne in a brown paper bag.

"So?" said Mason, just a little too sharply.

Dale didn't seem to notice. "Why don't the teachers at our school look like that?"

"If they did, would you be able to walk around without a textbook in front of you?"

"Probably not."

Despite his feigned indifference, the tantalizing thought of Ms. Emily asking him to stay after class, wearing just a pair of glasses and a smile, was cut short when he noticed his buddy staring at him with a big, goofy grin spread across his face.

"Uh . . . may I help you?" Mason asked.

"So?" said Dale.

"No."

"What?" said Dale with confusion.

"No . . . I don't sew," said Mason with a cheesy fake chuckle. "Get it?"

Dale groaned. "Another one of Rose's?"

"Yessir. Anyway, what do you mean, 'So'?"

"You and Jules?" Dale asked out of the corner of his mouth, motioning toward where Julie was finally speaking to the pharmacist.

"Oh . . . right." Mason waved him over to a rack of greeting cards, as if the few extra feet of distance somehow put them in a Cone of Silence. "Yeah, we talked. I'm not sure what's going on exactly, but I think something's happening."

"Like?"

"Like, remember how I said at first I thought she might be freaked out . . . you know, because we didn't really talk that much while she was in Cleveland?"

Dale nodded.

"Well, apparently I was wrong."

Dale flexed his eyebrows a few times. "Good thing I had to piss when I did, hey?"

"Oh, I see now," Mason said as the pieces fit together. "Took your time so we could have a little chat, did you?"

"Bingo," said Dale.

"Clever. Much obliged."

"So where did you guys leave it?"

Mason shrugged. "I think we're just going to see how things go."

"That's pretty vague."

"I'll say. Any advice?"

"Not really, except for . . ." Dale rubbed the grainy stubble on his chin as if deep in thought. "I say just go for it."

"I plan to," said Mason with enthusiasm. "It's just . . ."

"Yeah?"

"I mean, it's not like we're brother and sister or anything. But it's . . . Julie."

"And if shit goes south, it . . . ?"

"Sucks."

"I get it. But you'll never know unless you give it a shot."

"I know, I know." He watched her, pondering, as she tucked her hair behind her ear and paid. "Okay, so that's the grownup advice. Now, gimme the typical guy-to-guy advice."

Dale thought for a moment. "Quit being a pussy."

Mason's face went blank. "How helpful."

"Besides," Dale continued before Mason could ask again. "Who better to lose your V-card to?"

"I'm not a virgin!" Mason said—a little too loud, so that a few ears pricked up nearby. Quieter now: "I'm *not* a virgin."

"Yeah, but a halfie with Chelsea Olsen that one time just barely counts."

"No halfie! Fullie, man."

"That lasted thirty seconds."

"Still counts."

"Barely."

"At least I didn't lose my virginity to my cousin."

"Hey!" Dale stage-whispered. "I told you that in confidence."

"And I'm *keeping* it in confidence."

"Whatever. Anyway, just do it. You know . . . *do it*. Get down. Knock boots. Boogie. Diddle."

"Diddle?"

"Shag. Bone. Do the beast with two backs—"

"Now, *that* one I do know. But I'll bet you don't know where it comes from."

"Where?"

Mason was about to explain, but Dale dug a lighter from his pocket.

"Here, let's go outside. Less ears out there anyway."

Mason turned and took two steps toward the door, taking one last glance behind him to see Julie taking a white paper bag from the pharmacist.

Dale fumbled a flattened pack of cigarettes from his pocket and pulled one out for himself before holding it up in front of Mason as an offering.

"No, thanks," said Mason as he put his weight into the door, looking behind him while he did, and swung it out into the sidewalk.

WHUMP!

The door connected with something. With some*one*. The last person on earth—or anywhere else in the universe for that matter—Mason would have wanted to bump into, at all, much less literally.

Eric Riley.

Six feet of burly, square-headed rhinoceros with a crew cut and a green Packers jersey that, large as it was, didn't show much slack on his bulldozer of a frame.

"You little fucker!"

Eric grabbed Mason by the hair and pressed him up against the window of the drugstore. His face was frozen in a tight-lipped scowl, a beefy fist cocked back, poised to strike, while Mason was still trying to process what just happened.

Dale sprang into action. "What the fuck is your problem?" he shouted.

"He started it!"

"It was an accident, asshole! Chill!"

Eric clearly wanted to hit him, ached for it, but when he caught the baffled looks of people inside the store, he knew it was true. The question was whether or not he cared.

He let go of Mason's hair. "Watch where you're going next time, Jew Boy!" he snarled, and stormed off, no doubt looking for another nail to hammer.

Julie came rushing outside. "What was *that* about?"

"Your boyfriend nearly flattened him," said Dale snidely, as if it were somehow her fault.

Julie's face twisted. "Is that supposed to be funny?"

Dale shrugged and lit his cigarette.

She turned to Mason and put her hand on his shoulder, looking sympathetic. "Are you okay?"

Mason was trying not to look directly at her. The physical pain had already diminished. The hit to his dignity, however, was another story. He could still feel the tight grip of Eric's fist in his hair. It hadn't let go yet, and he was beginning to wonder if it ever would.

"I'm fine."

"Forget about it, man." said Dale, blowing out a long plume of cigarette smoke. "Fuck him. He's a douche-bro. A Brock."

Mason nodded. "A Chad." He repeatedly ran his hand through his hair, attempting to smooth out the feel of invisible fingers.

"Yeah! Total fuckin' Chad."

Something else bothered him though, and it had nothing to do with pain or humiliation. It was because, secretly, Mason *wanted* Eric to hit him. That would be all he would need.

They made their way back to the car. No one spoke for awhile until Mason tapped Dale on the shoulder.

"I'll take that smoke now."

SIX

"ARE YOU OKAY?"

That voice. It followed the whine of the locker door—shrill, as if it had been sealed for a century. He had been listing world capitals to himself to pass the time. All of them. Alphabetically. His personal best was twelve minutes. He had already made it through the list once and was about two-thirds of the way through a second time. So he figured he had been shoved into the locker about twenty minutes ago. When stuck in a 12"x18" tin can with nothing but someone's long-forgotten gym socks for company, twenty minutes is an eternity.

His eyes squinted for a second as they adjusted back to the fluorescent light.

The girl was unfamiliar but pretty. She had a backpack slung over one shoulder and a binder under the other arm. Even back then she had the same brown hair that turned the color of honey in the sun. Same habit of brushing it back behind her ear during an awkward moment.

"I'm fine," he said. "Just a little joke between me and some of the guys."

"I'd say the joke's on you," she said with an uneasy smile. "Is this yours?" she asked, holding out the loose combination lock in her hand.

He took it from her, admiring the charm bracelet she wore. "Thanks. Uh . . . you must be new here?"

"I am," she said as she looked both ways down the school's empty hallway, surveying the land. "This is my locker."

"Oh, sorry . . ."

"Why? Did you put yourself in there?"

"Well, no."

She shrugged. "Then don't be sorry. Besides, what better way to meet people?"

He liked her already. "I'm Mason," he said, and stuck out his hand.

"Julie," she replied, and shook it.

It didn't seem like six years had passed since they met. Somehow it felt like they had known each other forever.

Julie had moved to town from Cleveland just before Thanksgiving that year. Stonehill was so small that if tourists passed through and stopped long enough to ask for directions, it made the front page of *The Grapevine*, the town newsletter. So, naturally, the arrival of a family as distinct as the Walshes—not to mention rich—got more than its share of attention. Not quite filthy, but definitely "shittin' in high cotton," as Rose put it.

He was on his way to the library to work on a science project with Dale Anderson, his new lab partner, when he saw a polished red Bentley cruise down the street. It was followed by not one but two moving trucks and so many stares and slack jaws Mason would have thought they were watching a giant robot stroll through town.

Mr. Walsh, as Mason called him the handful of times he'd met him in the half dozen years since, was in charge of PR for the Cavaliers and constantly away on business. Their interaction was not much more than a handshake and the occasional chat, which usually ended with Mr. Walsh saying, "Nice to meet you," as if every time were the first.

Mrs. Walsh knew Mason well, but she was often deep in a bottle of either Hennessy or Prozac. Or both. According to Julie, she had been a model once. But Dale swore he'd seen her in a softcore skin flick from the '80s one time on TV.

And, of course, Julie was their only child, so naturally she got away with murder.

Most homes in Stonehill were like their owners: modest and conventional. Only three houses could be considered luxurious. One belonged to Mayor Watterson; one to the Caldwells, who were town council members (and connected by marriage to the Rileys); and the last was bought by Julie's parents for a cool five million dollars.

One day she invited them both to her house when she found them shooting hoops at the school court, which didn't even have nets on the baskets. It gave Mason the impression that somehow a small corner of Beverley Hills had been chipped off and dropped in rural Ohio. There was a gate, a three-car garage, and a real stone fountain in the circular driveway that was definitely not there when Mrs. Van Wyck, the lonely old widow with more money than living family members, had lived there.

Mason had expected to find a plastic, store-bought net erected at one end of the driveway. He stood aghast when Julie punched the code into the keypad to reveal an indoor court with an honest-to-god scoreboard mounted above the net.

They spent many summer days and nights in that garage, the three of them. Doors open, radio cranked, playing until night and then playing some more.

It seemed like just yesterday and yet so long ago; an entire cosmos somehow expanding and imploding all at once.

When Mason was a boy, summer was a vast expanse of time that he knew would end one day, but not today. Never today. It was always a distant thing. Now, it seemed that all it took was to blink his eyes before it was September again. And after so many autumns followed by a return to school, he'd finally reached the last one—the last day of summer vacation ever. A prelude to the real world, whatever that was supposed to mean.

What a fickle thing time was. Ignore it and it speeds up. Pay attention and it lingers. When you want more, there isn't any, and when you want to be rid of it, there's no escape. Like a flighty lover, time is both loving and cruel. Even at a mere eighteen, Mason saw that the way to travel through time was to pretend it wasn't there. He wondered if other people his age thought of such things. Somehow, he didn't think so.

Most kids his age had sent their college applications before the end of last year. While Julie was seeing her guidance counsellor and going over schools with decent health care programs, he and Dale were skipping school to hang around the record store and smoke joints out back with Tony, the old hippie who owned the only record store in town, where Mason had worked until it closed.

Once or twice, he thought about becoming an English teacher, but that was about as far as it got. When he mentioned the idea to Rose, all he got was a lukewarm, "That's nice, sugar."

He hadn't thought about it since.

Though it was never admitted aloud, the reason any mention of his future was met with avoidance was no real secret: Sooner or later, Rose knew he would leave. And he could not blame her, really. He understood because she was all he had, too, and Stonehill, for better or worse, was home. Sometimes, though, he just wanted to get as far away from there as possible. It was a strange thing to both love a place yet feel stuck there.

California would have been good. Maybe Canada. Portugal. Azerbaijan. Anywhere, really. He could almost see it, the path ahead unfolding before him, opening up like a stretch of dark highway at night, lit by stars and a bright full moon. And then it was gone. It seemed that every time he tried to look just a little further down the road, all that stared back was a dead end.

It made him think of the sign at the town border—the very sign they were approaching now as they passed the apple orchard of the Ogilvie farm.

STONEHILL, OHIO
A NICE PLACE TO VISIT

Every time he saw it, Mason couldn't help but make a little addition.

A nice place to visit . . . but I wouldn't want to live there.

He used to live in Israel. His parents were grad students from NYU. By the time he was six, they had already lived in Mexico City, Frankfurt, Istanbul, Athens, and, finally, Tel Aviv. They were visiting Jerusalem to research the synagogues, churches, and mosques for a book his parents planned to write.

That all changed on April 13, 1996. The day the world knew well from then on, for it was when the ancient city of Jerusalem vanished from the face of the earth.

They called it the Great Quake. Seismologists said that an earthquake of that magnitude had never occurred in recorded history. The whole city dropped into the bowels of the earth, along with over one million people—including Josh and Molly Cole. It was several days before teams could be sent down into the rift to assess any possibility of salvage and rescue in the devastation. But in all the rubble there was only one survivor.

One.

Most kids learn about death when their goldfish or hamster dies. Me? I got a crash course. Pun fully intended.

The way the relief workers told it, there was this little voice coming from somewhere in the dark, twisted remains of the city, crying and sobbing for help. Suddenly, there he was, little five-year-old Mason, wandering in the dark. Aside from some cuts and bruises, he was not seriously injured.

He didn't even recall the trip from the hospital to Stonehill. Not at all. Just woke up one day in what had been his bedroom every day since. And Rose's face was the first he saw.

People from all over the world sent flowers, cards, money; he received letters from strangers, foreign dignitaries, even the Pope. Rose read them to him before he could read for himself. They called it a miracle, said the Lord had a plan for him and every day was a blessing. A gift from God. But every once in a while, Rose would begin skimming through a letter and her face would darken before crumpling it up and throwing it away.

People in town were the same at first, offering condolences and inviting them to church service. And when Rose politely declined, they accepted it graciously, but there was an awkward tension that hung in the air from then on that even a child could detect.

Naturally, when he was old enough to ask about it, he did. Rose did her best.

"Why did God do this, Gramma?"

"Oh, sweetie, God didn't do it. Some people believe that God or the Devil are responsible for things because there's no other way to explain it."

"Then why'd this have to happen?"

"I just don't know, sugar. Sometimes bad things happen."

"That's stupid!"

"I know. I know it is. The truth is that no one really knows for sure. It's all just a part of life. The only thing we can do is look for answers and make up our own minds about things. But no matter what, we've got each other now. Right?"

"Right."

"Then that's all that matters."

"M'kay."

She gave him a big hug and said: "And don't call me Gramma. It makes me sound old."

From then on, it was just the two of them. Rose said that made them special to each other. Two peas in a pod. Bread and butter.

He heard people whisper about her when they thought no one could hear. About him, too. Said she was a witch and that the two of them were weirdos who worshiped spooky things, blah, blah, blah. The truth was that Mason praised only one thing above all others—the fact that he was alive.

As for God? Well . . . God was a tough sell.

If there is a God . . . I have questions. Like how or why could he allow things to happen the way they did? If he's all powerful, all knowing, and all good, why would he allow so many people . . . my parents . . . to die?

And let me live?

He asked Rose those same questions as well.

"Because he must see something pretty special in you."

Rose never said a word about religion, unless it was in response to someone in town who didn't like her "godless fortune-telling." One time Marcy Burgess, the pastor's wife, called her a heathen and spat at her as she walked by. Rose just smiled and said, "*She* that is without sin . . ." Marcy fired something back but was quickly silenced when Rose mentioned the Seventh Commandment and kept on walking without another word.

Religion was never her thing, but she believed in being informed. Somewhere in her Mason was sure there was a place for God in one form or another, but he got the sense that the relationship was not as strong as it once was.

Grief forces us to ask why. For surely there must have been some reason for something that powerful, that crippling to our very core . . . right?

And so he tried. He really did.

At night he would offer a little prayer. It started off with the impossible. "Dear God, please send my mom and dad back to me." He wasn't sure what he thought would happen since he knew that, even for the Almighty, that was impossible. Something simpler, then. "Please let the other kids quit picking on me." That wasn't much to ask, was it? Eventually it became: "Please just respond to me. Doesn't

46

matter how. Give me some sign that you're really there." Please *this*. Please *that*. Something that should be easy for the omnipotent creator of the universe. Always ending with a "Thank you. Amen."

But each time he tried, the result was the same.

No answer.

He realized that he was just talking to himself. And so the prayers stopped.

Time magazine's cover story following the tragedy showed the enormous hole where the city used to be with a despondent, dust-covered rescue worker carrying little Mason in his arms. But thirteen years later, the letters from strangers had long since stopped, and though most people in the world would certainly recognize that photo, much like *National Geographic*'s Afghan Girl, the Napalm Girl from Vietnam, or the Tank Man who stood in Tiananmen Square, no one remembered his name. He was just the Jerusalem Boy. A nickname with a few too many syllables for his plebeian peers, so it was shortened to just Jew Boy.

Mason and Rose were invited back to Israel three years ago for the ten-year anniversary. He considered it briefly, if for no other reason so that he could thank Levi Zurer, the rescue worker from the photo. Unfortunately, Zurer had died of lung cancer a year earlier. Mason had no real way to know for certain, but he figured that the sheer amount of ash and debris from the wreckage had done him in. That was one thing he remembered most of the ordeal—the dry, life-less smell and feel of ash everywhere. Every once in a while, for no real reason at all, he could still smell it. Feel it choking his throat.

He became obsessed with the earthquake, read every story, every article, every bit of information there was about it. Before then, the strongest known earthquake was in Valdivia, Chile, in 1960, and measured a whopping 9.5 on the Richter scale. However, the last earthquake in Israel that caused any damage at all was a mere 6.5. The event had numerous geological effects in the region, compromising connected fault lines and opening fissures in Egypt, Jordan, and Syria, triggering tsunamis throughout the Mediterranean, but surprisingly no aftershock. It could even be seen from space: satellite images showed a cloud of dust so big that, thanks to strong winds that day, stretched across the eastern corner of the Mediterranean and actually covered part of Cyprus.

Naturally, all manner of experts studied the event. Their findings were inconclusive. Possible theories ranged from destabilization from oil drilling to the more exotic and widely balked "terrestrial fatigue" hypothesis, which stated the amount of fighting over the area throughout history put an added strain on the land. Triskaideka-phobes cited the date as another example of the unlucky number, right up there with the Templar Inquisition and Apollo 13. The tin-foil-hat-wearers claimed it was an attack by aliens that live inside the moon and use gravity as a weapon. But no matter how much Mason searched, how much he racked his brain, nothing he learned gave him any comfort from the loss of his parents.

He didn't remember them that much anymore. He thought he did. Told himself he did. But really it was more that he had a sense of them, and mostly from pictures and stories Rose told him. Single frames of memories surfaced now and then, but they were just frozen pictures faded by the sun.

His mom by the Aegean.

His dad tying his shoe outside Hagia Sophia.

The three of them strolling down the beach in Israel.

He couldn't remember what their voices sounded like anymore, because nobody can tell you those kinds of things. Either you're lucky enough to have them, or you're not. Such is the blessing and the curse of memories. Never gone; never really here. All he had to remember them by was the cross necklace they had given him the day they died.

He didn't remember much about the aftermath. Darkness. Dust. His own lonely cries for his parents as he was trapped by tons of rubble. Waking up in a hospital somewhere. And, eventually, coming to Stonehill.

He had no clue how he had survived the fall.

They say things got better following the Great Quake. That there had been nothing but fighting and hatred and bloodshed on both sides in that part of the world, only coming together in the aftermath. The silver lining in a mushroom cloud. All Mason knew was that *his* world would never be the same.

Life went on, as it does. But he was still woken up at night by the same nightmare since the age of five—a god-awful roar as the ground cracked open, disappearing beneath him as he plunged into an abyss of frightened screams. Falling deep and only waking when he hit, to find that the bottom was his own bed. And to this day he still could not bear being in the dark. For him it was anything but empty.

The very fact that someone had lived through such a thing, let alone a child, was a miracle. Even he would not deny that. Everyone said so. And they were right. It was. Every day since was a blessing . . .

One he spent pumping gas.

Someday that would change, that much he knew. But right now all there was on the horizon was the next car to pull into the station.

SEVEN

Seventy miles away from Stonehill, near the border of Pennsylvania, a trio of crows cawed and cackled at each other on a telephone wire. A gray Buick came clipping along I-90 when it suddenly pulled off onto the shoulder and came to a stop, carrying with it a blanket of gravel and grit, which had enough time to settle before it was kicked up again as the car spun around and disappeared back the way it came.

The crows resumed their mournful song, unimpressed with the bizarre world of humans.

EIGHT

At the rustle of turning pages coming from the backseat, Mason craned his neck. "What are you reading?" he asked, unable to see the cover.

Dale looked up from the magazine he was thumbing through, and held it up so that Mason could see the title—*Conspiracy Quarterly* in thick yellow letters. It showed George Washington being beamed down by a UFO with the headline: FIRST PRESIDENT, FIRST VISITOR?

"*This* is what's behind the wool that's been pulled over our eyes."

"Oh, I see," said Mason. "Does it say what happened to Jimmy Hoffa?"

"No." Dale frowned and sat back in his seat. "That was in last month's issue."

"Right."

"And what about Earth being flat," Julie said, "or the government not wanting us to know we can actually breathe in space?"

"First off, don't get me *started* on flat-earthers," said Dale without so much as an upward glance. "And second, I'm beginning to sense some sarcasm."

"Beginning?" said Mason.

"How do you know it's *not* true?"

"Besides common sense and basic intelligence?"

"All right, Mister Skeptic." Dale closed the magazine and tossed it into the seat next to him. "Ever heard of Militia Dei?"

"The bad guys from *The Da Vinci Code*?"

"Heh? No. They're a special branch of the Vatican that investigates the occult."

"What, like witchcraft and stuff?"

"Witchcraft, exorcism, telepathy, ghosts . . ."

Mason shook his head. "Some people have too much time on their hands."

"Good thing, too, because they've recently discovered that there may actually be some evidence for ghosts."

"This should be good," said Julie.

"When ghosts 'manifest' "—he made air quotes with his fingers— "they've been detected through use of heat sensors, ultra-violet cameras, and, more recently, highly sensitive electrometers, which pick up the same amount of electricity a human body produces. How do you explain *that*?"

"Transient static electricity, faulty equipment, or . . . wait for it, because this is a game-changer . . . a hoax!"

"Or it could be the bio-electricity of a dead person," Dale continued, unfazed. "In either case, it would explain why our hairs stand up on the backs of our necks."

"If only you put this much thought into homework," Mason said. "Then I wouldn't have to do it for you."

"Well, you spent so much time telling me what was wrong with it, I figured that was the only way to shut you up," said Dale, flashing a shit-eating grin.

Mason raised a finger in the air. "Um, actually, there is one other way. Who knows what it is?"

Dale raised his hand.

"Yes, Dale."

Then Dale raised a finger himself, but not the same one as Mason. "Blow me."

"No, I'm afraid that's incorrect."

"Now *you* two sound like an old married couple," said Julie, looking knowingly at Dale in the rearview.

Fake laughs from both boys, and then Mason grew quiet. He had fallen off the honor roll last year because, in truth, he had spent more and more time doing assignments for his friends to the point that his own grades had slipped.

"You guys can think what you want," said Dale. "It's what I believe."

"Incredible claims require incredible proof," Mason replied, "and this makes no sense considering there would need to be a body to produce the electricity to begin with. I don't buy any of it."

Dale raised an eyebrow. "Really? Even with a witch for a grandma?"

He didn't mean anything by it, but Mason hated when people called her that. "*Especially* with a 'witch' for a grandma."

"Do explain."

"Mostly she just listens to people," Mason said calmly, "reads their reactions and, based on that, tells them what they want to hear."

"That's it?" Dale said with disbelief.

"That's all."

"And she told you this?"

"Didn't have to. It's obvious."

"What about the Tarot readings?" Julie asked.

"There are lots of different ways of interpreting the cards. She gives people the best translation she can."

"Isn't that kinda . . . I dunno . . ." She searched for the right word. "Sneaky? Why doesn't she just tell them the truth?"

Just then Mason's phone vibrated in his pocket. "Hang on," he said, and looked at the display. *Speak of the devil,* he thought. Her ears must have been burning.

"What is it?" asked Julie.

"Nothing." He let it go to voicemail and stuck it back in his pocket. "As I was saying, who wants to hear that their husband is going to leave them, or that they'll lose their job or grow a tumor? People don't want the truth, they want comfort. Why do you think they believe in religion, astrology, and fortune cookies? She gives them exactly what they come to her for."

"At least fortune cookies are yummy," said Julie, visions of fried rice and moo-shu pork shimmering in her eyes. "I could sure go for some Chinese right about now."

"That does sound pretty good," said Mason. "Where's the nearest one?"

"Chow Fun's, just five minutes north of the Falls."

"Sold," said Dale. "Let's swing by there after we pick up the tickets and—"

Julie swerved hard to the right, into the next lane. She glared into her rearview at Dale with a cloud of daggers. *"Really?"*

Dale stared back blankly.

Mason, however, gave them a look of confusion. "Tickets?"

"Oh, balls!" said Dale. He slunk down into his seat.

Julie cleared her throat and said: "Okay, well, you were going to find out soon anyway, so . . . we're going to pick up something for your birthday."

"Which is . . . ?"

"Still three months away."

"Hardy-har-har."

"All right, all right," she said, and reached into her purse. She took out a piece of paper folded into quarters and handed it to him. Mason unfolded it and saw the word CONFIRMATION with an order number near the top.

Julie smiled. "It's Hellysium tickets!"

"Say what?!"

"Yep."

"Oh, you magnificent girl, you. I've been wanting to go forever!"

"I know. And now you can. *We* can. Halloween weekend. I figure we leave a little early, get a decent spot to camp."

"Oh, this is so awesome!"

"Right? Over thirty bands, including—"

"Metallica!"

"Actually, no, they dropped out. Sorry."

"Damn!"

"But they were replaced with Slayer," said Dale, "so it's all good."

"Meh."

"Please!" Dale balked. "Slayer makes Metallica look like the fucking Jonas Brothers."

"Kirk could shred circles around Kerry King any day."

"Eh, whadda you know? You like Elvis."

"The King of Rock 'n Roll, man." Mason cradled the piece of paper in his hands, marveling at it as if it were the Shroud of Turin. "How did you do this?"

"Called Ticketmaster."

"Not that. I mean these must have been . . ." Before Mason could finish, Julie gave him a coy sideways glance as she took something from her purse next to her. ". . . expensive."

At first he thought it was her fake ID, but instead it was Daddy's platinum card.

Of course.

"Thanks."

"What're friends for?"

"No, really. Thank you."

"Anytime," she said, and patted his knee.

And just like that, his troubles were gone.

Go on . . . tell her! Tell her right now. What difference does it make when or where? Tell her what you've wanted to say for so long but couldn't. Tell her what you're scared to death to say aloud . . . because she might not say it back.

No. Not now. Not right this moment, which was otherwise . . .

perfect? Yes, that's exactly what it was. Perfect. Driving down the highway on this warm summer day, wind flowing through his fingers. The sun turning all it touched to gold. Everything else just seemed to melt away, and in a single instant, it became one of the good times.

A happy memory.

NINE

"Aw, damn," said Julie as a familiar sight appeared in her rearview mirror—the flashing red-and-blue of the fuzz. She slowed and pulled over to the side of the road. "Don't," she warned Mason, clearly all but biting his tongue.

"Wasn't gonna."

"Yeah, right." Picking through her purse with one hand, she pointed to the glove box with the other. "Can you grab my registration for me?"

The cruiser pulled up behind them and came to a languid halt. Heat radiated from the road and the buzz of cicadas came from nearby trees. Out came two highway patrolmen in gray uniforms and wide, flat-brimmed hats. One tall and razor-thin, the other a teapot, short and stout. A strange feeling crept up Mason's spine as he watched them slowly mosey on over, their feet crunching the loose gravel as they neared. Even when innocent, a surge of doubt appears in the teenaged mind when an officer of the law approaches in the eerily collected way they do, forcing one to wonder for one fleeting moment what it is they did wrong.

Julie rolled down her window as Officer Stretch appeared next to it. A pair of big dark aviators sat atop his long nose, making him look like an oversized insect. Officer Fatso remained by the back bumper, thumbs hooked through the loops of his belt. A bushy mustache hid his top lip and his uniform looked uncomfortably tight against his round squash body.

"Afternoon, miss," he said with a slight tip of his hat. The nameplate next to his badge read R. PORTER. "Can I see your license and registration, please?"

Knowing the drill all too well, Julie handed it to him before he had even finished speaking.

"Do you know why we pulled you over?" he asked, and handed the plastic card and slip of paper to his partner, who returned to the cruiser to check them.

"No, sir. Was I speeding?"

"As a matter of fact, you were. Speeding *and* swerving."

"What? I wasn't . . ." She paused, catching sight of Dale in the rearview as he slunk even lower in the backseat. "Oh."

The officer paused, gauging her reaction. Though his eyes weren't visible, they were clearly panning the inside of the car, looking for signs of delinquency, shenanigans, or mischief—a highway cop's bread and butter. "You kids haven't been drinking or anything like that, have you?"

"No, sir. Nothing like that."

"Wait right here." He left the driver's side window and headed back to the squad car.

It was hard to tell for sure, but he didn't look entirely convinced.

"What are you going to do?" asked Mason.

"What my dad said to do if I want to keep my car . . . cooperate." Had there been any trace of conviction in her voice, Mason might have believed her. "But still . . ." *There it is.* "I couldn't have been going more than a few miles over the limit."

She watched the two cops discussing something in her rearview. Mason could just make out enough in the reflection of the mirror on his side.

"I wonder what they're talking about," said Dale, trying to watch them in the rearview without being too obvious about it.

"I don't know, but I've been stopped by cops, like, a million times before. They don't do much talking."

"Where's the ID?" said Mason.

She looked away from the mirror. "I . . . just gave it to them. Weren't you—"

"No, the *fake* ID. Where did you put it after we were done looking at it?"

"Back in my . . ."

Her face went blank and the tips of her fingers touched her lips. Her hand dove into her pocket and felt around. She checked the other one, then the first pocket again, as if it would have magically materialized in the last second. Mason could see her replaying things in her head over and over, wishing they could be paused and recorded.

"Don't tell me you gave it to the cop."

But the more he thought about it, the more sense it made.

"No, I couldn't have," Julie said as she began to root through the jumbled contents of her purse like an escaped convict desperately digging a tunnel to freedom. "Maybe I lost it at the drugstore."

Dale gave the back of Julie's seat a nudge with his knee. "He's coming back."

The shadow of tension spread through Mason's chest with each of the officer's approaching footsteps, adding a sprinkling of disdain and just a dash of panic to his already mixed mood.

Officer Porter darkened the window once again. "Miss, I'm going to have to ask you to step out of the vehicle, please," he said, his words stern and serious, before casting dual glances at the other two occupants of the car. "You boys, too."

Shit! What small sliver of hope Mason had was instantly crushed.

Julie huffed, undid her seatbelt, and got out. The boys did the same, came around the car, and stood next to her. They were joined by Porter's large partner. The nameplate pinned to his undersized uniform read G. GEARY.

"We ran your license and found that you have an outstanding warrant for a speeding ticket you received back in January of this year." It was said in such a way, a subtle hint of assertion: *I'm not asking . . . I'm telling.*

Mason and Dale clearly weren't expecting this, but were otherwise unsurprised.

"A warrant?" Julie looked as though a glass of ice-cold water had been dashed in her face.

"Yes, ma'am."

"For a ticket in *January?*"

"That's right."

"January what?"

"The first."

Her eyebrows raised as the information sank in at a glacial pace.

"So, there are two ways we can proceed. One, we can take you into custody. Two, we can escort you—"

"Hold on," Julie interrupted, and held up her hand like the Queen of Sheba commanding silence. "I didn't get a ticket in January."

Here we go . . .

"Or *two*," Officer Porter continued, unimpressed, "we can escort you to the courthouse to pay the ticket with an additional fine."

"I *said*, I didn't get a ticket in January." Her cool head was beginning to disappear faster than thin ice on a hot day.

"I have a driving record that says different, with a list of violations a mile long."

There was a beat followed by a dubious scoff from Julie. "Fine, let's see it."

Porter stood still and silent.

"If there's a warrant, I want to see it."

Mason rolled his eyes. "Julie, come on. Don't make it worse."

He was met with a glare that would cause weaker souls to burst into flames. A look men of all ages know all too well. *The* look.

"Excuse me, but I couldn't have got a ticket then because I didn't have a car. Remember? It was being cleaned because *someone*"—her glare traveled to Dale—"puked in the backseat on New Year's Eve."

"Listen, miss, we're trying to help you out here. Now, if you don't want to cooperate, that's your choice." Officer Porter took a pair of handcuffs from his belt.

"You know what . . . go ahead!"

"Hands behind your back," commanded the officer, and he read Julie her rights. The metal cuffs closed around each wrist with a short series of rapid clicks. "You boys will have to come too."

Officer Geary appeared behind them, along with his cocktail of body odor and Aqua Velva. He placed a chubby-fingered hand on each boy's shoulder.

This just keeps getting better and better.

The police officers led the three of them to the cruiser, securing them without a fuss. Mason and Julie on either side, Dale in the middle, separated from the cops by a barrier across the entire back of the car. There was a funny smell floating around the inside, the stale hint of vomit and beer mixed together, presumably from the last drunk to have sat back here.

Porter, back in the driver's seat, took off his hat, placed it in his lap, and started the engine. The whole right side sagged as Geary landed in the passenger's seat, forcing Mason to sag with it. The car lurched forward and down the road in the direction they had been heading not ten minutes ago, yet further and further away from their destination.

"I don't know about you two, but I'm having a great time," said Mason, feebly attempting some levity. It fell on deaf ears. He kept his eyes straight ahead, half on the winding road, half on Officer Geary's sweaty rolls of neck fat. He didn't need to see Julie to know she was fuming, the air practically filled with smoke slithering from her nostrils.

"By the way, thanks for nothing," she said to Mason.

"This is somehow *my* fault?" Mason stared at her, unsure how else to respond.

"You're supposed to have my back."

Go on, say it . . . *"Maybe if you could control your mouth for once!" Say it. You know you want to. It would feel so good!*

"And you," she snapped at Dale, sitting timidly next to her. "I'm never telling you anything ever again."

"I don't think they're taking us to the station," Dale whispered in a voice that was dead serious and quiet as possible. Mason could see that he was trying not to move his lips, to make it look like he wasn't speaking.

"How do *you* know?" said Julie.

"The highway patrol station is five miles north of town . . . we're going east."

"Are you sure?"

"Yes." Dale was still trying to keep his words hidden.

"Then where the hell are they taking us?" said Mason.

Geary slammed a meaty elbow against the barrier.

The three of them jumped in alarm.

"Hay, stawp tawking," he barked with a gruff Brooklyn accent.

Silence. Nothing but the hum of the car as it traversed the road, curving its way downhill and onto Route 422. Over the La Due Reservoir they went, the lazy, golden sunlight bouncing across the calm surface of the water.

When he thought it was safe, Dale turned and mouthed two words.

Not cops.

TEN

THE SUN SANK DEEPER AND DEEPER BEHIND THE TREELINE
along the road. They had been driving for what seemed like a lot
longer than ten minutes when the car turned off the freeway and into
a small gas station marked by an old, unlit sign. It looked deserted, the
neglected twin of Gus's Gas & Garage. Abandoned long ago and left
to the elements. Little glass remained in the windows. Overgrown
weeds and grass surrounded the foundation. The pumps were
chipped and faded and looked like they hadn't been in service since
the Kennedy administration.

"Where are we?" said Mason.

"What the hell is going on?" said Julie.

They pulled around the far side of the building and stopped next
to a black Lincoln Town Car.

"Look, guys," said Dale, just under his breath. "Whatever
happens, just do what they say."

Porter faced them and flashed a big, toothy grin as he took something out of his shirt pocket. "Now tha's good advice, innit." His stern
exterior replaced with the oafish tongue of a Cockney dock hand.

His hand opened. A clear white crystal at the end of a thin chain dropped and began hypnotically swinging.

Back . . . and forth.

Back . . . and forth.

Back . . . and forth.

Mason felt his eyelids getting heavy, the motion of the pendulum brushing everything else aside.

Porter widened his gaze, unblinking, seeming to peer into all three pairs of eyes simultaneously. *"Listen te me voice."*

Mason's mind was struck numb, as if he'd been hit firmly in the back of the head. But there was no pain. No joy. No anger. No sadness. No confusion. No anything. Everything darkened, as if somehow the sun had been dimmed. All color drained from Mason's vision: an old black-and-white photograph of the world rather than the real thing. He could hear and he could see, but he couldn't move.

"You'll not move unless told. You'll not speak unless told. You'll obey every instrucshun an' cause no trouble. When you 'ear da word 'sandman,' you'll be released. Is tha' understood?"

"Understood," they all replied in unison, blank as lobotomy patients.

The two men smiled at each other.

Geary removed his hat, along with the bushy mustache that had passed for real. He eagerly unbuttoned the strained gray shirt around his bulbous torso, fidgeting with the last before finally ripping it off altogether as he let out a sigh of relief. "Much bettah."

"Ain' tha' da troof," said Porter, taking a small vial of fine white powder from somewhere unseen. He produced a thin metal spoon with a tiny scoop at the end, dipped in, and snorted it up his right nostril, then again with the left.

"Wan' a bump?" Porter asked, handing over the coke. Geary answered by indulging in twice as much as his partner in crime.

Geary whistled and clapped his hands. "Now *that's* blow!"

"Plains ov Leng, mate," said Porter, lighting a cigarette.

They both eyed the three entranced teenagers behind them,

Geary lingering a little longer on Julie and a little further south of her pretty, docile face.

"So whadda we do now?"

Porter produced a cell phone, flipped it open, and began to dial. "Now we call the big man 'imself."

"Now?" said Geary, confused. "It's still light out."

Porter shrugged and moments later became alert, at attention. "Yes, sir." His voice shaky, nervous even. "No, sir. Nuffin' we can't 'andle." He said nothing for a few moments. "Understood."

"So?" asked Geary, slouched down in his seat.

"We're ter stow da brats an' 'ead east. He said 'e'll join us after dark. Oh, an' da *special one* ain't ter be 'armed."

"Whaddabout the other two?"

"Didn't say," said Porter.

Geary smiled with sick delight. "Is that so?"

Porter nodded. "It's so. So let's get changed aht ov dese fuckin' pigskins an 'it da road."

"Good idea." Eyes moving across Julie's body. "I think I'll have dis one here assist."

"We can 'ave ahr fun latah."

"No. *Now*." Geary got out and walked around to the trunk. It opened and, moments later, slammed closed. He appeared next beside Julie, holding a duffel bag.

"Well, don' be all day abou' it."

Geary opened the door and Julie rose from her seat like a good doll, doing as she was told. No expression on her face. No fear of whatever was about to happen.

"Gimme your phones, if you have 'em."

They did as they were told, watching helplessly as Geary pitched all three phones into the field of high grass behind the station.

"You too, lads. Let's go then," said Porter, pointing at the still-open back door.

Mason and Dale did as they were told, the same vacant masks on their faces. The lanky impostor took the keys from the ignition, left the wheel, and joined them.

"Don't get me wrong," said Porter, strolling merrily along. "I don't wan' you fer myself. I ain't no pooftah. But me associate dere"—he pointed in the direction Geary and Julie had disappeared to around the side of the station—"why, 'e'd fuck da spare tire. So I fink it's best I put you in da back, yeah?"

Porter flicked his cigarette away and opened the trunk, took a second duffel bag from inside, and closed it again. He made his way to the trunk of the Lincoln, whistling to himself and twirling his nightstick as he went. Mason and Dale followed right behind him, like baby chicks waddling after Mama.

With another set of keys, Porter opened the trunk. Inside were two men wearing nothing but their underclothes. They didn't struggle, didn't even look alive at first. Just lay there placidly.

Porter unzipped the duffel bag and took out two more pairs of handcuffs, snapping one around each boy's wrists. He left for just two minutes and returned in different clothes, carrying the uniforms he and his friend had been wearing.

"There you are, piglets," he said as he dropped the two piles of clothes just outside the trunk. "Outcha get." Once they had changed into their uniforms again, Porter locked eyes with them and said, *"You saw nothing."*

"I saw nothing," said both officers as one. They got in their cruiser together and drove off.

"'Ere we go, gents." Porter bowed and directed Mason and Dale to the now-empty trunk. "Your chariot awaits!"

In they got. All Mason could hear now was the muffled sound of his pulse under a low vibration, like the sound of the ocean through the bulkhead of a ship. The waves of it slowly washed over him as the sun above disappeared and he sank deeper and deeper into the depths of the spell.

. . .

Time stood still.

There was something else, though—a chemical reaction, the growl of a volcano gathering strength beneath an otherwise calm sea. A force welling up where seconds ago there was none, boiling inside him from deep down in the gut where fire dwells.

It got louder, clearer, until it was thundering in his ears. Pure white lightning shot hot and clean from a spot in his chest through every nerve and fiber of his body, every cell filled with it. The last sliver of light was shrinking into total darkness when finally, ferociously, he erupted.

The chain of his handcuffs broke like an overstretched rubber band. His fist struck the underside of the trunk lid and sent it flying open.

Darkness became light once again. He saw a pair of feet fly up into the air before the body they were attached to arched and landed hard against the ground.

DANGER!

He sensed it, drawn by its magnetic pull. As soon as his feet touched ground, they propelled him forward until he found himself outside the men's room at the other side of the building and then they kicked the door open.

Geary froze like a fat raccoon caught in the garbage. Even as her captor fondled one of her breasts beneath the raised hem of her tank top, Julie's face was still blank. The pressure in his head grew tighter and tighter, consumed by a rage so intense that it sizzled against the backs of his eyeballs. Everything moved in slow motion—twisted hands out before him like talons, Geary's bewildered expression as he was clutched by the neck and pulled closer while, at the same time, Mason's head thrust forward and mashed his nose flat and the fat man fell to the floor with a wet slap.

Mason towered over the body, lifeless and broken on the grime-covered tile. The nose was now little more than a red mass of ruined skin and cartilage in the center of his face, blood seeping from what remained of the nostrils.

At that moment Mason felt something wet slowly crawling its way down the slope of his own nose. He turned ninety degrees and saw his stricken reflection in the cracked, dirty mirror. A smear of crimson no bigger than a quarter on his forehead, dripping slowly down the slope of his nose until a fat drop gathered at the tip.

And yet there was no pain.

With the trembling fingers of his right hand, he touched it, held them before his face to admire the lovely red. His senses returned to him. Sick and dizzy the way one feels after a long day of heat, corn dogs, and roller coasters at the town carnival. He stood reeling in the doorframe, all feeling rapidly draining from his limbs and face.

A cluster of static formed in the center of his vision, expanding in every direction until he was overtaken by a dark wave. Everything went black and, like the man he had just wasted, Mason collapsed to the squalid bathroom floor.

On the road, a car drove by, unaware of the relic of a gas station or what had just happened there.

When Mason awoke, it was well past dark. It seemed no time had passed at all.

The broken handcuffs rattled as he tried to scramble to his feet and was immediately defeated by the crippling pain that had finally found him. Immeasurable and endless as the stars, agony throbbed in his right hand; his forehead felt as if it had been split down the middle.

Behind him, Julie was still zoned out. He lowered the bottom of her shirt to cover her bare chest.

He said her name. She didn't answer.

He shouted it. Nothing.

Snapped his fingers in front of her glazed eyes, still no response . . . but there was something, a hint of life in her puppet's eyes.

As if galvanized by a residual spark of the pure electricity he'd felt before, Mason's muscles sprang into action. He gathered his stunned friend up in his arms and carried her back to the car.

"Holy shit," Mason said, shocked, when he saw the battered trunk lid, twisted as used tinfoil. He had heard of people performing incredible feats of strength in the midst of a crisis thanks to height-ened adrenaline. But somehow folding a steel trunk lid back on itself with a blow from a human fist was beyond unexpected. Not to mention the fact that he had broken out of his handcuffs.

And how did the handcuffs get there? That's right, you stood there brainwashed while a psychic cokehead tried to stick you in the trunk.

Was he losing his mind? He didn't think so. But how else to explain all this?

He had to get home.

Mason flung open the back door and laid Julie down in the back-seat. If not for her eyes being wide open, she almost looked as if she were asleep.

Dale was still dazed and handcuffed in the trunk. It took some doing, but Mason finally dragged him into the backseat. He tried to close the trunk even a little, but it was far too warped, grinding hard against the inner bracket of the trunk.

"Keys. I need keys." Mason crouched next to Porter's crumpled body and found them still in his hand. The sight of his head, cracked open and seeping spinal fluid, caused a momentary queasiness, but it was barely noticeable thanks to the world of hurt boring through his own skull.

Pine trees made pointed spires against the deepened color of the sky. Even fewer cars could be heard now, everyone else far from this forgotten corner of the road. Mason hurried around the front, hopped in behind the wheel, and took off.

What the fuck?!

The thought darted across his consciousness as he flew down the highway.

Sonofabitchwhatthefuckisgoingonhere!

He swerved, almost hit by an oncoming car, honking and flashing its headlights at him. Mason flicked his own headlights on, unaware until now that he'd been driving without them.

Okay, calm down . . . calm down . . . CALM THE FUCK DOWN!

He caught his expression in the rearview mirror. He didn't recognize his own face anymore. Somewhere in his chest, in a cold hole just behind the heart that made it prickle, he had a feeling it would be a long time until he would again.

ELEVEN

"Shit," said Mason once he came to the end of Mill Creek Road. He stopped the car at the driveway, but not in it. Another car was parked behind his truck. One he didn't recognize.

There was no way to call the police, since their phones had been taken. Besides, what would he say? They would sooner believe the town was under attack by a horde of flying monkeys than what he had to tell them.

Who cares? Seriously, fuck what they think. You were abducted by fake cops and now there's someone at your house. That's all that matters.

He thought for a minute. His mind was a mess, but he knew he needed to get a closer look at the house, see what he was up against.

Mason carefully got out of the car and left the door ajar so as not to alert anyone with the noise. Clinging to the shadows and watching for any sign of movement, he moved as stealthily as possible until he reached the bay window of the living room.

The curtains were drawn, making a warm purple glow of the pane of glass with a yellow sliver of light right down the middle. Just enough space to see inside. He inched slowly above the windowsill and peeked inside, then ducked back down immediately when he saw a face through the window.

He screwed up his courage again, this time prepared for what he saw.

The Bible salesman, the one from earlier today, was sitting on his grandmother's floral sofa, one ankle crossed over the other knee, fingers clasped in front of him. Now he recognized the car in the driveway—it had pulled into Gus's this afternoon. He looked completely out of place in this setting, like he belonged in a glitzy lounge protecting Hollywood royalty rather than in an old lady's front parlor.

There was no sign of Rose. Mason couldn't decide if that was good or bad.

Then she appeared behind the stranger from the kitchen carrying two cups of tea and saucers. She set one down on the table in front of him. The man's lips moved, and though Mason couldn't quite hear what he said, it looked like "Thank you." Rose sat down on the sofa next to him. Bossy leapt up into her lap and she rubbed her under the chin. Casual as could be.

"What the—"

"What's going on?" came a voice from behind.

Mason let out a yelp. He faced the feeble voice behind him to see Julie who, if he didn't know better, looked like she had just been roused from a coma. Her eyelids were half open and her knees buckled. Mason kept her propped up by throwing one of her arms around his neck.

When he looked back at the window, Rose and her guest weren't there.

The porch light flicked on. Mason froze like a deer in headlights as the front door flew open. The salesman appeared on the porch and held his hand up for Rose to wait, the other tucked just inside his jacket by the side of his chest.

"It's them," the man said. Same deep voice, same soft British accent.

72

Rose ran past him, clutching her chest. "Great Caesar's ghost," she cried. "You two nearly gave me a—" The color drained from her face as Julie wobbled again. "Oh, sweet Jesus! What happened?"

Rose rushed over to help him, followed closely by their gentleman guest, who scooped Julie up as she went limp in his arms.

"Take her inside and lay her down on the couch," said Rose. He did as she asked.

It was a good thing they had no neighbors to witness this little scene. Boy, would there have been talk around town the next day.

"Mason?" said Rose, trying to get him to look at her. He simply stared into space now, lost and confused. "Mason!" Rose barked, snapping her fingers in front of his eyes. "Where's Dale?

"T-t-trunk," he stuttered, and pointed at the vehicle they had arrived in.

Rose glanced at the Lincoln and saw the battered remains of the trunk lid.

"Who did this?"

"Police."

"The police?"

"Pulled us over. Tried to take us. Tried to hurt them."

"The police did?"

"Mmhmm."

She put her hand to his forehead, wiped away the trail of blood. "Okay, I want you to listen to me." She led him toward the front door. "Mason, look at me."

He did, and a sudden calm came over him as his pupils locked with hers.

"I need you to go inside, go to the kitchen, sit down at the table, and wait for me. All right? Can you do that?"

". . . Julie."

"Julie's fine, sugar. Do as I say now."

Mason did as she said, practically sleepwalking until he was inside the house. The porch light cast a long shadow of him down the hallway leading to the kitchen. To his left, Mason saw the man knelt down by Julie as she lay on the sofa, his head bowed, eyes closed, a warm dark hand on her pale forehead. But Mason didn't stop. He kept moving until he entered the well-lit kitchen and took a seat exactly where he had eaten breakfast earlier that morning. Same spot, different place. This morning, he had been in a world of tedious but complete certainty. Now, up was down. Everything flipped on its end.

"They've had their heads played with, but I think they'll be all right," said the gentleman as he entered the kitchen. He sat in the Barcalounger, the one of the odd quartet that seemed to fit him the best.

Rose had made Mason a cup of tea. It sat untouched and steaming in front of him as he stared out the darkened window above the sink.

"Thank heavens." Rose sat where she had been sitting this morning as well, in the lawn chair to his left. She leaned in close. "Mason?"

He looked at her, this time without hesitation.

"Mason, this is Mister Blake Grimshaw," she said with a gesture toward the man across the table from her. "He's . . . a friend."

Mr. Grimshaw gave a curt nod and a polite smile as he took a silk handkerchief from his breast pocket to clean his glasses. On his right ring finger he wore a silver signet ring with what, at a glance, resembled the Swiss Army Cross and Shield.

Rose had raised him. She had been both parents when it came to clothing and feeding him, keeping a roof over his head, teaching him right from wrong, how to be kind to be people, how to listen. Eccentric as she was, Mason would say he was the one person in this world who knew her best . . . and for the life of him, not a single way in which she might have known this man came to mind. She had never spoken of him before. Rose had few actual friends, and the ones Mason did know were women—mostly widows—well into their sixties or seventies who she played bridge with on Thursday nights.

This friend seemed to be the yin to her yang.

"Hi," said Mason dryly.

"Actually, we've met, haven't we?" said Mr. Grimshaw.

"Yeah. I guess."

Rose put her hand on his shoulder. He flinched. For some reason it unsettled him, made him nervous. "Now I want you to just relax and tell me what happened. Take your time."

Something about the soft, silky strands of steam flowing up from the tea fixed his gaze and cleared his head. Next thing he knew, the whole ordeal, every last surreal detail of it, came pouring out in lucid clarity all over again. The trance. His Hulk-like strength. The whole thing. The most amazing thing was how fast it had all changed. Moments before they were pulled over, it was just another day. Then everything just happened.

"And then . . . and then . . ." He stammered while describing the way the fat officer's face looked like a squished berry. "I didn't mean to hurt him. Not . . . like *that*!"

Rose and Mr. Grimshaw exchanged glances. Again, he was lost in the place between thoughts, teetering ever so slightly in and out of reality.

"Mason?" said Rose, her hand on his. He didn't respond.

"He's in shock," said Mr. Grimshaw quietly.

"Okay, why don't you go sit with Julie and Dale," said Rose, gently helping him out of the chair and toward the living room sofa.

Dale was still sprawled out in the loveseat perpendicular to the sofa, where Julie lay. He passed them both and stared out the window in a stupor. Night had arrived, the orange glow of the street-lamp across the road now the only light outside.

That was when it really sunk in: he had killed.

Taken life.

Shed blood.

Surely, though, it was an act of self-defense. Protection. Yet, suddenly, he was hit with a bitter chill of sadness and fear. It was so final. So total. Even though those men meant to do them harm, grief struck regardless. Rising and crashing like a wave.

Who in all the world knew nothing of death? One need only turn on the television. In discussion we regard it with familiar distance and an occasional modicum of sympathy, but in reality it's very different.

Though the Ten Commandments were not exactly well quoted or strictly observed in the Cole household, the big one, number six, swirled around in his head like a merry-go-round out of control.

Thou shalt not kill.

But he had.

Twice.

What if the real police had arrived? Maybe some kids pulled into the old gas station to tailgate, get high, get laid, found the bodies, and called them. What if they combed the area and found their cell phones?

What if they were on their way here right now?

TWELVE

Out there in the night, something stirred. Not near the house on Mill Creek Road. Beyond the borders of Stonehill, at the old gas station, which had recently become the resting place of two fresh corpses.

The edge of the western sky was washed with red and purple ink, dark blue clouds flecked across it here and there. Already crickets could be heard with the occasional croak of a bullfrog. There was no wind at all, just the still evening air.

Suddenly the crickets went silent.

A spindly figure approached the station as if right out of the shadows themselves. He could smell the two bodies even before they were in sight. One on the ground, one in the bathroom. Already he could see the crumbling molecules. The decay. The cells had stopped breathing, changing the chemistry in the muscles and bones that would eventually lead to rigor mortis.

Amazing.

And old news. He'd seen it countless times before.

He wondered if there was any blood left. Not that he was used to suckling for scraps—such things were beneath him. But there was a time . . .

Comforting that there were still corners of this world so forgotten that dead bodies could go unseen by human eyes. And yet, they could be just around the corner. Right next door. It brought a smile to his white mask of a face.

He ran a pale hand through the tangles of his copper hair and crouched next to the broken body. Fascinated by the network of burst vessels in the whites of his lifeless eyes.

"You're fired."

And with that, he left the forsaken place.

Fast.

THIRTEEN

Mason sat on the cushions next to the bay window, looking out into the field of black beyond. Except for the lonely cone of light coming from the streetlamp, the night was void of any signs of life.

He couldn't tell what they were saying, but he heard Rose and her "friend" still talking quietly in the kitchen. He sat there, desperately hoping that any minute now she would come to him and explain all this.

A sharp intake of breath and a few mumbled syllables came from the sofa. "What . . . ?" Julie muttered, turning her head from side to side, confused by her new surroundings. "What's going on?"

"Easy." Mason got up and went to her. "Does it hurt?"

Julie sat up and rubbed her forehead as if she were attempting to scratch an itch on her brain. "No, it's more like . . . I'm having trouble . . . thinking. Like there's a . . . fuzziness." She heard the voices coming from the kitchen and peered that way. "How did we get here?"

Mason took a seat next to her. "Do you remember what happened? The cops that pulled us over?"

"Yeah . . . I remember getting in their cruiser and then they did . . . something. Then I couldn't move."

"They had these things, these pendulums that one of them waved in front of us and put us all under a trance."

"What? No. That's insane."

"I agree. But that's what happened."

Rose poked her head out the kitchen door. "Everything okay?"

"I guess," said Mason, unsure how else to answer.

Rose disappeared back into the kitchen.

Mason continued. "When we got back here, this guy was here with Rose."

"What guy?" said Dale, who was just rousing to consciousness in the seat next to Julie.

Mason chuckled coldly at what he was about to say. "*This* you're really not going to believe . . . he's a Bible salesman—or preacher or something. He came to the garage today."

"Oh, come on," said Dale.

"Seriously. He started going on about God and the Bible like there was free beer at a church raffle."

"Well, what's he doing *here*?" Dale doled out each question with a wave of his hand. "How'd he find out where you live? And why would she even let him in in the first place?"

"That's actually a really good question."

Whoever he was, this Mr. Grimshaw, clearly this whole thing had something to do with him. Rose was a lot of things, but stupid was not one of them. Careless when it came to her grandson's safety, also not one of them. One way or another, he knew she must have had a damn good reason.

"Oh, this is stupid." Julie abruptly stood and made to leave.

"No, wait," said Mason, placing his hands on her shoulders, just enough to steady her. "We don't know enough about what's going on yet."

"I know that we should be calling the fucking police."

"Don't you get it? If those guys can control the minds of those two cops, there could be more of them."

Julie let this unfortunate fact sink in and sat back down. "Fine. It's just . . . I don't remember anything. It's like I blacked out. Was it like that for you too?"

"Kind of." Mason strolled pensively to the window again, recalling the experience. "Except that I had thoughts."

"Well, *I* sure didn't," said Julie.

"Me neither," said Dale.

"Probably for the best," said Mason with a hard swallow.

Julie leaned in close to him and spoke as quietly as she could. "How do we know he's not manipulating her like those other guys did?"

Mason looked toward the kitchen, pondering the possibility. "I don't think he is. She's too . . . herself. You guys looked like you were zoned out, hypnotized or something."

Julie gasped. She curled into a ball against the back of the sofa as her hand shot to her mouth, eyes wide as dinner plates.

"What?"

She pointed at the window. "I just saw something move out there!"

Hurried footsteps approached from the kitchen.

"What is it?" asked Mr. Grimshaw, who joined the kids at the window, followed closely by Rose.

Mason listened, scanned the night, but found nothing unusual. Somewhere high above, a plane was on its way to far-off skies. Other than that, it was the way a late summer evening should be: still and silent.

Except for one thing. No crickets.

Were there any before? Mason couldn't remember, even though it was just moments ago.

The lights cut out.

Breath stolen from everyone inside the now-darkened house. Only the light from the streetlamp remained.

"I'm afraid we are no longer alone," said Mr. Grimshaw as he drew the curtains.

No one moved or made a sound.

"Crafty buggers," said Mr. Grimshaw quietly. "They're trying to scare us."

Mason scanned the night and felt a catch in his throat. "It's working."

A scream pierced the silence. Outside. Not far away.

Mason's heart shot ice water through his veins.

Another one. Louder. More like a word now.

"HELP!"

Mr. Grimshaw sprang from his spot, which alone was enough to make the others jump. He pulled something from inside his jacket and took a defensive stance by the front door.

Against his better judgment, Mason peered slowly through the gap between the curtains. A girl staggered into the orange light of the streetlamp. Frazzled and crying.

Grimshaw burst out the door and quickly crossed the lawn.

"Halt!" He raised a silver pistol that glinted in the faint evening light like a fiery dagger poised to strike.

The petrified girl stopped in her tracks just a few steps from the perimeter of the property. Mason got a good look at her. Roughly his age, perhaps a little younger, dressed in a denim skirt, a sleeveless top, and only one mud-covered boot on her left foot. Dyed blue hair in disarray, eyes glassy as a doe in crosshairs.

"Please . . . help," she begged, sobbing between breaths. "They're after me, those fuckers. Those *freaks!*"

Rose cracked open the door. "Is she one of them?" she called to Mr. Grimshaw, who was sizing the girl up with a sharpened gaze, keen to the slightest peculiarity.

"I don't think so," he replied. "But we can't take any chances." Slowly, he backed up, his gun still fixed on her.

"Are you kidding? We can't just leave her out there," said Mason.

"Oh, yes, we can," said Julie. Mason shot her a disgusted look.

"It's too risky," said Grim over his shoulder as he neared the door. "This is what they do. She's bait."

"No! Please, you have to help me," said the girl.

"I'm sorry, my child. There's no room for you at the inn." He crossed himself with his gun. "God be with you."

"No! Please . . . please . . ." Tenderly inching closer.

"I'm warning you." He cocked back the hammer of his gun. "Come no further."

"Please," she whispered with her last breath of hope, and lurched forward.

"Forgive me."

Her bare foot touched the cool grass of the lawn.

A brutal crack of deadly thunder shattered the air itself and the girl dropped instantly, a marionette with severed strings. Face down in the grass, limbs limp at her sides.

Julie squealed hysterically as she clutched tight to Mason, who barely noticed her. His eyes were fixed on Mr. Grimshaw as smoke snaked its way from the gun barrel. Hating him. Loathing him. He couldn't help thinking how he had just mowed that lawn earlier this afternoon.

Another figure appeared slowly, gradually, as if forming from dark clouds. Slender, bone white, and clad in black, he appeared in the soft cone of light beneath the streetlamp. Mason barely knew what he was looking at. It seemed to be a man, but like none he had ever seen before. The languid way in which he materialized from the shadows made him frightful to behold.

"Back inside!" Grimshaw commanded, moving swiftly until they were all finally safe behind the door. He slammed it shut and locked it.

Mason peered above the sill, saw the stranger move across the pavement to the edge of the grass and stand above the dead girl. He began waving his hand over the ever growing pool of blood beneath her head in a clockwise motion, holding something delicately between his thumb and forefinger, as a thin stream of liquid fell to the ground below.

At first, nothing happened.

Then, the ground began to smoke and spark like a lit fuse. It continued until the stranger was partially obscured by the smoke. Finally, there was a flash followed by a low rumble. A burst of energy shook the house, knocking everyone back a few steps but not off their feet.

Something had changed. A metallic tinge of smelting steel hung sour in the air.

When he looked again, Mason saw the stranger standing just outside what appeared to be a giant, smoldering circle surrounding the house.

With the calm manner of an old man out for a stroll on a lovely Sunday afternoon, the stranger put one foot out, stretched it over the blackened perimeter, and crossed the front lawn.

"Impossible," said Grimshaw.

"You said we were safe!" Rose's voice broke on the last word.

"I thought we were."

As the man approached, Rose pulled the curtains closed completely and huddled the kids in close to her, wrapping her arms around all three.

Nobody moved.

Nobody spoke.

Nobody breathed.

Quiet as a dreamless sleep. Waiting for whatever was about to happen next.

The doorbell rang. Whimpers came from them all—except Mr. Grimshaw, who began to breathe powerfully, his nostrils flaring with each inhale.

The doorbell rang again, followed by a few gentle knocks.

"Hell-OOO-ooo?" Practically no more than a whisper, as if a neighbor had stopped by.

. . .

84

A fist began pounding on the door loud enough that Mason was sure he heard splitting wood.

And then it stopped.

"What do we—?" Julie uttered in a single, shuddering breath.

The living room wall exploded in a hailstorm of splintered wood and glass as an earth-shattering crash rocked the house, the impact so hard that it shook Mason's bones. Dazed and short of breath, bits of drywall clinging to his hair.

When he lifted his head from his own trembling arms, he saw a giant hole where the window had been moments earlier. His surroundings were littered with dust and debris, broken wood strewn about the furniture. From the deafening noise he expected to see a wrecking ball but saw instead a car—the Buick that had been parked in the driveway—crashed at a downward angle as though it had somehow been thrown.

The others were coming to. Mr. Grimshaw, himself clearly shaken, helped Rose to her feet. Dale lay pinned to the floor by the bumper of the car like a nail in a centipede. Julie . . .

No Julie.

No sooner had he noticed she was missing, than Mason heard her strained voice coming from the front door. He hurried over to it, stepping past Rose and Mr. Grimshaw, to see the door wide open . . . and Julie, just beyond the threshold, held captive on the porch by the red-haired stranger.

Mason saw him clearly now. Aside from a few thin, dark veins snaking across his forehead, his skin was white as chalk. Hair the color of dried blood, wild as if ravaged by a violent squall. The eyes were crazed and empty. A pair of stone-washed jeans and a studded leather jacket that had seen better days were the only things covering his otherwise bare, emaciated frame.

He held Julie by the throat in front of him, her face twisted in pain, tears trickling down her ruddy face.

"Aren't you going to invite me in, little pig?" asked the stranger.

"Mason, get away from the door," Rose snapped, braced upon one of Grimshaw's shoulders.

"Well, now, that's not polite. Not polite at all." Sweet words in a sickening hiss. "I simply would like to come in and have a chat. A little chin wag, if you will. But if I'm not welcome . . ." Julie let out a cry as the stranger tightened his grip.

"Don't do it, Mason!" Mr. Grimshaw pleaded. "You can't help her now."

"You're hurting your friend, boy." A hint of pointed teeth just visible behind his thin lips. "Why would you do that? Do you want her to die?"

A metallic *click*. Mr. Grimshaw had drawn his pistol again and was aiming it at the open doorway. "Don't do it, son. I don't want to, but I will take her out to prevent you letting him in."

"*Wooool!*" The stranger's eyes widened with excitement. "*Now it's a party!*"

Thoughts swirled, each choice, each outcome clashing as both voices battled each other.

Do it . . .

Don't.

Do it!

Don't!

DO IT!

DON'T!

Julie managed to choke out a single, solitary word. "Please."

"Come in, goddammit!" Mason shouted. "*Come in!*"

Grimshaw fired.

Mason was knocked to the ground as something sped past him.

Where the stranger stood an instant earlier there was nothing but empty space. Julie had collapsed to the ground.

Mason turned over to see Mr. Grimshaw lifted clean off the ground, held by one of the stranger's clawed hands clasped around his neck, the other holding his gun.

"Olly olly oxen free," he called out with unbridled glee.

An echo of scattered yips sounded in the night like a pack of hyenas closing in. Several other figures appeared on the front lawn, moving in the same ghostly manner as their leader, and stopped just outside the front door. There was a blonde with purple shades, who gathered Julie up from the ground and held her, another man with mutton chops in a simple jacket and blue jeans, and a pair of identical twin women with cropped black hair. With their dark clothes they looked like mourners at a funeral—except for their demented, wide-eyed grins.

The blonde gathered Julie up from the porch. Still alive but clinging to consciousness.

"'Ello, Grimsy, ol' boy!" the stranger hissed in a faux-English accent, and handed him over to his gang.

"Novak," Mr. Grimshaw said with nothing but disdain.

"I've missed you. Like a burn in my piss." The stranger tossed the gun out the open door and felt around inside Mr. Grimshaw's jacket. "No more toys?"

"I wasn't exactly expecting company."

The stranger wagged a finger at him. *"Tsk! Tsk!"*

A pair of dirty bare feet approached. The stranger crouched, stared deep into his eyes, and whispered, "At last."

There was an oddness to the sunken eyes and sheer angles of his face that cut through the veil of humanity. A current of madness just below the surface of his smile, poised to crest into a wave of laughter that never quite seemed to crash. Though he had the form of a man, this stranger was anything but human. Mason had never before known the sensation he felt in this creature's presence. A sense of danger radiated from him the way Mason's body produced heat. How he imagined a rabbit must feel in the pit of its stomach when spotted by a wolf. That same basic dread, deep in his core.

The stranger stretched out his hand ever so delicately toward Mason's face. And for the second time in his short eighteen years, Mason thought he was about to die.

One long white finger tapped him at the end of his nose. "Boop!"

A sickening shudder went through him as if the Devil himself had just cupped his balls.

"Don't you touch my grandson, you filthy thing!" Rose spat.

As if suddenly remembering that there were others in the room, the stranger drifted over to her like a wisp of smoke. With nowhere else to go, Rose was backed up against the wall.

He cocked his head, considering her.

An unthinkable thought flashed through Mason's mind—the stranger plunging his hand into her chest, twisting and pulling out her bloody, beating heart.

Julie was lost in a fit of wailing. Grimshaw winced while his captors cackled around him.

Mason realized that what he'd seen was not in his head. It had happened.

The horrible *crunch* of her breaking bones played again and again and again. It wasn't until the stranger dropped the heart to the floor and began to slap his own face, leaving wet, red hand marks on his cheeks, that he was even sure it had really happened. The honesty of blood.

He got in nice and close to Mason, foul breath practically fuming from his open jaws.

"It is most unwise to insult me," he hissed, low and deadly.

A dull knocking sounded from the trunk of the car.

The stranger swept over in one move, dug his fingers into the metal like warm butter, and tore the trunk lid clean off. A loud *crack!* followed by a bright flash of light as thick white smoke filled the living room in an instant.

Mason felt himself being pulled out of the fog until he was safely outside in the untainted air. Reduced to a full-body cough, he doubled over and spewed the contents of his stomach onto the lawn.

Mr. Grimshaw, a handkerchief over his mouth and nose, hacked and choked into the wadded palm of his hand. There was no sign of the intruders now. After quickly taking the opportunity to collect his gun from the lawn, he lifted Mason up off the ground by the elbow and pulled him toward the Lincoln.

"Mason," said Grimshaw, making for the deformed Lincoln. "Hurry."

"Wait."

"There's no time."

"Wait!" he shouted, and stopped at the passenger's side door. "We have to go back for them—we have to—"

"They're gone, son," said Grimshaw forcefully, shaking him out of it. "As we should be. Now get in and buckle up!"

The car peeled away so hard and fast that a fat cloud of burnt rubber was whipped up by the screeching tires, particles reflected in the headlights for a moment before being left behind.

Down the dark road the car flew at breakneck speeds, around corners, past other vehicles so fast they were little more than streaks of brake lights. The engine revved . . . and with it came shrieks from above.

One landed hard on the roof, denting it in the middle. Grimshaw aimed his pistol at the shallow groove and fired until a body fell, slamming the bent trunk lid closed before hitting the pavement.

Something hit the back end and sent the car skidding. Grimshaw cranked the wheel hard to regain control and hung a right onto the highway. The interstate opened up, streetlights and green signs whizzing by as the car raced beneath an overpass.

Two of them appeared on either side of the car—the twins—running as no person could run. Their arms and legs jackhammered with mechanical fury, keeping pace with the speeding automobile. Both of them leapt skyward at the same time and hung in the air for just a moment before rocketing down toward them.

Grimshaw slammed on the brakes, put his hand out to brace Mason, and came to a gut-wrenching stop so harsh Mason could feel his bones press against his skin. Two bodies collided with each other half a second before slamming into the ground. The engine revved again and drove right over them.

"Wo' fa' thanagan!"

Words muted by the concussive shock of gunfire in Mason's ears. "What?!"

"*I said they won't fall for that again!*" Mr. Grimshaw shouted over the growl of the engine.

The crash of glass came from behind. A spare tire hit the window, shattering it as it went bouncing down the interstate. Mason braced himself and, without fully realizing it, clutched at the cross around his neck.

A ferocious, disembodied roar sounded above and the roof was violently torn from the car. Someone landed in the now-open back-seat. Grimshaw fired blindly behind him, each shot hitting nothing but air. The red-haired stranger flipped over to the passenger's side, hanging outside the car by nothing but a handful of upholstery.

He grabbed Mason by the collar of his shirt and spun him around. The cross around Mason's neck came spinning out toward the ravenous face, fiery and blazing brightly through its coat of tarnish.

The stranger let out a terrible howl, and with a frantic flurry of white hands, fell away into the night.

The deep purr of the engine had been reduced to a hacking cough. Ears assailed by the noise, all Mason heard now was a hum as the world around him began to dissolve.

Just the night road that stretched out into the distance. No destination, but no longer a dead end. If the moon was out, he did not see it in the sky.

And with that, Mason Cole finally got his wish and left Stonehill, Ohio.

FOURTEEN

Sheriff Bailey didn't think much of Rose Cranston or her grandson. He thought she was a loony who had somehow dodged the bin, and the boy? A doper, maybe a queer. He didn't particularly like the Voodoo crap she did for a living, either. Filling people's heads with all kinds of pagan nonsense that didn't do anyone any good. But as far as the law was concerned, they were no different from anyone else. Innocent until proven guilty.

But when reports came in from those who lived closest to the hill of loud noises—almost like a car crash and gunfire—he was sure tonight was the night.

The sheriff didn't like being disturbed when he was off duty, but he had been called by one of his deputies, who said there was something he would have to see to believe.

He'd heard that before. But sure enough, this time it happened to be true.

FIFTEEN

THE WORLD HAD BECOME AN EMPTY VOID. HIS MOUTH DRY AND full of dust. Eyes burning, caked with ancient sand. Bits of ash fluttered in front of his face and landed on his tongue.

He moved slowly, carefully through the emptiness, fingers unseen brushing against his little limbs. There were voices. Screams. Cries. Pleas in tongues he couldn't understand. He wanted to help but couldn't. He heard the clapping of invisible hands; not near, far too quiet for that, but off in the unknown . . . soft, flat applause, guiding him.

Something appeared ahead, faint and drowned like a light underwater. He walked toward it and watched it grow, the din clearing with each step before it pulsated and opened up, killing the dark altogether.

He heard before he could see. A flat patter of sound nearby, like the drumming of fingers on a cardboard box. Mason felt himself rising. A strong hand touched his chest and he sank back down to the bed.

"Easy," came a deep voice from somewhere unseen.

Eyes trying to focus in the bleached-white light around him. For a moment he thought of Heaven . . . but surely it wouldn't have such a sterile smell nor the coarse rustle of unfamiliar sheets. He rubbed the fuzziness from his vision until a rain-spattered window appeared on the wall next to him, each fat drop hitting the pane of glass that separated him from a cloudy gray afternoon. Outside he could hear the distant wail of an ambulance.

"Where am I?" he asked.

"Boston, Massachusetts," answered the voice of Mr. Grimshaw.

He was in a hospital room. Except for his, the other beds were empty. The floor was tiled in a black-and-white-checkered pattern that looked like a giant chessboard. He had not been in a hospital since childhood—since the earthquake—but even from one side of the world to the other, they all looked the same. There were two chairs next to the window: in one sat his neatly folded clothes; in the other sat Mr. Grimshaw.

This isn't happening, he thought. *It must be a dream.* Only you don't ever think that in a dream.

"They're dead, aren't they?" Mason said, his throat dry as a bottle of ash.

A moment of silence passed between them before the next words were uttered. "I'm afraid so." Mr. Grimshaw rose from his seat and peered out the window. "Do you understand what has happened?"

"I'm *aware* of what happened, but I wouldn't say I *understand.*" Mason fought back a catch in his throat while reluctantly recalling the events that led him here. "You're no Bible salesman, are you?"

"I never said I was," said Mr. Grimshaw.

"Then who the hell are you?"

Mr. Grimshaw turned and faced him again, arms crossed as he leaned against the wall. "I'm a member of a private sect of the Catholic Church called the Holy Order of Militia Dei. Have you heard of us?"

You gotta be fucking kidding me, he thought so loudly it showed on his face. "Actually, yeah, I have."

"What have you heard?"

"Not much," said Mason, rubbing his head in a vain attempt to clear his thoughts. "My friend Dale mentioned it . . . said you studied the occult and stuff like that."

"Stuff *like* that," said Grimshaw with a subtle but notable emphasis. "Yes, we study a great many things. Possession, spiritual phenomena, extrasensory perception—"

"Vampires."

Mr. Grimshaw's face went blank. He regarded Mason like a crippled thing, someone who would not recover from a severe injury. "God knows if you're not ready for this yet, I'll understand." He spoke softly. "But if you want to know what happened, why they were after you, get dressed and come to the church next door. Take all the time you need."

Out the rain-washed window Mason could see the steeple of a church tipped with a cross. There was a sickly pallor to the sky as it coughed rain and wind down from above.

Grim began to leave, the heels of his shoes tapping on the polished floor, placed his hand on the doorknob, and stopped and looked back over his shoulder. "I'm sorry."

As soon as Mr. Grimshaw left the room, Mason's head began to whirl. He couldn't tell whether it was a natural result of shock or the effects of painkillers doing their job. There was very definite pain in his neck and shoulders, but it was dull when it should have been unbearable.

This can't be real . . . can it? It felt as though he were trapped in an episode of *The Twilight Zone*. Only instead of being curious to find out what would happen next, he dreaded it.

His breaths grew to rapid, panicked rasps as he fell back on the bed.

"No!" Mason forced the air in his lungs out to form this single word. Inhaled again: "Not again . . . not again . . . not again . . ."

He wept, rocking back and forth. Halfheartedly, he expected to see their faces come bursting through the door any second. Just some sick joke, a terrible, thoughtless prank at his expense. That would be just fine. That he could live with. It may take years of therapy and a nice cozy pill addiction, but he could learn to cope with such an experience if only he knew that everyone he cared about was actually safe and sound.

With a nice cold place to grow now, it seemed his worst fears had spread from their home in the shadows to the vacant corners of his heart like a nest of cockroaches. While others have faces, shapes, and sounds we can try to block out, the unknown is the most insidious of fears, for it turns our imaginations against us.

On the other hand, if this was real, he had to know.

SIXTEEN

"DOESN'T LOOK LIKE HE'S COMING," SAID FATHER COFFEY, WITH a nip from his flask.

Blake Grimshaw, seated in the front pew of St. Augustine's Church, patiently looked away from the silver crucifix of the altar to his wristwatch. It was 5:40, nearly an hour since he left Mason in the infirmary.

"Have faith," Grimshaw said with an uncertainty he was trying to keep hidden. Then one of the church's double doors groaned open and Mr. Grimshaw's frown inverted to a smile.

Damp and chilled, Mason made his way down the middle of the church. Wooden pews lined the nave beneath low-hanging light fixtures. High, intricate windows of stained glass every color of the rainbow stretched toward the vaulted ceiling. He passed the confessionals and approached the pulpit to see Mr. Grimshaw with a stout, spectacled man with a white beard and hair thinned to wisps behind his ears. He had a kind, grandfatherly face, round nose between flushed cheeks, and dressed in a clean black suit with a white clerical collar.

"Glad you could join us," said Mr. Grimshaw, beaming. "This is Father Coffey, our chaplain and custodian of St. Augustine's."

The priest gave a friendly nod.

"Hello," said Mason nervously. "Look, Mister Grimshaw—"

"Please, just call me Grim. Everyone does."

"Okay, *Grim*," Mason corrected himself. "I just want to know what's going on. That's all."

"And so you shall." Grim gestured to a spot on the pew next to him. "Please, sit."

"I'll be going now, give ye two some time," said Father Coffey with a lyrical Irish lilt, and he left through a door in the sanctuary ahead.

Mason accepted the invitation and took a seat. He remained silent, expecting something to follow. Instead, Mr. Grimshaw—Grim —whatever—was focused on the altar before them.

Carved of the same dark wood as the pews they sat on, it was clean and polished so that it glistened even in the scarce light. The gilded figure of Jesus was nailed to his cross, flanked by the Virgin on one side and Judas on the other, hanging from a tree. Above him an angel—Michael, presumably—shone down rays of light and clutched a sword to his chest. In the apse behind the altar was a triptych of stained-glass panels depicting saints whose names he did not know.

"What do you believe in, Mason?" Grim spoke at last.

The first thing that came to his mind was *In the beginning, God created the heavens and the earth*, followed not by the remaining verse of Genesis, but rather the sardonic wit of Douglas Adams. *This made a lot of people very angry and is widely regarded as a bad move.*

Mason sighed. "Haven't we covered this already?"

"I recall us discussing Shakespeare and 'old myths and legends,' as you put it."

"You asked if I had accepted Jesus as my Lord and Savior."

Grim raised his index finger. "Actually, the precise question I asked was if you had accepted *Christ*."

"What's the difference?"

"Oh, there is most definitely a difference." He gingerly pushed his glasses back up to the top of his nose where they belonged. "Do you remember what you said?"

Mason pretended to replay the conversation, searching his memory for the answer, when he really didn't need to. "I said I didn't need a savior."

"Do you feel the same now?"

Mason shrugged and breathed another deep sigh. "I don't know."

"That's a good answer."

"I feel so many things at the same time they're kind of canceling each other out."

"Not surprising. You're likely still in shock, not to mention a mild case of whiplash. You'll have to take it easy for a while, but it should clear up in a few days."

"What are you, a doctor?"

"Yes."

"Really?"

"Who do you think treated you?"

"Oh." Mason bowed his head as if in prayer. "Thank you."

"The questions I asked before were intended to gauge your responses rather than to preach."

"What for?"

"To see whether or not you were open-minded."

"Given the things I've seen in the last . . ." Mason's hands shot to his pockets, feeling around for a phone. "Wait, how long has it been?"

"Two days," said Grim.

"Well, I think it's safe to say that my mind is wide open for business now."

"Glad to hear it. How do you feel about providence?"

"We talking about the capital of Rhode Island or matters of divine intervention?"

Grim grinned. "The latter."

"That would require a belief in God, wouldn't it?"

"More generally, then. What about fate?"

"Not really, no."

"Because?"

"Because, aside from its existence being unproven, that would still mean someone or something is mapping this all out—you, me, every animal, every bottle of ketchup, every dog turd, the world and the way it works, everything and everyone in it. And by extension it would mean that each decision made by fate, however bad, has a purpose. There are things I just can't believe that about."

His words prickled with venom.

"And by even *further* extension, it would mean that that same someone or something has made recent events unfold as they have, meaning the deaths of my friends and grandmother were a conscious, deliberate choice, making this mysterious custodian of fate as guilty for their deaths as the one who killed them."

"How interesting." Grim sat back, pensively stroking his goatee as though he hadn't picked up on the anger in Mason's voice. "I've always thought of fate as an equation with infinite, ever-changing variables, constantly shifting, creating remainders that accumulate over time and result in random events. Meaning fate needn't necessarily rely on God, but merely on *balance*. So despite the existence of a mostly harmonious equilibrium, sometimes anomalies occur which we might refer to as 'luck.' "

Mason considered this a moment. "I've never heard it described that way." As the drugs wore off, and his patience with them, pain slowly began to return. "If it's all the same to you, could we skip the philosophical musings for now?"

"Yes, of course. My apologies." Grim stood and leaned casually against the pulpit. "I'll explain everything as best I can for you, but first I need to ask you a few questions."

"*You* need to ask *me* a few questions?"

"It will help clarify certain matters."

Mason shrugged. "Fire away."

"Do you have any relatives with whom you're not very familiar?

An estranged uncle, a distant cousin whose name you know but have never met, anyone like that?"

"No. Both my parents were only children."

"To your knowledge, are you related to anyone with the surname Graves?"

"No."

"Marlowe?"

"No."

"Darkhölme?"

"No."

"When I treated you, I noticed that you wear a cross around your neck."

Mason's hand jerked as though he instinctively wanted to touch it, but stopped.

"May I ask how you got it?"

It was innocent enough, though for one fleeting moment Mason thought the question sounded like an accusation.

"My parents gave it to me."

"I see. The reason I ask is because it just so happens that I've seen it before."

"Where?"

"Around the neck of an old friend of mine named William Graves."

Mason took it in his fingers finally and looked at it. No bigger than his pinky finger, simple, and blessedly spoiled by time, so much so that it was difficult to tell exactly what material it was made from. Its arms extended from the top half of the central beam. He knew there was an engraving on the back, but due to the amount of wear and tarnish he never could quite make it out. "I'm not sure what you're seeing, but this was given to me by my dad when I was six, just before . . ." Mason trailed off.

"I know . . . about the earthquake, that is."

"Join the club."

"I also know that cross when I see it. It's unmistakable and for centuries has been the symbol of the Messiah of the Archangel."

Mason shrugged, waiting for him to go on. "I don't know what that is."

"Not many outside the Order do. The lore and scripture of Militia Dei is a bit more . . . unconventional compared to the rest of the Church, which worships Jesus of Nazareth as the Christ. Of course, we revere Jesus as a teacher and prophet, but it is another holy figure we regard as our Savior, or Christ, which of course comes from the Greek word *khristos*, meaning—"

" 'The anointed one,' I know."

" 'Anointed one,' 'sacred one,' 'chosen one'—all interpretations of the translation of the Hebrew word 'messiah,' which, in its broadest sense, means a divinely ordained figure. But there is no *one*, any more than there is one teacher or leader. There have been many."

"Great. I'm still waiting for the part where you tell me what the hell any of this has to do with me."

"I believe *you* are the messiah."

Silence. Total silence.

"Well . . . *a* messiah. *Our* messiah. It's a long story. I'll give you the abridged version." Grim crossed his legs, took a breath, and continued. "You already know we study the occult, paranormal, and supernatural, and as you have no doubt gathered by now, this goes a bit beyond the realm of mere mythology."

"No shit."

"And one thing we take a particular interest in is miracles."

"Miracles?"

"Anomalies and occurrences of a potential supernatural origin. Stigmata, near-death experiences, inexplicable recovery from sickness or injury, et cetera.

"It was a miracle that spawned our order when God sent the Archangel Michael to Saint Philip, the First Messiah. Will Graves was one of his descendants. Unlike his father and brother, who lost their lives in the line of duty, he chose to be a servant of God rather than a soldier.

"Thirteen years ago, Will—then known as Brother Graves—left our chapter quite suddenly. He wouldn't say why, only that there was a threat which only he could see to."

"Let me guess: Werewolves? Sasquatch? Aliens?" said Mason sarcastically.

"So far as we know, werewolves are extinct, same with sasquatches. And as for aliens—"

"Whoa, whoa! I was kidding." To describe Mason's expression as dumbfounded would have been a gross understatement. "You're really serious, aren't you?"

"Cross my heart."

"Hope to die?"

"Stick a needle in my eye."

"What about ghosts?"

"Real."

"Zombies?"

"Oh, yes. Trust me, you don't want to muck about with a zombie."

"Leprechauns?"

Grim laughed. "No, that's silly. I must say, you're taking this quite well. Most people have a hard time accepting it."

"Guess I'm not most people, then."

"No, you certainly are not. Where was I? Oh, yes . . . having been trained by his father, himself a prior Messiah of the Archangel, Will hung up his collar and took up the sword. Unfortunately, missionaries such as he are tasked with investigation rather than intervention, and so this act resulted in his excommunication from Militia Dei."

"That seems a bit extreme," said Mason. "I get someone breaking the rules, but to kick them out?"

"We take our vows quite seriously. Shortly after, we received a call from our Motherhouse in Jerusalem. The Head Chamberlain said Will had showed up claiming that there was to be an imminent attack on the city. A search was conducted, but nothing was found. And so—"

"Wait . . . what are you saying?" asked Mason, hands clutched to his visibly trembling arms.

"The Great Quake of Jerusalem was not a natural disaster but rather the result of a coordinated attack which Will lost his life trying to prevent. And with him, centuries of history and countless innocent souls."

Mason could hear them, all of them, screaming in a chorus of terror.

"Our prime suspect for that atrocity"—Grim reached into his jacket pocket and produced a cell phone, tapping the display a few times until an image appeared—"is him."

Mason flinched. The shot was blurred and monochromatic, as if taken from a surveillance camera, but that face, that horribly white face he last saw smeared with his grandmother's blood, now appeared in front of him in the palm of Grim's hand. Same cruel grin, same hollow eyes as he waved at the camera.

"His name is Novak," said Grim, who could see how unnerved Mason was by it and quickly flipped to the next image.

Novak . . . the word floated hungrily through his head, *Novak . . .*

"After I left Stonehill, I received a call from Father Coffey informing me that our former chaplain, Father Abbott, had vanished the night before." Grim held the new image up for Mason to see. A lone finger bearing a ring identical to the one Grim wore, severed and placed upright in a bloody puddle on a desk. "This is all that was found of him."

Mason squinted for a better look. "Is that . . . ?"

Grim gave a slow nod and put the phone away. "His middle finger. It's Novak's calling card. After the Great Quake he disappeared, and not so much as a whisper was heard of him until now."

"And how would this Novak be able to destroy an entire city?"

"Well, we're not entirely sure, but according to the late Overseer of our Motherhouse, Will said that Novak was in possession of a device of some sort."

"A device?"

"That's right. I can't stress enough just how exotic a claim this was. Vampires favor stealth and secrecy above all, opting to remain hidden so as not to draw attention to their activities. But over the last century their numbers have dwindled considerably, which apparently forced such a bold and unorthodox move. But *how*, I'm afraid we just don't know for certain.

"We can only guess that Novak has been in hibernation ever since, and upon waking to discover that there had been a lone survivor of the incident, set out to find you, believing, as we did at first, that you were the new messiah. In the wake of the tragedy Father Abbott was convinced it was you, and I was sent to ascertain whether his suspicions were correct."

"You were in Jerusalem after the Quake?"

"I was. However, I found no sign to indicate that you had possessed the Holy Spirit. Had you been wearing that cross at the time," he said, pointing to it, "I would have thought differently. It must have been kept with any other personal effects on your person upon admittance."

"Aha," said Mason. "So when you said we had met before, you didn't just mean earlier that day."

"Right you are. At any rate, Father Abbott became obsessed with finding the next messiah and resigned as our chaplain. He spent the next thirteen years researching the different possible bloodlines, none of which bore any fruit. Turns out his first guess was right after all."

"No. I can't be. How can *I* be a part of *this*? I told you, I'm not related to any of these people."

"To be completely honest, we're not exactly certain. Since the fourteenth century, each messiah has been a direct descendant of Saint Philip. For now, at least, it is a mystery."

"I can't be. I mean, I just *can't* be."

"Lux in tenebris."

"I beg your pardon?" Mason, being the good student and proper nerd that he was, not only getting straight A's but doing extra credit in both his Spanish and Latin classes, actually knew exactly what it meant—*light in darkness.*

"It's a reference to the Christ in the Gospel of John, the motto of Militia Dei, and you'll find it engraved on the back of your cross."

"How could you . . . ?" Mason took it out from under his shirt and turned it over. "I can barely make it out, how could you . . . ? You looked at it while I was out. You must have." Even he didn't believe in the words as he said them.

"Tell me," Grim continued, "what do you recall from when you were abducted by the two thugs posing as policemen?"

"I already told you everything I remember."

"That's just my point. You *remember*. When properly hypnotized, you should have no memory of it at all, let alone have managed to break free."

"All I know is it felt as though someone stuck their fingers in the back of my brain and made me do things. Like a puppet. Like being trapped in my own body. I could see everything going on, but I couldn't control it. Next thing I knew there was this . . . I don't even know what to call it . . . this *storm*," said Mason, recalling the memory of the warped trunk lid. "Erupting. Driving me forward. I just thought it was an adrenaline boost."

"Oh, no doubt," said Grim. "There must have been massive amounts of adrenaline coursing through you. But I can tell you that, from a medical standpoint, no amount of adrenaline can explain a feat such as that. In all likelihood, it would have killed you. And surely you remember what happened when we fled from Stonehill, after Novak turned our getaway car into a convertible."

That's right! He had almost forgotten and at the time was barely aware of what was going on. He only remembered a burst of light from his cross before his assailant was driven away into the rushing shadows of the highway.

"But this can't be. It just can't be."

"Why not?"

"Because . . . it just . . . *can't*."

"However it happened, it seems God has chosen you."

"I don't believe in God."

"Well, He believes in you."

"But why? I'm nobody."

"Jesus was a poor carpenter, the first Dalai Lama a shepherd. An orphaned apprentice named Arthur became the once and future King of England. It matters not one wit who you are now, but rather who you can become."

"Has anyone ever told you that you sound like a fortune cookie?"

"I know how difficult this must be for you."

"Difficult?" Mason's voice wavered. "No, *difficult* would be watching my grandmother and friends murdered right before my eyes. This is *insane!*"

"Yet a minute ago you said your mind was open now. Perhaps it would help if you knew more of the story."

"No! I don't want to hear another word." Mason stood as Grim continued to lean casually. "Look, thanks for saving my life and all, but I've had enough of this. See ya!"

With that, Mason stormed off down the aisle back the way he came, and this time he was not idly admiring the architecture.

"Where will you go?" said Grim, a little louder now.

"Thought I'd start with the police," Mason called back over his shoulder.

"I wouldn't advise that." Grim's deep voice echoed through the church like the voice of the Almighty.

"And why is that?"

"Well, for starters . . . you're dead."

Mason stopped in his tracks. "What are you talking about?"

Grim left the pulpit and made his way toward Mason, tapping at his cell phone while he walked. He held it up like a badge. Mason took it from him and looked again. It displayed an article from the *News-Herald* website.

SEVEN KILLED IN AUTO WRECK

Mason's stomach churned as he counted frantically in his head, starting over each time he reached the same number as the headline.

Seven are dead following an auto-residential accident in the small town of Stonehill in Cuyahoga County, Ohio. Police described the scene as "unbelievable." Three adults and four teenagers were killed after a vehicle collided with a house around 9 p.m. Friday night.

Sheriff George Bailey, of the Stonehill Sheriff's Office, reported a Buick Regal with Massachusetts plates had passed through town and collided with a bungalow, driving right through the wall and into the living room.

While the identities of the victims have not been released, two men were confirmed to have been driving when the vehicle veered off the road. Impaired driving has not been ruled out.

It was the kind of thing that felt as though it had happened to someone else. His home had become a murder scene, the whole ordeal condensed to these few pitiful lines of black and white.

Something about this tiny blurb hit home in a big way, the attacks he had experienced after Jerusalem now returned. His heart began to beat against the walls of his chest, screaming to be let out of its cage of bone which had suddenly become too small, tightening around it. Somehow he knew this would happen again. He didn't know what would cause it, but he felt it. Dreaded it.

Grim said something about a cover story, and though he was standing right in front of him the only words he heard were those of King Claudius.

Help, angels. Make assay.
Bow, stubborn knees, and, heart with strings of steel,
Be soft as sinews of the newborn babe.

Except that all was *not* well. With little left he could do, Mason sunk to his knees in the middle of the church while all the saints and angels, even Jesus Himself, His expression frozen in mirrored agony, watched.

"Mason?" said Grim.

Brain overloaded to a point of meltdown, Mason was stuck staring into space. "Mason's not here right now."

A few minutes passed. Grim took a seat in the nearest pew and waited. Finally he spoke again. "I think that's enough for one day," he said, placing his hand on Mason's shoulder. "Come. Let's find you a room."

He rose from the pew, looked toward the rain-spattered window, and headed away from the double doors rather than toward them.

Mason followed, walking down the aisle once again, until they reached the altar. Through the same door Father Coffey had exited through earlier and right down a narrow hallway they went. It led to a much wider hallway carpeted in green and carved of the same dark wood as the rest of the church. Two doors on each side and one at the opposite end, and from there to a set of stairs descending into the church basement. It was filled with all manner of dusty, shrouded things. Dispersed along the walls was a faint glow of candles at smaller, more modest altars. Through the maze of sheet-covered objects they wove until they came to a door with chipped brown paint.

Grim took a set of keys from his pocket, inserted one into the lock, and twisted. From its appearance, Mason thought it would creak like hell, but instead it swung open almost silently.

They entered a narrow concrete tunnel lit by fluorescent lights. Grim closed the door behind them and locked it again. It was cold in here, but as Mason was already damp and chilled, he did not notice the difference. The hall went straight for about twenty paces, then a complete ninety-degree turn until finally reaching the end.

Mason and Grim emerged into a large garage with all kinds of vehicles parked in the spaces. Civilian mostly, but dispersed throughout were a few police cruisers from different states, two panel trucks, a SWAT van, and an ambulance. There was even a limousine with the diplomatic plates of Argentina. And sure enough, the deformed Lincoln, parked in a space next to a freight elevator.

Grim pulled the elevator gate down until it snapped shut and then pushed the third-floor button. When they reached their floor, Grim got out and Mason followed. But not for long, stopping between two rooms.

"Take your pick," said Grim with a sweep of his hand from the door nearest the elevator to one next to it in the middle of the hall. "Though, if I may make a suggestion, I'd take this one." He pointed to the more central of the two with the number 33 above the keyhole. "The elevator can be a bit noisy."

Mason nodded, barely registering the words. Grim took the keys from his pocket again and opened the door.

Simple and empty. A folded cot in the far corner and a pair of thick curtains hugging the window were the only signs of life in an otherwise barren, cement space. Roughly the size of a small apartment, it had a kitchenette with a small round table and mini-fridge, its own bathroom, and a desk. Bigger than his room—his *old* room, that is—by far, but devoid of its warmth.

Grim unfolded the cot and plunked it down.

"I know it doesn't look like much," he said, taking some linens and a pillow from the top shelf of the closet. "But with a little sprucing, a proper bed, perhaps a carpet or two . . ." He trailed off, looking at Mason as he stared out at the gray world beyond the window, lost in the rubble of his thoughts. "Mason. I promise you, we will find the monster responsible and bring him to justice. You have my word."

Mason continued to stare.

"I'll let you rest now." Grim left the room.

Rest. Would he ever know such a thing again? For surely these past eighteen years he had been resting, all the while perceiving them as burdens, and now he had been drafted into a holy war he never knew existed. The smell of its smoke clung to his skin, soured his tongue. To think that he actually dreaded his life just two days ago. Now it just seemed pathetic. Now he would do anything to trade places with his past self.

When his parents died, being just five-years-old at the time was both a curse and a gift. A curse because there was nothing more awful to a boy his age than feeling frightened and all alone in the world, but a gift because he was young enough to eventually adapt to his new life with Rose. Kids are resilient that way. Grownups often overlook it, but children are far more flexible and receptive to changes than any adult. Now that Rose was gone, taken from him just like his parents—and by the same person, no less—he felt like a six-year-old again. And he cried like one.

Rose was gone.

Not to mention his only friends.

Grim's words echoed in his mind. *We will find the monsters responsible.*

As children we're told that monsters don't exist. But they do.

He's out there, thought Mason. Wind sighed softly against the window. This creature, this Novak, may be standing on the street right now in the rain, looking up at his window trying to work out how to get to him. A sense of dread flooded him, the likes of which he had never tasted before.

Fear for his life.

Thin veins of lightning cracked the sky, followed by the soft rumble of thunder. Mason drew the curtains suddenly and went to the bathroom. He flicked the light on, closed the door just enough to cut a swath through the ambient dark-blue of the room, and sat within it on the cot. It wasn't the same, but it would have to do.

Arms hugging his legs, chin resting on his knees, rocking back and forth while staring at the covered window, he sat there as images of that horrible smiling face surfaced in his mind, just beyond the thin layer of cloth, making him never want to open those curtains. It was like believing in the boogie man again; he found himself resisting the urge to look under the bed.

Sleep was out of the question tonight, but if by some miracle it found him, he knew that he would only be met by nightmares.

Act II:
Slings and Arrows

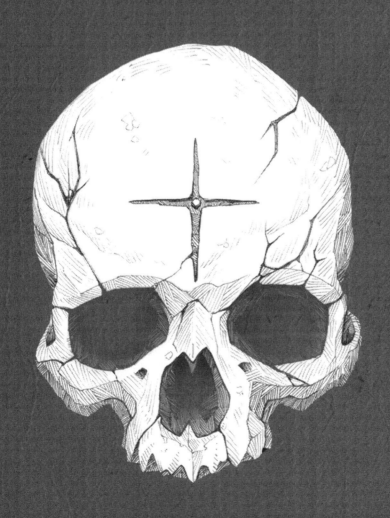

SEVENTEEN

BACK IN THE HOLE, THE CRIES HAD STOPPED. THE GLOOM PIERCED *only by a distant crack of gray light high above. He approached it, weightless. Climbing higher out of the ash. Darkness gave way to an endless wasteland as far as the eye could see.*

Sand-filled wind whipped at his face, ceaselessly whistling in his ears. His vision only penetrated the hazy air enough to see that there was nothing around to see. No distant hill or mountain, no outcropping or rock formation, not so much as a rise in the ground. A flat expanse of nothing.

Then, a sign of movement in this barren limbo: four stone-gray triangles, suddenly appearing in the dirt. A quartet of shark fins surfaced and began to circle in a tight perimeter, smelling his fear sweet as blood in the water. He was afraid to move lest he walk straight into one.

Trapped!

Footprints erased from the ground by the vicious wind when he heard something coming from all around. The clang of bells grew steadily louder until . . .

. . .

Mason woke up in a cold sweat.

At some point in the early hours of the morning he had finally fallen asleep from sheer exhaustion, though when he couldn't say.

He rose from the lumpy cot and went to the bathroom to splash some water on his face. His clothes clung to his clammy skin like cobwebs. In the mirror above the sink his face distorted, a smeared portrait. Hair a mess and matted to one side; eyelids horribly puffy and dark, as though he had not slept in days.

Why is it that every time we look in the mirror we wonder who that is looking back at us? Maybe that's the real me, and I'm the reflection.

Trying to smooth some of his hair back into place, he left the bathroom and went to the window. Yesterday it had only been spritzing, but now it had grown to a proper rain. Normally he liked rain. The feel of a cool breeze through an open window as each drop chatted away about nothing in particular. But today it just dampened him.

Unconsciously, he went about his normal routine. But having no clean clothes to change into, nowhere to go, and no one to go to, these reflexes became stillborn, dying before they could leave the womb.

What do I do? he wondered.

It felt wrong to just go about his day as if it were any other. But staying cooped up in this cold, empty room was out of the question.

Mason went to the elevator and pressed the button, forcing the gears inside to groan to life like an old man getting out of bed. When it arrived, he lifted the gate, brought it back down, and rode it to the only place he knew to go—the ground floor.

As he neared the bottom, he thought he heard echoes from his dream. Only these were different, clearer. Even cheerful. The voices of living people.

Men and women of varying ages, about half a dozen or so. Some sat on the sofas around a large TV screen mounted to the wall, others in front of computer monitors in a small cluster by the far corner of the floor. In another corner populated with game tables and pinball machines, two men casually shot pool. Mason had barely noticed all this yesterday in his vacant state, owing to the fact that it was dark and there were no people there to fill the space.

All eyes fell on him.

He froze, and suddenly felt like the new kid in school.

"You must be Mason," said a voice he didn't recognize.

One of the men playing pool approached. Sandy hair, stubble on his chin, wearing a Boston Police Department T-shirt. He stuck out his hand for Mason to shake. It felt rough and coarse, as if he'd been working with his hands since birth.

"I must be," said Mason awkwardly.

"Patrick Muldoon, but they call me Irish."

"Mason Cole. They call me when supper's ready." Mason felt a sharp, momentary tug of grief. There was no one now to appreciate Rose's sandpaper wit but him. "Um, where's Grim?"

"He'll be down in a minute. We're just waiting for the Bishop before we head over to the church."

"Right . . . the Bishop."

Irish raised an eyebrow. "You don't know who I'm talking about, do you?"

"Not a damn clue."

"Honesty." Irish clapped him on the back. "I like it. Bishop Strauss, he's the Overseer of our chapter."

"And he's a prick," said an athletic, young man in a black-and-red Miami Heat jersey as he knocked one of the balls into the corner pocket. Sporting a single diamond earring and a buzz cut that faded so gradually it was practically a work of art.

Irish gave him the crook eye. "A little soon for that, don't you think?"

The young man shrugged. "Just sayin'."

Irish motioned to him. "This is Silas Diaz."

"Hey hey, easy with the first name." He looked to Mason. "My pops thought it was a good idea to name me after his favorite book."

"Let me guess. Silas Marner?"

"You know it?"

"I like to read," said Mason with a shrug. "You're Grim's son?"

"Nephew. My pops isn't with us anymore."

"Oh. I'm sorry."

"All good. Anyway, just call me Diaz."

"Does everyone here have a nickname?"

"Just the best of us."

"Okay." The beginnings of a tiny smile curled the corner of his mouth. "From now on call me . . . *Mace*."

Both men burst with laughter.

"Nice!" said Diaz.

Mason shook his head. "Why do I think I'm going to regret that?"

"Because you probably will," said Diaz.

The elevator opened. Grim stood waiting inside as everyone began filing into the elevator. "Ah, Mason. How are you feeling?"

Mason unenthusiastically raised both thumbs. "Never better."

"We have a briefing at the church. Would you care to join us?"

"I guess," he said uncertainly. "I mean, I don't want to be a sore thumb or anything."

"Nonsense. If anyone has earned the right to be there it's you."

Mason joined the group in the elevator. They descended to the garage and entered the church through the same tunnel Mason took with Grim yesterday, far more cramped this time due to the number of people. He noticed a few things he hadn't before. The presence of security cameras at either end of the tunnel, for one. And a metal door with a keypad on it in the middle of the tunnel.

Upon entering the church basement, they passed through the labyrinth of covered junk. This time Mason peeked over the heaps to see a series of makeshift altars along the walls. Surrounded by candles in glass holders were holy cards, rosaries, and photographs. Some of them were not Catholic, not even Christian. One had a large penta-gram and an ornate blade of some kind, another with a ram's horn and Star of David, and one that appeared to be Shinto.

The stamping of feet echoed through the basement, kicking up loose dust that clung to the boards they stepped on. As Mason climbed the stairs behind the others, he emerged into the hallway through which he had passed yesterday. The stream of people poured into a door on the right.

Mason followed and entered a meeting room with a long table in the middle. Two men were already seated at the far end: one was Father Coffey; the other he didn't recognize but knew instantly that it could only be the aforementioned Bishop Strauss.

A strict-looking man with a gilded pectoral cross hung over a black cassock, he stirred a cup of coffee on the table in front of him as he watched Mason. Thin strands of hair slicked back beneath a violet zucchetto atop his head. From his hard, heavily lined face Mason figured he was perhaps in his seventies. Jowls hung at both sides of his mouth in a lazy frown, giving him the visage of an old toad. If he had ever smiled, it was a long time ago.

Mason took the nearest empty seat by the door.

Grim waited until everyone was in then closed the door so that it was still open a crack before joining the two clergymen. "We're still missing someone, but I think we'll get started," he said, scanning the faces as they took their seats around the table. "First, out of respect for our guest, I think introductions are in order." He gestured toward Mason. "May I present Mason Cole, formerly of Stonehill, Ohio."

Every pair of eyes twisted toward him again. He gave an awkward little wave and with a slight crack in his voice said, "Hi."

"You've already met Father Coffey, and with us today is Bishop Strauss, Overseer of the Boston chapter of Militia Dei."

The Bishop neither waved nor spoke but regarded Mason with quiet skepticism.

Starting counter-clockwise, on his left, the others began to speak.

"Lieutenant Patrick Muldoon," said Irish.

"Corporal Silas Diaz," said Diaz.

"Sergeant Gabriella Rodriguez," said a comely woman with a throaty voice which carried the slightest hint of an accent, the kind that lingers from acquiring a second language later in life. Wavy black hair slung over one shoulder in a single braid. Brown eyes and taut, tanned skin that gave her face a strong, smooth shape. Not a scrap of makeup. The plain white shirt she wore was stained with grease and dirt as if she had just come from working on a car.

"Corporal Miguel Rodriguez," said a bald, heavily tattooed man with a goatee who strongly resembled the woman beside him. His voice carried no accent, nor levity, at all. Broad-shouldered and muscular, most of his torso showed beneath the black tank he wore. A full, highly detailed portrait of the crucifixion was inked into one bicep; a pair of praying hands clasping a rosary on his neck; and a cross just below his left eye. One of the few tattoos that was not of religious origin were the letters M-I-G-G-S across his knuckles.

"Major Natalie Hirsch, Chief of Security," said a muscular woman in army fatigues. Loud and clear, with an Israeli accent. Short chestnut hair beneath a cap matching her uniform. Eyes dark and strong. Pure military.

A middle-aged Asian man next to her wrote quickly on a piece of paper. He was dressed plainly in a collared shirt, unbuttoned at the neck. Narrow, chiseled face and long gray hair tied back in a nub that swung slightly from the rapidity of his motions as he wrote: CORPORAL RAYMOND YEN, WEAPONS SPECALIST. Mason read to himself, noting the typo in the last word.

Perplexed as to the nature of his method, Mason gave a simple nod of acknowledgment, which was politely returned as Yen sat with his hands folded in front of his face.

Just then someone burst into the room.

"Sarah Vegesticka, blasphemer and heretic." It was a girl with a spiky green mohawk, and she took the empty seat next to Mason. "'Sup, Eli," she said, jerking her head toward the Bishop, who appeared to cringe at the sight of her. Her eyes were drowsy and dark with eyeshadow. Long neck. Wide mouth. One nostril of her slender nose was pierced. Her impeccably high cheekbones gave her face a contoured, if slightly gaunt, sort of appeal. She wore a Rancid T-shirt with the sleeves cut off, ripped red tartan pants, and a pair of combat boots. A circlet of chains and spikes around her wrist jingled as she moved her waifish arms, both of which were patterned with an eclectic mix of tattoos. She stopped chewing her gum just long enough to blow a big pink bubble until it popped.

Each more different than the next. There were two commonalities between them—they all looked bedraggled, as if they had just come off double shifts, and they all wore the same silver rings Mason had seen on Grim's right hand. Only the Bishop's differed in that, instead of a solid piece of silver, it had a violet setting.

"You're late," said Grim dryly.

"Sorry, Cap. But I have a good reason," she replied.

"I look forward to hearing it." Grim raised his eyebrows and took his seat. "The cover-up in Ohio. How did it go?"

"Piece of cake," said the female Rodriguez, sliding a manila file in front of her down the table toward Grim. "Story secure, fail-safes in place. Fortunately there were no actual witnesses, so containment was minimal. Only a few memory wipes were needed, namely the sheriff and his deputies."

Grim opened the file and began flipping through it. "Victims?"

"Two males, Clive Ballantyne and Randall Romano, both convicted felons. One female, Kimberley Manning, a runaway from Des Moines. Rosemary Cranston and Dale Anderson, present and accounted for. Mister Cole here has been replaced with a Doe, as has Julie Walsh, whose body still hasn't turned up."

"I want to know if it does," said Grim. His eyes didn't leave the pages.

"Her parents were hypnotized for a positive ID, so even if she does they wouldn't recognize her."

"It's more of a principle matter than a professional one, Sergeant." Grim gave Mason a sympathetic glance.

"Understood."

Mason felt a sickening tug of nausea at the thought of her body, stiff and cold somewhere no human could travel, an undiscovered cave or buried beneath the bottom of a lake. Poor Julie. And Poor

Dale. Gus must be devastated. His mom and brother, too. As for Julie's parents, he wondered if they would have even noticed. Maybe once her mother had to pick up her own Prozac from now on.

Don't! he willed, feeling the tears rising again. *You can't lose it. Later you can have the granddaddy of all breakdowns. But not here. Not now.*

"What have we got on Father Abbott's disappearance?"

Irish cleared his throat. "We searched his room at Saint Angela's. No sign of forced entry, no prints, no witnesses. One of the nuns brought him his breakfast to find that he wasn't there. Except for his finger, that is."

"Any thoughts on how Novak knew to find him in the first place?"

"Think we have a leak?" asked Irish.

Grim took his glasses off and rubbed the bridge of his nose. "It's possible."

"Yes, it is," said Bishop Strauss, his voice a low, gravelly croak. "And I believe it's obvious who it is." He took his time stirring his coffee before finally placing the spoon on the saucer, then brought the cup up to his thin lips. "Father Abbott," he said, followed by a thoughtful sip.

Grim's mouth hung open. "You can't be serious?"

"How else do you explain it?"

"With all due respect, the lack of an explanation doesn't make an assumption correct."

"Oh, come now, Captain. You know as well as I do that he'd been growing . . ." Strauss fumbled for the right word. "—*unstable* over the years. His work bordered on obsession, his methods questionable, leading him to consult with far less . . . *ethical* individuals than a man of his covenant should. Who is to say he hadn't been compromised?"

"Horseshite," said Father Coffey with a tipsy little hiccup.

"I beg your pardon?" said Strauss.

Father Coffey sat himself up straight in his chair and cleared his throat. "He was a man of God and once-chaplain of this very chapter, a station not easily assumed nor subverted. He devoted his life te Militia Dei and te finding the next messiah. And he just suddenly decides te betray us to our enemies for no reason at'all? Forgive my candor, Yer Eminence, but I don't believe that for a moment."

"He was obsessive," said Grim. "No argument there. And frankly, I can't say I blame him. But he was no traitor. Of that I have no doubt."

"Lord knows he wouldn't be the first." With another sip from his cup, the Bishop glanced toward Sarah which, if intended as subtle, certainly was not. It gave Mason a chill.

"Besides, that still wouldn't explain how Novak managed to break a sacred protection in Ohio," said Grim.

Irish spoke up. "We didn't find anything even close to a spell like that in any of the known spellbooks or grimoires."

"You won't find it in any spellbook," said Sarah.

"Why is that?" asked Irish, confused.

"It's a family secret." Sarah fidgeted, picking at her chipped black nail polish. "Or it *was*, until recently."

"Care to explain?" said Grim with a patient cross of his arms.

"I spoke to my aunt, and . . ." She paused, locking eyes with Grim. "It seems Syd has gone missing as well."

"Missing?"

Sarah nodded. "She was on assignment in London and disappeared around the same time as Father Abbott."

"Well, that settles it, then," said Strauss, reaching for his cup again.

"Settles what?" said Sarah gruffly.

Strauss took a loud sip. "Your beloved cousin must be our leak."

"Sorry, but didn't you just say that you thought Father Abbott was the leak?"

"That was before we had all the facts. If she's turned on us—"

"Way to jump to conclusions."

"Given the circumstances, a safe one, I'd say."

"Until we have something concrete, let's not assume anything," said Grim. "Could the spell have come from another source?"

"Like what?" said Sarah dubiously.

"Another family, perhaps? The Greenes? The Dvoraks?"

Sarah shook her head. "The Greenes are all earth children and the Dvoraks are nowhere near powerful enough. The Grimaldis, maybe, but . . . nah! This spell came from a rather nasty spirit that likes my family a little too much."

Grim grew quiet for a moment before voicing his realization aloud. "I take it you're referring to Earl."

Sarah shot him a finger gun. "Ten points to Gryffindor."

"Then Sydney must be involved in *some* way."

Sarah cast her eyes downward. "I'm afraid so."

"Do you think she's been corrupted?" Grim asked point blank.

"Aunt Kath doesn't think so. Says it's more likely *she* was abducted, too."

"That will have to do for now then, I suppose." Grim faced Irish. "Inform all eyes and ears, try to track her down. In the meantime, I have a feeling we'll see an increase in activity in the Boston area, so we'll double patrols, check all the usual places. You know the drill."

"Aye-aye," said Irish.

"Sarah, we'll need you to provide us with that spell. And it may even be prudent to . . . go to the source . . . in case there's anything else that may pose a threat."

"Goody goody," said Sarah without a shred of enthusiasm.

"The other chapters will need to be alerted as well. I assume you'll do the honors, Bishop?"

Strauss stopped the cup just before his lips. "A little informal today, aren't we, Captain Grimshaw?"

"Forgive me, Your Eminence."

The Bishop's eyes lingered on Grim for a moment, satisfied, before drinking what little was left of his coffee.

"If there's nothing else, we've got a lot to cover, so let's get to it."

Grim shuffled some papers back into the file in front of him and folded it shut.

Mason had about a hundred different questions but no clue where to begin.

"Before I go, I'd like to have a word with Mister Cole in private," said Strauss.

"Of course," said Grim, and looked to Mason. "I'll wait for you in the church."

If Mason was the new kid in school, he felt as if the principal had just asked to see him in his office.

With that, everyone rose from their seats and began to leave. As Diaz passed by, he bent down and quickly whispered in Mason's ear, "Told you he was a prick."

Mason tried to hide his amusement at this, but couldn't help letting a smile escape. Once everyone was gone, Bishop Strauss rose from his seat and closed the door.

"So," said Strauss as he came back into view, an unexpected smile on his face. "You are the new Messiah of the Archangel."

"If you say so," said Mason with a shrug, his eyes fixed on the table before him.

"You doubt this?"

Mason shrugged again. "I don't have nearly enough information to make a judgment."

"How interesting." The Bishop sat next to him, folded his hands on the table. "I admit that you're not quite what I expected. The last Messiah of the Archangel was a man devoted to God, even if he did have something of a fall from grace."

"Am I going to get the spiel from you now, too?"

"And what 'spiel' is that?"

Mason let out a frustrated sigh. "The one where I tell you I don't believe in God, then you tell me that I should because He's appeared to the world through miracles and prophets to show how wonderfully awesome He is. Then I would respond with something like 'If He's so great, why does He allow terrible things to happen?' which you would reply to with one of two possible answers: 'It's the Devil's fault,' or, my personal favorite, 'It's God's will.' "

The Bishop said nothing, frozen in a quiet calm that gave Mason the chills. The wrinkled skin around his lips sagged, the corners of his mouth nearly dangling beneath his chin.

"No."

Mason's eyebrow raised curiously. "No what?"

"No, I'm not going to repeat what you've clearly heard before, and the reason for that is simple." Strauss leaned forward. "You don't need any sermons about that which you already possess."

"I don't follow."

"If you truly are the Messiah of the Archangel, that means you have within you a power but a few degrees removed from the Almighty Himself." Strauss crossed himself. "My attempting to convince you on matters of the divine would be akin to convincing a bird it can fly."

"You truly believe that, don't you?"

Strauss considered the question. "I have faith."

"In what?"

"In Captain Grimshaw, and he has faith in you. And if he is correct, then that is indeed quite the miracle." He said the words, but his heart was clearly not in them.

"Well, I'll take trust over faith any day. And what I trust is my own eyes and ears, which have never witnessed any so-called 'miracles.' "

"Oh, now, that's not true at all, is it?" There was a little twinkle in his eye, and Mason felt that the Bishop's true intentions were about to be exposed.

"How would you know?"

"I don't believe there is a man, woman, or child who does not." He began to drum his fingers on the table.

Mason's eyes fell on the tabletop again. "I don't want to talk about that."

"In fact, it is a perfect example."

"Of what?"

"An event that tragic, that destructive, and yet one single soul—an innocent child, no less—survives. What else would you call that if not a miracle?"

"Bad luck."

"Oh, Mister Cole. You disappoint me."

"Sorry, *Your Eminence*, but I don't see an earthquake as a miracle. Not even a natural one, either. One caused by a monster."

"The Lord works in mysterious ways."

Mason scoffed. "I was wondering how long it would be before I heard that."

Strauss cleared his throat and straightened the cross around his neck. "I advise you to choose your words carefully under this roof. At one time, admittance to the Holy Order of Militia Dei was granted only to the most pious of followers, and while over the years we've had to . . . *evolve* by opening our doors as well as our minds"—so flat were his words, no heart in them—"every member believes in God, or at least a higher power in one form or another. If you're going to remain here you may want to consider that."

"Are you telling me to believe or leave?"

"I'm saying that when it comes to whatever subversive views you may have, a modicum of discretion would go a long way lest you offend the very people who saved your life."

Whether Mason liked it or not, he had a point.

"In any event, arrangements have been made to determine if you truly are our long-sought messiah."

"You just said you had faith in Grim."

"And I do. But even faith must be tested from time to time."

He continued drumming his fingers on the table. Mason found it quite annoying.

"Well, great . . . Can I go now?"

Strauss regarded him again in that chilly manner of his. Mason lingered a moment, all but waiting to receive a week's worth of detention. The bishop gave a dismissive gesture. Nothing more.

He got up to leave when he was stopped again by Strauss's guttural croak. "Has it ever occurred to you that perhaps God doesn't take kindly to being forsaken by someone whom He has spared?"

"I refuse to believe in a God like that."

"One who dislikes ingratitude?"

"One who holds grudges."

Mason closed the door behind him.

EIGHTEEN

MASON RETURNED TO THE CHURCH TO FIND GRIM SITTING IN the front pew clutching a rosary close to his chest, eyes closed and head bowed. He heard the approaching footsteps and looked up from his prayer. "Have a nice chat with the Bishop?"

"He truly *is* a prick."

"Hmm." Grim gave a weak smile, clearly not going to deny that. "He is, however, the head of our chapter." He stood up from the pew. "What did he say that upset you so?"

"In so many words, he implied that God is displeased with my lack of belief in Him when He could have let me die."

After a few moments, Grim said, "Consider this instead: While true that many believers have shared very powerful experiences which, to them, prove the presence of the Almighty, God is, first and foremost, a mystery. Something which cannot be calculated or measured. We can only truly come to know Him once we've shuffled off this mortal coil, as it is meant to be.

" 'Bless the Lord, O my soul and all that is within me. Forgetting not His benefits, nor forgiveness of iniquity. Bless Him who brings healing and redemption to our lives, crowning us with living kindness and with blessings, satisfies.' *That* is the God I believe in."

People had quoted scripture to Mason in the past. Principal Sadler had quoted Proverbs 22:15 to him while looking down upon him with self-righteous condemnation—*Whoever loves discipline loves knowledge, but whoever hates correction is stupid.* Ironic, considering that the reason he had been sent to his office in the first place was for pointing out that you can't actually see the Great Wall of China from space in history class. Mrs. Crouch—called "Mrs. Crotch" by most students—had straightened out her glasses and forced her tight, wrinkled lips apart. "And how would *you* know? Have you ever been to space?" He probably should have left it alone right there. But, relishing a good argument the way he did, instead he mirrored her tone and said, "No. Have you?"

This was different. This he actually found beautiful. Poetic.

"And that being the case," Grim went on, "perhaps God believes, as I do, that power belongs not to those who crave it, but to those who would use it wisely."

"Why would He choose me, then?"

"He must see something good in you."

Once again Mason was at a loss for words. Only this time it was from the certain sense of comfort that came with Grim's statement.

"Put it out of your mind for now and let me show you around," said Grim.

Mason followed Grim through the church basement and into the underground tunnel. There they stopped at the metal door he had seen earlier. Grim punched in the code on the keypad (which Mason did not catch) and the door clicked open. From there, they descended a flight of stairs that came to another metal door at the bottom. This one had no keypad. No lock. Not even a door handle. Only a small circle of glass that appeared to be a peephole.

Grim took off his glasses and went eye-to-eye with it.

"Grimshaw. Blake."

A tiny red light blinked in the small circle on the door and it slid open.

"Retinal scanner," said Grim, placing his glasses back on his face. "Works in tandem with voice print to ensure no one can get in or out without authorization."

"Cool," said Mason, both amused and amazed.

It felt like entering the bowels of Area 51, and he half expected to see a chamber filled with aliens in fluidic tubes. Grim flicked on the lights to reveal not a secret lab but a simple shooting range. Ten lanes stretched across the space behind a wall of glass, each with its own stall where safety goggles and earmuffs sat on small shelves.

"This is the Tactical Area. We're twenty feet underground, right below the graveyard. Completely soundproof." He pointed to an open area behind them. "Back there are the weapons lockers."

Mason saw a door at the far end with a sign that read: AUTHO-RIZED PERSONNEL ONLY.

"What's through there?"

"The holding cells."

"I see . . ." said Mason uncertainly. His imagination spun with visions of just what sort of prisoners they might hold. To think, all of this was below the pedestrian streets and sidewalks of Boston.

They went back to the garage and rode the elevator up to the second floor, which consisted mainly of a kitchen, laundry room, and gym. They continued on their way up, past the third and fourth floors, which Grim said were all living quarters, and stopped at the fifth, home to the infirmary where Mason had first awoke to this new world on one side and a lab on the other. Brightly lit but otherwise empty, it looked much like the science lab at Stonehill High, complete with beakers, Bunsen burners, and microscopes. Then there was much more sophisticated equipment, such as a biochemical scanner and a piece of equipment which resembled a projector with a glass orb on top that Grim had referred to as a hemaspectroscope. There was also a cold-storage that held blood samples and other biological specimens.

"Hell of a place," said Mason.

"With your permission, I'd like a sample of your blood."

"Why?"

"To determine if in fact you do share a lineage with prior messiahs, however distantly."

Mason was reluctant but intrigued. If nothing else it would put this question to rest. "Okay."

Grim snapped on a pair of rubber gloves and approached Mason's right hand with a small needle no bigger than a thumbtack. There was a little pinch as it pierced the tip of his ring finger, making him wince. Immediately a drop of bright red formed above the puncture. Grim touched it with a metal syringe of some kind, only instead of a long needle, it had what looked like the tip of a fountain pen that drew the drop of blood into it. After placing a small circular bandage over the puncture, he fed the syringe into an open port at the side of a nearby device. A three-dimensional image of the red drop appeared suspended in the glass orb on top.

"Whoa," said Mason. Wonders he saw before his very eyes. A microscopic universe in which cells became as clear as clouds in the sky.

"What would normally take weeks to analyze, we can do in a matter of hours."

"Wicked!"

"If you want to see something truly wicked . . ." Grim rolled his chair over to where a microscope and a small collection of glass slides were set up near one of the sinks. Grim took a slide, placed it in the microscope, and motioned to it, silently inviting Mason to take a look.

Mason peered into a dark red ocean, thick and soupy. Little black eels swam through its murky depths feeding on the healthy life-raft-shaped blood cells.

"What am I looking at?"

"Type V. Otherwise known as vampire blood." Grim placed an elbow on the counter next to Mason as he marveled at the insidious elegance of it. "High in platelets, which increase their healing factor, but low in plasma, which requires them to feed on healthy nourishment. The cells attach to healthy ones, actually propelling themselves while they feed, thus reducing the role of the heart in circulating blood throughout the body."

"Like a parasite."

"In a sense, yes. Only in this case they convert the consumed cells into metaproteins which rewrite the genetic code to generate new, more complex components, such as additional neural pathways, superior musculature and bone structure, enhanced optic nerves, and, of course, their distinctive fangs. It's a mutagenic agent unlike anything else known to exist. Unfortunately, there is still so much we don't know that science has yet to reveal."

"Funny, when we first met I wouldn't have ever figured you for a science man."

"I am a physician, after all, and biology is essential to medicine. As is science to nature. When God created the cosmos, I guarantee you that science is the code in which it was written."

Mason looked back into the microscope. "Very profound."

"And sometimes that code is organized into dangerous things. The cancers and choleras. Venoms and diseases and pathogens. Much like Type V here. It's simple, elegant, and deadly."

"So they're not actually *dead*."

"Well . . . yes and no. Many traits by which we would class a living organism don't apply to them, such as sexual reproduction, growth and aging, natural death. And every test conducted so far has yet to explain why that is. On the other hand, they are highly adaptable and resilient, and possess DNA like any other form of life. But here's the interesting thing: they have no unique genome. Unlike humans, who require the genetic material from both parents, vampires all appear to share a common heredity. So if a sample were taken from two separate individuals, their genetic makeup would be identical. It really is quite the marvel."

"You sound like you admire them."

" 'Admire' may not be the way to put it. I *understand* them. I'd also say I feel sorry for them."

"You must be kidding." The image of Rose's heart being pulled from her body flashed in his mind.

"Truly, I do. Each one starts out no different than you or I until they are turned. After that, they crave blood like a drug. It takes over them, consumes them. Killing them doesn't sadden me. What does is the fact that they cannot be saved. They may not be dead, per se, but damned? Absolutely."

"Couldn't there be a way to cure it?"

"It's been tried, but I'm afraid it just adapts to antibodies too quickly. If some day we had a living specimen to study, things may be different. But for now, the best we can do is protect ourselves and pray for the souls of their victims."

"And there are ways to do that? Protect ourselves?"

"There are." Grim spun around to face a computer screen behind him. "But perhaps we'll come to that a little later."

"Too bad. I was enjoying the biology lesson."

"Well, I have another one for you: chemistry." Grim tapped a few keys. "I'm examining a sample of the substance we collected in Stonehill used by our friend Novak. Do you remember when he broke the protection around your home?"

Mason's stomach churned at the memory. "How could I forget?"

"After he sacrificed that poor girl—"

"You mean after *you* sacrificed her."

Grim grew quiet, pensive. "I sense you have some hard feelings toward me about that."

Mason didn't answer.

"You have to understand, Mason. I've seen those devils use innocent people for all kinds of horrible things. She could have been hexed or possessed or God only knows what. At the time, I had no other choice."

Mason still didn't answer, but now it was because he knew it was true. "I'm sorry."

"You needn't apologize. It's not easy to sort out."

"There's something I don't understand."

"Please," said Grim with an inviting gesture.

"If the protection was broken, how come he still needed to be invited in? I would have figured that one for a myth, anyway."

"I'm afraid not. And thankfully so! The protection on the land surrounding the house was but one barrier. The protection I and your grandmother placed on the house itself is one that can only yield to an invitation."

"*Rose* did that?"

"With my instruction, yes. Wardings work best when performed by whomever lives there."

"What exactly happened again? I don't think we covered that yesterday."

"Quite right. After hearing of Father Abbott's disappearance, I turned around and headed back to Stonehill. You see, a letter was found in Father Abbott's quarters."

"A letter?"

"In his desk drawer." Grim reached into the breast pocket of his jacket and took something from it. An envelope that had been sealed and opened. He handed it to Mason.

There was no sign of postage, no return address, and was addressed only to Father Abbott. From inside it, he took a single piece of paper folded into thirds. The few words were written in a thin, slanted handwriting.

Forgive me, Father. For I have sinned . . .

"Am I supposed to get this?"

"Not yet," said Grim. "Being a learned man, I assume you know the meaning of an ellipsis?"

Mason stared at the three dots at the end of the writing. "Sure. It indicates the omission of a word, or words, from the preceding text. Commonly used nowadays to imply that one is trailing off or that there is more to come."

"Very good," said Grim, taking a small flashlight from the same pocket from which he took the letter. "Another way it is used, specifically by the Holy Order of Militia Dei, is as a signal. It means that there is a hidden message. Sometimes in the form of a code, sometimes in the form of a covert shorthand. For example, 'all is well' followed by an ellipsis means just the opposite. And other times it means there are more words right before your eyes."

Grim clicked on the flashlight and cast its purple circle of light upon the page. Before his very eyes, Mason saw a new set of words appear.

Mason Cole. Stonehill, Ohio.

"But where did this come from? Who gave it to Abbott?"

"Well, I can tell you for certain that the handwriting you see at the top of the page belonged to Will Graves. And the method in which the message was conveyed is consistent with that. You see, with the advances in technology over the years, we don't really rely on this to convey sensitive information anymore. But thirteen years ago it was still in use. Sometimes old ways are best."

Mason sensed a "but" coming.

"However . . ."

Close enough.

"Some things don't add up."

"Such as?"

"Such as the fact that if Father Abbott received this letter from Will after the Great Quake, it means that Will somehow knew who the next messiah would be and sent the letter to Father Abbott before he died, and that Father Abbott then held on to it for thirteen years and said nothing. *That* I have great difficulty believing."

"Maybe he didn't realize that there was a secret message on it?"

"Possible, but unlikely, since Father Abbott was well aware of this way of passing secret messages. Even used it himself."

"What other explanation is there?"

"That Father Abbott only recently received the letter. It still wouldn't explain how Will knew that you would be the next messiah, but it's the only other alternative I can think of.

"Whatever the answer, it was more than enough to tell us who to look for and where. But by the time I arrived, you had already left with your friends. As you can imagine, your grandmother was alarmed to find a stranger at her door claiming her only grandson's life was in danger. I attempted discretion at first, but after she brandished a freshly used pair of shears at me, I decided to entrust her with the truth."

"And what did she say when you told her?"

" 'Why didn't you just damn well say so?' Verbatim."

"Sounds about right." Mason shook his head.

Figures. If a stranger comes calling, speaking of goons, monsters, and miracles, she's all ears. But the minute I say anything about leaving home someday, that's when she becomes hard of hearing.

"After that," Grim continued, "she helped protect the house with holy water and blessed silver medallions planted in the north, south, east, and west points of the land and waited.

"During my second cup of tea, I noticed the same car pass by the house for the third time and intended to make sure that it was the last. Turns out it was another of Novak's men watching the house. I managed to subdue him, put him in the trunk of my car for questioning later."

"Oh Christ! I didn't realize there was somebody in there." The moment of impact as the vehicle came hurling though the wall of his home replayed in his head, followed by the knocking on the trunk interior just before everything turned to smoke.

"He should have been out long enough for the trip back to Boston, but I dare say the jolt from colliding with your house would be enough to wake anyone. He's fortunate to have survived, let alone escaped."

"Was that tear gas that came out of the trunk?"

"Close. A mixture of highly pressurized holy water, silver nitrate, and essence of garlic, which acts as a pacification agent to vampires."

"Garlic? *Really?*"

"Oh, yes. But only insofar as it inflames their highly sensitive olfactory receptors, causing temporary disorientation. As do a number of other things: ginger, certain spices. But they're no protection against them."

"Good to know." The thought of all this suddenly took its toll on him, made him uneasy. "I think I've seen enough for one day."

"Very well. There's still one last place you should see. Let me just get things put away here." Grim took the slide off the microscope and placed it in the box with the rest of them. "Would you mind putting these back in the freezer?" Grim asked with the snap of latex as he took off his gloves.

The little slides of glass jingled a bit in their holder as Mason carried them to the freezer. He opened the door and knelt down to stow them safely away. Tucked inside the freezer door was a translucent plastic container. He took it in his hands a little too fast and felt something roll across the inside. He peeked under the lid and saw a severed finger. It looked waxy and fake. The skin had grayed in color and the severed end had a small piece of bone poking out from the wound as though it had been pulled out rather than cut.

He wondered about its former owner. What was he like? What kind of man was he? Where did he get this letter with Mason's name on it? Had he ever been in love? Did he have friends and relatives? If so, would they miss him now that he was gone? Or would his existence be erased from the world the way his own was?

Out of morbid curiosity, Mason picked it up.

A spark! It burned his fingers like the charge of a live wire and shot through the bone of his arm faster than the speed of pain. Pure white electricity connected with the dead cells of the finger, reanimating them for a millisecond in which he saw an entire lifetime.

A birth, a memory, encoded in the very fabric of his being: First steps as a little boy, followed by his first fall. The faces of friends and siblings. Birthdays and weddings. The mother that dotes upon him and the father that beats him when he's had a few too many. The loss of his first tooth. The loss of his virginity at the tender age of twelve—"I've never done this before"—to a girl named Jill, nearly fifteen at the time. The loss of both parents from one form of cancer or another. The loss of his wife, with whom he couldn't have children, but whom he loves anyway. And finally the loss of his own life. The sound of water. A metal maze all around him. Something rattles nearby. One hand draws his flashlight and swings it toward the sound. "Hello?" No answer. His pulse quickening, chest growing tight. Approaching the nearest cargo container, holding his breath as he peers around the corner to see nothing but shadows. He stops and listens. Just the waves lapping against the dock. Must have been a seagull, or maybe a stray cat. Nothing to be afraid of. He is on the ground before he knows what hit him. The last thing he ever sees is the evil, smiling face of a red-haired devil . . . his empty eyes.

The next thing he knew, Mason was looking up at the ceiling, cradled in Grim's arms.

"Breathe, Mason. Breathe!"

His whole body convulsed from the unbridled shock that coursed through him. Yet somehow the pain itself was minimal. Mason mumbled, dazed and staring into space.

"You saw him, didn't you? You saw Father Abbott."

Mason coughed as the convulsions ended and his lungs slowly regained their usual rhythm. "Not . . . Abbott."

Grim said nothing, his face blank with shock.

Mason continued to mutter under his breath. He saw Grim take out his cell phone, heard him speaking frantically.

The dead finger lay on the floor in front of him like a missing piece of a puzzle, ugly to behold, yet he couldn't look away. It was the strangest, most foreign thing he'd ever experienced—to see through another pair of eyes as he would his own; to feel as they felt, to think as they thought, to live in the life of someone who no longer lived all in the span of a heartbeat, and to share the visceral weight of his death.

Diaz and Irish rushed into the lab, followed closely by Rodriguez, who carried a medical kit. The four of them stood over him, staring down with confusion and concern.

Rodriguez took a penlight from the kit and shone it in one eye then the other. Mason squinted. She held the penlight vertically. "Follow this with your eyes," she said softly. He did as he was told, tracing it through the air as it moved from right to left, left to right. She put the penlight away and put her thumb to his wrist to check his pulse.

"What happened?" Irish asked.

"There was a psychometric reaction when he picked up the finger," said Grim.

"Are you sure?" said Rodriguez.

"Positive."

"We should have Sarah check him out just in case."

"Agreed." Grim took his handkerchief from the pocket of his trousers and delicately picked the finger up off the floor. "Who collected this?"

"That would be me," said Diaz.

"Did you print it?"

"You kidding me? You'd never get a print off a finger."

Grim shook his head. "Did you take the print *from* the finger itself?"

"No," said Diaz with a hint of confusion.

"May I ask why?"

"It was in a pool of Father Abbott's blood. Didn't think it was necessary."

"Are you sure it was *his* blood?"

"*That* I am sure of. Tested it myself. What's the problem?"

Grim exhaled a long breath. "Next time, check the print too."

"Yes, sir." He seemed unsure what to make of this.

Grim handed Diaz the finger, which he took from him as if it were a normal thing. "I want to know as soon as you have a match."

NINETEEN

THEY TOOK THE ELEVATOR TO THE THIRD FLOOR WHERE MASON followed Grim past his room to the last one on the left. The discordant musical defilings of GG Allin came from inside, and a sign hung on the doorknob that said ALREADY DISTURBED.

Grim rapped "Shave and a Haircut" quickly but firmly on the door. A few seconds later, "two bits" was knocked into the other side before it swung open.

A shock of green hair appeared above a half-finished cigarette dangling from the pierced lips of Sarah Vegesticka. "Ahoy, Cap'n," she said with a salute.

"Mason here just had a rather unpleasant experience," said Grim. "I'd like you to have a look at him and perform a cleansing if necessary."

"Aye-aye," Sarah said, and stepped out of the way so Mason could enter.

"I believe I've asked you not to smoke in the building."

"Sorry," she said with one more quick drag. "It's raining bats and frogs out." She crushed it out on the door, leaving a black mark, and let the butt drop to the floor.

Grim gave her a stern look.

Sheepishly, she knelt down, making her knobby knees show through the rips in her red tartan pants, and picked it up.

"Bring him to the roof when you're through," said Grim as he went through the stairwell door.

Sarah closed the door behind her. When Mason thought of a witch's quarters, he expected a dimly lit room that smelled of tea and incense with heavy drapes, crystals, and candles all around. Instead he found a room full of reptiles. Shelves lined the walls with glass tanks filled with geckos, bearded dragons, and snakes. A mesh cage held a chameleon clinging to a stick with its zygodactylous feet. Next to it, a baby turtle swam through a bowl of water. Where there weren't living specimens, there were prints and photos of anacondas, tortoises, Komodo dragons, and crocodiles. A terrarium that blocked the window held an assortment of rocks baked beneath a heat lamp, but there was no one home. A moment later he saw why. A great green iguana sat on a cabinet next to the door. So still was it that Mason thought it was stuffed, like one of Rose's cats, until it twitched its head and looked at him.

"So . . ." said Mason. "You're a witch?"

"Uh-huh."

"Are you a good witch or a bad witch?" A nervous smile creased his cheeks.

"Congrats," she said dryly as she went about collecting things. "That's the millionth time I've heard that."

"Yay. What do I win?"

"A swift kick in the nards," she said, craning her foot back. "Wanna cash in now or space it out?"

"Jesus, sorry!" Mason skidded back a half step to avoid the kick that never came. "I was just kidding. Are you off your meds or something?"

"Yeah. I am," she replied, deadly serious. "Something about the term 'witch' gets the Church's panties in a twist, so officially I'm an

'Occult Specialist.' " She made air quotes with her fingers. "Personally, I'm not jazzed about either one."

"Why do it then?"

"Beats waiting tables. Let's get on with it. I can feel lots of bad mojo around you already and it's bumming me out." She motioned for him to sit on the bed. She gathered up some things from the cabinet on which her reptile friend sat, picked it up, and handed it to Mason.

"Here. His name is Igor," said Sarah as she sat cross-legged on the bed next to him.

"Uh, okay." He had never held an iguana before. Much softer than it looked. In pictures they seemed smaller, but up close Igor was the size of a small cat. He twitched his scaly head, blinking at him inquisitively and giving him the sense that he was studying Mason as much as Mason was studying him.

"He likes you."

"I'm flattered."

Sarah took what looked like a big nugget of ganja and held the flame of a lighter to it. As soon as Mason smelled it, he knew it was sage. Rose used to burn it now and then. White smoke began to spill from it as she made several circles with it in front of Mason's face before placing it in a small metal dish. She took two bottles from the bed next to her, poured a little from both into the palm of her hand, and rubbed it all over her hands until they were slick. They smelled pleasant and sweet. With her thumb and index finger she pinched a spot at the top of Mason's head, then his forehead, then his throat. She told him to put his hands out, which he did, letting Igor rest in his lap, and she proceeded to rub the excess into his palms and wrists.

Silently, Sarah took Igor from Mason's lap, placed him in her own, and took a long, deep breath.

"Should I close my eyes?"

"Doesn't matter."

He kept them open and fixed on her deep, half-moon eyes, which he only now noticed were two different colors. One blue, one hazel.

"You have a lot of company," she said, "a lot of death. It hovers around you like a dark cloud."

Mason had never heard anyone say that, but he'd always felt it. He'd never had any cause or even the right words to speak it out loud, but as soon as he heard her say the words, they made perfect sense.

"Describe it for me," she said.

"Is it really necessary?" he asked with a hard swallow.

"Yes."

Immediately his mind went somewhere wholly unexpected. "I killed these two men who were trying to steal my friends and me away." He never thought there would be any hint of blame at this. But there it was. So strange how tumultuous a thing it was to kill. What a disruption it causes in the mind and soul of the killer. Even when necessary to survive, to prevent ourselves from being killed, it gnaws at the very thing that makes us human.

And then it dawned on him just how sick a thing it was for those who killed not only without remorse, without compassion, without so much as a second thought, but enjoyed doing so. Got a thrill from it.

Sarah made a quick swipe at the air near his face. Mason ducked, unsure what this was about. "Keep going," she said.

He told her about how Julie and Dale were killed during the attack, how he watched Novak break Rose open like a porcelain doll. It still didn't seem real.

Unable to guess what it was she was doing, Mason watched her snap at invisible flies with imaginary chopsticks. "Who is the old man?"

"What old man?"

"Square face, big nose, died on a pier . . . you carry the weight of his death now, too."

Mason's mouth hung open, astonished. "I . . . saw that maybe ten minutes ago, in the lab when I touched Father Abbott's finger. Or, what I thought was Father Abbott's finger."

"No, it wasn't. It belonged to a man whose name starts with a T."

"Tom." He felt the loss as if he were a loved one, even though he had never laid eyes on him. "His name was Tom."

Sarah continued to snap around his head. As she did, weight lifted from him with every swipe of her fingers. The burden of worry. The sadness of death. Not gone, but the sting of it lessened.

"Keep going."

"That's it."

"Oh, no. Not even close. There are so many now I can barely . . . all of them . . . screaming . . . crying. You didn't cause them, but you feel guilty. Like you should have joined them."

Sarah winced, bearing the burden of his pain, and he was relieved of its weight for the first time in all his memory. It had been with him for so long that he knew not what it felt like to be without it until now. For the first time ever, someone else truly shared the weight, however briefly.

Everything became quiet and Mason rested, still, with only the sound of rain on glass. The air was light and warm now, full of fresh scents. He noticed that all the critters seemed to be looking their way.

When they were done, Sarah opened her eyes and said, "Better?"

"Yeah. A little." Whatever she did had worked. For now, at least.

"Wanna hear a joke?"

Mason gave her a surprised look. "Actually, yeah."

"What does a vampire do with a used tampon?"

Mason thought for a split second. "What?"

"Makes tea."

Mason groaned with disgust and then started to laugh.

"I'm very funny. Here." She stood, took something from her pocket, and placed it around Mason's neck. A beaded necklace with a pewter pentacle and white crystal dangling from it. "Wear this for the next day or so to keep clear. Dark energies attract misfortune, not to mention bad spirits. Take it from me—you don't want that."

"I'd feel kinda silly wearing this. Is there no other way?"

Sarah cast her eyes upward, thinking. "You could drink the

spiced blood of a she-wolf with your dick tucked between your legs until the next full moon."

"This will be fine. Thank you." Mason tucked it away under his shirt, next to his cross.

"Good." She kissed his hand and got up to put her stuff back in the cabinet. She picked Igor up off the bed and placed him back under his lamp.

Mason stood, his knees buckled, and he sunk back down to the bed. "I feel a little lightheaded."

Sarah looked to one side, away from Mason, as if someone else had just come into view. "That's normal. Just give it a minute, splash some water on your face, and you'll be right as dodgers."

Mason rose slowly, went to the bathroom, and closed the door behind him. He turned on the faucet and let the clear, cool liquid wash over his skin, marveling at the sensation, as though it were rinsing away the blood he'd felt on his hands the past few days. He studied his reflection in the mirror of the medicine cabinet above the sink, looking straight ahead. Still not quite himself, but definitely clearer than before.

He was about to leave when he saw the waste basket next to the toilet, and knelt down for a closer look. A full alphabet of empty pill bottles for everything from Abilify to Zoloft, with more than a few O's, courtesy of Oxycontin.

And you thought she was kidding.

Mason caught the sound of whispering coming from the other side of the door. For a moment, he thought someone else must have come into her room. But each string of hushed words from her was followed by nothing but silence. All he could make out were the last two words, much clearer than the rest.

"Go. Away."

There was a tap on the door, giving Mason a little jolt.

"Ready, Eddie?" said Sarah from outside.

Mason opened the door. "You know, I'm sure I can find my way."

"Do you know where it is?"

"The roof. I imagine that's hard to miss."

"Eh, suit yourself."

Mason left the bathroom and was just about to leave Sarah's room when he paused at the door. "One more thing . . . could I bum a smoke?"

She took a cigarette from her pack and handed it to him.

"Thanks," said Mason, and left her room, seeing the black mark on the doorframe she had left earlier.

"Stay gold, Ponyboy!" said Sarah, and she shut the door.

TWENTY

STILL RAINY. STILL CLOUDY. A LIGHT MIST MOVED ACROSS THE grass like a roaming ghost searching for a friend. Mason was beginning to wonder if the sun had died, but felt refreshed by the rain again as it brought the moist perfume of grass and leaves into the air. For the first time since waking up in this rain-spattered city, the sound of it brought a sense of calm rather than melancholy.

He stood hunched and under the awning at the front entrance to the building, puffing away at the cigarette he held between his thumb and finger. When he was done, Mason pitched the butt and took the elevator back up to the top floor. Climbing the single flight of stairs, he reached the roof and found a wondrously peculiar sight of a rooftop garden.

Surreal at first, then, a few moments later, as natural as could be. The rain had let up just enough to give a misty weight to the air, the ground covered with mossy rocks in triad formations. Small pruned trees and bushes surrounded a little pond from which he could hear the gentle trickle of water. Gone was the world of cement and metal, held apart from this lost corner of Eden. A little bridge went over a thin strip of gravel, raked in such a way to resemble ripples in a stream. The path led him to a wooden hut that stood in stark contrast to the surrounding gloom. It had a single pagoda at the other end, covered by translucent paper with a warm, golden glow coming from within, making it appear as a large paper lantern.

Lit white candles surrounded the interior, filling it with a drowsy warmth. Mason breathed in the perfume of jasmine incense, making his eyes momentarily droop. A smooth straw mat covered the entire floor, making each footstep sound like walking through sand. Framed calligraphy adorned the walls and in one corner sat a vase with a few pink blossoms in water.

And in the center of it all, Grim sat in lotus position on a cushion with his eyes shut.

"Welcome to the dojo," said Grim as his eyes opened.

"Never thought I'd see something like this here," said Mason, still taking it all in.

Grim stood and stepped over to Mason, who lingered by the door. "Nowadays it's used more for meditation and reflection, since everyone here has been trained for some time . . . until now, that is."

"What are you talking about?"

"You joining us, of course."

"Right . . ."

And there it was. He had been waiting for something like this. In one of his books, it would be known as the Call to Adventure, the point in a story in which the main character has to make a choice whether to accept the call and follow the path before him or turn around and go home.

But I can't go home, can I?

And then he remembered something he had read once, a quote, though he couldn't recall what it was from: If the path you're on should split in two, choose the third.

So what's the third option here?

"About that," Mason continued. "Bishop Strauss said there was a way to test me."

Grim nodded. "The Tritemptamen. It's a series of tests for each new Messiah of the Archangel. It's tradition. And, in your case, I'd say also a necessity."

"Meaning it's possible that I may not be this messiah you seek."

"It has been suggested that you may be a proxy of some sort, a temporary keeper of the Holy Spirit. Though how it found its way to you in the first place is still a mystery. I suspect it must have something to do with the way you got that cross." Grim pointed at Mason's chest.

The cross was tucked away, out of sight beneath Mason's shirt, but the contours of it showed through the fabric. Mason clutched at it. "I told you, my dad gave it to me in Jerusalem the day it was destroyed."

"Egad, boy! Don't you see how phenomenal that is?"

"Could just be a coincidence."

"True. And perhaps ninety-nine times out of a hundred, that's all there is to it. But that one-in-a-hundred, one-in-a-thousand, even one-in-a-*million* time is when incredible things happen."

"Well, I don't know what to tell you then."

"I know this is a lot to take in, Mason. But if you let me, I can help you. I can teach you how to defend yourself, how to fight, how to hone the power within you and make the bad things of this world fear *you*."

And so the path was laid before him: The young knight has to decide whether or not to pursue the savage dragon and see that he is slain. If he does, he meets with pain, peril, trials, and tribulations, but in doing so becomes a hero and saves whole kingdoms from being scorched to a crisp.

If not, no story.

He had seen this happen to so many others: Farm boys who follow crazy old wizards on a quest to save the world. Misfit girls who bound from one dimension to the next searching for something, finding themselves in the process. Brave sisters who are the one and only hope at restoring freedom. And fathers who would risk it all to show their children the meaning of justice in an unjust time. These and many more had he met. Laughed and cried with. Shared in their griefs and triumphs. Known better than he knew himself. But until now, it had never happened to him. To everyone else, it was just a story, the sort of thing you hear about and say, "Oh no, that's terrible," with no way to know what it's really like. To him, now, it was reality.

Mason went to the threshold of the dojo, crossed his arms, and stared off into the night. The dark sky above showed no sign of drying up anytime soon. In the harbor nearby, boats blew their horns before heading off to faraway waters.

"What do you say?"

Mason thought a moment, then turned and faced him.

"No."

Had a record been playing, it would have scratched to a halt.

"I understand if you feel confused by all this, Mason," he said sympathetically. "I can't say I blame you. God knows it's a difficult thing I'm asking of you."

"I'm not confused. I understand perfectly. My answer is no."

"Would you consider thinking about it, just for a day or two, while—"

"No . . . scratch that . . . *fuck* no! Sorry, but I don't want any part in this. Who would? So I can't go back home, fine. I get that. What else is there?"

"Theoretically there should be some way to draw the Holy Spirit out of you and channel it into whomever the next in line would be. We would then create a new identity, and you would be free to live whatever life you choose."

"Great. Let's do that."

"We could even modify your memory if you like. Convince you things happened another way."

"Would I forget about Rose and my friends?"

"If that was your wish."

"I don't know about that." The prospect seemed monstrous to him. As his memory was currently the only place in which they still lived, they wouldn't just be dead, they would essentially cease to exist. But if his aim was truly to start over, would not this be preferable to clinging to ghosts of his past? "I'll have to think about it."

"Of course." Grim adjusted his glasses, crossing and uncrossing his arms. "You're welcome to stay here, of course, in the meantime."

While you wear me down a little bit every day until I cave, right? Nice try.

"I can't force you into anything, Mason. It's not my intention to connive you into service with some long-winded series of words that sound good but ultimately don't mean much. Everyone in Militia Dei is here because this is less of a job and more of a duty. A calling, if you will. You have to make a choice that is right for you."

Mason's mouth hung open, feeling as if Grim had just plucked the thoughts straight from his mind. His words were sincere, he had no doubt of that. But he didn't have to be a mind reader to tell that Grim secretly hoped he would change his mind.

"Where would I be safest? I mean, aren't I in danger here?"

"If Novak wanted you dead, I'd say yes. But if I'm right—"

"*If* you're right?"

"—if you were killed, the spirit in you would simply pass to another, as it has done before, and we would be back to the drawing board. No, he wants you alive."

"Terrific."

"If you really wish, we can have you moved to a safehouse nearby. It's as well protected as the chapterhouse."

"But that can be broken."

"With methods that only worked because they got the jump on us. Trust me, that won't happen twice."

Mason pretended to consider this for just long enough to make it seem genuine. "Still, I think I'd prefer the safehouse."

"I'll make the arrangements," Grim said quietly. "If I could ask just one last thing. Would you mind waiting for our envoy from the Vatican? They'll be performing the tests I mentioned."

"When will that be?"

"Tomorrow."

"Fine. Tomorrow."

"Good," said Grim, relieved. "Thank you."

Something occurred to Mason. "What's the date today?"

Grim glanced briefly at his watch. "The thirty-first of August."

"I'm supposed to start school tomorrow," said Mason wistfully.

"Looking forward to it, were you?"

"Actually I was dreading it."

"What did you want to do after graduation?"

Mason wondered, a faraway look on him like someone lost at sea. "I don't know. Not *this*, that's for sure. I thought maybe an English teacher. Rose was one, you know."

"She mentioned it."

"My folks were teachers too. Or rather, they were going to be until . . . God, it's so stupid. A week ago I'd have given anything to get out of that town. Now I'd give anything to go back."

"It's not stupid at all. We never realize what we have until it's gone. Especially at your age. Granted, you definitely haven't had the most conventional of lives so far."

"You have a knack for understatement, sir," Mason sputtered. "No, you know what, the thing is that it started out unconventional for sure. But ever since I moved to Ohio it's been extremely conventional. One might even say too much so. Now . . . honestly, I don't know how I'm supposed to deal with this. It hasn't sunk in yet. It feels like there's just no . . ." Mason fumbled for the right word. "Balance. Everything is all to one side or the other, never in the middle. At least having my friends and Rose made it a little more bearable. But now I don't even have that. Now I'm alone."

"Son." Grim placed his hand on Mason's shoulder. "I promise you that that is one thing you certainly are not. I know how hard it is to see now, but this too shall pass. One of the hardest things to learn in life is patience. When you're ready, you'll find your balance."

"That's exactly what I'm trying to do."

"Then I respect your wishes. Unless you're really sure you wouldn't like more background on all this?"

Mason let out a heavy sigh. "I'm really not in the mood for a story right now."

"Well, let me know if you change your mind. Because a story is just what I've got."

With that, the two of them left the dojo and made their way through the dripping zen garden to the stairs on the other side.

When Mason returned to his room, he was greeted by a face he recognized. One with whiskers and big blue eyes.

"Oh my god!" Tears welled up in his eyes. "C'mere, girl."

Bossy jumped off the bed and trotted over to him. She had never done that before. Mason swept her up in his arms and held her, buried his face in her neck and let her whiskers tickle his face. He'd forgotten completely about her during all this, but now he would never let her go.

A duffle bag had been left for him, clothes neatly folded inside, on a chair by the window, along with some supplies and toiletries— soap, shampoo, tissues, toilet paper, toothbrush, the same stuff anyone would need. Beneath it all he found a pair of dishes and a flat of cat food. The corner of a handwritten note stuck out of a genuine leather journal. The front cover bore a design: an ambigram of the word *Journal*, same right-side up and upside down. The pages were of a decent-enough paper. Unlined. Clean and smooth as untouched snow.

IF YOU NEED ANYTHING ELSE JUST ASK.

It was unsigned.

After a long and much-needed shower, Mason changed into

clean clothes and sat by the rain-drenched window. Bossy came and curled up by his feet the way she used to with Rose.

He hadn't even considered Grim's offer. Not one bit. It wasn't that it seemed too impossible to believe. Just the opposite: It now seemed *very* possible. And that was the problem. He had no choice but to accept the existence of things he would have laughed at a few days ago. More than anything now he longed for a normal life, one far from all of this. Choosing to be part of it freely was a bridge too far, one he intended to burn before he could cross it.

You're doing the right thing. The smart *thing. If they can take this . . . this spirit, this power, whatever it is . . . out of me, great! Let them. Give it to someone who wants it and I'll be on my way. If this God of theirs has a problem with that, too bad. No reps, no spokesmen, I want to talk to the man in charge. Let Him come and tell me Himself. Until then, I refuse to be chosen.*

And what Grim had suggested about altering his memories, well, that was a dilemma. To lose the things from his past which caused him pain, but in turn risk losing himself . . .

No. Out of the question.

Whatever it said on a piece of paper or a computer screen, he must not forget who he was. Who he *really* was.

It would be the hardest thing he's ever had to do, even more so than the loss of his parents, but he could do it. He could start again. A new place. A new name. A new life. Only now did he fully realize that he had secretly been waiting for it.

I'm alive, he told himself. *I'm still alive. I'm here. Looking out a window. Petting Bossy. And no matter what happens, I will not forget. Not Rose. Not Dale. Not Julie. And certainly not myself.*

As the drops of rain pattered and dripped down the pane of glass, his mind's eye drew imaginary lines between them, connecting one dot to another until they formed shapes. He traced them with his finger and found not shapes but words. Two of them.

What if?

And just like that something inside him flickered, a stubborn flame that refused to die no matter how much darkness surrounded it. No matter how many tears sought to drown it. Breathed to life by that same voice which called from within. It was still there, still burning. And something told him that if he let it, that flame could become a bonfire. A blaze. A roaring inferno from which even the damned would recoil.

And he would enjoy it.

TWENTY-ONE

MASON WOKE THE NEXT MORNING TO A GENTLE RAP ON THE door, sending a flock of hummingbirds fluttering through his chest.

"Mason? It's time," came Grim's voice from the other side.

"All right," he answered, but did not get out of bed.

Ten minutes passed. Deciding he couldn't put it off any longer, he dressed and readied himself, hardly noticing the clothes that had suddenly appeared on his body. Generic garments that didn't belong to him, foreign as spots on a zebra.

Mason came downstairs to find Grim waiting for him. No sign of the others. They made their way over to the church with Father Coffey, who gave Mason a reassuring little wink. Reassuring but short-lived, for his mind was elsewhere in time, lost in worry about things that had not yet come, let alone passed. A place in time in which things both speed up and slow down, pulling him hard in opposite directions. Mason tried to stand still but couldn't, noticing that he was only pacing in a line that became shorter and shorter, until finally he stopped and took a seat in one of the pews.

The tickle of hummingbird wings inside him only increased with each passing minute. *This is so dumb,* he thought. *What have I got to be nervous about? I don't even know what these so-called tests are. And what will they prove, anyway?*

Mason regarded the altar again. Only this time he saw things a bit differently.

How lovely those rays of light seemed; how comforting would be their warmth if he let them. Not many times in his life had he prayed. His attempts as a boy to bend the ear of God were, in truth, half-hearted, knowing full well that no one was really listening. But there was one time that had been unequivocally sincere. The ground had disappeared beneath his feet. His mother's hand had left his as they both plunged down into the roaring darkness below. It wasn't even a proper prayer. Just three simple words.

Please. Save me.

There was no part of him that truly believed his pleas would be heard by anyone other than himself. But as he gazed longingly at the saints around him, at the Nazarene on the cross, the Virgin Mary, the traitor Judas, and all the angels, in his heart of hearts he wished it was not so.

Two cars arrived promptly at noon. Sleek and black, so finely polished they could have been straight from the factory. The drivers, two men dressed in matching black suits and slick hairstyles, got out and opened the doors for the passengers.

Out of the first car came Bishop Strauss and another clergyman Mason didn't know, plump and bespectacled, dressed in the same black cassock as Strauss but with trimmings of red instead of violet. From the second car, an elderly man with a sun-worn face and silk suit the color of wine, dark glasses, and a long cane which he tapped ahead of him with every step he took. He was led by a woman with rich dark hair and a modest yet stylish silk dress and heels. They looked as though they might be attending fashion week in Paris, clashing with the austere appearance of the clergymen.

The group approached the church entrance as the drivers rummaged through the trunks of the cars. Grim and Coffey greeted them, shook hands, exchanged pleasantries. Mason couldn't hear well but knew the kind of words they were saying: "Nice to see you," "You're looking well," "We're honored by your visit," and so forth.

They made their way down the aisle. The two drivers followed close behind, each now carrying two metal cases. Grim gave a discreet little gesture to Mason indicating that he was to stand.

He did so and stepped into the aisle, so nervous that he bumped his knee on the pew in front of him. He had to bite his tongue to kill the "Goddammit!" that got far too close to escaping his mouth. Christian or not, cursing in front of a whole troupe of clergy in a church would have been in poor taste even to him.

Grim shook the hands of the blind man and the woman at his side before bowing to the cardinal with a kiss of his ring.

"Mason Cole," said Father Coffey while motioning to the unknown clergyman. "May I present Cardinal Francesco Scagnetti, Head Overseer of the Holy Order of Militia Dei, first in command and liaison te His Holiness."

"Bonjourno," said the cardinal, his presence far more congenial than the Bishop's. His ring, bearing a red setting, glinted like a ruby when it caught the light.

"And these are two very distinguished guests," Coffey continued. "Dante Moretti, our Curator of Archives and Artifacts, and Head Docent Maria Di Pietro."

"Nice to meet you," said Mason to them both. The old man said nothing, but even through his dark glasses there was a twinkle in his eye that was hard to mistake.

"And of course you've met Bishop Strauss."

"Of course," said Mason, avoiding his scrutinizing gaze.

"Mister Cole," said Strauss.

"They're here to perform the Tritemptamen, which will test the Holy Spirit within you. With your permission, of course."

"So long as they don't involve a rubber glove," Mason said nervously.

There were fewer crickets chirping in a moonlit field. The only one who seemed to enjoy the joke at all was Father Coffey, who let the briefest of smiles escape his lips, along with the smell of whiskey, before bringing his hand up to stifle them both.

Everyone moved to the front of the church, where the two drivers snapped open two cases and set their contents near the altar: a pair of candles, a censer set before Moretti as he donned a ceremonial sash of some kind, a bronze pitcher, a gilded chalice, a small bell, an ornate plate, and, lastly, a candlestick-sized silver cross identical to the one Mason wore. Two other cases, smaller than the first, had not been opened yet.

The Curator turned to Mason and spoke a few words in soft Italian.

"We'll need to perform a brief ritual," Maria relayed in flawless, unaccented English. "But first Signor Moretti requests, please, to examine the cross you wear around your neck."

Mason hesitated at first, but then, reluctantly, slipped it over his head and placed it in Moretti's open hand. He held it delicately, as if it were made of glass, moving his thumb slowly across the metal, feeling every contour.

When he was done the Curator handed it back to Mason and smiled. "Grazie."

Cardinal Scagnetti paced around the group, waving the censer back and forth like a pendulum, fragrant white smoke spilling from it as he did. Mason was expecting some form of a prayer or blessing but was taken by surprise when Moretti began to sing.

Where this man had once been quiet and small, he was now a powerful tenor belting out a Latin hymn in a voice so magnificent it made the walls of the church tremble. The others around him all either had their eyes closed or their heads bowed, hands clasped before them. It was so beautiful that Mason could not help but feel moved by it, the tiniest tear gathering in the corner of his eye. He quickly dabbed it away before anyone could see.

When he was done, Moretti ended with a melodious "Amen."

The Curator faced the altar and was handed the bronze pitcher by Cardinal Scagnetti, who slid the chalice across the table in front of him. His hands looked frail and weathered, but he steadily poured water into the chalice until full, cupped it in both hands, and held it up in front of Mason.

"Tocca questo," he said.

"Touch," Maria translated.

Odd. Mason thought he would want him to drink from it. He extended his index finger and placed it in the water so that the tip was submerged.

From somewhere behind him, Mason heard the locks of another case snap open. One of the drivers appeared, now wearing thick black gloves covered in strange white symbols. Cradled between them he held the small stone figure of a dragon with a human face.

Mason took a step back.

The man placed the figure at the altar atop a cruciform seal. Moretti tipped the chalice slowly toward it. Not meaning to, Mason held his breath, unsure of what to expect. A light trickle of water fell upon the grotesque stone figure.

Nothing happened. Moretti, watching expectantly, looked disappointed.

The other driver approached carrying a square case of lacquered wood in his now white-gloved hands. He set it down on the table, snapped open the latch, and took out a human skull from inside. Ancient by the looks of it, rough and brittle. The deep brown color of wet parchment. Few teeth remained, and those that survived were little more than tiny nubs. And on the forehead, as if branded by holy fire, was the symbol Mason wore around his neck. He placed it on the ornate plate before the large cross.

"Hold," said Moretti via Maria. "Gently."

Mason approached the skull and placed his hands carefully upon it. Smooth as if it had been polished, cared for. Though the sockets were dead and empty, he could very much feel its eyes on him.

That's when he noticed that everyone was watching him, clearly expecting something to happen.

Again Moretti looked disappointed.

Mason stepped away from it and one of the men picked it up, returning it safely to its bed of velvet.

Maria stepped forward, lovely black curls springing across her shoulders as she moved. She looked him deep in the eyes as if studying the patterns of color in them. "What would you say if I told you vous êtes mon véritable sauveur?"

Mason's mouth hung open. "I'd say . . . I don't speak French." He didn't have to look at the others to know that this was clearly not the answer they were expecting.

An awkward beat passed between everyone present. There was a glance between Father Coffey and Grim, who finally stepped forward. "Thank you, Mason. Why don't you wait outside? We'll be along shortly."

Translation: We have things to discuss that we don't want you to hear.

"Okay," he said. But he had no intention of missing this.

Mason left as quickly and quietly as possible, catching the stare of Bishop Strauss, who had not said anything during all of this. He went out the doors and into the foyer, pressing his ear to the narrow slit between them as soon as they'd closed. It was hard to hear, but fortunately the acoustics were enough to get most of what was said.

"Well, Signore Moretti, what is your assessment of the boy?" It was Cardinal Scagnetti speaking, his words difficult to make out thanks to a thick Italian accent.

"It seems there has been a mistake," said Moretti in English, his accent much lighter than the Cardinal's. Mason was confused as to why he'd relied on a translator with Mason if he didn't have to.

"A mistake?" said Grim.

"The angelic spirit, I'm afraid, is not within the boy as previously believed. I sense no other presence in him of any kind, aside from his own."

"Forgive me, signore, but that's just not possible," said Grim. "I saw it with my own eyes, saw it manifest in holy light when his life was in danger. He managed to escape from his captors in a feat of unprecedented strength. Not to mention his vision when coming into contact with what we believed to be the finger of Father Abbott, a belief that he himself disproved."

"Was he wearing the cross during these occurrences?" said Moretti.

"I believe so."

"And that is most definitely the cross of Saint Philip." Moretti paused to clear his throat. "Which the angelic spirit now resides within."

Silence at first. Then all voices spoke at once, mingled together in disagreement and disbelief.

"Please," said Father Coffey. "Signore, how can tha' be? The spirit needs a living vessel, one bound by blood te Saint Philip."

Moretti continued. "It would be possible for a living spirit to attach itself to non-living matter if it were channeled into a pure metal."

"And it has never been conclusively proven that there must be a shared lineage between messiahs," said Maria. "This is only how we know it has been passed down from one to the next. Since the blood-line has branched off many different ways over time, he may still be distantly related."

"No," said Grim. "I'm afraid the results of his blood tests show no genetic connection."

"You are certain?" said Maria.

"Yes."

"It is not important," Strauss croaked finally.

"Forgive me, Your Eminence," said Grim. "But it is most definitely important."

"As a matter of academic curiosity, perhaps. More important is what we do now. We must find whomever the rightful successor may be. Someone proper. Someone *worthy*."

The arrogance, the sanctimonious resonance in his words, made Mason want to spit fire.

"Then it is a matter of determining how to transfer the spirit to the new messiah," said Maria.

"And how do we do that?" said Scagnetti.

"One thing at a time," said Strauss. "First, we will need that cross. Then—"

He had heard enough. Mason left the church before he could hear any more.

And this time he would not be coming back.

TWENTY-TWO

MASON RETURNED TO THE CHAPTERHOUSE, SAYING NOTHING TO anyone and drawing curious stares as he all but stormed up to the third floor. As soon as he reached his room, he took the empty duffle bag from its resting place at the foot of his bed.

His thoughts raced. He didn't know what angered him more—that he wasn't this coveted messiah they all talked about or that he had only just started to believe it. When Grim told him about the tests, he found himself wanting it to be true. He didn't want to admit it, not even to himself. That nagging little flame, that one that still flickered and refused to go out. It would be dangerous, no question, but it meant a chance at justice. For Dale. And Rose. And Julie. Now there wasn't even that much comfort and, finally, he felt that brave little flame die.

It didn't matter whether the cross belonged to him rightfully or not. Whether it was a holy relic or a piece of junk found in the street . . . when something is all you have to remember someone by, a trinket becomes a treasure—and they were *not* taking this one from him!

Mason went about filling the bag with things he barely recognized. He was just about to collect the toothbrush he had used only once from the bathroom when it occurred to him that he wouldn't get far without food or money.

"I'll think of something. I just need to get away from here."

And then: *Wait . . . I can't just leave. What about Bossy? Who will take care of her?*

She sat next to her bowl, waiting for him to feed her, as if to say, *Never mind that . . . where would you go? Everyone you know is either dead or thinks you are.*

"Maybe I could go to Gus, or Julie's parents, and explain . . ."

Hello, Earth to Mason! They think you're dead. If you show up all of a sudden, there will be police. Doctors. Psychiatrists. Not to mention that they would figure you had something to do with the deaths of their children. How do you plan to deal with that small matter?

"I'd tell the truth."

And wind up in an asylum for the rest of your life.

"Better than this!"

Is it? Think about it for a minute. Oh, and let's not forget that there's a vampire out there who's probably got eyes on this place—yes, even now, during the day—and who would just love for you to be alone and vulnerable.

"If I'm not what he thinks I am, he's got no reason to want me."

But he doesn't know that. Do you really want to take that chance? If he found you once, he can find you again.

"I can stay off the grid, go by a different name, go far away where no one will find me."

"Stay off the grid"? Listen to yourself. You have no experience at this. No resources. Nowhere to go. Not even a way out of town. Even if you did manage to hide from him, he only has to catch you once. Just once.

Then the panic really hit. The cross became an immobilizing weight around his neck. He was trapped. And there was nothing he could do about it.

"FUCK!"

Mason hurled his bag with all his might into the bathroom. It struck the mirror, which shattered into a million pieces across the floor. He yanked the cross from around his neck—for the first and only time in thirteen years—and threw it as far away from him as he could. It hit the wall and, with the muted chime of metal dancing across concrete, landed somewhere near the bed.

Bits of his own frantic reflection flashed across the last remaining wedge of mirror still in its frame. The rest lay in a jagged nest in the sink below and scattered across the floor. He collapsed, raw and wretched. Cursing the heavens and longing for Hell.

"Why, God?" he hollered. "Why? Why are you doing this to me? What have I ever done to you? What do you want from me?"

No answer, as always.

Nothing mattered anymore. Nothing at all.

He curled up into an unresponsive ball of sobbing flesh.

A shard of mirror lay close to his face. He reached out and touched it, gently, as though it were a keepsake, and turned it on its side toward his face. A tearful eye appeared. He sat up and ran his thumb along the smooth surface of it, felt the fine, lethal edges, which would only need to be pressed at the right angle in order to come alive with pain. He not only saw himself in this broken little thing, but the path to his salvation as well. It would set him free.

Mason smiled.

He raised his other wrist to eye level, angling the point of the glass toward the veins under the soft layer of skin, begging to be cut.

There was something else now in the reflection. A white light filled the shadows of the room behind him. Mason turned and saw for himself the concentrated point of light coming from under the bed, so pure and strong that its image remained burned in his vision even when he looked away.

He crawled on his hands and knees toward it, saw the light in a cruciform shape. A cross. Growing brighter the closer he got to it. Bracing himself on one arm, he reached out to grab it. The pain in his hand disappeared—and so did the very world around him.

· · ·

"Please. Save me."

Black explodes into white as he plunges through depths no hole in the ground can possess. Lost in a cyclone of fractured images, faces both familiar and strange howl all around him. A whirlwind of sharp air rushes past, biting at his skin, strong enough to throw him upward.

But he continues to drop.

His closed eyelids open in time to see the bottom. He reaches it, but does not stop. Instead, he falls farther still into another layer of space, fitting snug but firm into this new form.

Immediately he stands, unharmed. The fall alone should have killed him. He looks up to the corridor through which he fell only to see a rapidly closing aperture of some kind, a rip in the air sewn together with invisible thread.

Sight returns from the darkness of death and unveils a figure before him. Smokeless flame in the form of a person, red eyes burning in pools of black. Lightning surges through his limbs, igniting the blade he holds in his hand, and propels him forward, connecting with the figure's infernal core. A howl too abhorrent to be anything other than the mouth of Hell itself shatters the very air, shaking loose dirt from the rock around him.

The fire dissipates and then it is gone.

He sees his hands—but not his hands—before him: one holding the sword, its weight nothing to him now; the other clutching the cross he had brandished in an attempt to drive the fiend out. It is different now. Silvered, a hole in the center, and each end sharp enough to draw blood.

Mason returned to his body. Lying on the floor staring up at the ceiling, overcome with a kind of cold. Refreshing his senses, allowing him to momentarily hear voices again. Only they weren't the echoes of the ghosts of his past. They were the minds of every person in the chapterhouse.

He was connected with the other lives around him—even with

Bossy, whose energy he felt nearby, surveying him from under the bed to make sure if it was safe to come out after the commotion.

He clutched the cross so tightly that it left an imprint in his palm. When he opened his hand he saw not the tarnished metal he was so familiar with, but rather a clean, silver one, as if it were suddenly brand new. He turned it over and saw the engraving clearly—*Lux In Tenebris*. No particular style or script, and yet it bore one notable distinction from the Latin of antiquity; that of a *u* in place of a *v* in the first word.

Mason felt a warm, uncomfortable spot in the middle of his forehead. He reached up to touch it, but his fingers felt nothing there. Not in the skin, anyway. Had his mind been an eye, it had just opened.

He could sense Grim before he ever saw him, felt it like a breeze on his skin. He was on the roof, deep in meditation, bathed in the glow of candles. Eyes closed and legs crossed. He remained sitting as Mason approached and kneeled down before him on the floor.

Grim opened his eyes to see Mason's unfurled hand extended toward him, holding a clean, shiny silver cross.

"Okay," said Mason. "Tell me a story."

TWENTY-THREE

GRIM SAID NOTHING, JUST STOOD AND WENT TO THE NEARBY table, where his glasses lay atop a leather-bound book. Placing the glasses snuggly on his face, he sat back down and began thumbing through the pages.

"From the Gospel of Judas," said Grim. " 'And though my brothers saw fit to sup, I hungered not. Troubled was I by the words of my Lord that among us was a treacher. And so I sought my Lord, and in Gethsemane I did find him. Still and silent regarding the olive trees.

" ' "Come, Judas. Stand with me."

" ' "My Lord, I would stand with you unto the end of this world. If there truly be a snake in our midst, speak his name and I will see him hung."

" 'He turned to me and spake. "Judas of Kerioth."

" 'To my knees I fell and implored him. "My Lord, sooner would I part my own flesh than fall from your grace. I serve only you."

" ' "You will betray me . . . for I command it so."

" 'His words cut mine and he took my hands in his.

" ' "Judas, most beloved of mine, it must be you. For I can trust no other in this task. They will not understand."

" ' "My Lord, I do not understand."

" ' "To the church elders I am a false idol, to the Romans a threat, and to our brothers and sisters a messiah. I am none of these. So many have said that I came to believe it myself, but I am not the Son of God. Touched by Him, but not of His hand. I am not to be a savior of this world, but its condemner."

" ' "This cannot be."

" ' "I have seen it. I long only to make our church a compassionate one. To give hope to those in need of it. To let them know that a greater kingdom than any amongst those of men lies beyond, and the way to that kingdom is love.

" ' "And for my passion this world will suffer ages of conflict and oceans of tears. A seed to a field of blood where truth is as water in the desert. My very name will drive legions. Yours will be as treachery. But I have seen the light shed through ages hence. I have seen this and more that must come to pass. For through this fire is the path to true salvation."

" ' "If this truly be thy will, thy will be done."

" 'My Lord put his lips to mine. "Return this kiss with my accusers. And hate them not. Forgive them, for they know not what they do."

" 'And so I wept.' " Grim flipped to another section of the book marked with a red ribbon, looking up for a moment to gauge the response from his audience of one.

"So," said Mason, "Jesus and Judas, they were . . . together?"

With a long, thoughtful blink, he nodded.

"Really? Wow."

"A detail which still maintains a level of contempt among the more traditional circles of the Church."

"I'm sure."

"And this is a passage from the testimony of Sir Richard.

" 'I, Sir Ricard de Avignon, being of sound mind, body, and soul, hereby solemnly swear that the following testimony and all accounts within are true, so help me God.

" 'In September of 1300 *anno Domini*, I received word from the Grand Master himself that there had been reports of strange disappearances near a small village in the North of France called Àilean. Having not seen my motherland in many years, I immediately made ready to travel. This was of course highly irregular for a Knight of the Temple but, due to the mission I had been tasked with since Acre, one to which I had become accustomed.

" 'Disguised as missionaries, my men and I were sent to investigate. We arrived at the village and met with the resident friar. He claimed that people from the village had gone missing and there had been sightings of a figure cloaked in red at night who he believed to be the Devil himself. The next morning the friar was found on a nearby tree, hanged and disemboweled. Many of the villagers fled in fear, but the brave few who stayed behind joined us as we searched for the culprit of this unholy act to put an end to it.

" 'Death littered our path as we made for the coast: birds and small animals at first, then stags and deer, all drained of their blood and far too plentiful to be natural. As night fell, we came to a cave near the sea. I heard the sound of chanting coming from deep within. At last we arrived at an opening to the sea and beheld a most unholy sight: the naked body of a young maiden covered with profane runes and symbols painted in blood, surrounded by a circle of cloaked figures in black, all swaying and chanting. Above them, a woman cloaked in red stood atop a great rock at the edge of a precipice, clutching the maiden's heart in her hand. Instead of taking alarm in our presence, she bade us welcome and pierced the heart with a dagger. The heart caught fire, as did the Red Woman's body, burning away her flesh until she was clothed in a smokeless flame, emerging as something else entirely.

" 'Strange eons of time long before Christ was born, before the first sprig had sprung in Eden, when the earth was but a shapeless void, were beings such as this. A blessedly distant period when even God held doubt in his heart while manifesting his Creation, eternities of chaos when the stars were cold and all was maddening darkness as forms of which even nightmares cannot conjure took shape. Forms which in myth have been called titans, demons, and monsters. This thing was all three.

" 'A perverse mesh of male and female, possessing the sex organs of both, the skin was black as pitch with eyes to match, except for the middles, which burned red and white hot, shrouded in a shadow which I could feel within me, pressing itself against my will. It spoke in gibbering, mouthless sounds I couldn't conceive of yet somehow understood, a fathomless timbre which spoke of the yawning depths of the Abyss itself, countless souls crying out as one while tortured, unmade, and rewoven into the very fabric of Hell.

" 'God help me, I can still hear it!

" 'And I knew then what I could never have known otherwise: the oppressive, wholly unbridled terror of being in the presence of true evil.

" 'As my squire Philippe drew his sword, it reached out with its black hand and smote him invisibly as if he were no more than a fly. Life left him, words he uttered with his final breath.

" ' "Please. Save me."

" 'I charged forth and the dæmon pulled my very soul from my body, and as life slipped away I saw a bright light. I had failed in my mission but now it mattered not, for I was ascending toward the Kingdom of God, to be welcomed into the loving embrace of the Lord Almighty.

" 'However, the light fell not upon me. The sky above had opened, casting Heaven's light upon the lifeless body of my squire. And lo, a miracle occurred. He stood to his feet. His sword beamed with holy light. He plunged it into the dæmon, cracking the charred skin apart to reveal the flaming form that lay beneath, and vanquished it from the earth. The boy had been dead, but in his place stood a newly christened protector of the flock. A Ram of God. The

Messiah of the Archangel. And it was in this moment that I truly felt the hand of the Almighty at work. I knew then that He had bestowed upon us a true and righteous savior. And the fight had just begun.' "

Grim stopped and closed the book. Mason sat still and didn't say a word.

"Do you believe now?"

"Yes."

Grim smiled. He leaned forward and offered the book to Mason. "I think you'll be wanting this, then."

Mason cradled the book in his hands, scanning the title page.

BIBLE OF THE HOLY ORDER OF MILITIA DEI
REVISED INTERNATIONAL VERSION No. 138

Beneath it was a coat of arms, a shield marked with a cross on the front with crossed swords behind. It was the same as the setting on Grim's ring, only more elaborate. A banner with a the motto beneath it inscribed with elegant calligraphy—*Lux In Tenebris*.

"And you just hand this out like the Gideons or Mormons?"

"We make it available to those we feel may have need of it," said Grim.

"Aren't you worried about, I dunno, keeping this secret and hidden lest the human world find out and all that?"

"Heavens, no! Awareness of a problem is the first step to a solution. We can use all the help we can get. And most who would read its contents wouldn't believe it in the first place."

"Then why modify memories and engage in cover-ups?"

"Well . . ." Grim searched for the right words. "Authorities have a way of complicating matters. Not to mention that they are by no means impervious to, shall we say, corrupting influences. It's a lesser of two evils, one we employ on an ad hoc basis."

Mason flipped the page to the table of contents. It had some of the same books as the average Holy Bible, such as Genesis, Exodus, Proverbs, and Revelation, while others were completely foreign to him—Gnosis, the Book of Enoch, the Book of Jubilees, the Gospel of Mary.

"So how is this any different from any other Bible?"

Grim shrugged. "Aside from the bulk of its content, I suppose it isn't. Do you know how many gospels there are?"

Mason shrugged.

"Over a hundred, that we know of. The Old Testament is comprised of the same books of the Tanakh, and even those differ from one denomination to the next. The authors of the Holy Bible compiled the texts that they believed were most relevant to their faith and mission. That is exactly what we have done."

Yeeeeah . . . okay, Mason thought. *Like "No man whose testicles are crushed or whose male organs cut off shall enter the assembly of the Lord"? Or "Permit no woman to teach or have authority over men, she is to keep silent"? Real relevant.*

"I agree," said Grim. "Alas, they were products of an unenlightened time. And you'll notice that the books to which those passages belong are absent from our Bible."

"Can you not do that, please?" Mason asked with an awkward look on his face.

"Do what?"

"Read my mind."

"Ah," said Grim. "You are under the impression that I intentionally probed your mind for what I heard. I assure you, I did nothing of the sort."

Then something changed in Grim. As if the door to a soundproof vault had opened, letting a buzz of voices so jumbled they were practically white noise escape from inside. Mason heard it all. *Felt* it. And through the din, a single voice emerged.

Unguarded thoughts are as easy to hear as words spoken aloud.

Grim's voice. His lips had not moved, but it was his voice in Mason's head.

And just as quickly as it started, it stopped. All was quiet again.

"Wow," said Mason.

"It will take some time, but we'll get you sorted out. To return to your question, if there is one difference between our Bible and the usual one, it would be that this book, like Militia Dei itself, is not centered around Jesus of Nazareth but rather Saint Philip, who was the first Messiah of the Archangel, the holy presence which I am convinced now more than ever you possess."

"And let me guess . . . there was a prophecy that told of this occurrence?"

"No."

"No?"

"No prophecy, no prediction, no premonition. Not for the Inception of Saint Philip, nor now with you. However, I don't believe its bestowal upon you was entirely without reason.

"I believe that God meant for a change to occur long ago, but was obstructed by the Holy Spirit falling into possession of those who abused it, used it for avarice and vice—in essence, the very opposite of what it was intended for. What followed were generations of mishandling and misunderstanding, until it fell into a state of ill-repute. And in order to correct the course, it seems that He put the right people in the right place at the right time in order to achieve that."

"But . . . in the church today . . ."

"In the church today, it still resides solely within the cross. With your permission, I'd like to attempt an exploration of your memories using a technique called meditational hypnosis. Basically, I attempt to walk you through your memories while in a shared meditative state."

"Does that really work?"

"If done properly, yes."

"Okay."

Grim went to one of the walls bathed in light and returned with a single candle. He sat on the dojo floor cross-legged and gestured for Mason to do likewise.

"I want you to just close your eyes, let your hands rest on your knees, and relax."

He did as he was told.

"Focus on my voice. Think of it as a guide in a world without vision. Can you see the candle?"

"Yes." A warm red glow heated the thin flesh of his eyelids.

"I want you to breathe in through your nostrils, hold it for a moment, and let it out through your mouth."

Mason inhaled until his lungs were full . . .

. . .

. . . held . . .

. . .

. . . and let it out.

He could feel himself slipping into another layer of his mind, a place inside himself between the conscious and subconscious. Very aware of himself and his surroundings.

Mason began to perceive a fiery point the shape of a teardrop, flickering ever so slightly from his breaths.

"I see the flame."

"Let it open up. When it does, you will be back in Jerusalem thirteen years ago."

Mason closed his eyes, held the cross tightly in both hands. Concentrated on it. The flame began to grow both in size and brightness until it filled every corner of his perception, enveloping him, blinding his mind's eye until it expanded beyond the boundary of his inner vision. A moment later it left, but was not gone. It had moved to a point high above him.

"I'm there."

The scene unfolded before him like pages in a pop-up book.

. . .

Sun-filled sky. Blossoms on an olive tree at the first kiss of spring. Beneath him, the old stone roads and narrow alleyways where so many once walked over the centuries, ancient footsteps forever in the past, solid as can be. Tanned bricks of the surrounding buildings match those of a tall archway leading into the marketplace. The sweet smell of sesame bread drifts through the air. Brightly colored clothes and fabrics hang from the awnings of street vendors while a nearby flock of pigeons bobs and pecks at the ground for crumbs. People move through the market, itself a living thing, their voices drowned by church bells that ring loud and clear. Everything just as it was that fateful day. And there is Grim again, walking side by side with him as though they are old friends.

They come to an archway at the edge of the market and stop. The Church of the Redeemer looms overhead, its bell tower bathed in midday sun. Mason looks through the crowd and sees a woman at one of the nearby shops, one hand skimming through strings of beads, as a small boy clutches at the folds of her skirt.

He sees her, not with the vision of his form across from the market, but up at her from below. Even after all this time he knows he's looking at his mother, seeing her through the eyes of his younger self.

He is barely waist-high, his hair is light in color and soft. He hasn't even lost his baby teeth yet. He looks around at all the big people nearby, scanning their faces, some of whom meet his gaze and smile, others barely even noticing him.

There is no sign of his father at first. Then, from the throng of people, he appears, dressed in a linen shirt and cargo shorts, with a camera around his neck. He is holding something in his hand.

"Where'd you get that?" asks his mother.

"Found it inside the church. Cool, huh?"

"Put that back. It probably belongs to someone."

"It does," says his father. "This little guy."

"Let me see that." She takes it in her hands and looks at it.

And when she does . . .

. . .

Born in the same house her future son would grow up in, her room the same one that would one day be his. A house so full of cats they could be found in every corner: under beds, atop cabinets, peeking out from between the daisies in the garden. And loving every one of them.

"Pay them no mind, sugar. You'll be ten times smarter than all of them together."

Reading Little Women, *identifying immediately with Jo and the whole story, making her want to know so many other places than Stonehill. Her father killed in action while flying troops out of Saigon. They stopped going to church after that.*

Boys noticing her, asking her out. Saying yes a couple of times, but finding them all dull and stupid. Going all the way with one of them, Tommy. He seemed different than the rest, but it was all an act just to get with her. She doesn't say yes again after that. But she doesn't lose hope that someday maybe, just maybe, one will be different. The thought makes her start whistling a song. "Don't Stop Believin'."

Someone starts singing. She turns around to see a boy with straw-colored hair and steel-blue eyes. A mouth that looks like he's about to say something but doesn't. Not yet. She wonders what it could be. Some horrible pick-up line, no doubt. Instead, it is just one word.

"Hi."

Both of them smile—

And they're back in the square, his younger self and his parents.

A little smile bends the corners of her mouth. "Well, I suppose it's all right."

She hands it back. His father kneels down and slips a chain over his son's head.

A cross. The very same one adult Mason hasn't taken off since that day. It's terribly dirty and all but ruined, but young Mason doesn't care.

So strange seeing his father's face now in this way, both with his own eyes and through those he possessed as a child at the same time.

Not static and frozen in a single expression the way it is in a photo, alive as he hasn't seen for years. He's almost forgotten. Here in this moment, this reality, this memory, whatever it is, coexisting as his two selves simultaneously.

Mason swooned. His legs were beginning to lose their place on the ground.

"Stay with me," said Grim. "Don't look away. Focus on every detail. Hold this moment, Mason. Think about your father. What was he doing inside the church? What did he see? Who was around? Follow him back."

And as his father's hands brush the side of little Mason's face while slipping the cross around his neck, time scatters like a handful of puzzle pieces.

Mason glimpses those pieces of his father's life.

His mother dying of breast cancer when he was seventeen. The one person he could talk to about what he really wanted to do with his life. Seventeen was too young to realize that life was too short. He made up his mind and told his father the truth: that he wanted to quit football and become a teacher. His father's face looks as though he had walked up and told him that he wanted to herd gay cats for a living. If he wanted to, he'd do it alone, but he somehow hoped deep down his father would be supportive. That hope didn't last long.

Cashing in a bond he'd had since birth, worth quite a bit of money now. How much he wasn't sure. Enough to pay for school, that was all that mattered. Leaving home at last, not even bothering to say goodbye to his old man, for that's all he was to him now. An old man with whom he had nothing in common.

Whatever it took. And it paid off. Walking through the quad, he heard whistling, the opening of "Don't Stop Believin'" by Journey. Not even sure where it was coming from, but he starts singing the lyrics anyway. Then he sees her for the first time. The girl who would be his wife. Her lovely brown hair. Soft face with a touch of rosy pink in her cheeks. Glasses that framed her bright green eyes just right. Cotton dress bound with a leather belt. Everything about her gentle and warm. Happy and alive. He loves her instantly.

"Hi." *He smiles.*

She smiles back.

All of it whizzing by until it approaches the pocket of time they now inhabit. Inside the church while Mason and his mother went to look at the beads, the congregation that had gathered, most of them locals, some tourists. Mason's father was just about to leave when he stopped and spotted something on the floor. The cross. He picked it up and examined it.

"Focus now, Mason. How did the cross get here? This gift is different with non-living objects. They have no organic tissue to house memories. You have to find the emotion attached to a specific memory."

But Mason didn't have to search. As if reaching out from the depths, it found him, closed the gap between them and connected.

Time rewinds again. Before the floor, the cross had been resting on a nearby pew until a tourist sat on it without even realizing. Before that, it was placed there after being clutched in the white-knuckled hands of a disheveled, unshaven man as he prayed. The man sat there with his eyes closed, his face grief-stricken.

"Stop," *said Grim.*

Time freezes again. Grim kneels down next to the man and places his hands on him, touches the brow of his head to the man's shoulder.

He stays that way for a long while.

"Goodbye, my friend," *said Grim.*

This is him. Will Graves.

Time resumes.

"It's you," said the man, tears welling in his eyes as they stared rapt at the empty ceiling.

Mason saw nothing where he was looking. Just empty space.

"This is it, isn't it? What must I do?" A few moments of silence from the man before he took the cross in his hands and bowed his head. "Into my hands, I commit your spirit."

Mason closes his hands around his. It feels different than the time with his father. Ragged. Disconnected, somehow.

He sees the puzzle pieces of this man's life:

Eight years old. Same age his father was when he became the messiah. He and his brothers kneeling on the floor reciting their prayers. Two years later, he died. An orphan now.

The cross passed to Joseph, his eldest brother, next. Twelve years later, died.

Then to his brother Benjamin. He only lasted seven more years. Such was the passage of the Holy Spirit from one to the other. It was not seen as a curse but rather an honor. In truth it was both.

And finally, it came to him. He relived the same moment of the Inception of Saint Philip, but chose another path. A safer path. Or so he thought . . .

He hears a woman's voice.

"I never thanked you for saving my life." She brushes back her soft blond hair.

"No need, miss," Will says. "Just doing my duty."

She flicks her eyebrows at him suggestively. "You sure about that?"

It starts nice.

It ends with death.

A baby, one which was never alive, cradled in his arms as he sees a city, an entire city but which one he's not sure, swallowed by the earth. But he vows to find out.

The cross dropped from the man's hands and he staggered away as if wounded until he was out of sight. Mason's father, cross now in hand, left the church and returned to young Mason and his mother, and adult Mason watches as they stroll away from the market.

Time passes and the streets move on around them, blurry and less clear the farther his younger self moves away.

"Did you know it was possible? To do what he did with the cross."

"No. And I imagine neither did he until it was time. And that in itself is another one of life's miracles."

"What's that?"

"Of what you are capable when called upon."

High above the church, bells ring, startling Mason.

"This isn't going to be easy for you to see Mason, but you must."

A vibration goes through the ground.

"No, no. Please. I can't . . ."

But it is too late.

Things begin shaking and breaking apart. People begin to scream and run. A horrible roar sounds as the very earth itself opens up beneath them. Cracks eat their way across the city, spreading outward into massive chasms.

His mother picks him up and takes his father's hand as they run for shelter.

It's no use.

They fall, as do everyone and everything around him. The last thing Mason feels, through the eyes of his mother, his father, and his younger self all at the same time, is being swallowed by a roaring blackness below.

Please. Save me.

Destruction rains down upon them against the rapidly shrinking light. A car. A person. The side of a building. Whole uprooted chunks of earth plummet around him and farther into this upheaval in the earth. Consumed by darkness.

All goes dark.

His other self and Grim remain fixed in the very same spot as if held by invisible hands. High above, a small flock of birds can be seen circling in the sky just before being stained by dust so thick it blocks out the sun.

Everything silent now.

Grim places his hand on Mason's shoulder and slowly, far more slowly than should be physically possible, they slide down into the hole and through a crack in his mind he forgot was even there.

Deeper they go into the wounded earth.

Where it has split open there is now a gaping maw. Water bleeds from broken pipes and water mains. The rock face of the chasm holds none of the stark natural beauty one might find in a colossal cave or some other underground wonder. This is violent. Strange echoes and chthonic acoustics sound, the earth itself moaning in pain.

Split into a series of erratic shelves above a hopeless pit of black destruction and rubble. Scattered ledges dotted with the remains of vehicles. Buildings. And, soon, bodies. Everywhere there are bodies. Caked in a thick layer of dust. Fires burn all around, mixing with the dust into an acrid smoke throughout the pit.

In a word: Hell.

They descend to the ruined bottom of a ledge on the east side of what used to be the city. The terrain so destroyed that it is completely foreign. Twisted metal. Shattered stone. Erupted earth.

Sticking out of it all is a face.

His.

Five-year-old Mason lies broken and dirty. Sleeping—or so he appears. At no point does his eyes open or his lung take a breath. Then, adult Mason is sure of it.

He died.

How much time passed he cannot say. The tiniest sliver of light is just barely visible after the sun rose. Then, dark again.

Suddenly the cross around little Mason's neck glows. Just a little at first. Then brighter. Enough to make his eyes glint as they fly open. His lungs take in a painful, dust-filled breath.

He starts to cry.

. . .

When Mason returned to his body this time, it was as if he were connecting with the ground from a high drop with ease. Short of breath, he dabbed at his forehead, wiping away thin beads of sweat. Grim showed none of the same signs as him, simply awakened from his pose and stood. He offered Mason his hand and helped him to his feet.

"I . . . I didn't know I had any of that in me," said Mason.

Grim said nothing, but the look on his face was one of deep satisfaction.

"A week ago I had to strain even for the slightest memory of them, and now . . ." Mason clasped his hands before him and, watered by thankful tears, a smile grew.

"Quite the gift, isn't it?"

Far from perfect. There were vast gaps in what he saw. But it was a damn sight more than he had before. And so he cherished it.

"What did you get from Will?"

"I saw him with his brothers. Praying. Each one became the messiah."

"And?"

"And . . . something else . . . a woman. Kendall something?"

"Kendall? One of the last assignments we worked on together led to a woman named Kendall Schumacher, if memory serves. But he didn't even really know her."

"I think he did," said Mason with a small grin, pleased that just for once he knew something that Grim had not. "And . . ." He described the vision of Jerusalem falling as he held the stillborn. "Do you know what that was about?"

"No." Grim's brow furrowed. "Not a clue." After a beat, he looked at his watch and placed his hand on Mason's shoulder. "Come, you must be hungry."

They left the dojo and stepped outside into the night air.

Mason noticed two things. First, that his senses were alive like he had never imagined they could be. The lights seemed to dance in their own reflections on the wet pavement. The edges of the buildings had sharpened, when before they were dull and distant. The plants of the zen garden surged with an energy as if it were the very blood in his veins. Every sound clear and clever. And mingled amongst the chorus were voices that now sang rather than screamed.

And the second thing, though far from the slightest, was that it had finally stopped raining.

TWENTY-FOUR

AFTER A BITE TO EAT, CONSISTING MOSTLY OF LEFTOVER spaghetti and meatballs from the previous night's dinner, Grim made a phone call to Bishop Strauss. It wasn't easy, but he had managed to convince him to let Mason retake the Tritemptamen tomorrow afternoon.

When asked what had happened, Grim replied, with great satisfaction: "A miracle."

"Very well," said Strauss, and hung up. He did not sound convinced. Hard to tell for sure as Mason was not even sitting near Grim during the conversation, but rather, to his surprise, could hear it all from the solitude of his room.

His senses ran wild, stretching out in all directions. He heard things that he could not possibly have before. People typing away on keyboards, the organ playing in St. Augustine's at the other end of the compound, even people talking in the surrounding buildings. He caught new chemical smells which were completely foreign to him, and he realized they were endorphins, hormones, pheromones, and the various other chemicals the body produces. His sight had not improved, per se, but what he saw he could later recall with amazing clarity; he'd read an article from the daily newspaper and recite it word for word hours later. He picked up the residual body heat of someone who had been leaning against the cold metal carriage of the elevator well after they left. But it was not all at once, seeming to come and go at random.

Mason and Grim returned to the church the next day to find Bishop Strauss, along with Father Coffey and the visitors from the Vatican, already waiting for them. As he approached, he could sense them. No words, no stray thoughts—just the shape of their minds. Halls upon halls of closed doors. And there was something else from each of them as well: a presence . . . that was the only way Mason could describe it. There was a new quality to the church itself as well. Fresh and pure as a golden mist in sunlight.

"Everything all right?" Grim said.

Mason snapped out of it and continued forward to the altar.

Without needing to be asked, he offered the cross to Signor Moretti, who was waiting there patiently for him to approach. At the first sight of the renewed silver symbol, tears welled up in the man's eyes and he crossed himself. So did Maria. So did Cardinal Scagnetti. Strauss, blessedly silent, simply watched.

After the candles had been lit and the incense burned, Moretti sang his lovely Latin song again. Only this time Mason understood the words:

"O Heavenly Father,
    Come forth and bless us in this our time of need.
    Bestow upon us your most sacred gift, your holiest of soldiers.
    Wherever our travels take us, whatever land we defend,
    May you guide us in our quest and keep us from harm's way.
    Amen."

. . .

He could both simultaneously tell that the words were not English and understand them. Their meaning, their images, the feelings attached to them, fed directly into his mind. This, he realized, was the first test.

Same as yesterday, the silent bodyguards unpacked their macabre cargo while Grim, Strauss, and the others watched.

Next test. Signor Moretti presented Mason with a cup of water. He touched the tip of his finger to it, and this time he felt a brief discharge of energy, like the tiny prick of static electricity. He positioned the chalice above the idol, which had been set upon the makeshift altar, and once again let the water trickle down.

The stone immediately began to smoke and hiss as if acid had been poured on it.

"Holy shit," Mason said aloud, placing his hand over his mouth. He thought he'd draw stares for cussing in a church, but the others just looked on with awe.

Third test. The other guard took the old skull from its wooden box, placed it atop the ornate plate, and gestured for Mason to approach it. His chest became light, his nerves wrinkled by what he had just witnessed. Again he felt the overwhelming sense of the empty sockets of the eyes looking at him, locked together with his. And as he slowly moved his hands toward it, a warm weight settled over them. He looked down to see that another pair of hands were touching his, spectral and glowing with a dim light, guiding him in his movements.

After a short pause, he took the skull.

The church vanished. Gone, just like that. He was not in Boston anymore. Not even the same country. Not even the same century.

Death. All around him, everywhere. The ground soaked with blood, so completely it splashes with each step, its rusty smell mixed with sour woodsmoke. A battlefield long ago, littered with the bodies of soldiers.

Their soiled tunics and broken armor forming the very shape of the land. A sky so thick with black smoke that it chokes the sun. He is not in his body anymore. Not holding the skull. He is the skull, replaced with his eyes and his skin. His face cradled delicately.

Another face looks down on him from above. Her beautiful eyes and soft mouth framed by a linen veil around her head. He knows her. Intimately. Body and soul. She is crying as she runs her fingers through his curly black hair, stroking what little of his face isn't caked with blood. It is faint, but as the life drains from his body the world as he knows it begins to dissolve and grow ever darker. He hears her voice.

"Vous êtes mon véritable sauveur." You are my true savior.

"Es tu es la mienne." And you are mine. The last words his lips will ever utter.

Mason returned to the present to find tearful faces all around. Not sad, but elated. Moved. He didn't know what they saw, but from their minds he sensed a collective happiness. A blessing of grace. They had witnessed something so spectacular that it had revitalized their faith and warmed them to their very core.

When the ritual was finished yesterday, Signor Moretti had clearly been let down. Now, his face was practically brimming with admiration. He took Mason's hands in his own and brought them to his forehead while he muttered a prayer.

There was one face, though, which did not match the others.

Bishop Strauss sat in the front pew, his face partially obscured by his hand, knuckles locked beneath the nose; but the drooping jowls of his signature scowl were clear nonetheless. Very calmly, he stood, smoothed his cassock, approached Mason, and extended his hand to him.

"Welcome to the Holy Order of Militia Dei," said Strauss. There was more warmth in a gust of wind. And for an instant, Mason caught a whiff of something close to burning hair from him.

"Thanks," said Mason, and shook his hand.

With that Bishop Strauss left along with the visitors, leaving Mason with Grim and Father Coffey.

"So . . . what now?" asked Mason.

"Now," said Grim, looking at his watch. "We get to work."

Father Coffey cleared his throat. "Before that, I wonder if I might have a word in private."

"Of course." Grim turned to Mason. "Come find me at the security building when you're through." And he left.

Since he'd arrived, Mason and Father Coffey hadn't spoken to each other much at all, certainly not one on one. He wondered if this man would be any different than the Bishop.

"Shall we sit?" said Coffey, gesturing to the pew next to them.

"Sure." Mason wasn't crazy about church pews. They felt hard and cramped. But he accepted and took a seat.

Father Coffey unbuttoned his suit jacket, folded his hands, and sat next to him. His beard was a tad on the scraggly side but not unkept. Fine lines creased the corners of his eyes, but none so deep as those of Bishop Strauss. Sixty, sixty-five at the most, Mason figured. It was his wispy white hair that showed any true age.

"I just wanted te take this opportunity te welcome ye formally," said Coffey.

Mason fidgeted. "Oh, well . . . thanks. I'm honored."

"The honor is mine." Coffey's voice was soft and sincere, his breath thick with whiskey. "I'm sure ye've been told by now that our sect worships the Messiah of the Archangel as our savior."

"I was told that, yes." Mason paused, pondering this and all implications therein.

Coffey folded his hands, showing a slight tremor in the right one, either from age or drink. "And ye also must be aware that while we are part of the Church, we accept members of various faiths?"

"Yes, I am." Wondering where he was going with this.

"I understand that you yerself are not a believer."

"Well, that was true."

Father Coffey cocked his head. "Was?"

"Honestly, I'm still processing all this. Faith, particularly blind faith, is a difficult concept for me. It requires a suspension of reason in order to believe something that all other signs are pointing away from."

"Such as?"

Mason sputtered, not because he had nothing to say, but because he didn't know where to start. "Okay . . . for example, take something like poverty. Disease. Famine. War! Why would God allow such things to exist?"

"Those are all problems we have created fer ourselves as a species. Why should He prevent them?"

"Because . . . He could."

"He could. But *should* He? Should He clean up our messes fer us, or let us learn from our mistakes?"

"But we're not learning from our mistakes."

"But of course we are," Coffey said with fervor. "People used te die in the streets in masses, they were so poor. Before modern medicine, disease was so common that it decimated whole populations. The numbers for famine today are but a fraction what they were even a century ago. And as fer war, well, o' course it's still around. But it's not what it once was. Since the Great Quake, Israel and Palestine are one nation now, and there has been a lasting peace in the Holy Land fer the first time ever."

And all it took was for a million people to die. A drop in the ocean compared to what came before, but considering the personal toll it took, Mason still couldn't bring himself to see this as a comfort.

"And why? Because, slowly but surely, we're learning. We're far more compassionate today than our forebears. Is there still work to be done? Absolutely. But any way you look at it, lad, today is the best time there is or ever has been."

"Okay then," said Mason. "What about something like torture?

Rape, abuse, murder. Pain and suffering. Why does God allow them?"

"Well . . ." Father Coffey folded his hands and placed them in his lap. "A traditional catechist would tell you that these are a result of Original Sin. But the truth is so much simpler than that." Father Coffey paused for a nip from his flask.

Mason waited, then finally said, "Which is?"

"Because every light casts a shadow. Fer one thing te exist, there must be a counterbalance. And so God has given us this world in pairs. Life and death. Day and night. Pleasure and pain. The scales may sway from one side te the other, but destroy one and ye destroy them both.

"Now, if yer seeking a reason for it—a purpose, if ye will—consider this. By knowing yer own pain ye can know that of others, and through that, gain compassion. I don't know that I'd go so far as te say that pain is a gift. But a lesson? That ye can be sure of."

Mason let this sink in. "You're certainly not like any priest I've ever met."

"I was once like you," said Coffey. "Full of confusion and doubt. But I knew there had te be another way. And that was the key, really. By believing it was possible, I found it. A better way."

"Then, I guess, so can I."

"That's wonderful," said Coffey. "That's all I needed to hear."

"There's something I'm confused about," said Mason.

"Tell me," said Father Coffey.

"I killed two men in Stonehill and, even though it was in self-defense, I have to admit that I've been feeling the burden of their deaths. But since they were bad men, I can't figure out why."

"All that means, m'boy, is that ye have a conscience. I don't believe that any of us here want te kill. But ye can believe that if anyone threatened the safety of my flock and that was the only way to stop them, I wouldn't have te think twice."

"Isn't it still a sin, though? I mean, don't get me wrong—I've always thought God has better things to do than care about touching yourself or which hole you like to stick it in. But 'Thou shalt not kill' seems pretty cut-and-dry to me."

"A common misconception. The original translation of that particular commandment is 'Thou shalt not *murder.*' God protects not the wicked. Therefore, the killer of a wicked man has committed no sin."

Mason thought a moment. "Well, they were wicked men, no doubt about that. So where do you draw the line?"

"That's a question I'm sure every soldier in history has asked of themselves at one point or another. My advice t'ye would be te follow your orders and follow your heart."

"And when they conflict with each other?"

"Then come to me and receive the sacrament of confession. Mind ye, I wouldn't expect ye to feel comfortable doing so straight away. Just know that should ye ever need to unburden yourself, m'door is always open."

"Thanks, Father."

"As a token of good faith between us, may I confess something to ye?"

"Sure."

Father Coffey stood from the pew and took a few steps, thoughtfully regarding the altar. From his inside jacket pocket, he took out an old, scuffed metal flask. Spun the top off and took a swig.

"A man of the cloth I may be, but I have often found m'self plagued with doubt. When I was a boy, my sister became possessed. I'll never forget how terrifying, *truly* terrifying it was te see, how the thing within her twisted and perverted her body. She saw doctors, of course. Psychologists. But in the end it was a priest who was called upon te save her, a priest who bore this ring." He held up his right hand and Mason saw what he had come to recognize now as the same signet ring the others all wore, except that the setting on his was black and white.

"He did everything he could, but despite the priest's efforts he was unable te deliver her before . . ." Coffey stopped abruptly, and

Mason could make out a small sniffle. "I remember wondering how God could let such a thing happen. *Why* He would let it happen. If everything truly is according te His will, why? It has caused me te question m'faith many a time since." He turned and faced Mason, a smile beaming across his gentle face. "But ye have restored it today."

In an unexpected gesture of humility, Father Coffey knelt before Mason and kissed a ring that was not on his hand. Awkward, but Mason allowed it.

"Here," said Father Coffey, and took something from his pocket. He held between his thumb and forefinger a tiny silver object. An oval holy medal. On it a haloed saint enclosed in carved darkness clutched a sword to his chest with a burning heart on top of the hilt. Mason recognized the imagery even before Father Coffey spoke. "It's Saint Philip, Patron Saint of the Soldiers of God."

"What exactly did you see today, when I took the skull?"

"The same thing you did, laid out before us in vivid clarity. The culmination of a battle that raged throughout the entire month of September in the year of our lord, thirteen hundred and seven. A clash between Militia Dei, the faithful brotherhood of the First Messiah, and the vampire clans of old. It became known as the Red September, so named because the land, the water, even the rain itself, turned red with blood."

Yes. Mason knew this now. Just as he had when reliving the life of Tom Mayhew. And his parents. And Will Graves. And now Saint Philip.

"And you found it beautiful, seeing all that?"

"Exquisitely so. Not the carnage itself, o' course. But rather the sacrifice of the brave souls who had the courage te defy the ecclesiastical conventions of the time. Which was the law, mind ye. Remember, this was during the Crusades, when such things risked penalty of death. All te follow a path they knew to be right."

"Why would it be considered wrong, though? It was a miracle. A *real* miracle."

"Not te the Church. Te them it was heresy and sparked suspicion that the Templars had been corrupted by the Devil. It caused a rift between them, which led to mass arrest of every knight and, in most cases, their execution. Strange te deny a miracle right before their eyes in favor of one from centuries before they were ever born.

"Ye spoke earlier of sin. Te deny the divinity of Jesus of Nazareth was exactly that—te say nothing of accepting another as Lord and Savior, much less one supposed te have entered this world, not through the grace of God, but from a hellish ritual. Saint Philip was dubbed the 'pariah messiah' and openly hunted as a heretic."

"That's so wrong."

"It is. It was a blessing and a curse. A miracle and a sin."

"A blessing in demise," said Mason, amused with himself.

Coffey gave a short chuckle. "It just goes te show ye that what is right is not always what is rightful. Above all else, God wants us te do what is right."

"Well," said Mason, "I think I can do that."

"Bless you, lad," said Father Coffey with a little hiccup. "Oh my, and bless me too."

"What was her name, your sister?"

"Caitlin," said Father Coffey. "Her name was Caitlin."

Mason felt a welcome sense of calm as he left the church. It was refreshing to hear a priest speak the way Father Coffey did. Outside, the sun was still fighting the good fight, struggling for every sliver of warmth that made it through the persistent clouds, lighting one of the stained-glass windows as his hand fell on the door. He paused to look at it: it depicted an angel, bright and beaming and dressed in armor and clashing with a fiery sword upon a winged black serpent. That's when something occurred to him which, in earnest, had not even when Father Coffey mentioned possession, not even at the sight of blackened skin and red eyes last night.

If demons exist, so does the Devil.

. . .

Mason wanted to put the holy medal Father Coffey gave him away before meeting Grim, so he took a quick detour up to the third floor. As he held it, running his finger along its smooth sides, a wave of nausea came out of nowhere and hit him on the way up. He thought perhaps the elevator carriage had moved a little too quickly for his liking.

The elevator door opened, but he didn't get out. Just stood, staring helplessly at the source of the mysterious sickness.

An impossibly tall man at the end of the hall, waiting outside Sarah's room. His feet not touching the floor. Naked aside from a crooked coronet on his head, with skin the color of ash. Face sickly and brimming with vacant menace. Wide, flat hands like rakes at the end of each bony arm. The stomach distended, sagging almost to his knees. There was no problem with the lights in the hallway, yet he seemed to be surrounded in a cone of shadow. Curls of smoke rose from his skin and between the strands of greasy white hair dangling at the sides of his head.

Tap, tap, tap . . . with one long finger he pecked at Sarah's door . . . and stopped.

Slowly turning his horrible face toward Mason, showing a lipless slit of a mouth. Orange eyes that burned like the lit tips of cigarettes in the dark. Heat glowing from between his ribs with each breath. The only term that came to mind was one Mason had glimpsed in the pages of *The Exorcist* . . . "unclean spirit."

They glared at each other. Then the mouth curled into a sneer, spreading so far it seemed to overtake his entire face, revealing rows of blackened teeth like the bars on a roaring furnace. Mason had been in darkness before, but until now he had never known what it was to feel it *inside* him.

The door opened and the man disappeared right before his eyes.

Sarah entered the hall and began walking toward him. "I see you've met Earl," said Sarah casually. No big deal.

Mason didn't say anything. He wanted to move, he *needed* to move, but his whole body was so stiff that he thought his bones had fused together.

Her gazed dropped from his to the crotch of his pants where a warm, wet stain was soaking through the fabric. "I . . . think I'll take the stairs."

TWENTY-FIVE

After a long and much-needed shower, Mason headed for the security building. The graveyard sprawled out before him, at the end of which sat a small concrete building at the southeast corner. All the markers were in neat rows, a few autumn leaves clinging to them like fat brown leeches. They were properly groomed, no weeds or overgrowth. Most were the type of simple plaques one sees in military graveyards, but dispersed across the yard far older ones of cracked stone poked up from the ground. The names and dates had become as worn and faded as the memories of the people who lay in the ground beneath them. A little rudimentary math was all it took for Mason to come to the realization that none of the graves he saw belonged to people who had lived long, healthy lives.

Mason saw a security camera perched atop the perimeter wall. It swiveled toward him as he neared the building.

He raised a fist to knock.

The door flew open. A grizzly-looking man in a camouflage hunting jacket filled the doorway. He sported a horseshoe mustache and an aged Red Sox cap.

"Who are you?" he barked in a Boston accent, and approached, forcing Mason to take two frightened steps back. "What do you want? What are you doing here? What is your quest? What is your favorite color?"

"I . . . huh?" he stammered, and froze, hands up in a defensive gesture.

The tough guy's exterior cracked and reduced him to laughter. "I'm just fuckin' with ya. C'mon in."

Skeptically, Mason followed the man inside.

A plump woman looked up from behind a console. Curly ginger hair pulled back in a ponytail revealed freckled cheeks and full lips, eyes wide with alarm. She wore a windbreaker over a sweatshirt that said DOG MOM in varsity lettering.

"You're an ass," she said, her voice flecked with surprise.

The man shrugged.

She placed her hand over her heart. "You scared the poor kid half to death."

He waved it off like a fly buzzing too close to his face. "I was just fuckin' with him. He's fine. Aren'tcha, slugger?" he said with a wave of coffee breath as he clapped Mason on the back.

Mason hated being called "slugger" and couldn't help letting it show.

"Sorry if I made you wet yourself." He stuck out his hand. After a second, Mason shook it. "Lloyd Leary. This is my wife, Michelle."

She stood and offered her hand as well. "You'll have to forgive my husband's infantile sense of humor."

"Sure," said Mason. "Grim told me to come here."

"He's in there, sweetie," said Michelle in a motherly tone, pointing to a door to the left. "Go on in. As for *you*," she said to her husband, "that's enough coffee for you."

"Eh, maybe your right," said Lloyd, and took a seat next to her.

As Mason passed the console, he caught a glimpse of its many monitors displaying different areas of the grounds—ones he didn't even realize had cameras.

He found Grim standing behind a collection of monitors in the next room, Hirsch standing stock still with her hands on her hips. Two young men sat in front of computers, tapping vigorously away.

"Ah, there you are," said Grim, looking over his shoulder. "Everything all right?"

"I . . . saw . . ." Mason stammered, unable to spit out the words.

"Earl?"

"Yeah."

"Mmm, I was afraid of that," said Grim, just as casually as Sarah. "I asked that Sarah commune with him to find out if there were any other spells that could be used against us. A side effect being that once invited in, his presence tends to linger for a while afterward. It's quite harmless though, I assure you. Just a reflection."

Well, shit! Thanks for—

Mason halted, stifling the thought, remembering that it could be heard.

"Okay." Mason shook his head, confused. Questions upon questions upon questions. "I wasn't going to say anything, but the other day Bishop Strauss kind of hinted at Sarah having betrayed the Order or something. What's up with that?"

"A slight misunderstanding. He was referring to a relative of hers, her aunt Olivia. As it turned out, she was . . ." He rolled his next words over like a tongue probing a canker. ". . . not as trustworthy as previously believed. Something of a sore subject among us, I'm afraid."

" 'Was,' " said Mason. Past tense. "What happened to her?"

Grim considered this for a moment or two. "She was dealt with."

Due to the scarcity of his words, Mason sensed there was more to it than that. It could have just been his imagination, but with Grim's mind closed it was hard to tell.

"What about this cousin of hers?"

"Sydney," said Grim. "There's never been cause to suspect her of any misdeeds, and I'm not about to start simply because Bishop Strauss embraces the time-honored, albeit flawed, axiom that an apple does not fall far from the tree."

With his third eye open now, it was a different thing altogether being in the presence of Mr. Grimshaw. His mind was a well-crafted maze to which only he knew the path. But for the first time ever, Mason caught a stray thought from him like a bubble of air rising from a body of water.

I just hope she's all right.

"Fair enough, I guess." With all Mason currently had on his mind —information, grief, new senses, new thoughts, and voices that seemed to gravitate to him, he decided to let it go. But oh, how his curiosity was piqued.

He should have noticed much sooner that his face adorned at least a dozen different images on multiple computer screens. Birth certificate, driver's license, social security, school records. He had once entered a contest online in which the grand prize was a restored '67 Mustang, and even that was there.

"What's all this?"

"Everything that proves you're you," said Hirsch.

The gentlemen in front of them spun around in their chairs and looked at Mason. One skinny, acne-ridden, with long greasy hair, and a shirt with HAN SHOT FIRST across the chest, the other podgy with light-brown skin, an afro, thick glasses, and chipmunk cheeks, wearing a yellow golf shirt with the command insignia of Starfleet on the left breast.

"Mason Cole, may I introduce the cyber soldiers of our team," said Hirsch, gesturing to each. "Chewie and IQ. While some aspire to get their driver's license at the age of sixteen, Chewie here had the FBI's Cyber Division knocking on his door by that age."

"How 'Zero Cool' of you," said Mason.

Chewie raised his eyebrows above the thick frames of his glasses. "I'll take that as a compliment."

"And IQ here," Hirsch continued, "won the 2002 DEF CON CyberBowl by managing to hack the Vice President, making it appear that the VP was a Ukrainian spy."

IQ drummed his fingertips against one another in front of his face. "The NSA actually detained him for twenty-four hours. It was glorious."

"Together they perform their own special brand of magic," said Hirsch. "For example, making people disappear."

The two hackers continued their digital wizardry, attuned to a force most people could barely perceive, let alone understand as they did. Multiple codes simultaneously processing through their heads at warp speed, anticipating variables of encryptions, countering, bending the laws of programming, all with the ease of a child riding a bike. They didn't simply use the machines at their fingertips. They became one with them.

"Voilà!" said IQ.

Mason looked at what they had done. Anything that had his picture on it—his driver's license, for example—had the same name, same details, but a different face.

"Who's that?" Mason asked.

Hirsch folded her arms. "To the Kentucky State Police, John Doe. His real name was Jeremy Burnquist. A mechanic by trade, until he got on the wrong side of a gang of meth dealers. Soon he'll be occupying a plot in Stonehill cemetery under the name Mason Cole."

"What the eyes see and the computer confirms, the mind believes," said Grim. "For security purposes, we'll need scans of your fingerprints and retinas."

"Uh. Okay."

Hirsch led Mason to a nearby seat in front of a contraption that looked a lot like an eye-exam phoropter and asked him to place his chin on the rest below it. A thin beam of green light passed back and forth horizontally and then again vertically. When that was done, Hirsch placed a flatbed scanner in front of him and instructed him to place his right hand on the glass. He did so and a similar green light scanned it from wrist to tip. All together it only took about five minutes.

"What happens to my house?" This was a question which had

occurred to him yesterday, but he'd hesitated in bringing it up until now.

"It will be repossessed by the bank, at which time we'll purchase it. When you're old enough you can take possession yourself. If that's what you choose to do, of course. What would you like done with your truck?"

"I don't care. Scrap it," said Mason without so much as a second thought.

While IQ was putting the finishing touches on things, Chewie created his new identity. Mason's face slid in next to information completely foreign to him. He wasn't born in Latham. He didn't attend Boston Catholic school. And his name wasn't . . .

"James Hawkins?"

Grim offered a coy smile. "Thought you might like that."

"Pretty good." It was accurate, too, in its own way. "Does that make you Long John Silver?"

"Aye," said Grim in his best rum-soaked tongue. "But the treasure we seek is not of silver and gold, m'boy."

Mason's face darkened suddenly.

"It's nothing to worry about, really. Merely a public cover. We won't be calling you Jim."

" 'He's dead, Jim,' " said IQ, eyes still fixed on the screen in front of him.

"It's not that," said Mason. "What happens to Rose?"

"What would she want?"

Not to be dead, for a start. "I'm not sure. She was from Georgia, originally. But somehow I don't think she'd want to be buried there."

Grim rubbed his chin thoughtfully. "Georgia is awfully far away."

"I was just thinking that. Did you read my mind?"

"I didn't have to." The timbre of his deep voice gave the words he spoke a sense of understanding that he needed desperately. "Would you like us to find a spot for her here?"

"In the graveyard?"

"No, I'm afraid that space is all spoken for. But somewhere nearby. One you could visit whenever you like, place fresh flowers on."

Mason nodded. "I think she would like that."

"I'll see to it personally. In the meantime, would you care to go for a ride? I thought I might show you around Boston."

"Sure, why not?"

"What about the pups?" said Hirsch.

"Oh yes, quite right," said Grim. "Before we go, there are a few more members of the team we should introduce to you."

Hirsch escorted them back to the entrance of the security building and through a door behind the security console. They entered a kennel and were met instantly by eager yips and whimpers from the five dogs before them—two Rottweilers, a pit bull, a Doberman, and a German Shepherd that was maybe only a few months old.

"Attennn-TION!" Hirsch commanded.

Each member of the pack sat immediately, without so much as a peep. Hirsch identified the two Rotties as Duke and Daisy, the Doberman as Lola, the pit bull as Boomer, and the Shepherd pup as Max.

"Now, without making eye contact, approach Duke and Daisy and offer them your hand with a closed fist."

When he did, both dogs remained seated and extended their snouts toward him. After a few sniffs, they began to wag their tails.

"Okay," said Hirsch.

The whole pack surrounded Mason in a swarm of sniffs and sagging tongues. The one that seemed the most taken with him was little Max, who, even when they left the kennel, tried to follow Mason out the door with a wagging tongue.

Grim flinched and took his vibrating phone out to answer. "Yes?"

A voice on the other end buzzed away.

Grim looked at him. "I'm afraid that ride is going to have to wait. Silas found the finger's owner."

But Mason already knew.

TWENTY-SIX

"Thomas Mayhew," said Diaz. "Age sixty-two. Born and raised in Boston. Worked as a guard at Conley Terminal. Widower. No kids. Reported missing a week ago."

The rest of the team joined them at the security building—all except Father Coffey, who Mason could hear puttering around the church.

"Priors?" Grim asked.

"Drunken disorderlies, public urination, that sort of thing."

"Family?"

"Not much."

"Who reported him missing?"

Diaz flipped through his notes. "His boss when he didn't show up to work."

Mason found it sad how a person's life could be quantified into such thankless facts, lacking the details that made them who they were. There was no mention of how his friends called him Tommy, that he had a dog named Barkley whom he and his late wife adopted as a stray. That he was a reserve firefighter—even played the trumpet in the Reserve Firefighter's Marching Band on St. Patrick's Day—

because at his core he wanted to help people. Yet despite all that, there were dark things in him, things he was aware of but couldn't help, for they had been engrained in him early on in life. They hadn't consumed him enough to hurt others, but they were there, just present enough to torment him his whole life.

"And, Mason, you saw Novak kill him?"

Mason closed his eyes, replaying the tape. "I saw him strolling down the dock, at night, doing what guards do, and then Novak just pounced on him."

"He coulda just been in the wrong place at the wrong time while Novak was out for a midnight snack," said Diaz.

"Perhaps. But then why leave the finger?"

"Maybe it's a warning," said Irish.

"Maybe he's fuckin' with us," said Diaz.

"Or maybe it's bait," said Rodriguez.

"Maybe it's the Fratellis!" said Sarah.

"Oh, it is most definitely bait. The question is what's on the hook?" Grim thought long and hard for a considerable amount of time before speaking again, stroking the gray hairs on his chin. "I want to talk to Mayhew's boss."

"Think he had something to do with it?" Irish said eagerly, crossing his arms.

"If Novak killed him on the dock, that means two things—one, Mayhew was on duty when he died, and two, there's a crime scene at Conley that no one even knows about."

"And yet his boss didn't know either?" said Rodriguez. "Not likely."

"Set it up."

"You got it," she acknowledged.

Hirsch handed Grim an envelope, who handed it to Mason.

"What's this?"

"ID, driver's license, passport . . ."

"Oh . . . right," said Mason. He had almost forgot. He was a new person.

"There's important information in here, so be sure to familiarize yourself with it."

It felt heavier than just a few papers and documents. He looked inside and found a brand-new phone as well.

"So, officially, I'm dead?"

"Correct."

"And I can never contact anyone?"

"Who would you contact?"

"I don't know . . ." Mason paused. "My friends' parents, maybe?"

"I'm afraid that won't be possible." Grim didn't say any more. Didn't have to.

He expected as much, but it was still hard to hear. "I understand."

"I know how you feel, but it would jeopardize your safety, not to mention blow your cover. Remember, they think you perished with your friends."

"You don't *know* how I feel."

"I just mean that I sympathize with your desire for closure. In that sense, I do know how you feel. All too well." Grim's gaze wandered.

"This may sound crazy, but what if we . . ." Mason fumbled for the right words. "Un-hypnotized them? Just for a bit so that I can at least talk to them, tell them how sorry I am. Would that be possible? Could you do that?"

The others exchanged skeptical glances.

"That would be highly unorthodox," said Grim, considering the idea. "But, then again, nothing about your situation so far speaks of normality. It would have to be cleared by Bishop Strauss. No promises, but I can try."

"Thanks," said Mason. A slim chance was better than no chance.

Grim looked at his watch. "Good lord," he said. "It's almost time for supper."

And he was right. Mason saw by the clock on the wall that it was nearly five o'clock already.

"Why don't we go see what we're having?"

"How does that work around here, anyway?"

"Most of the time we fix our own meals, but now and then Father Coffey doubles as our cook."

"Really?" Mason suppressed a smile at the image of a priest wearing a chef's hat and an apron that said KISS THE CHEF.

"Actually, he's quite good. And," said Grim with a ping of realization, "I believe tonight he was planning to make his famous shepherd's pie. Let's go see."

They headed up to the second floor, which smelled instantly of cooking. The sound of pots and pans, clinking dishes and silverware came from the kitchen. The table had already been set and the food was being brought to it by Miggs and Yen.

Father Coffey stood by the stove, sleeves rolled up as he slipped on a pair of oven mitts. He reached into the oven and pulled out a steaming tray of shepherd's pie. "Evening, lad. Hope you're hungry."

"Famished," said Mason, realizing that he hadn't eaten anything all day.

"Oh . . ." Coffey handed him a large basket of rolls. "Would you mind taking this over to the table?"

"For sure," said Mason. He felt the warmth from it in a way he had never known before. Strong. Tempting. Begging to be part of his hand. Mason allowed it, let the heat go into his palm, up his arms, and through the rest of his body just before setting it down between a dish of buttered green beans and scalloped potatoes.

Miggs took one while filling up his plate and gave it a curious look.

"Everything okay?"

"They're cold already," said Miggs.

"Huh. That's . . . uh . . . weird."

Then Miggs gave *him* a curious look.

Once everyone was present, they all took their seats. Mason was just about to take a bite, a forkful of meat and potatoes dangling before his open mouth, when he saw everyone join hands.

Without a word, he set it down and took Diaz's hand to his right, Sarah's to his left.

Father Coffey made the sign of the cross, closed his eyes, and bowed his head. "Heavenly Father—"

"Or Mother," said Sarah.

Coffey opened one eye and looked at her. "Or Mother," he continued. "Bless us and these thy gifts which we are about to receive from thy bounty to our bodies. Amen."

"Amen," they all said in unison—including Mason, if a shave later than the rest. He never used to say grace with Rose, but he knew the gist. Even as a nonbeliever, it was one thing he didn't mind. Regardless of who, what, or where it was given, he found thanks always worth giving with a meal in his belly and a roof over his head.

He looked at the faces of these people as they began to eat. There was a bond between them, an intangible tether that connected each and every one of them. They were a team. They might have even been a family. And at this thought, he felt the absence of those he loved more than ever.

"Gabby," said Miggs. "Pásame las papas, por favor."

Rodriguez picked up the potatoes, rose a bit from her chair, and passed them to him. "Aquí."

"Gracias," he said.

Even if Mason's Spanish wasn't better than average, he would have been able to understand what they said. Now, he picked up on little mental exchanges between most others at the table, faint as tiny ripples through water, but he couldn't make out what they were saying to each other. Words muffled behind closed doors. One between Rodriguez and Irish, another between Sarah and Diaz, and another between Grim, Father Coffey, and Hirsch. Just Miggs and Yen remained silent.

Mason thought of how nice it must be to be able to eat and talk at the same time.

"How is it?" said Grim. Father Coffey looked his way with an eager smile.

GOOD, THANKS! Mason said with his mind.

Everybody winced as if he'd just shouted in their ears.

Mason dropped his fork, mouth hanging open. "Oh shit. Sorry," he said, and began gathering up his plate and cutlery. "So sorry."

"It's all right," said Grim with a still-surprised laugh.

Father Coffey waved it off. "No need for that. Please, stay."

"No, really, it's fine." With that, he took his plate and left the kitchen, never having felt quite so stupid in all his life.

TWENTY-SEVEN

THE NEXT MORNING, MASON WOKE TO SOMEONE POUNDING ON his door. There was no clock next to his bed as he was accustomed to, but he didn't need one to know that it was not yet dawn.

"What the hell?" he shouted at the invisible fist, hoisted himself out of bed and flung open the door. He found Rodriguez standing on the other side, dressed in athletic gear and holding a gym bag.

"Rise and shine, valentine," she said. "Nice skivvies."

In his hurry to answer the door, Mason didn't realize that he'd done so wearing nothing but his underwear. "Do you mind?" said Mason, half covering himself with the door.

"Yeah, actually, I do," she said plainly, and tossed the gym bag into his arms.

"What's this?"

"Your gear. I'm supposed to whip you into shape."

"You?"

Rodriguez folded her arms. "That a problem?"

"No," he answered with a yawn. "What time is it?"

"Six. I let you sleep in 'cause I'm nice.

"*This* is 'sleeping in'?"

"Yup! Get dressed and meet me in the gym." She disappeared down the hall toward the elevator.

Mason unzipped the bag. Inside was a sweatshirt, sweatpants, shorts, running shoes, a water bottle, pads, wrist guards, tape, a few granola bars, and—he felt a lump in his throat and wondered what he'd need *that* for—a cup. He'd never used a cup before. Never had a reason. Basketball was the only sport he had ever played, and even then it was usually just a friendly game of one-on-one with Julie. For a flicker, he had once considered joining the team at school, but it was soon quashed when he remembered the other names that would be on the team roster—names like Troy Keenan, Jay Brubaker, and, of course, Eric Riley. None of whom he'd want to spend any amount of time in a change room with.

Unsure of what he would need, Mason changed into the sweats and brought the rest with him, scarfing down two of the granola bars as he made is way.

When he reached the gym, Rodriguez was throwing jabs into a canvas punching bag that hung from the ceiling in one corner of the room. The place smelled of rubber and sweat mixed with the chemical smell of wet wipes. The wall was lined by a mirror spanning the length of the room, where there were rows of weights, treadmills, a StairMaster, exercise bikes, and a few other machines he didn't recognize. Mid-punch, she saw his reflection behind her own in the mirror and faced him.

"I didn't know what I'd need, so—" said Mason.

"Just drop it there," she said, dabbing herself with a towel.

They walked toward each other and met in the middle of the floor, covered by a large mat. Rodriguez removed her gloves, along with the hooded sweatshirt she wore. Suddenly Mason felt his nerves flutter.

Sublime, sculpted to peak condition. Her arms were toned and firm. Her midsection trim, leading to svelte hips and thighs. Beneath a spandex top, a swell of ample bosom, where his gaze lingered a few seconds longer than it should have.

"Hey." She snapped her fingers and pointed at her face. "I'm up here."

"Sorry."

"Let's make one rule, okay?" She got in close. "Do what I say and don't piss me off."

"Isn't that two rules?" Mason said.

"Whatever. Just do it."

"Yessir . . . I mean . . . ma'am?"

" 'Ma'am' is fine. Now." She took two steps back. "First thing's first. Drop and give me twenty."

"Can't, I left my wallet in my room," said Mason with a little awkward laugh.

She didn't laugh with him.

Tough gym. Take my life, please.

I can hear you, came her throaty voice in his head.

Mason dropped to his hands and knees.

She had him do sets of pushups, crunches, and squats, then started him on the weights—nothing big, sets of ten with twenty-pound dumbbells, followed by a nice, healthy bout of dizziness and a desire to throw up. They moved to the punching bag, where Rodriguez showed him how to punch properly, to line up his shoulder with the target and turn his body into it. After the first hour, his muscles had already begun to stiffen. After the second hour, they felt like limp noodles.

Exercise was not exactly his thing. He could practically hear "Eye of the Tiger" being played in his head, only this version was sluggish, as though someone were holding down the Pause button. Perhaps it was fate that, had things been different, he might have been in gym class right about now.

Funny how things worked out.

It was nearly nine when Grim found them in the kitchen, both at one table near the window, Rodriguez sipping a cup of coffee while doing a crossword in the newspaper, Mason across from her with his head down on the table next to an empty bowl of Cheerios and two banana peels.

"How's our student?" he asked.

"A regular Karate Kid," said Rodriguez with only a momentary glance upward.

"May I borrow him?"

"All yours," she said, chewing on her pen.

Grim tapped Mason on the shoulder. He didn't stir at first, opening his eyes only after a few more shakes. As he got up to follow, he turned to Rodriguez and said, "Denmark."

"Excuse me?"

Even half asleep, he had heard her wondering about that one for the last ten minutes. "Eight down, seven letters. The answer is *Denmark*." And he disappeared out the door.

She stared at him, unaware until now that he had heard her unguarded mind wonder what filled the empty squares as he snoozed. "Thanks," said Rodriguez, and wrote in the missing letters.

At the front entrance of the building, two gorillas, one with a shaved head and a neck tattoo, the other with a lazy eye, moved large cardboard boxes from a truck parked outside.

"What's this?" said Mason.

"Your things," Grim replied. "For now the furniture, appliances, and whatnot will have to be stored in the church basement, but I thought you might want your own clothes at least."

"You thought right. Thanks."

Grim's cell phone began vibrating in his hand. "Why don't you spend some time unpacking and come find me when you're done?"

Mason made a pile of boxes in the elevator and took it up to the third floor. As soon as he entered his room, he could smell the acrid stink of cat piss. Bossy's litter box in the corner was untouched, and it wasn't long before he found the smell coming from the cot.

"Seriously?" he said to her, and threw up his arms.

She just sat there, looking pleased with herself.

He gathered up the sheets in a big wad and dropped them in a pile out in the hall for the time being.

Just as well, as it turned out. In addition to boxes, the movers had brought his own bed.

It was a good thing that he just had boxes to deal with for now, or else he'd have a hell of a job on his hands. Mason considered Grim's comment about the other items being stored in the church basement. That was when it occurred to him for the first time that the maze of cloth-covered things he had seen there must have been made up of the remnants of other former lives, tucked away like the ruins of a lost city. Scars too painful to remember. There was something oddly comforting in that; something that, however small, connected him with the rest of them.

He surveyed it all. There was more than he thought there would be. His guitar, clearly unable to fit in a box, rested on top of it all. It was strange seeing his things like this, packed up neatly in boxes that, instead of block letters in black felt marker, were designated only by labels with barcodes which made him unsure where to start.

The first box he opened was filled with clothes for which he was extremely thankful. The garments he'd been wearing the last two days felt too generic, too "standard issue," the type of thing patients of an asylum would get. He longed for the feel of his own shirts with the tags cut off and jeans with rips and wear in just the right places. Shoes he had walked miles in.

Ah, and there was the alarm clock that sat next to his bed. He plugged it in and reprogrammed it immediately, followed shortly by the lamp he kept on at night.

The next box was filled with CDs; the one after that, a mixture of rock magazines and old school papers covered more by doodles than information about covalent bonds or trigonometry. And at the very bottom was a copy of *Hustler* that he had swiped from work and kept hidden in his closet. He looked quickly over his shoulder and stuffed it away, along with a momentary twinge of embarrassment, in one of the desk drawers.

Finally, he found the books. The next three boxes he opened were filled with them. Of all his earthly possessions, they made up roughly half. He could trace the course of his life by them.

Most of the classics—*Frankenstein, The Lord of the Rings, To Kill a Mockingbird, Charlotte's Web,* and the like—he had only read within the last year or so; except for *Treasure Island,* which he'd read for a book report in fifth grade. Stephen King he discovered by accident when someone left a copy of *Misery* behind in the restroom at Gus's. He'd decided to give it a whirl, and to this day it still held the record for fastest he'd ever read a book. Rose gave him a copy of *Where the Sidewalk Ends* one year as a birthday gift and he always kept it close. He read *A Wrinkle in Time* because Julie said it was her favorite book, but when he tried talking to her about it, she couldn't seem to recall most of the details.

And then there was Shakespeare, which occupied no single, set time in his past. No matter what was going on in the real world, there was no time when Mason didn't find the characters bold, the dialogue poetic, and the effect powerful. It was at the very core of him. There was no sign of *Hamlet,* though. The last time he had it for certain was at the gas station, but beyond that he couldn't recall what had happened to it. His heart sunk a little more.

He had a subscription to *National Geographic* at one point, and while he couldn't keep them all, there were a select few he'd held on to. The mountains of Asia. Rainforests and deserts. The oceans, in particular, he found fascinating. Anything about dinosaurs. And several issues down he found one he could never forget. He was on the cover. There were a few that he had not read yet. And then he came at last to the first book he remembered: *Love You Forever* by Robert Munsch. So clear was his memory of the first time hearing this story of the relationship between a boy and his mother. Except that it was not his mother who read it to him. It was Rose. If he had any books before that one, he didn't remember.

Once he had his books put away, sobbing at the memories each one brought, he felt something like himself again. But there was a catch in his throat at seeing the empty space between *As You Like It* and *Twelfth Night*.

Mason opened a smaller box, one he could hold comfortably in his hands. Inside he found Rose's African violet. Soil had spilled all over the inside. The stem was bent and several of the petals had withered and fallen off. No "Handle With Care," just stuffed into whatever fit.

He took it to the window, where it would get some light, and poured water from his own water bottle into the soil, which he had gathered up from the bottom of the box.

"Don't worry," he said to the flower. "We'll get you fixed up."

He looked around at what was now his room. It wasn't much, but it was a start.

The sour stink of cat piss lingered in the air.

Oh god, what have they done with all of Rose's stuffed cats? A bizarre thought, but a valid one.

Figuring he had better take care of it before someone complained, he gathered up the soiled sheets, vainly trying to hold his breath, and left the room.

With his first step out the door, he came face-to-face with that of an old man. His stomach churned. Skin on the backs of his arms rippled.

"Oh, jeepers!" said the old man, clutching at his chest. Not the horrid visage of Earl, but a man. Just an old man. Hunched, dressed in coveralls, carrying a push broom in one hand and pulling a wheeled garbage can with the other. Hooked nose. Rheumy eyes. Gray hair swept aside into a combover. "Ya gave me a start there."

"Likewise," said Mason.

"Just came to collect the trash, if ya have any." His voice soft and cordial.

"Oh, uh . . ." Mason looked behind him into the room. "Not at the moment. Just some empty boxes."

"What's 'at now?" he said, one hand cupped behind his ear.

"Just some boxes," Mason repeated, louder this time.

"Oh, you betcha. Just leave 'em outside in the hall here when yer done."

"Sure, thanks." Mason stuck out his hand. "I'm Mason, by the way."

The old man leaned the broom against the wall and offered his hand in return, all knuckle and bone. "Joe. Nice to meet ya," he said with a wink.

Another wink. Father Coffey's wink flashed in his mind. *What's with old people and winking?*

Mason took his sheets and made for the laundry room on the second floor. He found it empty; however, there was a load spinning in one of the machines, a white plastic chair placed in front of it. There were two rows of machines each, washers on one side of the room, dryers on the other. Between them, a single door which opened to a walk-in closet. Shelves full of enough detergent to fill the ground floor with suds. Fabric softener, bleach, dryer sheets, anything one could think of, including a mop and bucket. As he took a bottle from one of the shelves, liquid sloshing around inside, a machine lid slammed behind him and he nearly jumped clean out of his skin.

He poked his head back into the laundry room to see Miggs throwing his stuff in the dryer. He was dressed in a burgundy track suit with white stripes on the pants that Mason thought made him look like a Russian wrestling coach.

"Oh, hey," said Mason with a hint of relief. "Sorry, didn't know anyone else was in here."

No response. He just sat down in the plastic chair Mason had seen earlier, crossed one foot over the other knee.

"Knowing my luck," Mason said to fill the silence, "I'll probably leave a red sock in by mistake."

Nothing. Miggs began reading a copy of *Guns & Ammo.*

Not a big talker. Got it. In truth, neither was he. Just trying to make conversation in an uncomfortable moment of silence for reasons even he couldn't name.

Awkwardly, Mason put his sheets into a machine three down from Miggs, poured a generous amount of detergent in, closed the lid, and cranked the knob.

"Well. See ya," said Mason as he passed Miggs on his way out of the laundry room.

"I wouldn't get too comfortable here, kid."

Mason stopped at the door. "Excuse me?"

"If I were you," said Miggs with a brief upward glance. "I wouldn't get too comfortable here." If an award existed for most restraint shown in suppressing a sneer, he'd be taking home the gold. He went back to his magazine.

"Oookay," Mason said to himself, confused about what had just happened, and left. He returned to his room and decided that when it was time to dry the sheets, he'd put them in a machine as far as possible from whichever Miggs was using.

TWENTY-EIGHT

With his clothes hung up and most of his stuff unpacked, things almost felt like home.

Well, not really. Better, though. Either way, it was home now.

At home he'd had nowhere near enough space for all his books, just one decent-sized bookcase, and the rest he'd put in piles against the wall or on the floor of his closet. But here at least there was a table and a desk to put them for the time being.

He thought of the note that had been left for him.

If you need anything else, just ask.

How literal was that supposed to be? Was there a price cap, or was the sky the limit? Of course he wouldn't have space for just anything, but could he get bookcases if he needed them? A couch? A stereo system? Maybe a cat tower for Bossy?

He felt bad for her. In Stonehill she'd had free reign over not just the house but the land around it too. There were no other houses on their hill overlooking town, no fences, no other cats to compete with. Now she was cooped up in this room.

He threw the empty boxes out into the hall for Joe—all but one, which he left behind for Bossy to sit in (which, of course, she did).

Enough unpacking for one day. Whatever was left would just have to wait.

Mason clapped the dust off his hands and set out to find Grim.

After checking a few places, all of which were empty, Mason finally found Grim in the security building. Duke and Daisy pricked up their ears when he entered, wagging their tails and grinning with their tongues hanging out. From around the corner of the desk, little Max came flopping over. He patted them all.

"Oh hi," said Michelle, poking her head from around one of the monitors. "Here for the brief?"

"Uh, yeah, I guess so," he answered, relieved that there was no sign of Lloyd this time.

Her vision darted back to the monitor. "Just in there," she said, pointing to the same door as before. "Be advised, we have kids spray-painting the northwest outer wall."

Mason could heard Grim's voice coming from around the corner. He walked toward it.

"This morning I spoke to the former supervisor of the late Tom Mayhew, Chief McElroy."

Mason entered and saw Grim speaking to a small crowd. Irish and Rodriguez. Diaz, Miggs, Yen, Hirsch, and Father Coffey. Even IQ and Chewie were listening. Sarah was the only one missing.

"Or rather, *Detective* Grimshaw of Boston PD spoke to him to ask some questions about a possible homicide. I asked the usual—problems at work, performance issues, conflicts with co-workers—all the while probing his mind for anything dodgy."

Heh heh. Probe, Mason wanted to say, but though better of it.

"I'm quite certain he had nothing to do with Mayhew's death," Grim continued. "Furthermore, he was actually distraught upon hearing that foul play was suspected. But before I informed him of this, I found something amiss. As soon as he saw a badge, an alarm went off in his mind which took the form of two words. *Gibraltar Express.*" Grim gestured to the geeks. "Gentlemen?"

A square of light flickered above them on the flat cement wall as

Chewie and IQ commanded the projector to life, their fingers flying across their keyboards in a ballet of altering images and lines of code.

A set of specs appeared for a large ship.

"The Gibraltar Express," said Chewie. "Herzog-Schmidt fleet. Launched in 2005. Callsign: DCL-19 IMO-31375 . . ."

The superfluous information drew blank stares.

Chewie cleared his throat. "It's a container ship."

"A ship I suspected the chief was being paid to take interest in," said Grim. "So I hypnotized him and, sure enough, found a memory of a visit from this man." He leaned over Chewie's shoulder and tapped at a few keys. A mugshot of a pudgy, grumpy-looking man with no neck and a scraggly goatee appeared overhead. "Wayland LaVey. Attorney-at-law and representative to those who give a bad name to scum."

"And what was *his* interest in the ship?" asked Father Coffey.

"As it turned out, none. Quite the opposite. LaVey paid him to ignore it completely."

"Interesting," said Hirsch. "Unnecessary though, considering how routinely cargo goes un-inspected at Conley."

"Perhaps. But if they wanted to be certain that a specific shipment goes unmolested, it's worth it—not to mention the added benefit of an accessory to take the fall should things go south."

"You've got to be kidding me!" said Rodriguez.

Grim was surprised but calm. "Sergeant?"

"Sorry, but this has got 'bad news' written all over it," she said. "Usually we need to rely on informants and luck for the smallest shred of credible intel. Now suddenly we stumble upon all this practically gift-wrapped for us *and* right under our nose. Why?"

"I haven't the foggiest," Grim said honestly. "Maybe Novak's trying to provoke a move from us out of desperation. What I do know is that, like it or not, this is our only lead. When does the ship arrive?"

IQ tapped at a few keys. "Day after tomorrow."

"Which means it's time to go camping. I want surveillance on that dock as of yesterday."

"On it," said Irish.

"In the meantime, see if you can find the cargo manifest."

"No problem," said IQ. "But I doubt that's where we'll find what we're looking for."

"So do I, but maybe we'll get lucky. That's all."

Everyone dispersed except for Mason. He stood there, locked on the image of the ship still cast upon the wall.

What's in there? he wondered. *What's so important about it?*

After a few moments, he realized that he had been left standing there with just IQ and Chewie. They looked at him skeptically.

He looked back. "Uh, hi."

"Whom do you worship?" IQ asked.

"Wow," said Mason, unsure how to respond to the query. "Wasn't expecting to get that from you guys."

"Lucas or Roddenberry?" Chewie added.

"Oh, I see." Mason considered the question for a moment. "Actually, I'm rather partial to Doctor Who."

They both looked stupefied by this, brains attempting to process the data.

"A moment please," said IQ.

They talked in hushed tones amongst themselves for a minute. And, unless he was mistaken, in flawless Klingon, no less.

They turned back to him.

"This is acceptable," IQ said. "Welcome."

"Thanks!" said Mason, pleasantly taken aback by this exchange.

IQ sat back in his chair, folding his hands thoughtfully. "We hold a weekly Soldiers and Scoundrels game on Thursday nights. Seven p.m. Bring a snack."

"Circumstances permitting, of course," said Chewie.

"Oh, that's okay. I don't really know how to play, so—"

"Oh, you'll be there." IQ leaned in closer with a grin on his face. "You'll be there!" And winked at him.

"What's with all the winking? Why is everyone winking at me all of a sudden?"

. . .

Mason went to the roof, where he sensed Grim had gone. As he approached the dojo, a flurry of shadows showed on the warm orange glow of the rice paper that covered its walls. He slid open the door and found Grim fending off a gang of invisible attackers with a clean katana. His bare torso showed a patchwork of scars. Writ upon his very skin in cuts and wounds was a story of one close call after another. The blade glinted with each swipe as it danced through the surrounding candle light, whistling as if cutting the very air itself. Even though he was nowhere near enough, Mason's balls retreated instantly back into his body for fear of being severed. If the other protruding parts of his body could have done the same, they would have. Grim made a wide diagonal swipe with his blade and spun around so that he faced the entrance to the dojo where Mason stood.

"Ah," said Grim, slightly out of breath. "You found me." He went to a circular table with an array of weapons positioned around it like points on a clock. He sheathed his sword before placing it down next to the rest. Also on the table were his glasses, which he put back on his face.

"I'm afraid to ask, but is that our exercise?" said Mason, pointing at the table of weapons.

"Not quite," said Grim with a chuckle. "There are many steps you'll need before picking up an actual sword."

"Then what are we doing?"

"Dancing."

"Excuse me?" said Mason with disbelief.

Grim took two lengths of bamboo leaning against the wall and handed one to Mason. "Any thug can shoot a gun. Sword fighting is a craft. An art. And, in many ways, much like dancing. It depends on poise, footwork, timing, and an ability to anticipate your partner—or, in this case, your opponent."

Mason felt the bumps in the length of bamboo. "Then I take it you don't kill vampires with wooden stakes?"

"You could most certainly kill a vampire with a wooden stake . . . just as you could kill a person with one," said Grim, adjusting his glasses. "With the exception of sunlight, most things that would kill a person will kill a vampire. They are, however, far more resilient. Faster. Stronger. Facing one in hand-to-hand combat is a challenge, to say the least."

There was a memory behind those words. More than one.

"Any adversary worth their salt will look for openings in your defense, waiting for you to look away or get distracted in order to strike." Grim twirled the bamboo. "And when they do, you must know how to block. For instance, if I were to attack like so—" In one motion he raised his staff above his head and brought it down an inch from Mason's nose so fast he didn't even have time to flinch. "How would you respond?"

Mason drew a blank. "Um . . ."

"No," said Grim. "I'm sorry, but 'um' would be less than useless." He tucked the bamboo under his arm. "You would respond like this," he said, guiding Mason's hands up above his head so that the bamboo was parallel to the floor. "A horizontal high block. Try it."

Mason repeated the motion, on his own this time.

Grim stepped back. "Your stance is a tad rigid. Stiff. And that which does not bend, breaks. You must be as a tree, firm but flexible. Place your legs shoulder-length apart, and bend your knees."

Mason did as instructed.

"Better." Grim raised his length of bamboo. "Let's try again."

Grim repeated his strike, slower this time so that it connected softly.

"Good. Again."

Grim repeated the strike. Mason blocked.

"Again."

Grim repeated the strike. Mason blocked.

"Again."

And again and again until Mason began to feel comfortable with the move.

Grim made a flourish with the bamboo, followed by a series of rapid movements. Strike after strike, straight toward him.

Mason flinched and closed his eyes.

When he opened them, Grim was no longer standing in front of him.

He felt a tap on the shoulder, spun around with surprise to see Grim standing behind him.

"Lesson one: Eyes open. Always. Never look away from your opponent." He took up a defensive stance. "Now you attack."

Mason stood the same way he had seen Grim stand, tried to hold the bamboo in the same way he had. Fists one on top of the other, elbows bent so that the bamboo stood beside his face, pointed upward at the ceiling. He bent his wrists back and slowly brought the bamboo down in an arc in front of him.

Something not quite right about it.

Grim blocked. "Space your hands apart a bit," he said.

Mason repositioned his hands two inches apart from each other and struck again. Much better.

"Good. Again."

Mason repeated the strike. Grim blocked.

"Again."

Once more, they repeated the motions several times. The better part of an hour went by. Repeating the same moves. Attacking and blocking. Blocking and attacking. At the end of which Grim imparted lesson number two: repetition, repetition, repetition.

Easy enough, but around the ten-minute mark a problem presented itself.

"What's wrong?" Grim asked.

Goddammit, bitch! I said—

Will you marry me?

I'm afraid it's getting worse . . . doctor says it's just a matter of time . . .

—don't burn the casserole! Is that so hard?

Who's a stinky baby? Who's a stinky baby?

Oh my god, yes!

Unique New York. Unique New York. What a to-do to die today. What a to-do to die today.

Since bonding with the spirit yesterday he had become hypersensitive to the presence of others around him. With those whose minds were shut to him, like the other members of the team, it was only a general feeling he got from them. Either way, there was still a vibration that radiated from them. A resonance. A frequency to which he was now attuned.

But right now he got just the opposite, a smattering of voices swirling around him like debris in choppy waters, coming from all around. Coupled with the rush of cars below, the sounds of trains and trucks, the squeal of seagulls, and the stray voices around them, it had become overwhelming.

Mason pinched his forehead between the palms of his hands. "It's . . . too much."

"Ah, yes," said Grim.

He took a seat on the dojo floor and motioned for Mason to do the same.

"I'd like you to place your hands on your thighs, take a deep breath slowly through your nose . . ."

Grim inhaled. Mason did the same.

". . . and out through your mouth."

They both exhaled.

"Again, but slower. Breathe in . . ."

Inhale . . .

". . . hold it . . ."

. . .

Everything froze. Held tightly between one moment and the next.

. . .

"And let it out."

. . . exhale.

"Wow!" said Mason. "I felt . . . lighter. Like everything had slowed down."

"That's because *you* slowed down. Now I want you to close your eyes."

Mason closed them, his vision cut off by a colorless blur. The noise immediately seemed louder.

"Breathe in . . ."

Then something else happened. Everything became clear, sculpted out from the marble of his blind sense in chiseled definition. The voices and the mouths they came from. The flap of wings in the air above him. Footsteps on the floors around him. Even without sight Mason knew where it all was, as if he were the center of the world with tendrils connected to everything in motion.

Moved by the experience, Mason didn't wait to exhale and opened his eyes.

But for one instant, he'd seen without seeing.

"How?"

"It's an awareness all people have, a remnant of our primal ancestry that need only be honed. Like instinct. But as we adapted to the comforts and protections of civilization, our need for such senses all but disappeared. Unfortunate that we so seldom see what is right at our fingertips."

"I just figured it would be much more difficult."

"Which was part of the problem. You assumed it would be difficult, but it's no more an obstacle than what you make of it. Controlled breathing allows you to control yourself, and that's what we have to work on if we're to make progress. You must learn to harness and wield what's inside you at your command. And when you are done, you must learn how to quiet it."

See the noise in your mind.

An odd instruction, Mason thought. But he didn't have to try too hard to do just that, and there it was, all the noise, taking the form of a nebulous cloud of static and muttering mouths.

Now reach out with your inner hand and close a fist around it.

And just like that, he saw the cloud surrounded by a hand in his mind.

All went quiet.

"It worked."

"See?" said Grim. "With practice and proper instruction, it'll become second nature to you soon enough. And so you've learned lesson number three: patience."

"What's lesson number four?"

"Repeat lessons one, two, and three."

Mason allowed himself a little smile at this. It would take some work, but it could be done. No matter what he faced, no matter who stood in his way, it was possible.

They broke for dinner. Near the end, Grim dabbed the corners of his mouth and spoke. "Everyone ready to go?"

They all answered in the affirmative.

Mason wasn't sure what he meant at first, but then remembered that earlier he had said something about a stakeout where the ship was supposed to dock.

Everyone left their dishes piled up in the sink and headed off.

"What do you want me to do?" Mason asked Grim, who was the only one left, scraping his plate into the trash.

"There's one thing I'd like you to do tonight, Mason. Try the meditation technique I've shown you on your own and write down anything about the experience you can think of."

"I'll do that."

"We'll be back by midnight if there's no immediate matter to attend to."

With that, Grim left the kitchen as well, leaving Mason on his own.

The first thing he did was the dishes. Once they were all clean, dried, and put away he just sat for forty minutes or so, looking out the nearest window as the sun set. Dark shapes of the surrounding buildings cut into the dimming sky as lights began to show in their windows.

Still. A quiet moment to reflect on the many shapes and colors of this situation he found himself in. Vampires. Secret societies. Demons. God. Conspiracies. Gay Jesus. And in the middle of it all, him.

Somewhere, be it in the afterlife or as a mere figment of his memory, he knew Dale was laughing his ass off at him.

Mason chuckled at this. He knew he shouldn't, but couldn't help it. It seemed Lord Byron was right. The truth really was stranger than fiction.

Returning to his room on the third floor, he found Bossy sitting right near the door, waiting for him. He fed her, and as he did he saw the new phone he was given sitting there on the desk, its face blank. Devoid of light. He spent the next few minutes setting it up. When it powered on, he was surprised to find that he already had a text waiting for him.

Hey homie. Diaz here. Hit me up if you want later. I'll be in the shooting range.

Tempting . . .

"No," he said to himself. "Homework first." However rare it may be, wherever he could keep to the same routine he knew in his former life, he would. "Okay, I can do this."

Mason sat on his bed, rested his hands on his thighs, closed his eyes, and breathed.

That was all.

He waited, tried everything Grim had shown him. Relaxing as it was, he did not return to the memory of Jerusalem, nor sightlessly experience his surroundings, or anything else for that matter.

The noise had returned. Not as loud as before, but more than enough to be a nuisance. He saw it, just as he had left it before. He reached out, attempting to grasp it like he had done earlier, when whiskers tickled his elbow. It was Bossy nuzzling his arm.

"Are you kidding me?" he said.

She nuzzled against him again. Funny how cats were. Sometimes, when they stared, Mason could swear they were about to open their mouths and speak.

With a roll of his eyes, he got up and scooped the rest of the can he had opened into her dish.

It felt too cramped in here. Maybe somewhere more open. Mason suddenly remembered that there was a large common room on the main floor. With everyone gone, it might just do the trick.

Aside from the lights in the vestibule and a glow coming from the bank of computer monitors along the far wall, he found it dark and deserted.

There's something, though . . .

The spit of burning sulfur sounded in the shadows to his left as a flame spontaneously sparked to life.

Mason dropped the candle he was carrying.

A face etched in yellow fire appeared, fading back to black before it could spread further. Sitting in one of the chairs of the sitting area, holding a lit match up in front of her. Peering into it like a crystal ball. Sarah.

"Hi," said Mason awkwardly.

She said nothing at first. Then, slowly, Sarah looked up at him and smiled. "Howdy."

Mason swallowed a hard lump in his throat. "I . . . thought everyone was on a stakeout."

"Nope," she said. Her words slurred, head lightly bobbing. "No stakeout for me." She watched the flame as it burned. When it reached her fingers, Sarah blew it out and tore another match from the pack before smoke from the last one had even stopped. And then, staring intently at the head of the match, it ignited.

"Okay. Well . . . see ya."

She didn't respond.

Mason called for the elevator and left, seriously hoping that he wouldn't return to find the place a smoldering heap.

So much for that. Luckily he remembered the text from Diaz and called the elevator. He got in and took it to the garage, where he went through the metal door and into the underground tunnel.

He really didn't like it in here. Ever since Jerusalem he was uneasy being underground or in tight spaces. Especially at the same time. At least it wasn't dark—that would have been a problem. The fluorescent lights above him led forward in a straight line. At the junction, they took a hard left.

Mason came to the door with the keypad . . . only to realize that he didn't know the code. He took out his phone and texted Diaz.

Hey. What's the code for the door??

Mason waited for the dancing dots. He looked up at the security camera in the corner, for no other reason than because it was there.

The phone vibrated in his hand.

3387

Mason punched the numbers in and the door clicked open.

Down the flight of stairs he went until he reached the second metal door at the bottom. Recalling what Grim had done, Mason put one eye to the tiny circle of glass and said, "Cole . . . Mason?"

The same tiny red light that had blinked for Grim now blinked for him.

"Okay, *that's* awesome!"

Mason entered, the smell of gunpowder fresh in the air. It had an acrid bite to it, with notes of something familiar. Steely, almost like recently exploded fireworks. He saw Diaz behind the wall of glass, leaning against one of the stalls. Wearing a pair of safety glasses with a set of earmuffs around his neck. He acknowledged Mason with a little jerk of his head.

"'Sup, Mace?"

Mason winced. "Ohhh, I almost forgot about that."

"Not happening." Diaz stood with his arms crossed. "You okay? Look like you seen a ghost."

"Not quite. Sarah. Whacked out of her gourd on something, I think."

Diaz gave a short laugh through his nose. "Yeah, she does that sometimes. Says it keeps things *quiet*."

"I see."

"Ever shot a gun before?"

"Sure have . . . *not!*"

"Oof!" said Diaz with a squint. "A 'not' joke? Really?"

"Hey, it's an oldie but a goody."

"Well, half of that is right," said Diaz, picking up the gun from the stall he was at and pulling back the slide. "This is Mister Glock. Mister Glock is a semiautomatic weapon that does two things: kick ass and chew bubblegum. And he's all out of bubblegum."

"Huh?" said Mason, dumbfounded.

"Never mind. Anyway, Mister Glock is your friend so long as you respect him by following his three rules. Rule number one: never point him at anything you don't want dead." Diaz held the gun up so that Mason could see its side. "Rule number two: finger *off* the trigger until you're ready to fire." He rested his finger on the trigger guard to demonstrate. "Rule number three: keep the safety on until you're ready to fire." His thumb moved a mechanism near the sight down and a little red dot appeared. "Red means 'dead.' Got it?"

"Got it."

"Good." Diaz slid the magazine into place with a *click*. "Nobody needs blood and guts everywhere, which you'll have to clean up because you're the new guy, and I don't think you want that, right?"

Mason laughed. "No, I don't want that."

Diaz turned and aimed at the target.

BANG!

The very air around them shattered in an instant. Mason was amazed at just how loud it was even when muted.

Diaz shot again. Muscles on his arms flexed with each shot. When he was done, Diaz brought the target in closer. There was a quarter-sized hole smack dab in the middle of what would be a forehead. Not a single shot out of place.

"Your turn," said Diaz as he reloaded and handed the gun over to Mason. "Use, don't abuse. Ya dig?"

"I dig."

He felt a tingle of anticipation as he took it in his hands. Like the first time he held a cigarette. Tantalizing danger. It was heavier than he expected. Not cold the way metal usually was.

Diaz grabbed him a paper target from a pad fastened to the wall, clipped it to the line above the lane, and pressed a button on the side of the stall, sending it zipping away from them. It passed the marks for five, ten, fifteen, and twenty feet and kept going like it was headed for a touchdown.

"You expect me to hit that?" said Mason.

"Don't worry about accuracy yet. Just give it your best . . . *shot*," said Diaz, and nudged him with his elbow.

Mason rolled his eyes and fake-laughed. Rose would have liked him.

He took the pair of glasses and earmuffs from the stall next door, put them on, and took his stance, cradling the grip in his left hand as he aimed at the dark-green silhouette of a person. Palms sweating as his breaths grew deeper. The sound of his own pulse in his ears.

He pulled the trigger.

The muzzle flashed and his arms jerked. An electric crackle of adrenaline surged through his arms and chest. He wasn't surprised by the sound this time as much as the recoil.

"Okay," said Diaz. "Now we just gotta work on your aim."

To say the least. The bullet hole he made was in the top right corner. Way off the mark.

"Center the tip of the barrel between the sights at the back, and once you have your shot squeeze the trigger."

Mason lined up his shot.

He fired once. Twice. Thrice. Hot shell after hot shell flew out and fell to his feet.

This time there was no target. Just Novak. Smirking from afar and dead in his sights. Each round sent bits of torn paper flying, which he saw as bone and brain, until there was nothing left of the face and the gun clicked empty.

Smoke coiled from the barrel. He felt alive and powerful in a way he had never known before.

"Damn," said Diaz as he brought the target back to the front of the stall. "That's . . . definitely better. I think."

Without meaning to, Mason had shot a crooked row of fangs into the target.

TWENTY-NINE

HIS FEET WERE STUCK, ROOTED IN PLACE AS IF THEY HAD FUSED *with the ground. He struggled, but it was no use. And the sharks. They were still there. Circling nearer and nearer. His dread was thick enough to taste. One of the sharks rose up from the sand by the tail. Adjusting his monocle, he smiled from gill to gill, each tooth stained a candy pink from the bits of flesh and viscera between them. Eyes as cold and empty as the darkest part of the ocean.*

He produced a glass of bubbling champagne in one flipper. "Are we having fun yet?"

A discordant electric chorus sounded behind him as the desert gave way to a carnival. A rave. A full-blown bacchanal.

A choir of skeletons clapped and sang gospel music while lasers shot through the air. Sheet-covered ghosts with holes for eyes and no feet beneath dry-humped one another. A group of dwarves—some with wings and glittering halos, others red-skinned with horns—battled each other with plastic swords and pitchforks. Corpses shambled by with glow sticks, colored bracelets, and rows of beads. A wolf with no legs rolled forward in a wheelchair, followed by a leprechaun on stilts. And a flying saucer passed through the sky overhead, landing behind the striped circus tent around which the crowd was congregating.

This was Mardi Gras in a circle of Hell even the Devil had disowned.

A nun in black leather and lace led the Pope behind her on a leash. "C'mon. You'll miss the show."

He followed her through the flap of the tent, met by the haunting hoot of a calliope. Sword-swallowers, fire-breathers, tattooed ladies, and Siamese twins appeared . . . but they were not part of the show. Just some of the many onlookers eating peanuts and popcorn, huddled around the center ring.

Then the ground began to rumble. It burst open as a dead tree rose in the middle of the tent. Only it wasn't a tree. Wooden, but not of natural make. Its beams were carved and refined into thick planks. And on them, a man. Long hair rippling gently as he rose higher. A generous beard. Clothed in nothing but his own blood. The heads of nails flew into each wrist at the ends of his outstretched arms. A crown of thorns wound its jagged way around his head, twisting his face with anguish. The final touch, his epitaph—I.N.R.I.—affixed to the top of the crucifix in flashing neon letters.

Even as he suffered, he managed to look down toward Mason, who watched.

"Forgive them," he choked. "They know not what they do."

Mason woke with a jolt. Bossy went scrambling off the bed, confused.

Bossy—?

Oh yeah.

He had let her sleep on his bed, which he had never done before. Never needed to. She always slept with Rose. It was strange to see her here in this place. She sat in the middle of the room, staring at him, two lamplike little eyes piercing the dark.

He stretched and yawned as he made his way to the bathroom, but not before pausing at the window. As he peeked through the curtains, Mason was greeted by a most welcome sight: the sun. A tough little sliver of dawn showed in the windows of the nearby buildings, warming a cold blanket of clouds.

Not much, but I'll take it.

Mason could feel his lizard begging to be drained and zeroed in on the toilet.

The door burst open—and his bladder nearly with it.

Rodriguez again, dressed as she had been yesterday. "Good, you're up."

"Could you knock, for Chrissake?"

"Nope. Get dressed and let's go."

"Where are we going?"

"For a run. I'd dress warm if I were you."

"How come?"

"Well, we're not running indoors." She nodded at the window. As pleased as he was to see his long-lost sun, it wasn't the type of weather to play outside in.

"Couldn't we do something else? What about target practice?" he said a bit too eagerly, remembering the feel of the gun in his hand.

She stopped and turned, dubious. "You won't go outside, so I should give you a gun instead? Please. Besides, it's not that bad out. Don't be a baby. Vámonos."

She left without a word and closed the door behind her. As soon as she was gone Mason went to the toilet and pissed, reminding himself to keep his door locked from now on.

Even with warm clothes, his hood pulled up, and the little sunshine they had, it was cold. Having never been to Boston before, Mason had no idea if this was usual or not. Either way, he'd already had his fill.

Don't be a baby, she says. Hmph! What a stupid-head.

They took a brisk walk for a few blocks until they reached an area full of bushes and trees. Birds chirped in the early morning air. Paths and stone bridges stretched over muddy waters. Mason thought this must be the area known as the Fens. He remembered reading about it in a book some time ago, though he couldn't recall which one. Under the gentle branches of a weeping willow they ran, passing a few tennis courts, a baseball diamond, a family of ducks, and a World War II memorial, but not a single other person.

His gym teacher, Mr. Connor, used to make him and any other students he felt like picking on run an extra lap around the track. "Gotta build those muscles up." That was what he said every time. Gotta build those muscles up, as if you were nothing without them. Muscles equaled manhood. That was how his brain worked. The truth was that he did it just to be a dick. Just so everyone would know that Mason was different because he had long hair, listened to heavy metal, and cared more about fiction than football.

But he had taken it in stride. If Mr. Connor wanted to make him run an extra lap, fine. He'd do it and in the process prove that it didn't bother him. His muscles would ache and sweat would soak his hair, but he would do it. *Could* do it. And if he could do it to show up an old jock on a power trip, he sure as hell wasn't going to wimp out now. Not in front of Rodriguez.

By the time they returned to the chapterhouse, Mason's chest hurt as if they had been running for hours when it had only been about twenty minutes. He may have run those extra laps for Mr. Connor, but not since June. Somehow this made him want a cigarette more instead of less. Oh, the human body and its contradictions.

When they returned, Mason collapsed onto one of the couches on the main floor, gasping like a fish out of water. Rodriguez showed little sign of having run at all: a misting of sweat, but otherwise he would have thought she had been inside this whole time. He, on the other hand, looked as if he had just tried to lift a house.

"Nuh-uh. It's not naptime yet, chico," she said with a firm but playful nudge with her leg. "Today we start basic training."

"Then what was yesterday?"

"A warm-up."

"Gabby, darling, how about we give it a few minutes, hmm?" he said as his eyelids began to droop.

Next thing he knew, he was vertical. Lifted upward as one end of the couch was raised clean off the floor, sending Mason tumbling with eyes as wide as dinner plates.

"You're *really* pushing rules one and two." She was not happy.

"Fine. Sorry!" said Mason.

"And who said you could call me *Gabby?*"

"I heard your brother—"

"*You're* not my brother. It's 'Rodriguez' or 'ma'am.' "

"All right, goddamn."

"Let's get something straight. You stuck around. That means you chose to live this life, and that's not going to happen if I go easy on you. You sure as hell won't get it easy from *them*. Got it?"

That got his attention.

"Got it."

"Take a quick break, fill your water bottle if you have to, and be at the gym in five minutes."

As she strode powerfully away, Mason finally got the message. This was not just friendly advice. This was not a suggestion.

It was an order.

"Yes, ma'am," said Mason.

He spent most of that five minutes rubbing a bruised knee from the tumble. The bruise on his ego, however, was too deep to touch. He hoisted himself off the couch, got his gear from his room, and headed to the gym.

Rodriguez had shed the jogging clothes, hoodie tied around her waist, the single braid in her hair hidden behind her back. She took the roll of tape from his bag and began wrapping his hands. After that, he put on a pair of padded gloves he found inside and awaited further instruction.

"This is probably a ridiculous question, but do you have any self-defense or martial arts training? Karate, kickboxing, wrestling, anything?"

She stood there with her arms crossed, waiting, while Mason thought.

"I took Taekwondo once," he said.

"Good," she said, pleasantly surprised. "Then you must have learned how to block, at least?"

"Well . . ." Mason sheepishly folded his arms across his chest. "When I say I took it once, I mean *once*."

The glimmer of hope on her face vanished. "Okay, then. You've heard the saying, 'The best defense is a good offense,' yes?"

"Yeah."

"Well, it works both ways. If you can't defend, you can't attack. And if you can't attack, you can't win."

Mason sniggered.

"Something funny?"

"Sorry, I just find it a little hard to believe that there's a way to fight a vampire hand-to-hand."

She raised an eyebrow. "Who said anything about vampires? This is just what you'll need to engage the goons who do their dirty work."

The faces of the two highway cops—the two he had killed with his bare hands—flashed in his mind. The thought made him uneasy. The proximity, the personal nature of the act as he robbed them of their fragile, pathetic lives. Whatever guilt he had felt toward them was beginning to shrink.

Took care of them without training.

"Couldn't I just shoot them?"

Rodriguez threw her hands up. "Fine. Shoot me."

"What do you mean?"

"Arms at your side, then draw like you would if you were holding a gun."

Mason flattened his arms against his body, imagined that he was a gunslinger waiting for the first chime of high noon. Rodriguez stared him down in a way that looked as though she were watching not just his arms but every part of him at the same time. A complete state of readiness.

He drew.

She stepped forward, blocked his arm with her own in a sweeping motion, and struck him in the chest with the palm of her hand without so much as batting an eye.

The force of the hit emptied his lungs immediately and sent him skittering backward until his legs gave out beneath him. He fell hard on the mat, face beet-red as the world spun around him. There was no actual pain, but no matter how he tried Mason couldn't catch his breath. She had knocked every bit of wind out of him.

Again, he felt a fire stirring in him, a heat from somewhere as deep as the bowels of the earth, welling up in the pit of his stomach. He could practically taste the smoke.

Rodriguez appeared above him. "That was just a love tap."

"This . . ." he said between gasps for air, feeling like he might pass out, ". . . is bullshit!"

"You had a gun, didn't you? How did I beat you with nothing but my hands?"

Mason said nothing as he let lungful after lungful of sweet oxygen into his body again and again.

"A gun is no good if you can't fire it. You hit hard when you have muscle. You get muscle by training. *Then* we move on to other stuff. Not before. You've got to crawl before you run. Comprende?"

She offered her hand to him.

"Sí, comprende." Mason took it and reluctantly let her help him up. "Just don't do that again."

"You're welcome to stop me," she said with a playful flick of her eyebrows.

"How?"

"Thought you'd never ask."

Rodriguez motioned for him to follow her over to the punching bag.

"Legs shoulder-width apart, bend your knees a little, and keep your hands up to guard your face."

Mason complied.

"In a fight you want to stay loose, so your stance should be a balance between structure and flexibility." She moved to the opposite side of the punching bag and grabbed a handful of it. "Now make a fist with your thumb on the outside and punch."

Mason threw his fist and connected with the canvas.

"Not bad. A little wide, though."

Rodriguez positioned herself behind him and put her hands on his waist—an act which sent a little tingle through the rest of his body.

"When you punch, turn that whole side of your body into it, like this, to put your weight into it."

She pushed on his hips. She smelled nice. Lotion of some kind. Mason felt a sudden swell of heat in his cheeks as he punched again, this time in slow motion.

"Better. Now line your arm up with your shoulder and punch."

Mason hit the bag, straight and true, sending it wobbling.

"Again."

Mason hit it again.

"Again."

He threw a fifth punch.

"Again."

This time with his left. Then again with his right. Then his left. Soon one hit was thrown after the other with such rhythmic succession that his fists made a beat like a brave pounding on a war drum.

Rodriguez's phone beeped in her pocket. She held it up to her face. "Just keep doing what you're doing, and I'll be back."

Mason continued throwing punches for ten minutes after she left. Once his knuckles grew sore, he stopped for a breather. After twenty minutes, he wondered what was taking her so long.

Maybe . . .

He sat cross-legged on the floor as he'd been shown, rested his hands in his lap, and closed his eyes. With the first few breaths he saw the contoured terrain that was this new sense. The noise was still there. He loosened his grip on it—not all the way, but just enough to bring things into focus, slowly adjusting it until things cleared up, like tuning a radio to the right station.

Everything could be heard now. Heartbeats, voices, traffic, people flossing their teeth, all clear as a day without cloud. And all jumbled together. Mason waited for one particular sound, as if listening for a single note in an orchestra. And then he heard it: a throaty voice speaking from somewhere in the floors below.

"*¿Qué piensas de este chico nuevo?*"

He narrowed his focus in on that one point and all the other sounds dimmed to background noise. It was Rodriguez, all right. She was speaking to someone.

"*Él es débil.*"

Her brother, Miggs. Mason didn't catch what they were saying at first, but after a few moments, he understood in midsentence.

"*Puedes verlo in his eyes. I give him a week before he runs.*"

"*If he even is the messiah.*"

"*He's not.*"

"*How can you be so sure?*"

"*Because Jesus is the messiah. The one and only.*"

"*Then why are you here?*"

. . .

"*Seriously, you've never said why. You obviously don't like it here, or believe in our mission. So why?*"

"*You know why.*"

Several moments of silence passed before either of them spoke again, and then Rodriguez said:

"*You know I don't blame you, right?*"

"*I blame me. You're all I've got and I'm never letting—*"

"Oookay, this sounds like a private conversation," said Mason. As he stood back up, his empty stomach made its displeasure known to him. "And I'm not waiting around here all day."

He left the gym and headed for the kitchen. Halfway there, he had a thought.

What if I want to go out instead?

And just like that, his feet carried him toward the elevator. A short ride later he found himself at the main entrance of the building, facing the clear glass double-doors beyond the vestibule. Daring himself as though he were standing at the edge of a cliff.

"Going somewhere?" came a voice behind him.

Mason turned. Irish approached from the sitting area, wearing a fall coat with the collar turned up and jingling a pair of keys, which he then tucked away into one of his pockets.

"Uh," said Mason, unsure how to respond. "I was thinking about it. Is that allowed?"

"Are you allowed to think about leaving?" Irish answered with a wry grin.

"You know what I mean."

"Where did you want to go?"

"To grab coffee," said Mason with a little shrug. "Maybe a bagel."

"Oh, I know a great place. Best breakfast sandwiches in town." Irish made for the door. "How about I grab you one and we can have a chat when I get back? Sound good, big guy?"

"Yeah, okay," said Mason, and watched Irish leave.

He knew how this would go. He'd return with a sandwich and coffee and explain in dulcet tones that it wasn't safe for Mason to go out on his own. It wasn't his fault, Irish would say. He was just doing his job.

But that didn't stop Mason from wanting to shoot the messenger.

THIRTY

When Irish returned, Mason followed him out the side door to a picnic table in the shade. On it sat a coffee can. A stubbed cigarette butt sent its last few coils up like smoke signals from within. Irish picked up the can and placed it on the ground, replacing it with a tray of coffees and a full brown paper bag with grease stains. They took their seats across from each other. A piece of the sun, blocked moments ago by a stubborn bit of cloud, broke through, kissing all it touched with its warmth.

"Here we go," said Irish, placing one of the coffees in front of Mason. "A Conan EspressO'Brien and a Breakfast Club Sandwich."

Mason unwrapped the sandwich and took a bite. "Oh wow." Peppered turkey, sausage, cheese, and lettuce on a toasted sesame bagel.

"Not bad, huh?" said Irish, who hadn't even touched his yet.

"Pretty damn not bad." Mason finished the rest with a few big mouthfuls.

Irish raised his cup in a silent cheer. "Like I said, best in town."

"Are you from Boston?"

Irish nodded. "Born and raised."

"Huh. You don't really sound like it."

"Not everyone in Boston sounds like they're straight out of *Good Will Hunting*."

"Right . . ." He already knew the answer to his next question. "I can't leave here, can I?"

Irish gave him a sympathetic look and matter-of-factly said, "Trust me, you don't want to leave here. Not yet, at least."

"Right." Mason took his sweet time eating the rest of his sandwich, spinning every wheel in his head for something to change the subject. "How did you wind up in all this?"

"I was a cop." He took a pack of Marlboros from his coat pocket and lit one. "Six months out of the academy. Wanted to be a detective, like Columbo. You know Columbo?"

"I know Columbo."

"A man with taste, I like it," said Irish with a short smile. "Back then people were going missing in Boston. Hobos and druggies mostly, the odd hooker, so basically no sweat off the PD's back. But when a pair of college students went missing, that got their attention. No suspects, no witnesses, no leads. Zip.

"One night my partner and I get a call. A noise complaint near a subway station downtown. Reports of kids drinking and carrying on. So we check it out."

He took a long drag and blew it out slowly in a steady stream of smoke.

"We found five kids. Four of them dead, all with their throats mangled to shit. But the fifth was still alive. Bleeding from the neck, not quite as bad as the others. Barely able to talk. My partner went to call it in while I stood guard. It didn't even look like something a person could do. This was . . . *raw*."

Irish made a tight claw of crooked fingers to drive the point home.

"The kid tried to speak as he choked on his own blood. Then, finally, he said: 'Look out.'

"I looked up and saw something clutching to the alley wall. A woman, white as a ghost, with the eyes and fangs of an animal. She dropped down on me like a bat out of Hell. I don't think I've ever drawn my gun so fast in my life. I fired, got her right in the head, and ran as fast as I could. When backup finally arrived, we went to check for the body . . . nothing. As if she were never even there."

"Grim said that a regular ol' gun could kill them."

"It can, but that doesn't guarantee that it's going to. They're tough, man! You usually have to empty the clip before they'll stay down. And you always have to destroy the remains, or they'll come back.

"So I tell all this to my CO, and of course he—along with the whole precinct—thinks I'm nuts. My partner was no help, since she had been calling for backup at the time. But *she* believed me. Only one who did, actually."

"I started looking into it some more—which, by the way, being a rookie, I was absolutely *not* supposed to be doing. Wouldn't have even been able to if I didn't have a clerk who owed me a favor. Turns out there were a bunch of similar cases being quietly buried in the unsolved files. I didn't know what to do. If I said anything, I'd get in trouble, likely fired. But if I didn't, it would continue."

"So what did you do?"

Irish smiled. "I went to confession. The priest—who was Father Abbott, by the way—he said I should do what I thought was right. So I spoke with Captain Garrity—which, again, not supposed do. He suggested we discuss this down at the *bah*," said Irish, affecting a Boston accent, then gave Mason a wry look. "Because he actually did sound like he was straight out of *Good Will Hunting*."

Mason noticed how Irish referred to him in the past tense.

"Over the course of a few beers, he gave me a whole spiel about there being things we can't explain in the world, and on this job you see your share of the unexplainable. And that the real truth of it is that no one wants to know. They're scared to look into dark corners for fear of what they might see.

"I had just started saying how I wasn't afraid even if everyone else was when everything began to blur. As if God had smudged the world with His thumb."

Irish fell quiet.

" 'Ya couldn't just leave it alone,' " he said in a deep voice that was not his own. "That's what he said to me. That muthafucka!"

His Boston showed more clearly now, whether he liked it or not.

"Garrity led me out into the alley and dragged me over to a dumpster. Took my wallet, hoping to make it look like a mugging gone wrong, I guess. I didn't even have time to pray . . . when who appeared behind him?"

Mason gave a little shrug, unsure whether he was actually supposed to know somehow.

"None other than Blake Grimshaw. Knocked the captain out cold, cleared my head up, and offered me his hand. Been with him ever since."

Irish trailed off, watching a group of chickadees flutter to the ground and peck at the grass.

Mason reflected on Irish's story. It was not so very different from his own. For that he was unexpectedly grateful. "What happened to him?"

"Garrity? We altered his memory and managed to pin the victims on him, which is really not far from the truth."

"How many were there?"

"All together, fifty-two."

Mason blinked, surprised. "Wait a minute . . . when was this?"

"Nine years ago. You probably heard of him. Robert Wayne Garrity."

It rang a bell. And after a few moments of thought, the whole belfry clanged to life. "The Massachusetts Mangler?!"

"That's him. Currently enjoying a padded room and three square doses of Thorazine at Saint Jude's."

"Holy shit."

Irish scoffed. "The irony is that *he* tried to make me believe *I* was crazy. Because that's what they do, see. They have all the time in the world, so they wait. They plan. They turn people against you and try to destroy your life before they take it. And then"—Irish snapped his fingers—"disappear into the shadows. So here's the best advice I can offer you."

He eyed Mason, deadly serious.

"Be careful."

Mason shifted uncomfortably in his seat, suddenly feeling very exposed. A fist began to tighten in his chest. Not all the way to a full-blown attack, but enough to be a bother.

"Guess I should get back." Mason stood and brushed the crumbs off his hand. "Thanks for the sandwich."

"Anytime."

And back inside he went, very aware of how much closer the walls around the compound felt than they had just minutes ago.

THIRTY-ONE

GRIM REPEATED THE STRIKE. MASON BLOCKED.

Mason repeated the strike. Grim blocked.

Again and again and again.

Then, somewhere around the hundredth time, Mason dropped his guard.

"Problem?" Grim asked.

There was. It had been on his mind all through the rest of his workout with Rodriguez and now during his time with Grim, gnawing at him until he could no longer focus.

"I'm not sure how else to put this, but . . . why in the hell don't people know about this shit?"

Then Grim dropped his guard.

"Sorry," Mason went on, "I don't mean to be rude or anything, but we're talking monsters. Actual monsters. People's lives are at stake, yet I'm forced to hide here while those *things* run around free. Why aren't you—we, us, whatever—why aren't we telling *everybody* that these things exist right now?"

Grim's face went blank. A moment passed. Mason thought he was angry at first, but then his eyebrows flicked, as if the dawn of an epiphany had just broke within him.

"You're right."

"I am?"

"Yes. Absolutely right. Come." A wave of his hand as he made for the stairs.

Down to the fourth floor they went, stopping at a room which he could only assume was Grim's. He stepped inside without Mason and emerged a minute later in his usual attire of a jacket and slacks, then made for the elevator.

"What are we doing?" Mason asked on the ride down.

"We're going to tell people the truth."

Straight out the front entrance he marched, Mason closely in tow, and walked up to the first person he saw on the sidewalk: a young woman carrying a latte in one hand and a phone in the other, her thumb darting across the screen.

"Excuse me, miss. Do you have a moment to—?"

"Sorry," she said without even looking up, and kept walking.

Grim went to the next person, a man carrying a briefcase. "Excuse me, sir. Do you have a minute to hear about our Lord and Savior, Saint Philip?"

"Beat it, weirdo!" He waved Grim off with a scowl and kept walking, a little more rapidly than he had a moment ago.

A woman approached with two children, a young boy tugging at her hand and another fussing in a stroller. She pushed the stroller as if sleepwalking through her day.

"Excuse me, ma'am. Sorry to bother you, but do you believe in ghosts?"

"Oh," she said, taken aback. "Well, yeah, actually, I do."

"Really?" Now it was Grim's turn for surprise.

Mason watched with rapt attention.

"Oh, yeah. I believe in all that stuff. Ghosts, crystals, palm reading, chai energy. My yoga instructor said—"

"Hi!" interrupted the young boy at her side. "I'm Jason. I'm five.

How old are you? I'm five. Blah-lah-lah-lah-lah." He stuck his tongue out several times in quick succession.

"Well, that's marvelous," said Grim, straightening his glasses. "Then you're in luck, because I'm part of a special sect of the Catholic Church that studies ghosts, among other things. And if you just follow me"—he gestured toward the chapterhouse—"I can show you—"

The toddler in the stroller began to cry while his brother continued to make faces at Grim.

"You know," said the woman, feigning eagerness as she began pushing the stroller forward again, "that all sounds great. Maybe another time."

They disappeared down the street.

Grim turned to Mason. Not smug. Not gloating. Just the face of a man who had made his point.

"Okay," said Mason. "But surely there must be another way."

"Another way, indeed. I think this calls for a more conversational setting."

Mason followed Grim back inside and rode the elevator up to the fourth floor. He hadn't seen Grim's room until now, and what he saw made his jaw drop.

Books. The entire room was filled with them. Custom-made shelves of fine wood held tome upon tome from the floor to the ceiling. Some were battered and falling apart; others looked brand new. It was hard to believe that it all could fit in the space afforded by standard quarters, and yet it did not feel cramped.

There were paperback novels, hardcover textbooks on psychology, philosophy, and languages, leather-bound medical journals, several holy texts from various cultures, an entire set of encyclopedias, the complete works of Shakespeare, and many others he couldn't determine at a mere glance. In one corner sat two leather wingback chairs on either side of a round mahogany table, upon which sat a green reading lamp next to a copy of *Moby Dick* with a pipe resting on top.

His bed was a simple futon, the sort one might find at a Japanese inn. The wall above it was the only space besides the window not covered with books; instead, five framed pieces of kanji calligraphy hung in a T-pattern. He had no idea what they meant but found the intricate black ink on the clean white paper pleasing anyway. Mounted above them, a katana; sheathed in a rosewood case with lotus inlays, it stood guard over the bed. No sign of the doctorate or degrees Grim surely possessed, which Mason found both uncommon and refreshingly modest. There was also no sign of pictures of family, friends, loved ones, nothing like that—which Mason also found uncommon, but he supposed it wasn't everyone's way. Everything was neat, clean, and polished, giving the room the cozy, meticulous quality of a library reading room. It suited Blake Grimshaw.

"Please," said Grim, gesturing to the two chairs.

Deciding that the one that sat beside *Moby Dick* must be where he usually sat, Mason took the other one. Its crisp leather was soft but unbroken, squelching like a ripe tomato as he shuffled around in it trying to get comfy.

"May I offer you anything? Tea? Coffee?"

"Nothing, thanks."

Grim hooked one knee over the other and began packing his pipe with tobacco from a pouch he took from the table drawer.

"You were saying that there must be another way to make people believe in the unbelievable."

"Well," Mason said, "you said yourself that seeing is believing, right? Surely there must be recordings, video, documents, yes? Why not post it all to the internet?"

Grim lit a match, let the flame hover just above the bowl of the pipe, and puffed. "It is."

"It is?"

Grim took out his phone, tapped it a few times, and held it up.

A video played. Immaculate white: a lab. A hunched, naked figure in one corner of an area walled off with thick plexiglass. The time index now read 11/05/97 8:08 AM.

"I give you specimen three twenty-seven."

Two men came into view sporting priest's collars and white lab coats. When they did, the hunched figure sprang toward them, smacking right into the glass barrier. The men flinched. The creature proceeded to hit into the invisible wall between them, vainly trying to attack. To call the sound it made *inhuman* wouldn't even come close. A growl and a moan twisted into one impossibly guttural noise that made Mason's insides pucker.

"What you're seeing is a ghoul. An aberration that manifests in those who consume human flesh."

A few seconds passed before he felt an internal hint of surprise at how casual his response had been, as though he were getting used to all this.

"Useful to anyone with need to dispose of bodies, they live mostly in sewers. I'm sure if you looked beneath the streets of Boston you would find one." Grim held up the phone again, insistent. "I found this one via the clerical portal on the Vatican website. I didn't even have to log in."

He tucked the phone away.

"These terrible wonders have existed as long as the world has, Mason. They go unseen because no one *wants* to see them. And when they do, it's rounded off into something acceptable. And that's the truth of it, really. We all know such things exist, but they don't become real to us until they enter our lives. Then we are forever changed. That is the true horror of this world. Not that bad things exist, but the level of willful blindness we show to them.

"We rationalize it however we can and go on with our lives, only recalling that we've seen behind the veil once in a rare while. Or perhaps never. It becomes a repressed memory, something we convince ourselves we dreamed or imagined—or, at best, something we can't explain. When the truth is that the supernatural is so much more *natural* than we've come to believe. And those who do believe, who either stumble upon these things or have been directly affected by them, we recruit."

Perturbing, but Mason knew it to be true. "So there's no hope, then, of bringing these . . . *terrible wonders* to light?"

"No hope?" Grim scoffed. "Egad, boy! You're living proof that there's hope. Did anyone ever have to tell you that there are no such things as vampires?"

"No, of course not."

"Precisely. You just knew that they were imaginary. But you believe now."

"Sure do."

"And why is that?"

"Because I've seen them."

That knowing smile creased Grim's face again. "And that's how it is done. That is how it *must* be done. One at a time. You untie one knot, and then the next. Little drops of water make an ocean." Grim turned his pipe over and tapped the contents into an ashtray on the table beside him. "You know, there was a time when what we call the 'supernatural' was seen as absolutely real."

"There was?"

Grim nodded. "For thousands of years. Up until not so very long ago, relatively speaking. Just the same as sea monsters, which, in the time of Magellan, were a legitimate danger for any mariner with the sense God gave a codfish."

Mason nodded. "Oh, I see what you mean. The days when women were burned at the stake for witchcraft was because they were in fact witches, not simple healers or freethinkers as they would have us believe today."

Grim cast his eyes upward, considering this. "Rather that it was a combination of the two. Like so many things, the truth is somewhere in between. It's how such things have entered into our ethos as the figments of imagination we take them for that is truly the wonder of all this.

"It was only around the time of the Industrial Revolution that vampires even deigned to be covert, or at least started to take care not to be noticed. As cities grew, electric lights lit the night, and the unexplored corners of the globe began to disappear, they kept their numbers smaller, their profiles lower, hibernating for long stretches of time, obscuring facts with false details until they became campfire stories and horror movie fodder.

"Meanwhile, those who knew of their existence could only watch as the world's view dimmed around them. There was a time when even Militia Dei began to question whether they ever really existed, shrinking our numbers and resigning us to the furthest fringes of our faith. We became the kooks, while they became invisible."

" 'The finest trick of the Devil is to persuade you that he does not exist,' " Mason said, quoting Baudelaire.

Grim nodded. "Apropos. And that's just vampires. There are still reports of ghosts and past life experiences and demon possessions all the time, are there not? It's there for anyone to find. And we rely on witnesses to tell us what they've seen. That's why we have the hotline."

"What hotline?"

Grim gave him an understanding look, with a hint of something else. Not quite all the way to reproach, but in a neighborhood just down the road from it. "I take it you haven't looked through the file you were given."

Mason shifted in his seat. "Not yet."

"It's important that you do. Be sure to make some time for it." Grim began packing his pipe again. "We have a hotline expressly for the purpose of reporting supernatural experiences."

"Is that really wise, though?"

"It's not only wise, it's *essential*. The more a problem is known, the better the chance of finding a solution. Consider everything you've seen so far and, if you can, everything you have yet to see. If I came to you and said flat-out that vampires exist, you'd have thought I was insane or pulling a prank or something to that effect, yes? Just as you saw not ten minutes ago.

"If I simply told you that there was no point in trying to disseminate our knowledge to the public, you'd have challenged it. Same as if

I'd told you that Shakespeare's works were written by someone else. Or that there were lizard people from another dimension in the government. It's why morals are divined more easily from stories than by flat-out telling people what to believe. Stories allow us to see from another point of view and actually experience the lessons we're meant to learn. And, in the process, to find ourselves.

"That's why we hand out our Bibles. Some will dismiss it as nothing but nonsense, yes. But others will see it as an affirmation of that which they already know. Then some will be genuinely curious, and just like that the seed is planted, opening their minds to possibilities that would have been inconceivable before."

"What about the government?" And just as predicted, Mason wondered if the comment about the lizard people was real. But surely it was just an example.

. . . right?

"Governments ask questions. Point fingers. Interfere. And due to a measure of diplomatic immunity we enjoy as an official prelature of the Vatican, I'm afraid we're not abundantly popular in most political circles. So, for the most part, we avoid them. But there exist among them ones like us. Ones we can trust. And that's really what it comes down to: who to trust. Whose eyes will be forever opened and whose remain closed. I put it to you: If you could go back before you knew about any of this, would you?"

"In a heartbeat," said Mason without so much as a pause.

"Exactly. And, to be honest, I couldn't blame you. Ignorance truly is bliss."

"I can understand that, actually," Mason said, nodding. "Wanting to forget. There were times when I just didn't want to think about Jerusalem. Or talk about it or have anything to do with it. Because if I did, it meant looking for an answer that, deep down, I knew I'd never find. I don't think I could even comprehend it most of the time. It felt like something that had happened to someone else. So I pushed it out."

"But even then there was a little voice, wasn't there? Telling you that in surviving something so phenomenal, there had to be some reason behind it. You had a duty to strive for something more."

Mason grinned. "Now you're starting to sound a bit like Bishop Strauss."

Grim grinned back, chuckling. "Don't mistake me. I'm not saying you *owe* us. I'm saying you owe it to yourself. You've been given a second chance. And as it turns out, so have we."

"How so?"

He stood and began to pace. "For the past few generations, the Ram of God had become a position of ill repute. You see, the title—and the power that comes with it—has been passed down the bloodline of Saint Philip thanks mostly to his only son, Joshua, who lived to a ripe old age and had many children. Eight, that we know of. Unfortunately, not all of his descendants turned out to be, shall we say, paragons of Christian virtue."

"I see," said Mason, thinking, *Whatever that's supposed to mean.*

"Some used it to amass wealth and privilege, gain prominent positions in society, even become Pope."

"Really?" said Mason with utter astonishment.

"Well, an *anti*-Pope, technically. And naturally, like any power, its possessors feared losing it, so attempts were made to keep it within the family via inbreeding."

Mason grimaced. "An Old Testament solution if ever there was one."

"It was a dark spot, no doubt. Thankfully it finally passed to other, more worthy descendants. But even then it was hardly smooth sailing. The purity of the Holy Spirit had been dealt such a blow that its strength had greatly diminished. Still powerful, but not to the magnitude it had been even a generation earlier. This, coupled with the untimely deaths of certain messiahs and their families, gave rise to the belief that the title and the power it held was more of a curse than a blessing. It wasn't long before the sanctity of the role was called into question.

"The point being that there could still be dozens, perhaps even hundreds, of possible descendants alive today to whom it could have passed. Why, my own family is a part of the lineage."

"They are?"

Grim nodded in acknowledgment.

"And you're not upset that it passed over you and to me? With no connection and no earthly explanation as to why?"

"Of course not," said Grim sincerely. "He decided to resurrect you as He did Saint Philip, which is the surest sign that you are the rightful Messiah of the Archangel. I accept God's will, whatever it may be."

"But how do you know that this was all God's doing? How do you know that it was a matter of Him choosing me specifically, not just a fluke? We saw what happened—the cross fell where it fell and someone was bound to find it. It just so happened that that someone was my dad, who gave it me. What if he kept it? Would *he* be the messiah now instead of me?"

"But he's not."

"And it didn't even take proper hold of me until a few days ago. What if I had lost the cross or it had been stolen? What if any other person, any other time, had found it?"

"But they didn't. It's you. As I said before, the truth is often somewhere in between. And I believe there has to be a reason for that."

"Seems like an awfully big coincidence to me."

"Some say that coincidences are God's way of remaining anonymous. I, however, believe that they are His way of letting us know He is there."

"Well, you could explain *anything* like that."

Grim nodded emphatically. "You could explain *everything* like that. Is it possible that it was a random occurrence with no divine intervention whatsoever? Yes. As a scientist, I can't deny that. But now ask yourself, with everything you've experienced so far and everything still yet to come, is it possible, however incrementally, that it was a willful act of God—a higher power, a divine intelligence, call it whatever you like, but something that has a plan for you? Is it at least possible?"

Mason opened his mouth to speak.

"You don't have to answer that. Just think about it. In the meantime . . ." Grim stood and retrieved a leather satchel and a wooden box from a shelf behind him. "What do you say to a game of chess?"

"You know what?" said Mason. "Yes. I'd like that."

Grim moved the table between the two of them and unbuckled the satchel. From it he took out a chessboard, its checkered pattern faded and chipped. He slid the top off the box and set up the pieces, each beautifully carved of black and white marble. Two armies on a battlefield upon which they had fought countless times before. He took two pawns from the board—one black and one white—shuffled them between hands, and then held his fists before him.

Mason picked the one on his left, Grim's right.

Black.

Grim set the pawns back in their place and, since he had the white pieces, went first.

Knight to C3.

Mason heard Grim's voice, though his lips did not move. The knight, however, did. The little horse hopped over the pawn he had just put back and landed in front of it. All without so much as lifting a finger. He sat back in his chair and puffed away at his pipe, grinning at Mason's askew expression of disbelief.

"How did you do that?"

"Think it in your head," said Grim, out loud this time.

"That's it?"

"No, that's a start."

Pawn to D5.

Very good. Now move it.

How?

See it in your mind. Stretch your inner hand out toward the piece. Feel it *in your hand as if it were.*

262

Mason did as instructed, staring at the pawn he wanted to move. It remained where it was.

"Try closing your eyes. They tell your brain something that your inner eye is confused by. It helps until you can reconcile the two."

Mason closed his eyes. Breathed. Saw the world with his inner eye. Sensed the chessboard and the pieces on it, their shapes solid in the space before him. And in the space Grim occupied, an energy, a core of nebulous light, effervescent with particles, that seemed to hum from inside his skull. Within was an opaque pocket of static which his mind could not penetrate.

Still the pawn remained where it was.

I can't.

You can.

A series of images were projected into Mason's mind. A multiverse of particles and planets. Supersized networks of immense stellar bodies to the firing neurons in his brain. Everything big and small, connected as one.

All matter has mass, and everything with mass has a gravitational effect on other objects. Every atom in the world around you and every atom in your body are entwined in the same energy field. The same one that causes Earth to orbit around the sun, and the sun to orbit around the galaxy, and so on.

It all coalesced into a single moment of lucid coherence, and Mason could now feel the pawn in his empty hand as if his fingers were wrapped around the marble. The round head, the narrow neck that flared downward into the base, the smooth bottom touching the board beneath it as it slowly began to slide into the square ahead of it.

He felt the piece next to it. And the one next to it. And then all of his pieces. And then all of Grim's pieces. The board they were on. Multiple sensations flooding into him. Everything became louder—the noise, voices near and far, ships in the harbor across town—the sheer volume of the input his mind was receiving overwhelming him. Growing out of control.

The table at which they sat lifted an inch off the ground. Then the chairs. Then the full weight and form of the man in front of him, and even himself. And for a moment he was weightless.

"Easy . . . *easy!*" Grim barked with alarm.

Everything dropped.

Mason opened his eyes to see a look of astonishment on Grim's face. Pleased, but shocked. The chess pieces had all toppled over, a few having rolled onto the floor.

"I'm sorry," said Mason, scrambling to pick up the fallen soldiers.

"That's all right," said Grim, a little flustered as he righted the pieces that had tipped over, while Mason placed the missing ones back on the board. "It is a difficult thing to master, but then so is the first time you tie a shoe, or type at a keyboard. And now I'm sure you can do so without a second thought. So too will it be with this. Until then"—moving his knight back into position—"how about we stick to using our hands?"

"Agreed," said Mason, the lapping of waves still fresh in his mind as he moved his pawn forward. "What do you think will be on that ship tomorrow?"

Grim took a final puff of his pipe and placed it down. "Nothing good."

THIRTY-TWO

TOMORROW BECAME TODAY. DAY BECAME NIGHT.

The night.

The arrival of the *Gibraltar Express.*

After supper, the team made their preparations and left the chapterhouse. Mason joined Grim in the security building, where they found Chewie and IQ gazing at the three different displays projected on the wall of the comms room. One was a digital map of Conley Terminal and its surrounding area, one a camera feed from a rooftop across from it, and the third all black with the words SLEEP MODE in the center.

Grim looked at his watch. "Any sign of her?"

"Should be any time now," said IQ. "She's due at 6:50 and Herzog-Schmidt are notoriously punctual." He had barely gotten the last syllable out when a yellow dot appeared in Massachusetts Bay at the outer edge of the map.

An air of doubt clung to Mason like clouds of mist around a hill. He wasn't even sure why this bothered him so. He was just watching. But, as had been pointed out, none of this added up. That was enough.

Grim raised a two-way radio handset, clicked it, and said, "Team One, looking for a visual."

"*Roger, Base,*" said Diaz.

The image zoomed in on the harbor and focused on a massive vessel looming in the distance, its deck packed with stacks of cargo containers. Mason scanned them nervously. Inside one of those ships was the answer to a mystery he wasn't even sure he wanted solved.

His imagination reeled with obscure images of what it might hold. Was it a weapon? A giant albino spider with a human face? A dildo in a jar of mayo?

God, no! Anything but that!

The ship moved so slowly that it was hard to tell it was really moving, but surely it maneuvered into position and docked. The name Gibraltar Express could clearly be seen in bold white letters across the stern. Before long, people appeared; not long after that, overhead cranes began shifting and sliding into position and offloading the containers onto rigs which carried them away.

Like most people, Mason had no idea what a laborious process this would be. Never had he felt any interest in the goings-on of shipping vessels until now—and that was a very liberal interpretation of the word "interest." More like an unbearable anxiety prolonged by the endless cycle of *pick up, drop off, drive, repeat* that went on all . . . damn . . . night. He tried to stay awake, willed his eyelids to stay open, drank one cup of coffee after another so that he wouldn't miss whatever it was he was supposed to see. But before long, he'd drifted off and was lost to a dream. This time it was a nice one.

Julie sat next to him on the detached backseat of an Envoy in her garage—only the garage had stone pillars now and a view of the ocean. They drank wine and ate fresh fruit.

"Whatcha thinkin' about?"

He noticed her smooth, crossed legs. Recognized the cutoff jean shorts she wore. But the unbuttoned white blouse, that was new.

He met her gaze, the same one he saw the night they had snuck a bottle of Merlot from her parents' Fourth of July party and made out like the world was ending yesterday.

"Home."

The contour of the shirt collar around her smooth neck drew his gaze downward to her chest as one delicate hand gently teased the fabric and it was pulled back and . . .

The door slammed shut as Lloyd entered the building. "Wakey, wakey, eggs and steaky," he said.

Daisy and Duke rounded the side of the desk and into the room. Cursing the fact that his dream was just a dream, Mason rose to his feet and gave each dog a scratch behind the ear as they began nosing and licking him—especially little Max, who broke into a fit of excited hops upon seeing him.

Mason returned to Grim's side, still in the exact same spot watching the display, which showed a lone red cargo container conspicuously set aside from the rest.

"What now?" he said, still groggy.

Grim crossed his arms. "Now we wait."

"Isn't that what we've been doing so far?"

"Jolly good," said Grim with a slight chuckle.

"Hey . . ." Mason shifted his gaze from one thing to the next, running a hand through his hair. "I don't know if you had a chance yet or not, but did you ask the Bishop about my request? To let me see my friends' parents?"

"I did." His face told Mason the answer before his lips did.

He knew that would be the answer. *Did I really expect that stiff to say yes?*

But he was disappointed all the same. "Oh well. Thanks for trying at least."

Mason stared at the monitor, all but willing the container to open, when Sarah appeared next to him, eating tuna fish right out of the tin. "Ahoy, Commodore Schmidlapp."

"Hi . . ." said Mason with a bit of a start, "Captain Nemo?"

She didn't seem high, at least not that he could tell. She wore an old flannel shirt, frayed and terribly worn, thick with the burnt smell of cigarettes. Slender fingers brushing through her thin, swooped-back strip of green hair.

"And how are we today?" she said. "Tonight. Whatever."

"Better."

"Oh." Sarah put her fork down, took a folded piece of yellow construction paper from her sweater pocket, and handed it to him. "Guess you won't be needing this, then."

Mason unfolded it. His eyes reeled, trying to help his brain process what he saw on the page. "How interesting. What is it?"

"It's a buffalo."

"And . . . what's he holding?"

"*She* is holding a fruit pie in one hand and a fetus in the other."

"I see. And why those two things?"

She looked at him with disbelief. "Because they're both delicious."

"Of course," said Mason. "Thank you."

Sarah pointed at the display. "Showtime."

The camera panned to the left, revealing a pair of headlights. *Finally!*

The radio crackled to life. *"Be advised, Base. Be advised,"* came Rodriguez's voice, hushed and garbled. *"We have an unmarked panel truck on approach. Two visible occupants."*

The truck pulled up, idling for a moment as the passenger got out, and then the driver repositioned so that the backdoor was aligned with the opening of the lone cargo container. Two more emerged from the hold. All men, all darkly clothed. Even zoomed in it was too scarce to make out detail in the image, but these were definitely guys you wouldn't want to mess with. The first man unlocked the container, flung open the door, and returned to the passenger's side as the other two disappeared inside. They returned less than a minute later carrying a large wooden crate.

Mason squinted at the screen. "What in all the hell could that be?"

"I haven't the foggiest," said Grim. "But whatever it is, Novak wanted us to see it for some reason."

"This is fucked!" said Sarah.

"Quite," said Grim.

Cargo in tow, the truck spat back to life and left the terminal.

Grim picked up his radio. "Okay, Team Two. You're up."

The text of the previously black monitor blinked to life, showing a vision of the night-world through the green eye of the drone. It showed the face of Raymond Yen briefly before rising high above the surveillance van and then flew west, positioning itself directly above the truck. A pair of crosshairs appeared. After a few rapid blinks, the drone fired and a red tracking dot hit the roof of the truck, distinctly visible now through the maze of green roads and buildings below.

"Are you receiving, Base?" asked Irish through the radio.

"Receiving. Good job, team," said Grim. "Return to Base."

"Ten-four."

Mason looked back and forth at Grim and the monitors. Grim, monitors. Grim . . . was leaving the room. "What . . . that's it?"

Grim paused at the door and looked back at him. "For now."

THIRTY-THREE

THE TEAMS ARRIVED BACK AT THE CHAPTERHOUSE JUST IN TIME
to see the truck's final destination. That same red tracking dot
blinked on a digital map of the city, stopping somewhere in
Cambridge, not far from Harvard. Chewie quickly checked the location and found out that it had been bought by Rance Financial
Group, a shell company owned by none other than Wayland LaVey.

Mason had managed to get a good couple of hours' sleep before
Rodriguez got him up for their run. His mind so preoccupied with
unanswered questions that it barely registered. Trees of the Fens
went whipping by in an unimportant blur of greens and blues. His
footfalls, in sync with his running partner, beat a rhythmic path on
the pavement which he could not help but follow. An odd shiver
went up his spine, and not just from the weather. The tingle of uncertainty. All he could think of was what had been in that crate.

A question the team intended to answer today.

. . .

It was Sunday. The days were much harder to keep track of with none of the usual touchstones that marked them. No classes, no bells, no weekends. They existed—he was just no longer part of them. And, it being Sunday, Mason did something which he'd never done before.

He went to church.

He had been *inside* churches, of course. Seen them. Studied them. Appreciated their artistic and architectural value. But attended a sermon? Never. Not even with his parents. His mother believed, though not really in a get-up-and-put-on-your-Sunday-best type of way.

After about an hour into their workout (which now included chin-ups and planks), Rodriguez looked at her watch and said it was almost ten o'clock, as if he should just know what that meant. She told him to go change and come to St. Augustine's when he was ready.

When he arrived, the mournful sound of an organ spilled out of the open doors. He entered to find a woman with a puff of snowy white hair coaxing a tune from the keys, and was surprised to see not just the team, but others as well. Scattered amongst the pews, they appeared to be common church-goers, plain as unbuttered toast. Families even, with small children.

But here and there he spotted one that stuck out. A biker with a beard down to his chest, wearing sunglasses even though he was inside. A young girl with pigtails, sitting alone and quietly singing "Jesus Loves Me" to herself even though that was not the song being played. A teary-eyed woman with unnatural green bruises on her neck, who looked away when Mason met her gaze.

Sarah was the only one he didn't see.

Mason spotted Grim sitting up at the front and took a seat next to him as the organ's song slowed and came to an end. Father Coffey ascended the pulpit and began to speak. He started with the Parable of the Prodigal Son. Courtesy of passages like "Your brother was dead and is alive again. He was lost and is found," Mason got the distinct impression the Father had chosen it because of him.

When the service came to a close, everyone except for the team filed out, stopping briefly to shake hands with Father Coffey, who closed the church doors as soon as the last of the flock had left. When that was done, he joined the rest of them near the altar.

"Okay, team," said Grim, his deep voice resonating through the church walls around him. "We have a search op this afternoon. I'm thinking ACS cover. No need to worry the neighbors. Agreed?"

He looked to Irish and then Rodriguez, both of whom nodded in agreement.

"Everyone clear on their assignments?"

Nods all around (except for Mason, who had no clue what, if anything, he was supposed to be doing).

"Any questions?"

Yen's hand flew into the air and he began signing away when Grim shifted attention to him. His face curious, eager for a response.

"Honestly, we don't know," said Grim, all but throwing his hands in the air in frustration. "That's the truth of it. I wish we had more to go on, but we're pretty much walking blind. So eyes and ears on full. Understood?"

They all answered the same. "Yes, sir."

"Then let us pray."

Grim made a welcoming gesture and everyone joined hands. Mason took Grim's firm hand to his left, Rodriguez's strong but soft hand to his right. He saw that her hair was now done up in a tight bun, not so much as a loose strand.

Father Coffey stepped forward, closing his eyes in silent prayer to himself, before he spoke it aloud. "Lord, guide our hands in this, thy righteous work. Grant us the courage and strength to brave the dangers we must face, and lead us safely home. In Heaven and on Earth. Lux in tenebris lucet."

"Amen," everyone spoke in unison (even Mason).

"So what do you want me to do?"

"Just watch and learn," Grim answered. "Head to the security building. Hirsch is expecting you."

"Ten-four," Mason said with a jaunty little salute.

It was nearly noon when the team was all ready to go. They emerged, all in Animal Control uniforms, caps, and windbreakers to hide their firearms. Harder to conceal were the blades they carried, either at their sides, or, in Grim's case, strapped across his chest, the hilt jutting out behind his shoulder. Each one stepped forward and spread their arms as Father Coffey sprayed them from head to toe, side to side, and front and back with a canister while muttering a prayer in Latin. Irish was first, and stood beside Mason when he was done.

"Holy water," he said. "Masks our scent."

When that was done, they got in a plain white panel truck—which Irish had fixed with a magnetic Animal Control Services decal—and drove away.

Mason made his way to the security building, where he found Chewie and IQ in front of their monitors with several different feeds showing at once, only this time they were feeds from body cams worn by the team. At first Mason saw nothing but the lot of them sitting across from each other in the truck, rocking as it navigated the city streets. Finally the rocking stopped and they all got out in a neighborhood that could have been inhabited by teachers and Harvard professors. Families. People who drove kids to soccer practice in minivans and attended PTA meetings. Not somewhere you would expect evil to dwell.

Isn't that always the way? thought Mason.

It was a Tudor-style house, intricate and charming, with a SOLD sign on the front lawn. Other than a car passing by as they exited the truck, not a soul was in sight.

"Team leader to Base," said Grim. *"Anyone home?"*

IQ tapped away at his keyboard as an infrared layout of the house and property came up on the monitor before him. The team showed in six yellow-orange silhouettes near the bottom of the screen. Near the center, two more were near each other inside the house, one orange and one blue.

Hirsch clicked the radio she held. "Thermal scan shows one warm body and one at a frosty fifty-six. Both in the basement."

"How's our footprint?"

Chewie reviewed his monitor, which had several windows of various internet sites open, before giving a thumbs-up.

"Nothing on police scanner or social media," said Hirsch. "Good to go."

"There is a security system, though," said IQ. "Give us a minute to disengage."

"Copy. Securing perimeter."

The team moved toward the house. Irish and Rodriguez took canisters of holy water and began spritzing the outside of the house. The team rounded the side of the house and through a gate in the chain-link fence to the backyard. Grim tried the back door to find it locked. Diaz crouched down and began picking the lock.

"How's that alarm coming, Base?"

IQ's fingers sped up as they flew across the keyboard, tapping the Enter key with satisfaction like punctuation on a sentence. "Open Sesame."

"Copy that. Radio silence from here on out."

The team entered through the kitchen. All the windows were covered with thick drapes, casting a dim brown light throughout. Miggs guarded the front door while Diaz watched the back.

It was spacious and modestly furnished, mostly with pieces from IKEA. Ideal for a family of four. There was something off about it all, though. Nothing felt . . . alive. All the pictures were the ones that came with the frames they were in. Rodriguez paused at a futon in the living room. Mason could see that it still had the tags and plastic covering—just like everything else.

Grim made a short series of hand signals indicating that they were to proceed to the basement. He took a flashlight from his belt, clicked it on, and began to lead Irish and Rodriguez down the staircase. The lone window, which let in a brave little rectangle of light, was just enough to see that it was unfurnished and bare as a jail cell.

Most basements look ancient, lived in, like a tomb that's been rediscovered after centuries of absence. This one, so far as Mason could tell, was brand new. Sure enough, the walls were lined with pink fiberglass insulation. Had he been there himself, he was sure it would smell of fresh paint and recently cut wood. No sign of bodies, living or otherwise. The team looked around at each other in the dark, confused.

"Base, are you sure about those signatures?" Grim whispered into his wrist, breaking his own order.

IQ and Chewie looked at their monitors, which clearly still showed the two heat signatures next to the three blips of the team.

"Affirmative. Six feet to your left, against the west wall."

The team all aimed their weapons in that direction and approached with caution toward a space that looked like it might be a wine cellar when finished.

Grim ran his hand along the wall. *"There's something behind here,"* he said, braced his body against the wall, and pushed with all his might. No good. *"I think there's a pressure switch. Give me a hand."*

Rodriguez and Irish joined him and all three put their full weight into the same spot.

Finally, a whole section of the wall clicked and slid back.

The team aimed their weapons again into the pitch-black space beyond. Grim stood back while the other two took point, scanning the room with their flashlights.

Against the far wall stood a dusty black coffin. Old-fashioned, the type one might use as a Halloween decoration. Wide near the top, narrow near the bottom. No locks or clasps. It was nailed shut.

Flashlights continued to scan the room. Mason jumped when they found a face. A young boy huddled in the corner of the room. Wide-eyed, shivering, barely dressed, and completely scared out of his wits.

Rodriguez crouched down and began swinging a pendulum in front of the boy's face. Back and forth . . . back and forth. Just like the fake cops. *"Sleep."*

And that's just what the boy did. Eyes closed, face relaxed, he fell limp into her arms and she laid him gently down on the floor.

"What's the plan, cap?" said Rodriguez.

Grim holstered his weapon and placed the tips of his fingers at either side of the coffin, giving it the slightest nudge. He paused and placed his hand on the lid, thinking.

"Rodriguez, you get the other end. Muldoon, you cover us."

"What?" said Rodriguez.

"We're taking it with us."

"In broad daylight?"

"We're most certainly not coming back later tonight. Now snap to it. Miggs, get the truck ready. Diaz, keep six."

"Cap, I . . . I dunno . . . I've got a bad feeling about this."

"Duly noted."

Carefully, they lowered the coffin down into carrying position. Rodriguez grabbed the top end, Grim the bottom, and once Irish had backed out of the room with his pistol still drawn they lifted it off the ground and out of the dark room.

It was hard to tell, but Mason thought it looked heavy. How could it not be? The feed from both body cams shook as they started up the stairs, proceeding with the kind of caution one would expect when carrying a crate of nitroglycerin.

Irish, now at the top of the stairs, holstered his sidearm. *"I'm not sure it will fit around the corner."*

"Well, they had to get it down here some damn way." Strain clear in Rodriguez's voice as she struggled with her end of the coffin.

"We'll have to tilt it—"

Grim was cut off as Rodriguez lost her footing and slid ass-first to the step below, the full weight of the coffin falling upon her and blocking out her camera. Grim put his shoulder into it to prevent it from sliding all the way back down.

"Jesus!" said Irish as he rushed to lift it off her. *"Are you all right?"*

The lid of the coffin broke open with a bone-crunching snap. A white hand shot through the fresh hole and grabbed Irish by the neck. His camera spun out of control for a second and then went dark.

There was yelling and four cracks so loud they rattled the speakers, followed by flashes of gunfire from Rodriguez as she shot blindly into the coffin. Grim let go of it completely and stepped out of the way, sending the coffin sliding the rest of the way down the stairs.

He drew his sword as the creature inside broke the rest of the way through.

All Mason caught was a fleeting vision of a pale face with gnashing fangs and eyes darker than an empty crypt sail past Grim before his blade separated the head from its body.

It bounced down the steps and landed next to Irish.

Grim hauled the broken coffin out of the way and caught a blurred flurry of motion from inside as a pair of limbs flailed about— much like that of an insect when separated from its head.

Rodriguez rushed to Irish's side. She said his name, panicked yet trying not to be.

"Diaz! Miggs! Somebody get the stretcher, quick!"

From just the monitor alone Mason couldn't tell or even imagine what state Irish was in, but from the few short contractions of his ribcage with each desperate breath, clearly he was alive.

But for how long?

Diaz hurried down the steps carrying a simple stretcher of two poles bound together by canvas straps. He laid it down next to Irish and with the help of his teammates gently turned him over onto it.

Rodriguez gasped. *"Oh, fuck me."*

His neck, little more now than a mass of deep purple flesh, had been crushed and bent at an angle no one should have survived.

"Just hold on, papi. Hold on!" said Rodriguez while she and Grim secured him to the stretcher before picking it up and carrying him out of the basement.

Grim barked orders for Diaz and Yen to stay behind and handle the police as they made their way to the truck.

Irish began to choke as his feeble gasps for air grew fewer. *"Shit, shit, we're losing him!"*

Miggs hurried to the driver's side and started the truck.

"Is Mason there?" came Grim's voice.

"I'm here."

"I need you to get a gurney and an AED kit from the infirmary and meet us in the garage."

"A gurney and a what?"

"An AED. A defibrillator. There's one in a red pouch mounted to the wall next to the door. Got it?"

"Got it."

Mason fled the security building as fast as his legs could carry him, past the Learys, past the dogs, which yipped excitedly after him from the commotion, through the graveyard, and into the building. His heart pounded and there was a sick feeling in the pit of his stomach. He didn't even bother with the elevator, instead bursting into the stairwell and flying up each of the five flights. He found the red kit—right where Grim said it would be—grabbed it from the wall, tossed it onto the gurney against the wall next to the row of beds, and pushed it out into the hall.

It was bulkier than he'd expected, but he barely noticed from the adrenaline. He hit the button to call the elevator. All ten seconds it took to arrive stretched on forever. Once inside, he hit the button for the garage. A welcome deep breath flooded his lungs and, foolishly, he hoped to see the truck already there waiting for him.

Ten. Whole. Minutes. That's how long it took for the rattle of the garage door as it opened.

The truck tore down the ramp, tires screeching, and came to a halt. Mason pushed the gurney to the rear as the back door opened. He'd expected assistance, but instead Diaz jumped out, raised both hands to his head, and strode off, pausing after a few steps and then bursting of rage, kicking the nearby trash can.

Mason rounded the side of the truck and reluctantly peered inside.

Rodriguez, knelt beside Irish, silently weeping, one of his hands clasped in both of hers. Grim sat on the other side of him, his head hung. The look on his face told Mason that it was too late.

Irish was gone.

THIRTY-FOUR

MASON'S JOURNAL – (undated)

I SAW A MAN DIE TODAY.

Mason stopped and put down the pen, pondering this.

He had seen a few people die by now. More than a few, actually. He felt differently about each one. None of it good. He'd barely even known Irish, so why was this time special?

He didn't know. It just was.

THIRTY-FIVE

TWO DAYS PASSED. FOR THE FIRST TIME SINCE HE'D STARTED training, Rodriguez didn't wake him.

He had never been to a funeral before. Not for his parents. Not for Julie or Dale or Rose. He didn't even have anything to wear that would be fitting for such a thing. Diaz let him borrow a jacket that was a bit wide in the shoulders but did the trick.

The exact wording of Irish's last will and testament were for his ashes to be spread from a plane across Fenway Park during a Sox–Yankees game. But if that was not in the cards—which, as Grim put it, "most certainly is not"—an acceptable compromise would be for his ashes to be poured into the Charles next time the two teams played each other. Until then, they sat in an urn in St. Augustine's, candles burning softly all around.

Fewer people showed up for the service than he expected. There was the team, of course, all dressed in black; Father Coffey, presiding and delivering the eulogy; Bishop Strauss, who Mason was beginning to think was incapable of looking anything other than dour; a few additional Militia Dei members who were later introduced as missionaries; a tall, dark-haired woman Mason didn't know; and himself. That was it. Mason found this quite sad. When he asked Grim if his family would be coming, he gestured to one of the missionaries.

A solemn, clean-shaven man, several years older than Irish and with the same strong jaw and sandy hair, stood near the altar, staring at an enlarged picture of Irish in his police uniform. Dressed in a black button-down, jacket, and dress pants, he looked almost like a priest minus the white collar, crossing himself as Mason saw his lips move but couldn't hear what he said.

He met and shook hands with the team as they left the church. When he came to Rodriguez, who Mason saw wearing her hair down for the first time, they openly embraced and held each other for a long while.

Finally, he approached Mason and Grim, tucking a rosary into his inner breast pocket. "Captain Grimshaw," he said. His grief was palpable, a dark anchor around his neck pulling everything in him down with its weight.

"Kevin," said Grim. "My deepest condolences."

"So, tell me . . ." He did his best to keep the tremor in his voice or the tears in his eyes from showing. "Who killed my brother?"

"Bartok," said Grim quietly, almost in a whisper.

Kevin's expression changed only with a sad lift of the eyebrows.

Who? Mason thought.

Grim turned to him. "Laszlo Lukavic Bartok, one of our more notorious usual suspects."

"Not so usual anymore," said Kevin. "He hasn't been seen in a century. And even then, he was already a ripe old three hundred, wasn't he?"

"Thereabouts. Bartok was never one for subtlety or laying low, so we figured him dead."

"I guess now that part's right, at least." Mason felt a hidden anger flare up from him, wishing in vain that it had been him to swing the sword instead. "So what was he doing here?"

"It seems Novak led us to him. Intentionally. To do his dirty work. My guess is Bartok was here to establish a new lair for the winter."

Kevin fell silent, his face hard as stone before he blinked a few times. "... your guess."

"We're pursuing every lead," said Grim quietly.

A cold, awkward silence frosted over between them.

"Let me know if you find anything."

"Of course," said Grim with a nod, and shook his hand.

Kevin's glassy eyes shifted to Mason. "So you're the new Ram of God." It was more of a statement than a question. He offered him his hand.

Mason shook it, finding the same rough hands Irish had.

"Godspeed. You'll need it." And he left.

Grim removed the glasses from his face, pinching the bridge of his nose. His usual buoyant demeanor was visibly weighed down by everything that had transpired.

"What leads?" Mason asked.

Grim stayed how he was for a moment after the question, appearing not to have heard him, before he placed his glasses back on his face. "Hmm?"

"What leads are we following up on?"

"At the moment, the boy found at the house in Cambridge is all we've got. But ..."

Mason waited for him to continue. "But?"

"He doesn't appear able to speak."

"At all?"

Grim shook his head.

"How come?"

"Brain damage, some sort of aphasia, perhaps?" He shrugged and let out a deep, troubled sigh. "Whatever the case, he hasn't said a word so far."

Mason sensed something in him. Something he desperately to say but dreaded. That's all he could tell, his mind was so tightly sealed.

"There's something else...I'm sorry to have to tell you this but... Rose's body has been taken."

Mason's brain sputtered. "Taken?"

"I'm afraid so. While we were at Bartok's."

"Why? I-I-mean," he stammered, "Why? What would they want her for?"

"We don't know."

Mason felt the very blood drain from his heart as every sick, profane, perverted, unnatural thing possible defiled his mind.

"We're pursuing ev—" Grim started to say.

"Every lead. Right."

Grim straightened, smoothed the lapels of his jacket, and made to leave.

"Can I have a minute?" Mason asked.

"Of course," said Grim. "Take your time."

In truth, he didn't need a minute. Just wanted to be left alone. It was an odd thing, this mourning, this sense of loss for someone he had met only a week ago. But in truth, it wasn't Irish he mourned for. He hadn't been able to do all this for his loved ones. To bury them, place flowers on their coffins, or even say goodbye. Now he wouldn't be able to. And connecting them all was the same red thread weaving from one point to the next.

Novak.

The name burned in him like never before. No rage or outbursts of anger this time, just a beautifully silent lump of hate so hot that it forged the first molten layer of an iron-hard shell around his heart.

He swore to himself, then and there, that he would find Novak and cut his fucking head off.

Mason had dozed off in the pew at some point during his ruminations, and was awakened by the sound of rain softly pelting the stained-glass windows. His neck, good and stiff, cracked like a walnut as he stretched it.

He sat up and jumped at the sight of Rodriguez sitting next to him. "Um . . . hi."

No response. She appeared the same as she had for the funeral. Hair still down, cascading down her shoulders like the dark waves of a nighttime waterfall. The exception being Irish's fall coat. She produced half a bottle of tequila from beside her and took a long swig.

After a few seconds she offered it to Mason. The hair in his nostrils wrinkled from just a whiff, but he put his lips to the bottle and tilted it back anyway.

Oscar de la Hoya, that's strong drink.

It simmered in the joints of his jaw before spreading through the rest of him. Good stuff.

Even in the gentle glow of candlelight, Mason thought she had been crying. Not because there were tears on her face—she'd never allow that—but then, not all tears show in the same way. He saw none around the chapterhouse after Irish died. But he heard them. Felt them mingled with his own. Like so many tears, they existed in private. Behind closed doors, when no one was around. How sad that something so common was so often hid from one another.

But hers showed. It was in her expression, the way her bottom lip seemed poised to quiver if someone but mentioned his name.

"I take it you were close?" he said with a pinch in his throat from the tequila. Mason had never had tequila before and could already feel lovely waves of it radiating inside him. He helped himself to another swig.

"Close," said Rodriguez. "Yeah, you could say that."

"Sorry, I . . ."—the full implication of it hitting him now—"didn't know."

"Of course not. Why would you? It's forbidden, you know. For teammates to . . . *fornicate* . . . out of wedlock."

Mason believed words themselves were innocent, no more responsible for their regard or standing in language than a snake is for being poisonous. But he had always found the word "fornicate" to hold such lewd overtones. Judgmental, even. Implicative of unbecoming behavior. It told a secret without telling, one that risked exposure and condemnation.

And yet, there was also something very arousing about it. Careless abandon. The thrill of something you know you shouldn't do. And since the way she said it seemed to imply the same, he couldn't help but think of Rodriguez in such a way. A twinge of guilty pleasure when he suddenly found himself lost to what could be referred to as "impure thoughts." Electricity tingled through him, and suddenly his neck was no longer the only part of him that was stiff.

"It doesn't feel like he's gone, does it?" said Mason, shifting in his seat. "I still keep expecting to see them around every corner like it's just a matter of walking into the right room."

Them. You said them, *dummy.*

He had of course meant to say *him*, but without realizing it had been thinking about Rose and his friends too. And it was true. No matter how much he wanted to see them just one more time, it would never happen again.

And Julie. Oh, Julie. I never told you. I should have told you. And now I never will.

"I know what you mean. It was the same when my parents died," she said, and took another swallow.

"Your parents are dead too?"

She nodded.

The hardness he had felt for her moments ago softened into something much more tender. The guilty pleasure had become just guilt.

"But we won't, will we?" she said. "See them again?"

"Aren't you supposed to tell me that they're with God and we'll see them in Heaven and all that?"

Rodriguez looked at him, serious as could be. "Irish believed that. Just like most of us. I looked into his eyes when he died, heard his thoughts as they slipped away into nothing. He wasn't just scared, he was *terrified*. So what, if he truly believed in God and Heaven, was there to be afraid of?"

Mason shrugged. "Nothing?" he said uncertainly.

"Exactly. Nothing." Rodriguez resumed her gaze into space, her last word and all it implied echoing in his mind until it became a comfortable silence between them. "Faith is a funny thing. In many ways it's the opposite of trust, takes no time to gain, and is damn near impossible to destroy. But when it's gone, it's a gift you never know if you'll get back. Know what I mean?"

He sensed a strain in her that, while unfamiliar, was not entirely foreign. A missing piece replaced with the confused anger of injustice, filling the empty space left vacant with that which we cannot explain. Not all that dissimilar from how he'd felt as a lonely child, wondering why God would have taken his parents from him before refusing to believe at all. And then he realized that what he felt from her, the burden they shared in that moment, was a crisis of faith.

Mason sat in stunned stillness, moved by the truth and clarity in her words. Then he spoke. "No. I don't know. Not really. I get my strength from books. Stories about people who don't even exist . . . though, in a way, I guess they kind of do, as aspects of the people who write them. I've learned more lessons that way than any other because, to me, that's real. Or rather it *was*, until this gift of mine allowed me to relive the lives of others."

Mason thought about each one. "From Tom Mayhew I learned that he wanted to help people but instead just wound up working a job. So when things don't turn out like you plan, do your best to make the most of them.

"From my dad . . . if you really want something, go for it. It might not be easy, and people might tell you that you can't or shouldn't, that you might not get it. But if it's worth it to you, that's all that matters.

"From my mom? One that kind of complements my dad's: Don't stop believing. Because if you give up, you sacrifice certainty for success.

"And from Will Graves . . ."

I learned that even when you try to do the right thing, life can still fuck you over.

Mason put the bottle to his lips again.

"Well, let's just say that I think I'd prefer *Hamlet*."

Not that he could re-read it if he wanted to. It had been lost the day he left Ohio, and he imagined it laying on the road somewhere. Dirty cover fluttering harshly as cars drove by. Just another thing lost.

He felt the need to say something comforting. Every platitude in the book came to him, each more cringeworthy than the next. *They're in a better place . . . Time heals everything . . .* He had heard them all himself, and none made him feel any better. Facile sympathy-card fodder that accomplished nothing except to give the speaker the illusion that they were helping, ruining a perfectly good moment of quiet in the process. Or, his personal favorite: *God must have needed them more.*

No, he thought. *Flat out, no.* Especially that last one. *What could the all-knowing, all-powerful creator of life, the universe, and everything possibly need them for more than their son?* Given and then taken away without any real reason—not that there was such a thing. If those were the intentions of a divine being, he found them greatly lacking indeed.

And so he said nothing. Just sat next to Rodriguez and let the moment doze like a cat in the afternoon sun. Alike in their grief, each mourning for that which was missing. Still, whether out of sympathy or the tequila working its magic, he felt compelled to say something.

"So what do we do?"

Rodriguez didn't speak. Didn't move or acknowledge that she had even heard his question as she stared into the flickering flame of the many candles before her. Bottle of tequila in hand, she abruptly stood and began powering down the aisle toward the door.

"Let's go!"

"Huh? Where?"

She didn't answer.

Mason hung his head, already sorry he had asked.

THIRTY-SIX

A SHORT CAR RIDE LATER, THEY PULLED UP IN FRONT OF A small building. The rain, while not quite in full downpour, was enough for lights and street signs to become washed with a watery blur. Mason could just make out the words HOTEL ALEXANDRA above the entrance. Both he and Rodriguez got out and hurried to the front door. He slipped on the wet pavement, shaking like a pile of dishes that had been stacked too high, but quickly regained his balance.

She leaned into the door and held it open for him . . . but he didn't want to go in. He couldn't go in. Even as the rain pummeled him, he sought not the shelter a few short steps in front of him. There was nothing in there for him. He was far more interested in a laundromat about halfway down the block, drawn toward it inexplicably.

"Oh . . . you may enter," said Rodriguez as he began to walk away.

With the effect of the protection gone, the fog around his mind dissipated all at once and Mason ran up the steps and through the open front door.

They entered a lobby with a few old chairs and sofas to one side of a staircase, a lounge area in the next room beyond French doors. Patterned carpet. Vaulted ceilings. An antique elevator he half expected to have an operator. Old, no doubt, but recently restored to some vestige of its former glory. And to the immediate right a reception booth, behind which sat a lump of a woman with cat-eye glasses reading a book of the cheesy Harlequin-romance variety, complete with a bare-chested stud cradling a swooning woman on the cover. Behind her, lining the wall, were rows of mail slots with their corresponding keys.

"Evening, Marge."

"Rodriguez," the woman answered back, lifting her eyes from the page just long enough to get a gander at Mason.

"Room Eleven."

Marge spun around in her seat, scanning the numbers of the slots with her index finger, and located the one for Room 11.

Rodriguez took the key and went up the stairs. Mason followed, and they stopped when they reached the first room on the second floor.

"You're clear why we're here then, yes?" said Rodriguez, tequila fumes filling the air her voice traveled on.

"Clear? You said 'Let's go,' and next thing I knew we were here."

"You're going to link with the boy we found in Cambridge."

The pit of his stomach turned hollow and dry. "Oh . . . I'm not so sure about that."

"Well, you better get sure fast, because we don't have a lot of choices here. If you have the ability, you have the *responsibility*."

Each time had been different. He lived the entire life of Thomas Mayhew from just touching his finger, yet only the moment of death from the ancient skull of Saint Philip. Perhaps it had something to do with the age of the remains which allowed for a clear experience. But so far he had yet to try it out on a living, breathing person. Would it be clearer? Cloudier? More ordered? More chaotic? Or maybe there was no rhyme nor reason to it at all. The luck of the draw. Mason had found it daunting enough to experience the full scope of regular life events alone, to say nothing about the moment of death. And that was just from a regular Joe. What fresh terrors might await in this boy?

"Chico, this can't go on." She got close, her hair dripping wet, smelling of rain, lips recently kissed by Jose Cuervo. "We've lost one of our own. And he was hardly the first. If we don't stop it . . . don't stop *him* . . ."

Lost one of our own. Her choice of words was the very affirmation he needed. He was part of the team now. Mason took a deep breath and summoned his courage.

"Okay."

Rodriguez put the key in the doorknob and twisted.

The room appeared empty at first. Quite basic, as hotel rooms go. Light from outside cast the shadows of rain along the floor like snakes swimming downstream. By the wall next to the bed, Mason spotted the top of a blond head. He stepped past the foot of the bed to see the boy, ten, maybe eleven years old at most, clutching his legs, bruised knees obscuring his face from the nose down. Eyes wide as pools of milk.

He took a step closer.

The boy flinched. His breathing grew faster, matching Mason's own quickened heartbeat.

"It's okay," he said, and held out his hand as if coaxing a stray cat. Mason stretched out with his mind as much as he could, finding it just a tad more difficult thanks to the tequila. He directed his thoughts toward the boy, looking for the inner voice in him to calm and convey that he meant no harm.

But there was none.

Not so much as a stray thought or even a word or two floating in the current of this boy's unprotected mind. Like touching the thin top of a puddle to find no water beneath. Not even images. Just darkness and silence and the ever-stinging swarm of bees that was his constant fear.

Mason stood and grabbed a chair from one corner of the room, placed it in front of the window, then stepped away, inviting him to sit. The boy lifted his face from behind the cover of his knees so that he could see his mouth and quivering chin.

"We're not going to hurt you," said Mason, and as firmly as he could he pressed that thought into a single stream and directed it at him. He could almost see it cast out to the boy like the line of a fishing pole.

Hesitantly, very hesitantly, the boy rose to his feet. Dressed in clothes like the ones Mason had been given upon his arrival in Boston, the boy took one bare footstep after another toward the chair and, gripping his elbows, slowly sat down.

Mason approached.

The boy shuddered as if it were the natural reflex to such a movement, but remained calm. Mason stood before him now, towering above him by comparison. And then, trying not to move too suddenly, Mason knelt down on the floor before him. A gesture he hoped he would recognize. The boy's body language and expression said he was still cautious, but he seemed to soften just enough.

"My name is Mason," he said, patting his chest with one hand. "Mason." He then pointed to Rodriguez and said her name. "Can you tell us your name?"

The boy just stared blankly back at him, nervously fidgeting with a hospital bracelet around his left wrist. On the other were black circular marks of some kind. Mason skewed his head to the side just enough to see that it was a tattoo.

DC

Mason racked his brain, thinking of what it could mean. *District of Columbia? DC Comics? David Copperfield? . . . Of course!*

"Are those your initials?" said Mason, pointing to it.

Nothing from him.

"Do you speak English?"

. . .

"Can you speak at all?"

Worth a try, but there didn't seem to be any other way. Mason gently reached out his hand toward him. The boy grew agitated again, breathing rapidly.

"It's all right," he said as his hand came nearer.

The boy tensed right up and clutched the seat of the chair by his fingernails.

"It's all right." Nearer and nearer.

The boy pulled away.

The tips of his fingers but a hair's length away.

Lightning struck, filling the room with a bright strobing flash, followed closely by rolling thunder.

Then another glint of light, getting closer and closer.

The window exploded in a hail of glass and flame. A clear bottle, fire spilling from its neck, came hurtling toward them. Time slowed to almost nothing as the fiery hail crashed against the back of the chair. Christened in flame. It was almost beautiful.

No time to think, let alone move. Heat from orange claws reached out, singeing the hairs on his hand. A strong, invisible force whooshed past him. One powerful gust of energy and the inferno that was a boy moments ago flew back and out the broken window into the rain, wailing like a banshee as he disappeared from view.

Rodriguez ran past him, little more than a blur as she leapt out the window to the adjacent roof.

Shaken, Mason stamped the fire that was burning away on the carpet until it was out. He hurried out the room and back down the stairs so fast that his knees buckled and almost went tumbling down.

Marge shouted something as he rushed past her, but he didn't answer. She took a shotgun from beneath the desk and marched upstairs.

Panting heavily, Mason opened the front door cautiously, scanning for any sign of movement. Rain and rain and rain. The night was drowned by it now.

A body fell to the drenched street before him. A bundle of limbs hitting the ground with a wet slap.

Mason shouted as he ran down the steps to her, stopping dead as she rose slowly to her feet. She turned and revealed herself to be a beaming she-devil with eyes that matched the night, a row of pearly-white daggers spread across her white face all pointed at him.

This wasn't Rodriguez. "Oh shit," said Mason, realizing his error.

Her hair, black and slick as oil, clung to her face and neck. She wore a biker jacket, which at a glance Mason had mistaken as the coat Rodriguez wore. It slid off her shoulders, dropping at her feet to reveal a black halter top between taut, tattooed arms. A chain dangled from a studded belt over leather pants as she crouched like a cat, ready to pounce.

Mason turned to run for the door. He slipped so fast, virtually in the same spot he had before, barely recognizing that he had fallen until he was staring at the ground. The night turned from black to white. His breath shot out from his lungs, sending him sputtering into painful coughs.

The crack of gunshots sounded from somewhere above, followed by a series of empty clicks.

A pair of motorcycle boots landed firmly on the sidewalk directly ahead of him, blocking his path to the door.

He scrambled to get away from her as she towered over him, reaching out with a thin hand that seemed to stretch ever closer no matter how quickly he tried to move away.

A knife shot through the air and pierced through the pale skin between knuckles.

The vampire wailed, but it was short-lived. The cut didn't even bother to bleed. She pulled the blade out and tossed it away with no more regard than someone plucking a splinter. It clinked along the pavement and landed in a nearby pothole that had become a puddle.

His eyes darted to where it had fallen. This was his only opportunity, his only way to defend himself. He knew it.

So did she.

Mason crawled on his elbows and knees toward the discarded weapon, threw a hand desperately at the handle sticking out of the puddle . . . only to have a boot fall upon it like a hammer to a nail. The palm of his hand splashed down into the puddle under the weight of her heel. He winced in pain and his eyes shut tight.

This is it, he thought, expecting a killing blow to follow.

It didn't.

He still drew breath, still heard the flat clap of rain.

"Mason?" he heard called from above.

Come on, already! Just get it over with. Let this be over.

"Mason?"

This time he recognized it as Rodriguez's voice and slowly, reluctantly, he opened his eyes. She was in the delicate process of climbing down the fire escape of the building next door to the hotel, stopping periodically to check on him. Finally she reached the street and crouched down next to him.

"Hey! You okay?" she asked.

"I dunno," he replied. "What happened?"

Rodriguez pointed to a spot behind them with a look of near disbelief. There, sprawled out on the blacktop, was the vampire, still and harmless. She didn't appear to be injured or conscious.

"You stunned her."

Mason's face twisted with confusion. "Huh?"

Rodriguez dipped her fingers into the puddle and made the sign of the cross, playfully flicking a bit of it at him. A smile, the first Mason had seen grace her face, spread far and wide until it reached his as well. Before he knew it they were laughing uncontrollably in the rain like a couple of drunks.

Soaked but steady, she stood and helped him to his feet. His hand ached, but had his attacker succeeded in stomping it into the ground, there would have been nothing left but flattened meat and shattered bone. They both stood over her body, sprawled out as though she were making a snow angel. Her eyes remained closed but her chest moved up and down, much more slowly than that of a human.

"What are we waiting for?" said Mason, and reached for the knife.

Rodriguez held up her hand. Thinking. "We're taking her with us."

"Alive?"

"Yep."

"Yeah, that didn't go so well last time. In case you forgot."

"I remember perfectly well, *cadet*. I was there." Whatever levity there had been was quickly rinsed away. "In case *you* forgot."

"Yes, ma'am. If you say so. But somehow I don't think just throwing her in the trunk is the best idea."

Just then Marge appeared at the top of the stairs. Shotgun in hand. Panting. Grumbled something about "goddamn suckheads." It was faint, but the sound of sirens could already be heard in the distance.

"Hey, Marge," said Rodriguez. "Got a hose we could borrow?"

Grim had only been asleep for about an hour when his phone began to vibrate. It was 2:00 a.m. No one ever calls at 2:00 a.m. with good news. He tapped the green button on the display and pressed it to his ear.

"Yes," he said groggily.

"It's Hirsch," said the voice on the other end.

Grim sat up immediately. His eyes were barely open, but his hands were already getting him dressed. "What's the problem, Major?"

"It's the boy. And Rodriguez."

His heart sank as he slipped on his glasses. "What about them?"

Hirsch uttered a single syllable, then said, "You'd better come down to the garage. You have to see this for yourself."

Grim hung up without another word, finished dressing, and took the elevator to bottom. When the doors opened, it was as if a fish hook caught his eyebrow and reeled it all the way in at the sight before him.

Mason and his lieutenant, surrounded by Hirsch and the Learys, all with guns pointed at them as they stood dripping wet behind a female vampire on her knees, glowering. Tied up with a rubber hose. Mason held the nozzle, pointed at their captive's head, and waved sheepishly.

Grim just stood there, baffled. After a few moments, he tucked one hand under his arm, placed the other in a fist beneath his chin, and took a deep breath.

"This had better be good."

THIRTY-SEVEN

TENSION, IT IS SAID, IS OFTEN THICK ENOUGH TO CUT WITH A knife. A chainsaw would have been needed to split that which filled the elevator.

Miggs and Hirsch had taken the vampire away while Grim escorted Mason to the fifth floor, followed closely by Rodriguez. They didn't say a word to each other the whole ride up. The elevator doors opened. Each step taken by Mason and Rodriguez brought wet squeaks against the linoleum of the otherwise quiet hallway. When they reached the infirmary, Grim finally broke the silence between them.

"Wait here," he said when Rodriguez tried to follow them through the door. She didn't seem shocked or hurt by this, simply planted her feet, placed her hands behind her back at attention and waited.

Grim shut the door behind them and went to the counter, gathering materials from the cabinet. He uncapped a bottle of rubbing alcohol and dabbed its contents onto a cotton ball.

"Are you all right?" Grim asked as he disinfected the cuts and scrapes on Mason's face.

The sting of the alcohol swabs only now made him aware of the wounds. The truth was that he felt more alive than he had in days. So why was Grim so worried? The disappointment in Grim's face was plain: Not only the disappointment but conflict, buzzing around his head like static. What admonishment could he bestow for following orders when they're given to you? Rodriguez had already made it clear that this would not fly.

"I dunno, am I?"

Mason winced and hissed as Grim took the hand in his own, testing it delicately with his thumb and forefinger.

"Bruised knuckles, but nothing looks broken." Grim unrolled a tensor bandage and wrapped it tightly around the hand. "Won't feel great, but it should be back to normal in a few days."

Mason nodded. Grim shook two white pills out of a bottle and handed them to him, along with a glass of water. They made eye contact for the first time. He opened his mouth to say something and stopped, letting out a barely audible breath instead.

"Just take those and get some rest. You're dismissed."

Down the hatch went the pills. Mason hopped off the bed as Grim opened the door to the hall for him. Rodriguez stood firm, exactly how she had been when the door closed with one exception— her damp hair was now tied back.

He looked at her—she didn't return the gaze—and made for the elevator, which thankfully was already there when he pressed the button with his good hand. When he reached his room on the third floor, he was met by Bossy, who meowed away, wondering where her dinner was.

Too tired and in far too much discomfort to do it properly, Mason peeled back the lid of the tin and plopped all of it into her dish. She immediately began munching away.

"I'm fine, thanks for asking," he said.

Undressing was no easy task with one hand, let alone with soaked clothes. He let everything fall to the floor with a slap and went to the bathroom for a towel. Once he had dried himself as best he could, Mason slid into bed and sank stiffly into the mattress.

Rain continued to pelt the windowpane. The tequila and adrenaline were beginning to wear off, and with them the dullness of the throb in his hand, sharpening now to a persistent pain in each bone. Considering the hand could have been mashed into jelly, he was grateful to be feeling anything at all.

Either from the fact that he was, as he believed, following the orders of the team's second-in-command or the blissfully generous swigs of the bottle (or both), Mason hadn't even considered that he might be in any trouble. And what was his excuse?

Rodriguez and I were drowning our sorrows, which somehow led to me getting wood, so when she told me to follow her, I did.

No matter now. The painkillers had begun to do their job, stealing him away from the burdens of consciousness. All he remembered of the next several hours was bed. Darkness. Pain. Both looking forward to and dreading what was to come.

At least this time he didn't dream.

THIRTY-EIGHT

MASON AWOKE AT A QUARTER TO SIX TO THE SOUND OF BOSSY scratching and digging in her litterbox. His hand didn't feel bad—but it didn't feel great, either. After dressing slower and much more awkwardly than he would have with two hands, he went downstairs.

The place was virtually empty. He could hear voices, but they were far off. Down below. Only one was nearby, and he didn't need any concentration to hear it. It was Diaz at the tail end of a phone call.

"A'ight, talk to you later . . . okay . . . bye." He ended the call and jerked his head at Mason. "What up, Mace?"

They bumped fists.

"The opposite of down, Dee."

"Aha, you think you slick, huh?"

"Just trying it out. What's going on?"

"Was just on my way to get you when I got a call."

"What for?"

"My ex just wanted to let me know our baby girl was feeling better. She came down with a cold, so—"

"Oh, I meant what were you coming to get me for?"

"Oh! Right."

"Sorry. I mean, that's great, of course. Glad to hear it."

"Thanks," said Diaz, tucking the phone away in his pocket. "We're interrogating the vamp we caught—or should I say, *you* caught. And Grim said you should be there."

"Okay . . . is this, like, an order?"

"Pretty much."

Without even realizing it, Mason's shoulders tensed. He grabbed hold of the wrist of his bad hand and began fidgeting.

"It's cool. Trust me. She's not going anywhere," Diaz reassured him.

Not that it mattered. They could have had a firing squad, an electric fence, and a pack of rabid dogs between them. It wouldn't have made him feel any safer.

Mason followed Diaz into the elevator and down they went.

"So, you've got a little girl?" Normally when nervous he went quiet, but right now it was the last thing he wanted.

"Yeah. Mya," said Diaz, and took out his phone. He pulled up a picture of a beautiful smiling baby lying on her back in a crib.

"Now *that's* a cute kid!"

"I know, right?"

"She in town?"

The elevator door opened to the garage, where they headed through the door which led to the tunnel.

"Naw, back in Miami with her mom. It's tough, but it's for the best, you know? This ain't no life for them."

"Do they know what you do?"

"Mya's not even a year yet. And Keisha . . ." Diaz laughed through his nose as he punched in the code for the door. "Told her I work for the Church."

Mason considered this for a moment. "Well . . . that's the truth. Kinda."

They made their way to Tactical to find Grim, Rodriguez, and

Father Coffey already there. For a split second he wondered where Irish was.

Mason was hesitant at first, but Grim reassured him that it was quite safe. They were surrounded by this-many-feet of concrete in every direction, behind this-many-inches-thick of glass, protections had been placed around the cell, et cetera, et cetera.

Slowly he tiptoed around the corner.

And there she was. The horrid thing from the night before, now confined to a cage of stone and glass.

She was hard to see in the dimly lit space, pacing back and forth through the cell, visibly agitated, like a captive tiger. Shadow seemed to follow her every move. It gave him the feeling that he was looking at both a person and an animal. A snake in a human suit. It made him fascinated and uneasy at the same time. It commanded an uncomfortable sense of unrest in the brain, a sort of vertigo with reality that what he beheld should not exist but did.

Every time he had laid eyes on one of her kind, he'd been overcome with fear and thus unable to properly study them. While not the same impossible white he'd seen in Novak, she was still very pale and dull. The lifeless pallor of a corpse. Ironically, her tattoos seemed more alive than the skin that bore them: a cackling skull that shook with laughter; a wreath of fire burning around a dragon; a smiling little girl in a baby-doll dress, holding a bloody knife in one hand and a severed head in the other that Mason could have sworn he saw blink.

There was one thing, though, that he certainly wasn't imagining: her eyes—her inhumanly glinting eyes, which had swelled to great black pits in the murk of her surroundings—were fixed on him.

He felt every bit of them.

As she continued to pace the length of the cell, Mason could see her scratching at her forearm in long, slow strokes. Thick red marks appeared beneath each fingernail, followed by drops of dark blood. Retreating to a corner at the back of the cell, a chill crept up his spine as she brought her forearm to her mouth and began to suckle at her own blood.

"She's hungry," said Father Coffey.

Grim just nodded.

Mason swallowed hard, his mouth dry as a bottle of ashes. "So what happens now?"

Grim cleared his throat. "First we feed her. Then we interrogate."

"Feed her?" said Mason. "What do you feed—?"

Just then the security door slid open and shut behind him, followed by mingled footsteps through the shooting range. Sarah entered carrying a baby pig, so pink it could have been born today, untouched by the world. Where they found a piglet in the city of Boston he couldn't imagine. Its ears flopped downward at either side of its head, little snorts coming from its twitching snout. Sweet and unsuspecting. Once it entered the cell bay, it began to fuss and squeal. Mason felt a twinge of sadness for the poor thing.

Sarah reached the cell door, struggling to keep her grip on the pig. Miggs and Diaz took up positions behind her, drew their sidearms, and aimed them at the door. Grim picked up a walkie-talkie and brought it to his mouth as it bleeped to life.

"Open cell two."

A loud click sounded as the door slid open. The piglet wailed its little heart out as Sarah shoved it through the opening and immediately stepped back. Miggs and Diaz stood at the ready, pistols trained on the door, until it slid closed and locked again. Mason had never heard sounds like this before—from a pig or any other living creature. Its shrieks echoing through the cell were hard on the heart as well as the ears. Running from one corner of the cell to the other, desperately hoping to find a way out, it sounded almost human.

The vampire stayed eerily still in her corner at the back right of the cell. Then, in one fell swoop, she shot clear across the distance between them and sank her fangs in, cutting off its cries. When it was drained, the vampire tossed the body—now little more than a pale husk—behind her, hitting the ground with a dull thud.

She stood before the glass, staring hard and cold. Noticeably less aggravated, she seemed almost calm now. A single drop of blood dangled from her chin.

"More," she rasped. So quiet, yet Mason felt every bone in his body rattle with it.

"Here's what's going to happen," Grim said. "We're going to come in. We're going to restrain you and then you're going to tell us where we can find your leader. If you behave, we'll feed you and you won't be harmed. If not, well, I think you know what will happen."

"You won't kill me." She spoke, yet her lips hardly moved. "You need me."

"What I *don't* need are injured team members, and believe me, I value their lives more than yours. What's it going to be?"

After a moment's contemplation, she took a few steps back, bowed her head, and stretched her arms out in the Jesus pose.

Grim raised his hand and held her there with an invisible force. Mason stood back in awe. Miggs and Yen went in and took up position on either side of their immobilized prisoner while Sarah stayed by the door.

Just then something caught Mason's eye: tiny sparks flecked off of Sarah's fingers as she rubbed them together like two pieces of flint.

Grim brought the fingers of his own hand together until they were touching, and as he did the vampire's arms pressed against her body.

Diaz entered carrying a pair of shackles, a muzzle, and something that looked like a thick rubber belt. He snapped the shackles, which were really just a single piece of metal that opened up to cuffs at either end. When they were securely around her wrists, they dropped to the floor with a *clunk* like a brick in a swimming pool, taking her hands with them. Diaz moistened his lips, stretched the piece of rubber apart with all his might, and proceeded to place it around her head.

Mason's breathing quickened as he felt the apprehension in Diaz. An image of the vampire lashing out and biting whichever hand was nearest flashed through his head, and he prayed that it was nothing more than the product of his paranoid mind.

Diaz brought the belt down below her nose, making sure to keep his hands at the sides of her head rather than in front of her mouth, and let it go. The belt squeezed firmly around her face, covering her mouth and every nasty little fang in it.

He checked his work, saw that the top hem was crooked, leaving a corner of her upper lip exposed.

Slowly he reached out.

He flicked at it quickly with one finger.

No change. Thin beads of sweat gathered on his brow.

He tried again. His finger grazed her lip enough to move it.

"Ah, fuck!" said Diaz, shaking his hand like it had been cut. He grabbed the belt with both index fingers and thumbs. It flipped up and finally covered her whole mouth. He then fixed the muzzle on her as quickly as he could and promptly left the cell with a sigh of relief.

"Did she bite you?" said Mason as he passed.

Diaz winced. "Naw, just touched the inside of her mouth."

"You okay?"

"Will be once I find me a shit-ton of Purell."

She didn't take her eyes off of Mason the entire time. Not until Grim himself finally entered the cell and stood between them.

"I'm afraid in all the excitement we seem to have skipped introductions. My name is Blake Grimshaw."

No response. No hum of muffled words beneath her gag.

"What are you called?"

. . .

"Angel," said Grim. She was responding, just not with her mouth. "Well, Angel, I'll be very honest with you. It's not often that we manage to capture one of your kind, and when we do they usually take their own life rather than endure captivity."

There was a longer quiet this time, leading Mason to believe she was saying something lengthy. Her eyes had narrowed to deadly slits.

"Yes, well, be that as it may, I'm at a bit of a loss as to how to proceed. So how about this?" He began circling her with wide, patient steps, past Miggs and Yen, who still had their weapons drawn and ready, prepared to fire at the first sign of aggression. "You tell us where to find your leader, and come dinnertime I'll see that you get some of the real thing. AB negative. The good stuff."

Her eyes lit up.

Grim clapped his hands together. "Splendid. I'm all ears."

Mason had no idea what she was saying, but whatever it was made Grim's expression sink and the light drain from his face.

"There's no need for that kind of language."

Her eyes narrowed to sly, mocking slits.

"Very well." Grim looked to Hirsch and flicked his fingers upward.

She turned a dial on the wall. The lights in the cell intensified to such a point that even Mason squinted.

Angel squirmed and writhed in place, her wrists still anchored to the floor by whatever invisible force held them. Muffled cries could be heard beneath the mask, loud enough that Mason realized another purpose of the rubber gag: without it her screams would surely be ear-piercing.

Miggs and Yen backed out of the room, keeping their pistols up until they were clear.

Grim crouched down next to her. "Hope you liked the pig." And then he casually strolled out, like a man walking through a park on a sunny day.

Mason saw the dead piglet behind her. Little eyes closed. Hardly any blood. It looked as though it might just be sleeping.

Then, suddenly, Grim stopped, turning abruptly back to the cell. He nodded and Hirsch killed the deathly white lights.

A few moments of silence passed. She gasped for air, her head facing the floor, eyes turned upward.

Grim seemed satisfied. "Thank you, Angel. You did the right thing."

No sound, but her whole body shook with laughter.

"Something amusing?" asked Grim.

Mason wasn't sure what she said, but it was enough that he felt a spike of anxiety in him. Grim didn't let it show, of course, and signaled for everyone to clear out. Everyone but Hirsch, that is, who stayed behind, watching her intently.

"Where to?" Rodriguez asked.

"Sixteen oh one Fifty-fifth Street. It's an abandoned dive bar in Hyde Park. Or so she says."

"We'll check it out."

As Mason moved quickly through the shooting range he saw Miggs and Yen returning their rifles to the weapons locker. He followed after Grim, who had disappeared ahead of them. To his annoyance, he found Sarah taking her time climbing the stairs to the parking garage.

"Sorry, can I sneak past you?" Mason said, angling to get by.

She stopped dead halfway up and gave him a sideward glance. "No."

Mason huffed with frustration. "Okay." He stayed put, only resuming the climb once the gap between them had grown.

"And stop looking at my ass."

"What? I wasn't!"

"Really? Why not?" said Sarah, disappearing around the corner.

"Oh my god, whatever." He hurried up the stairs, taking them two at a time, until he had reached the top. Sarah kissed the air and let out a giggle as he passed. He pretended not to notice.

Relieved, Mason caught up with Grim by the elevator.

"Uh, Grim?" he said, timid as a mouse. "I mean, captain. I mean . . . sir?"

Grim turned on his heel and faced him, his expression blank.

"Can we talk?"

"Certainly," said Grim. He didn't move.

"Oh, right here?"

"Something wrong with here?"

"I . . . guess not." A slight break in his voice. "So . . . I guess the first thing I ought to say is that I'm sorry."

"Whatever for?"

"Well, bringing a vampire here, for one. We honestly thought that's what you would have wanted since the other one—Bartok, was it?—he didn't quite work out, if you know what I mean, and . . . of course you do. Stupid. And . . . it wasn't her fault or anything, but Rodriguez was upset and she said—"

Grim held up a hand for him to stop. "I think I know why you did what you did."

Mason froze, his eyes wide. "You do?"

Grim closed his eyes and nodded. "She told me everything. That she ordered you to accompany her to the safehouse and while technically she should have cleared that with me, as lieutenant now she does have that authority."

"Oh," Mason said, not quite sure how to continue. *Lieutenant? Right. I guess she would be now, wouldn't she?* But second-in-charge or not, that still wasn't how things went. Not exactly. "Well, good then. I mean, if I knew we'd run into trouble, I doubt I would have gone."

"I know it's not easy, Mason, but you're going to have to get used to being around them sooner or later. And believe me, there are worse things than vampires."

"Worse?" A wave of nausea followed by an unclean shadow passed through him.

"Far worse."

THIRTY-NINE

With most of the team out following up on Angel's lead, the building was relatively quiet. Even with the absence of most of its residents, taking their footsteps, heartbeats, and voices with them, there were still sounds. The soft buzz of electricity. The biting wind passing through leaves of the plants on the roof.

He did as Grim had instructed and isolated a single sound in the din. First the traffic. As he did it grew louder, while everything else diminished. Then he chose the sound of pigeons. Their cooing was so clear he could have had a pair perched on his shoulders.

"*Sorry, Ephraim,*" came a boxed echo from somewhere below. "*I can't just leave the embassy.*" It was Hirsch talking on the phone, still standing guard in the holding cells. "*I wish I could, but it's not that easy . . . I know, I miss you too. How's Mother?*"

Even though she was speaking Hebrew, he understood everything she was saying. She began to sob, very quietly so as not to let whoever was on the other end hear. But Mason heard. And *that* he didn't need a translation for. He tuned her out, giving her privacy.

Nothing from the cell itself. He heard things outside of it but couldn't penetrate beyond whatever barrier surrounded it.

The stillness of the chapterhouse suddenly broke—and with it, his concentration—disturbed by the distant rumblings of engines, followed by the grating of metal on metal as the garage door opened. Doors opening and slamming shut.

The team had returned.

He tried to swallow the lump in his throat, but it resurfaced immediately.

The elevator kicked into gear, going down and then back up, carrying someone up to his floor.

. . . fucking waste of time! was all he caught from Sarah's momentarily unguarded mind as the stomp of her boots passed his room and then the door to her room at the end of the hall slammed shut.

I wonder what happened, he thought, debating whether to go investigate or not.

Elsewhere, he caught the sound of a ringtone as someone got a call. It was Grim.

"—*Coffey say?*" He found Rodriguez's voice and focused on it, but not too hard so others could get through.

"*That was the Bishop, actually.*" The tearing of Velcro straps as Grim removed his Kevlar vest. "*I told him what we found—or* didn't *find, I should say. He said, and I quote, 'Perhaps your lieutenant had the right idea when she decided to put the boy to work.'* "

Even tempered by the warm timbre of the voice that spoke them, Strauss's words made his jaw clench.

Rodriguez said nothing at first, just a series of short beginnings of sentences she would never finish. "*I . . . that's not . . . but . . .*" And then, finally: "*He wants him to link with the vampire?!*"

"*Either that or we try the more aggressive approach on her.*"

"*Pfft! That won't get us anywhere.*"

Mason waited with bated breath.

"*No, it won't. And I'm afraid he has a point. We need to use every tool at our dispos—*"

Mason shook himself out of it and shot up from the bed. He started for the bathroom, stopped, pivoted, and headed back toward the bed. Then back to the bathroom. Back to the bed. Bathroom. Back and forth.

"Okay, calm down," he said to himself as he paced the room.

Grim's choice of words notwithstanding, he knew what he meant. Even agreed with him. That wasn't what bothered him. Had it been Grim's idea, Mason likely wouldn't have had a problem with it. Though he hadn't known him long, Grim was obviously not the type to recklessly or needlessly put anyone in danger. But there was something about it coming from the Bishop. He couldn't help but wonder if every time Grim had asked something of him it was nothing more than orders being passed down the chain of command.

Even that wasn't the issue, not really. It meant that the time had come for him to get up close and disgustingly personal with a vampire. And if he didn't like some of the things he'd experienced while reliving the lives of others, what rotten horrors awaited in hers?

The *ping* of the elevator, and footsteps sounded from the hall. Mason scurried about frantically for a few seconds, sat at the desk, then, as the inevitable knock finally came, he shot up from the chair, sending it swinging around in lazy circles.

"Come in," he answered.

The door opened. "Mason," said Grim, his face already apologetic.

"Hi. I was just, uh, doing the . . . you know . . ." *Snap, snap*, went his fingers. "But anyway, what's up? What happened? Did you find Novak?"

"No." Grim crossed his arms and rested a shoulder against the doorframe. "No, we didn't. The bar was empty. Rundown and abandoned, as it has been for ages. Perfect place, but alas, nothing to be found."

"Then she lied to us."

"It's what they do, I'm afraid," Grim said with a shrug, clearly frustrated. "Although there is the chance that she was telling the truth and Novak just wasn't foolish enough to remain there. Either way, it gets us no nearer to finding him."

"So what now?" said Mason, doing his best to feign ignorance.

"Ah. Well." Grim stared off toward the window, though he wasn't really looking at it. "How would you feel about trying your gift on our prisoner?"

"I dunno. How *should* I feel about it?"

"Nervous. Scared. Apprehensive. All of the above."

"Your other pep talks were better."

"If it were my first choice, I'd have mentioned it well before now. But the truth is that we don't have many options, and if she *was* lying to us, we need to know."

"Will it even work on her?"

"So far as I know, it's never been tried before. We're in untrod territory now."

"Undiscovered country."

"Right you are."

Mason thought about it some more, though he had already made up his mind.

"She'd be restrained," Grim added. "Under heavy guard. We'll even sedate her."

Mason cocked an eyebrow. "How do you sedate a vampire?"

"Snake venom."

"Really?"

"Really. Regular tranquilizers don't even scratch the surface, so we need something with more of a bite. So to speak."

"Hardy-har-har."

"What do you say?"

"I say . . . what are we waiting for?"

"Very good." Grim straightened and made to leave. "Whenever you're ready."

Mason spent the next twenty minutes meditating, calming his nerves, before returning to the holding cells. He found Angel still bound and gagged and Rodriguez preparing a syringe, filling it with a milky yellow fluid.

He approached. "Hey."

"Hey," she said back.

Okay, that's a start . . . what next?

"Looks like we caught us a live one, huh?"

It was a dumb thing to say, he knew that. But he didn't have anything better.

"Mm-hmm," she said, pulling the needle from the bottle. "Look . . . last night I was upset and a little drunk, and may have said some things that I probably shouldn't have. So I'd appreciate if you kept it just between us."

"I don't know what you're talking about." He offered a wink and the tiny twitch of a smile.

To Mason's pleasant surprise, she winked back. "You're all right, chico."

"You too . . . chica?" His voice curled into a question mark.

"Don't push it," said Rodriguez, brandishing the needle tip at him.

"Hey, watch where you stick that thing."

"That's what he said," said Sarah, standing nearby, looking pleased with herself.

Rodriguez entered the cell and came around Angel's right side, studying her white skin. Once she found what she was looking for, she slipped the needle into a dark vein on the side of her neck and pumped the contents in. Angel's eyelids fluttered and her eyes rolled up as if they were trying to get a look at the inside of her skull.

"If anything happens, you know what to do," Grim said to Sarah.

She offered a little salute, the tips of black-nailed fingers flicking away from her forehead. "No sweat, Joan Jett."

Grim turned to Mason and gestured for him to enter. He could feel his heartbeat in his ears. Before he crossed the threshold of the cell, without really meaning anything by it, he crossed himself.

One foot in front of the other, he stepped inside.

And there was that same sickening miasma of fear he'd felt before in the presence of one of these things. It struck him immediately once past the threshold of the cell. The very air prickled at him from all sides and as both his feet touched down he swooned momentarily, feeling like he might pass out. It passed and everything came back into focus, taking no more time than when an elevator halts a little too fast.

He stepped right up to her, close enough that he could have spat in her face if he wanted. "Not so tough now, are you?" Mason took a deep breath and steadied himself, his fingers trembling as they drew nearer and nearer to the white skin before him.

Angel's eyes bored upward, making imaginary cuts into him, fantasizing about every drop of blood.

Good, he thought. Let her. With the dead, he had to focus on whoever they had been while alive; with an object, emotion was the key, and he had not gotten the chance to try it on someone living. But with vampires, perhaps this was the key right here. Fury and thirst.

His skin touched hers and the spark he was coming to know so well burst forth.

It was different this time.

Ragged.

Chaotic.

Instead of a single stream of consciousness, fragments of her memories whirled around in the dark like a hail of shattered glass.

It starts with crying, as it always does, only this time it doesn't stop—tears on the back of her hand while Mama and Daddy fight, more when he hits her. Hard tears, the kind that leave a stain on the skin. He leaves and doesn't even look at her. Doesn't even say goodbye. Mama doesn't cry though. "What are you looking at?" she shouts, and slams the door. She cries in the bathroom when the other kids call her fat. She cries a little—only a little—when Tommy, the older boy, convinces her to put his thing in her mouth. She doesn't want to . . . but he told her she was pretty. "Raylene Jeffries, get your pimply ass in here!" She leaves Billy, his sweet lips still fresh on hers. "This instant!" She's not fast enough and feels the swat of Granny's hand on the back of her head as she enters the trailer. "Get in there!" No, not the prayer closet! "I'll not have you sluttin' around with boys as long as you're in my care. Now get!" The door slams. She's forced to kneel on a broomstick. It's dark, but the candles burn. Always burn for Jesus. "I can't hear you, girl!" She begins to pray. "Hail Mary, full of grace, the Lord is with thee . . . pray for us sinners, now and at the hour of our death . . ." When Granny lets her out, her knees are so bruised she can't even walk and so she crawls to her room. Granny catches her sneaking back in, sitting there in her chair, in the dark. She didn't know an old woman could hit that hard. She tastes blood. Granny sends her to Reverend Powell. He's old but not bad-looking, speaks in a genteel Southern tongue with an undercurrent of righteousness. He says that it's not too late, that he can help her. He can save her soul and redeem her wicked ways. He leads her to the baptistry. He tells her to undress. She does. Ribs showing through her skin to a congregation that isn't there. He lowers her gently into the holy water. Cold but nice. He places his clothes next to hers and joins her in the water. His hands go all over. He tells her there's no joy in this, that it's his duty, the bathing of the young, cleansing the sin from her body. She thanks him. "And in return, you'll cleanse me of mine." He said she was pretty too. She's late. She tries to tell Granny whose baby it really is and gets put in the prayer closet again for telling lies. For good. No food. No water. Not even a bucket. Caked in her own filth, she breaks out of the closet with strength she didn't know she had. The door hits Granny in the face and she hears the sound of her hitting the trailer floor. She doesn't look back. She just keeps on running. She hitchhikes her way out of Kansas. Goes by Rachel now. Raylene is dead. Like the baby. She waitresses at a crappy truckstop diner on I-70. The pay is shit. The customers are the kind of trash even she looks down her nose at. She makes her way to Dallas. "How old are you, kid?" asks Al. "Eighteen," she says. "Eighteen or 'eighteen'?" He flicks his fingers twice to make air quotes. She shrugs. "Look, I won't get you in trouble. I promise." She starts unzipping his pants. "I'll be good." He puts his hand on the back of her head. "All right, angel. All right. I'll give you a shot. In fact, I think that's what we'll call you . . ." She learns from a spunky little rougette called Trixie. How to dance. How to work a room. How to hide the real her and keep it safe. "That's just for you, darlin'. That's the one part you can't let them see." It's weird at first, showing parts of her body that only she and the Lord know about to a room full of men, but at least the tips are better and the pervs cheer when she dances. A part of her secretly likes it. (The attention, at least.) "You're my Angel, aren't you, baby?" says Tony. "Fuck yeah, I am." She grinds her meagre booty into his lap as he slips something gently into her unholiest of holies. She reaches down and fishes out a small vial of white powder. "Whoa, whoa," she says to a customer whose hands begin to wander. She could smell the drink on him the second he walked up to her waving a wad of fifties. He's had too much. Way too much. "Hands off the merchandise, m'kay?" He doesn't listen. Rough hands graze her thighs and begin to curve inward. "I said cut it out, asshole!" She slaps his hands away. The backs of her arms bristle with goosebumps. Before she can even turn around, he grabs her by the waist and pulls her back into him. "You little bitch! I paid for you. You're mine!" She pries his hands loose and elbows him in the chest. He teeters backward and lands hard on his ass. "Raoul!" she shouts, and flees the room. Raoul barrels in like a gorilla on the warpath. She only sees a blink of the drunk man as the curtain billows away. Eyes wide. Hand over his heart. Gasping for breath. Her hands steeple in front of her face as she realizes what she's done. This is bad! Raoul gets on his radio. "We need you down here." She sits in Al's office, trembling. Wet eyes. Knows what's coming. "We'll cover for you, say he just collapsed . . . but you can't be here when the cops arrive." He and Raoul stare at her, expressionless. "Sorry, Angel," He almost seems sorry, but there's no love in his voice as he hands her the envelope, a small stack of hundreds inside. "You're done." Even she couldn't disagree with that. Some shithole honkytonk. Neon lighting the puddles of the cracked pavement. The money was *gone weeks ago. She hangs by the row of motorcycles outside, dressed in what clothes she has. Tube top. Tight jeans. Heels. Usually the crank bikers are horny as hell when they come in from the road. But tonight no one's biting. She follows a stocky guy with a trucker cap and a horseshoe mustache as he leaves the bar. "Lookin' for a date, honey?" she says half-heartedly. His face lights up. "Well, well! And what's yer name, darlin'?" She flicks her hair. "Whatever you want it to be." Doesn't matter anymore. "Mmm, mmm." He looks her up and down. "Ya know who you remind me of with yer dark hair and baby-blue eyes like that? Lynda Carter. Ya know Lynda Carter?" She has no idea. "Sure. Whatever you want." He's practically licking his chops. "Well, hot dog! Let's git 'er done then." They get in his truck and drive down the road a piece until they find a secluded spot. There's something off about him. She can feel it. It's not in what he says or what he does. It's his eyes. He parks the truck and is all over her in an instant. "M'kay, slow down there, big boy. It's twenty to suck, fifty to f—" He puts his hand over her mouth.*

She kicks and screams and cries "NO!" into his palm. No one hears her. She doesn't even see the other hand as it starts tearing off her clothes.

This wasn't the first time . . . but she's pretty sure it will be the last.

She's already letting go . . .

Crunch!

Quiet but clear. The John gets off her and she collapses to the ground, gasping for air. A pale boy with hair the color of grimy pennies is sitting on the hood of the truck, casually cross-legged. Eating popcorn.

"Sorry," he says with a dismissive wave. "How rude of me."

"Who the hell are you?!"

The red-haired one stuffs a handful in his mouth and says, "Just a spectator. Pay me no mind. Please, continue."

The John turns to flee . . . and runs straight into a blonde with violet glasses and the same ghastly white skin. She is smiling. "Howdy, pardner. How 'bout ridin' me instead?" He swings at her. She doesn't even bother to block it. Her fangs are in his fat neck before his fist can even land a blow.

Gentle fingers touch her chin. Cold fingers. He locks eyes with her.

"Please, just make it quick."

"Is that really what you want? Or would you turn your back on God forever more, as He has turned His back on you? Would you be a predator of predators, put fear and fury back into the night where it belongs, and make both sheep and shepherd alike tremble before you? If you would drink rather than die, speak now."

"I will."

A trickle of blood appears from his wrist, dripping down into her open mouth. An unholy communion. It slithers through her veins. Sizzles and consumes her from the inside out, burning away the mortal cells and replacing her living body with a damned one.

She breaks through the hail of broken memories . . .

. . . and lunges for him with her claws out . . .

Mason didn't even have time to wonder how her restraints were gone and her mouth unmuzzled. Next thing he knew, Angel was on top of him. He was only vaguely aware of shouts and the sound of scraping against concrete before the room spun around at an incredible rate. He resisted, but it did no good.

"Gotcha!"

She held him tight by a fistful of his hair. Her other hand held a sharp fingernail to his throat as she backed them up against the wall.

He could feel her strength. Her thirst. He'd never felt anything like it.

"Drop him, bitch!" It was Miggs, the business end of an automatic weapon aimed at them both. "We don't want to shoot him, but we will if it means keeping him out of your hands."

"See? See?!" She tugged his hair, forcing his head back to look at the others, all pointing their guns at them both. "They would rather kill you than let you go. You're nothing to them. You're not their

Savior. You're their *mascot*. You freak. You weakling. You . . . *Jew Boy*." She *hissssed* into his ear and licked his cheek.

The fire, that raging, untamed fire, erupted from with him like a volcano. He broke free of her steel grip and with a speed he didn't know he possessed, swooped down and grabbed her by the ankle.

Angel howled with murderous rage.

Swinging down over his head, he hammered her into the cement floor with all his might. Her body split outward with a splat of blood and viscera in every direction.

Whatever secrets she held were now on display for all to see, but forever unreachable.

There was barely enough time to realize that her muzzle and shackle had mysteriously reappeared before all of her ignited with orange flame.

"Sarah!"

"You said if anything happens . . ."

Transfixed by the bouquet of burning, mangled flesh, Mason felt himself being rushed out of the cell. Seconds later his view of it was from the other side of the glass again. The vampire's remains burned away until there was nothing left but a charred black stain on the cell floor. Considering what she had done to the poor boy at the safe-house, he saw a sense of poetic justice in it.

Grim angled him around to make eye contact. "Mason? Mason, can you hear me?"

"How?"

"How what?" said Grim, confused.

"How did she get free?"

Grim raised an eyebrow high enough that it crested the frame of his glasses. "She didn't get free, Mason. You slammed her into the floor with no provocation."

No, he thought. *That's not what happened.*

Mason explained while Angel's remains were carefully gathered up into bags and cleaned off the walls and floor of the cell. Everything he saw, a wicked trick of her mind on his. He still reeled with every chaotic twist and turn, every lurid detail, even if only half glimpsed, making him nauseous as if he had just gotten off the most perilous of roller coasters. One he had no intention of ever riding again.

Grim checked him out upstairs. He could see that trips to the infirmary were going to be a regular thing. Aside from a headache, he was fine. Physically, anyway.

But that grip, that iron-tight grip she'd had on his hair . . . he could still feel it.

Once back in his room, he went straight to the bathroom and began frantically rummaging through the cupboard under the sink until he found what he was looking for. He removed the guard, clicked on the electric clippers, and began mowing strips through the field of hair, watching his reflection change before his eyes as he proceeded to push the whirring blades across his scalp. And as he did, he was reminded of something he had read in the Book of Job.

Then Job arose, and rent his mantle, and shaved his head. He fell down upon the ground and worshipped.

FORTY

THE NEXT MORNING, AT 4:30 A.M., RODRIGUEZ AWOKE TO knocking at her door. The bright light of her phone temporarily blinded her before readjusting to the dark. Even for an early riser, this was pushing it.

Knocking again. Not pounding, just loud and persistent.

She hoisted herself out of bed, cursing in rapid-fire Spanish at whoever was on the other side of the door, and flung it open.

There stood Mason, dressed in his running clothes, his hair completely shorn.

"I'm ready."

Act III:
My Thoughts Be Bloody

FORTY-ONE

I'm watching people from my window. Dressed in
costumes. Laughing. Now and then someone jumps
out and yells "Boo!" Parents trick-or-treating
with their children, probably remembering when
their parents took them out on the same night
many years ago. The one night of the year when
children are actually encouraged to take candy
from strangers. I keep thinking about the first
Halloween after Julie and Dale and I became
friends. I went as Marty McFly, Dale as Doc
Brown, and Julie--while I tried to convince her
she should be Jennifer--wanted to be the DeLorean
of all things, so we wrapped her in tinfoil and
made a flux capacitor out of some LED wire and an
old fuse box. We carved a pumpkin from Rose's
garden while she made a cake. It was chocolate

324

with gummy worms and bugs baked into it. We must
have cleared the whole town out of candy, because
we went from one end to the other. When we were
done, we went back to Julie's house and watched
horror movies till dawn. It's one of the happiest
memories I have. And now

Mason's hand stopped moving. His eyes darted to what he believed to
be the first of a flurry of snowflakes, but then he saw it was only the
last remaining leaf falling from a nearby tree. He breathed a sigh of
relief at this. Snow on Halloween was just wrong. But it wouldn't be
long now.

It got dark a lot sooner now. Colder. Not even six o'clock and
already night had fallen. Foggy, too—far more than he had seen
during his time here. A chill had crept into him. He reached behind
to the hoodie resting on the back of his chair, stuck his arms through
the sleeves, and zipped it up.

In truth, he couldn't see any trick-or-treaters from up here. He
had seen them earlier while passing through leaf-covered Beacon Hill
and the image had become part of the tapestry he was weaving
through the words in his journal.

Just then, however, he did begin to see people dressed in costume.
More than expected, though not many kids. Mostly dressed in old-
fashioned clothes from different time periods. In fact, they all were.
No Draculas or Frankensteins. No pirates, evil clowns, or Batmen.
Not a single witch, slutty nurse, or Lady Gaga. Instead there were
men in frock coats, three-point hats, and wigs; ladies wearing long
gowns and bonnets; some even in animal skins and eagle-feather
headdresses.

"That's odd," Mason said to himself, wondering if there could
have been a war reenactment or something taking place today.

Book and pen in hand, he stood to get a better look. Despite
appearing solid, their lower halves faded toward the ground, disap-

pearing to invisible at the feet. As intangible as a reflection in a pane of glass. Slow—languid, even—appearing for only a moment or two. Transparent skin showing cold bones beneath. Confused by their surroundings, seeing a world they didn't recognize.

A large black ink stain bloomed where the pen in his hand had been resting. Mason closed the journal for now and placed the pen on top of it.

He rubbed his hand, which still ached a bit from when it had almost been crushed beneath Angel's boot. Apparently one of his knuckle bones had been chipped and the only remedy was time. Bossy had tucked herself between his feet, purring hard enough for him to feel it in his ankles. He had finished training for the day and decided to take some time for himself before tonight.

After recent events, he really didn't feel like celebrating much of anything this year. There had still been no sign of Rose's body. Or Julie's. Grim said it was unlikely at this point, that and they were exceptionally skilled at making corpses disappear. Just the thought of it made his heart rot from the inside out.

It was hard to believe that nearly two months had passed, simultaneously seeming longer and shorter. Time was funny that way. And in that time, he got his shit together.

Every waking minute, every ounce of energy Mason had, he put into training. He grew focused. Determined. Edging on obsession, though that didn't matter. As far as he was concerned, there was training and nothing else. Amazing what can happen when one wants a change and puts the work into it. It was something else, though, as well, a fact he wouldn't let himself forget: it was a matter of survival. There was no other choice.

Every day he woke early and did twenty push-ups and crunches, ready to go before Rodriguez even came to collect him. Every day he could run farther and faster. Now he actually looked forward to it. It helped tone his body and clear his mind. Every weight he lifted felt lighter. He kept his hair nice and short (nothing for anyone to grab at). His diet had undergone a complete overhaul, which Rodriguez said was by far the most important part of getting in shape.

There was something about her he had really come to admire, a vigor that compelled him to push himself harder. She exuded the kind of strength and confidence he not only admired but aspired to. There was a comfort in her routine. Stability. A foundation he greatly needed. And of course there were other things he had come to notice. The way she always kept her hair in a single braid over her shoulder. The way she closed her eyes with each sip of Spanish coffee as if reliving her first. How she smelled like fresh rain.

Unfortunately, he rarely saw Rodriguez anymore. The demands of being second-in-command meant she had little time to train him. That duty now fell upon her replacement as sergeant, none other than her twin brother, Miggs.

There was nothing obvious to tell Mason that Miggs didn't like him. But then it usually didn't take much. Each disapproving look, each admonishment when he got something wrong (or lack of encouragement when he got something right), things which he only noticed due to the stark contrast of the other team members. There was definitely something different about Miggs. He didn't have the gift like the rest of them—trained to guard his thoughts like them, but lacking the unique resonance they possessed.

Rodriguez had not gone easy on him, per se. But Miggs seemed almost enthusiastic in his regimen, choosing particularly grueling exercises that inflicted the maximum amount of pain. Burpees. Flutter kicks. Three-minute planks. Five-mile runs.

But Mason didn't let it show. Instead of everything he wanted to say or do, he channeled his frustration and used it to mold himself. As a result, the soft parts of his body were already growing tighter. His muscles were constantly sore, but in a good way. And it was beginning to show.

No pain, no gain, right? And there was plenty of pain to work with.

If there was one area in which he was still lacking, it was the nonphysical side of things. Some feats were massively difficult for him to achieve while others took no effort at all. He didn't have to try to hear the many voices around him, but filtering them out was much more difficult. Channeling his thoughts in order to communicate with Grim was not hard, but containing them took time, more so to keep them contained once he had. And as for *moving* things with his mind —a few days ago he had managed to move a quarter about an inch across the table, but that was it.

As Grim often reminded him, though, patience was key. He suggested some mental exercises that would help flex these abilities. Playing chess with himself without knowing his own moves. Trying to picture a color that didn't already exist. Refusing to imagine certain things Grim would mention over and over to try and distract him, like a lemon or a carousel. Or thinking about absolutely nothing at all while meditating, which he often found hardest of all.

In a reversal of Matthew 26:41, the flesh was willing but the spirit was weak. Or perhaps not weak but definitely stubborn, at times seeming to have a mind all its own. Alive as he was alive. Whatever he reached for, it reached back, joining like two drops of water into one.

Grim had also been schooling him on some lesser, but no less important, powers of observation. Like being able to tell from subtle body cues when someone was about to make a move, an action he found paired with a scent of burning ozone that was the firing of neurons. Or the facial tics someone showed when lying, which he discovered was signaled by the burning-hair smell he had caught from Bishop Strauss when he had welcomed him oh so sincerely. It was like learning to spot someone's tell when playing cards, and he was getting quite good at it.

The week after he'd arrived in the city, he and Grim did finally get around to seeing more of Boston. They walked along the Charles, strolled through the Commons. Saw parks with statues and fountains and weeping willows. Neighborhoods of brownstones, gardens surrounded with iron fencing, and trees with leaves that had just begun to show the slightest of copper wrinkles in their green skin. And with that came his first real exposure to the minds of the so-called normal people.

Reading people's minds was a strange sensation, to say the least. Nowhere near as desirable as it may seem in theory. We think it would make us privy to some grand insight into the psyche of others, glean valuable information from them, tell us their secrets, maybe help us understand them and in the process ourselves. So far he'd found that, more often than not, people spent their time wondering if anyone had seen them pick their nose. The same part of a song they had heard earlier playing over and over. Trying to remember if they had forgotten to do something. Keys. Phones. Where they parked. Thinking about that person they shouldn't be thinking about. Guilty fantasies. Wayward memories. And a thousand other things that occur in daily life. And beneath those stray bits that hovered at the surface, a never-ending current of raw, rambling thoughts and emotions all jumbled together into a chaotic mess in which even the clearest of notes was hard to detect.

This was what he got just from passing people on the street. What he might find if he focused his will, he was afraid to discover. Occasionally in the surface thoughts, as Grim called them, he caught secrets. Hidden things a person would barely let themselves think of lest it consume them. While on the other hand, some reveled in them.

And then there were those who were truly hard to be near. The ones whose thoughts smelled like gasoline, who would find some nice quiet corner of the world to haunt after they died. Mason had dwelled so much on the blood-drinking type that he had almost forgotten how evil a plain old human being could be. He asked about them one day after catching the image of a dead boy's face in the mind of an old man waiting for a bus. Didn't even have to try. He just sat there thinking about it, fantasizing, relishing the things he had done to the boy. He was young—far too young—and the old man kept his underwear beneath a loose floorboard in his house . . . along with all the others.

Grim simply said they were "not a part of our mission." Knowing how much worse there was out there, Mason decided not to press the issue, but he didn't like that answer. Not one bit.

Is this it? Is this who we're protecting? Does no one stop to admire the changing color of the leaves or a bright full moon? Do any of them hope that the human race will continue to mature and thrive in the centuries to come, avert disaster, and make it to the stars and beyond? Does anyone else wonder what other people are thinking? Does no one else care?

"Does anyone else talk to themselves when they thought no one was around?" he asked himself.

"Probably not," he answered himself.

When Mason wasn't training, he spent most of his time reading. Which was nothing new. What *was* new was that he was branching out beyond the realm of fiction to the scripture of the Holy Order of Militia Dei. He had practically speedread through their Bible, taking particular interest in the Testimony of Sir Richard. It went on to detail how he'd managed to rescue Philip during the Siege of Acre. How the Grand Master had believed their defeat to be the work of the Devil and commanded Richard to form a fellowship of knights who held a similar belief and to then seek out the dark forces that worked against them. This led to many missions across Europe in the decade that followed, most of which were too numerous to print in their entirety (though Grim said he could find transcripts of them in their database). Following the Inception of Saint Philip, Sir Richard was excommunicated— by the Pope himself, no less—from the Knights Templar after swearing fealty to his former squire-turned-savior. Mason thought it seemed like a shabby reward for a lifetime of service and, heresy or not, revelation in light of his discovery. But considering the times, Richard had been fortunate not to have been burned at the stake. Following his excommunication he sailed north and went into exile, continuing his work with St. Philip in purging evil from Christendom. That led to the Red September, a time of black skies, battles that lasted for days at a time, and blood raining down from above.

That part Mason remembered clearly because it had reminded him to water Rose's African violet. He went to the windowsill and poured a bit of water into the pot . . . and next thing he knew, he was bawling. Either because he had been reminded of her, or because everything about her was just a memory now, or because he was already starting to forget what it was like to have her in his life, or all of the above. It was the first time of many. He would be going about his day, and then suddenly, sometimes for no real reason at all, he would be in tears. Then he would be fine again.

And that was how things went.

As for Novak, there had not been much to report . . . but not nothing.

Two weeks ago Mason had been reading quietly in his room just after dark. A pretty average day, as the new status quo went. One of very few nights he had opted simply to relax and not study after training. All he wanted to do was read.

Scanning through his books, still very aware of the fact that *Hamlet* was missing, he felt like reading something new. He flipped open one he had been meaning to read for a while now, *The Curious Incident of the Dog in the Night-Time*. It started off interestingly enough—with Chapter 2, no less, each chapter numbered with prime integers.

Lying in bed, Bossy curled up near him, as had become her custom. He remembered clearly having just taken a bite of peanut butter toast.

He stopped chewing—so faint at first—to hear a sad little jingle somewhere out in the night.

Then louder.

It was music. "Little Brown Jug," if he wasn't mistaken. Lurching closer with every electric note.

He got out of bed and looked outside. A pair of headlights appeared attached to a hulking frame on the dark road outside. An ice cream truck, rolling languidly into view so slowly that it was hard to believe.

Hirsch had gone to carefully approach the truck.

She found it empty. Appearing very much that it had just tiptoed over on its own. On the driver's seat, a finger. A middle finger. Later identified as belonging to a recently deceased ice cream man. Just Novak's rotten little way of saying "Hi...

"Haven't forgotten about you."

FORTY-TWO

THERE WAS A KNOCK AT HIS DOOR. HE COULD SENSE WHO IT WAS even before opening it.

"You raaaang?" said Mason, assuming his best Lurch.

"Goood evening," Grim replied in his most ominous Alfred Hitchcock, helped by the fact that he wore a similar black suit and tie. "In a merry mood today, are we, Mister Cole?"

Mason gave a whimsical shrug. "You know, Halloween and all that."

"May I?"

"You may," said Mason with a sweeping gesture.

Grim took two wide steps into the room and stood with both arms clasped behind his back. There was something closed in his mind though, besides the usual. Some tiny shrouded corner so that Mason wouldn't see what was in it.

"What brings you to my humble abode?"

"How do you feel about early birthday gifts?"

Not at all what Mason was expecting, especially since his birthday was still just under a month away.

"I, um, guess I would have to say . . . I'm pro them? In favor?"

Grim held both hands in front of him, clenched into fists. "Pick one."

Mason chose the left first.

Grim turned it over and opened it to reveal an empty hand.

Mason chose the right.

Grim turned the other fist over, and suddenly an object appeared cradled between the two. All that was missing was a puff of smoke. "Trick or treat," he said with a coy grin.

He held the object out toward Mason. A katana. Old and beaten, sheathed in a visibly worn but beautiful blackwood.

"How did you do that?"

"I was holding it the whole time. I just tricked your mind into seeing something else."

"I *knew* something was off."

"If you hadn't I'd be disappointed. Though it will be a while still before you're able to see through such an illusion, and longer before you can recreate it."

Mason pulled the hilt and sheath apart, revealing a winter-sharp steel blade, polished to gleaming perfection.

"What did I do to deserve this?"

Grim cocked his head slightly. "Does one need to deserve a gift?"

"Depends on the gift, I guess."

"Well, if you need a reason, let it be that this sword belonged to Will Graves. It was one of very few things recovered from the wreckage of the Great Quake."

"I guess that makes it another survivor."

"In a way, I suppose it does. It was passed down from one member of the Graves family to the next for generations. I decided I'd pass it on to you when the time was right."

Mason's whole face brightened. "Does this mean I'll be needing it for training?"

Grim nodded. "We start tomorrow."

"I don't know what to say." Mason gave the sword a flourish and winced at the pain in his knuckle. "Thank you . . ." He trailed off, lost in loss, the inevitable ache of remembrance that came with it. Losing one person was hard enough, never mind several. At first it didn't feel real. But the more time passed, the harder the truth hit.

"Everything all right?" said Grim.

"I just miss them. Rose. My friends. My folks. All of them."

There would never be another Halloween with them. Another Christmas. Another Fourth of July, another Leap Day, or even another Arbor Day for that matter. Could he remember exactly what he was doing on the afternoon of June 12th? Certainly not. Couldn't tell you if it was raining or sunny, what day of the week it was, or if there was anything special about it at all. But whatever it was, he had been with them.

"Does it ever get any easier?"

Grim sighed. "It becomes . . . bearable. Tolerable. You learn to live a version of your life without them in it. But easy? No. I'm afraid not."

Mason felt the empty spots in him, the void left by those who weren't there anymore. No faces, just sun-bleached silhouettes showing what had once been there.

"Just honor them. Remember them and they will never truly be gone."

That was something he was sure he'd have no problem with. When he first arrived, he'd had to will himself not to forget at the prospect of having parts of his memory erased. Now he was sure that nothing short of death itself could ever do that.

"What say we head downstairs and grab a drink?" said Grim.

"Can . . . I do that?" asked Mason, aware that he was still well underage, as he set the katana down on the desk.

Grim made a gesture of assurance. "The compound is Vatican soil after all, so yes, you can."

"Well, now we're talkin'!" said Mason, rubbing his hands together.

"Just remember, we still have training tomorrow, so let's aim for tipsy, not blotto."

"Aye-aye, cap. Just need to get dressed. I'll be down in about twenty minutes or so."

"Ah, all right. Until then." With that, Grim left, closing the door behind him.

Pleased as Mason was about the prospect of being able to drink without needing to keep it hidden, it was not what he was most looking forward to.

From the closet he took out a brown paper bag tucked away in the corner and dumped the contents onto the bed. A black frockcoat, white linen shirt, cravat, burgundy brocade vest, dark trousers, dress shoes, and black wig. He put the clothes on and tied the cravat loosely, grinning with sheer unabashed glee to himself as he did. The wig was short and he styled it to create a part on one side. When that was done, he took a makeup kit from his medicine cabinet and began applying it to his eyes and lower lip to create sunken eye sockets and a mustache. And for the final touch, he took out the last thing in the bag—a black-winged bird with pins in the feet—and affixed it to one shoulder of the frock coat. There staring back at him in the mirror was the somber visage of one Edgar Allan Poe. An old costume, but one no one here had seen before.

Pleased with his handiwork, Mason took the elevator to the main floor, where everyone had gathered. Every pair of eyes fell on him as he entered the common room, every mouth hung agape with surprise. At first he didn't understand—it was a great costume, but surely not that great—but quickly realized why when he saw that not a single other person was in costume.

"Shit," he said.

Sarah, fixing herself a vodka cranberry at the bar, turned and burst with laughter the second she saw him.

"Did you . . . ?" said Diaz. "Did you tell him it was a *costume* party?"

She managed to nod between breaths as her knees buckled, sinking to the loveseat behind her.

But Mason wasn't angry. He was amused. Impressed, even. "Well, what can I say? You got me."

"Hell yeah, I did!" Sarah wiped tears from her eyes.

A table was set up against one wall with food, drinks, a large bowl of punch on one end, and a another bowl filled with candy at the other. Next to it a self-serve bar had been set up with an assortment of liquor and spirits, a cooler next to it filled with ice and bottles of beer. He took one, popped off the cap, and took three good long gulps.

"What up, Money?" said Diaz, who clinked his bottle against Mason once he had lowered it.

"Dee to the -iaz," said Mason with a slight burp.

Diaz looked him up and down, quirked one corner of his mouth up, and gave a short shrug. "There are just no words."

"Well," said Mason. "Except for those, so . . . five words."

Grim clinked his glass. "Now that we're all here," he began to speak, waiting for any remaining chatter to die down, "I just wanted to thank everyone for coming tonight. This has been a very interesting and at times trying year for us. We've gained some new members"—Grim's eyes swept the room, lingering just a moment longer on Mason—"and lost some as well."

At this, the last time Mason saw Irish alive flashed through his mind, followed closely by Rose, Julie, and Dale.

"But that is what tonight is for, to come together as a group, as a family, and remember them. Those who are no longer here but never gone."

"Hear, hear!" chimed Father Coffee, raising an empty glass.

Everyone else did the same.

Grim took a sip of his own drink, paused thoughtfully, and then smiled. "Now let's have some fun, for God's sake."

It was met by laughter and applause.

.   .   .

Teenage parties are much different from adult parties. Unless you had cool parents, they're always a secret, something done while uncool parents were away. Or they might be held in the woods outside of town. This was a different beast altogether. More laid back. People mingled, talked to one another. No one was playing drinking games or doing keg stands. Music wasn't blasting through speakers; instead, a selection of vintage Halloween standards from the '30s and '40s played on the TV. There was no one passed out with a mustache drawn on them—though in Mason's case he was already halfway there. He was sure anyone else his age would hate it. He, on the other hand, found it refreshing.

Just about everyone was there, except for Rodriguez. She was still away on assignment, but supposed to be back tonight. He saw IQ and Chewie away from their computers for the first time, drinking wine coolers and clinging closely to the wall. And those he hadn't yet met came up and introduced themselves.

There were two missionaries, Manx and Woodbine. An older, tanned man with graying hair and a tall, dark-skinned man with a bald head, both dressed in the plain black clothes Mason had seen Irish's brother wearing. A bit on the quiet side, but they seemed nice enough.

Then there was Yen. He was a mystery to him. Or rather why he didn't speak was the mystery. Mason asked Grim about it and all he said was that Yen had taken a vow of silence, but wouldn't say why. Mason had been studying sign language and was making some progress. Last week he was able to understand *good morning* when Yen signed it. But later that same day he had signed again, asking if he knew where *Hujn* was. Yen gave a silent chuckle when Mason said it out loud and tapped out GRIM on his phone. Realizing he'd gotten the letters wrong, Mason stuck out his thumb and pinky, placed it beneath his chin and twisted—the sign for "Oops."

Mason thought perhaps with the libations and relaxed atmosphere everyone would drop their guard and he would finally be able to see beyond the barriers each member of the team had in their minds. He had no real reason to want this, other than that the mind inquires strongest with that which is kept hidden. Unfortunately, this was not the case. If anything they were stronger now than before, and his abilities were slightly dulled by drink.

But the minds of the team were not the only ones there.

A middle-aged blonde woman named Audrey who organized a support group at the safehouse for survivors of the things Militia Dei dealt with. She invited him to come some time. He said he would think about it, though in truth he had no interest.

A squirrely man sipping a Sprite, very nervous about the fact that he had let himself be convinced that going to the party would be good for him, didn't like that it required him to put on clothes; this went against the will of the Astralnauts who had rescued him from the Moon People and, without his Helm of Aluminum, people would be able to read his thoughts. No, this was not good, not good at all.

Another man, reviewing the events of his life, was thankful for the fact that he had three beautiful daughters who now had children of their own, giving him the chance to have a real family. Sure, he was still a little bitter about the fact that his real body had been snatched by a girl he had been cheating on his wife with, but who wouldn't be? He never saw his real body again, and the one he inhabited now—that of a seventy-year-old Hispanic woman—bore every wrinkle, stretch mark, and liver spot that came with it.

And then there was someone who, while watching IQ and Chewie hook up a karaoke machine, at that moment, and only for a moment, wanted nothing more than to sing. Mason could practically hear the percussion, trumpets, and keyboards common to the musical stylings of Gloria Estefan. Which in and of itself would not have been quite so shocking, until he realized that the wisp of a wish had come from Miggs. With a sip of his beer, which he actually hated, he put it out of his mind.

Right about then, "Monster Mash," having played for only about thirty seconds or so, came to an abrupt end, replaced by some light guitar notes in the key of A Major. IQ's voice sounded over the speaker.

"It's astounding . . ."

Then Chewie joined in as they performed a maladroit but passable version of "Time Warp." When they finished, IQ held the mic up and said, "Okay, who's—?"

Without hesitation, Sarah scrambled forward, practically swiped it from his hands, and performed a shrill rendition of "Girls Just Want to Have Fun." There were more than a few fingers in ears during that one.

Father Coffey slowed things down a bit with a slurry rendition of "Danny Boy."

Hirsch and Woodbine kicked things back up with "Shake Your Groove Thing." When they finished, the crowd started an actual chant for Grim to perform.

"Cap-TAIN! Cap-TAIN! Cap-TAIN!"

He seemed genuinely surprised at first, but then a peacefully determined look came over him. Placing his drink down, he took the mic and picked a song. A moment passed before the music started. Trumpets, disco guitar, and the thumping baseline of "It's Not Unusual." He performed with a sway and swagger that rivaled the real Tom Jones, each note perfect and towering, earning every ounce of applause that followed.

Mason felt a ping in his nerve—for what reason he could not say —until a second later when Grim looked right at him.

"Mason Cole, come on up here."

He tried to flee, but everyone in his path practically red-rovered him forward. With a dramatic roll of his eyes, he took the mic. He held it in front of his mouth for a moment as an idea dawned on him.

"Raymond Yen, ladies and gentlemen," he announced, and held the microphone out toward Yen with an expectant look on his face. Everyone burst into laughter.

Yen smiled and signed something.

"What did he say?" said Mason.

" 'Nice try,' " said Grim.

"Ah well, worth a shot."

He looked through the songs until he saw the one that practically leapt out at him. He made his choice and covertly turned the volume up a shave or two.

"Oh god," he said, and crossed himself.

A door creaked open and a howl sounded before the immediately identifiable synthesizer of "Thriller" blasted through the speakers. Mason let out a vocal hiccup and for the first time ever performed a song he had only sung to himself. Everyone clapped along. When it reached the chorus, he belted it out.

And his efforts didn't stop there. He parted the air, shimmied and shook, skulked with his claws up from one side of the room to the other. The whole shebang. All dressed as Edgar Allan Poe, no less. Mason had never received a standing ovation before. It felt pretty good.

The song ended and he returned to his drink, taking a seat on the loveseat next to Sarah.

"Not bad," she said with a lazy smile, hands clasped while dangling between her ripped, fishnet-covered legs in a tartan skirt.

Drink in hand, Mason gave an exaggerated shrug. "That's it?"

Sarah rolled her eyes around in a circle, thinking. "*Very* not bad."

Diaz stood from the couch, took the mic, said, "Okay, I see I have to show you how it's done," and kicked off Tone Lōc's "Funky Cold Medina."

"Hmm, y'know what you look like?" Sarah slurred with a mischievous curl to her pierced lips. "A kiwi fruit."

"Is that so?"

"Yep. You have a very nice scalp."

"Thank you." He raised his glass and gulped down what was left. "So, I've been meaning to ask . . . What's the deal with you and Earl?"

"Oh, you know how it goes: Witch meets demon. Witch makes pact with demon. Witch dies before pact is fulfilled, forcing demon to seek out and torment witch's descendants for generations until payment is made. You know, that old cashew."

"Sure . . . sure."

"He whispers to us, tells us things, says there's something about us he likes." She scrunched up her face in a fake expression. "Isn't that sweet?"

"Is there no way you can, you know, exorcise him? Get him to leave you alone?"

Sarah shook her head. "It's one thing to ignore a demon, take steps to keep them away. But when you commune with one, you invite them in, that's a whole different disco."

"How many times have you done that?"

"Twice."

"Only twice?"

"That's plenty! And believe me"—Sarah brought her drink to her lips and took a big gulp—"it takes its toll."

Mason did the same. As he raised his arm, the raven, pinned precariously on his shoulder and apparently on its last leg after his "Thriller" dance, fell and toppled to the floor. He cursed and bent forward to collect it.

Sarah leaned away from him and pointed. "That!" she said. "That right there is a bad omen."

Mason skewed an eye at her. "What is?"

"A fallen raven. Bad omen, for sure."

"Okay . . . and what is it supposed to mean?"

"The appearance of a raven signals a warning of some kind. A raven diving and hitting the ground like that, I'd say a warning . . . unheeded."

Mason raised his eyebrows. "If this were a story, that would be called foreshadowing."

"Oh, we are in a story, all right."

"Oh yeah? What kind?"

She thought about it. "Low-budget horror slash art-house with a dash of black comedy."

"Sounds pretty unique."

"Eh, I'm sure there's another one like it out there. Still a bad sign."

"Then I guess it's a good thing that this particular raven"—he banged it a few times on the table—"is fake."

"Your funeral," said Sarah with a shrug, and stood. "I'll be right back. Gotta see a horse about a man." She set her drink—little more than pink ice cubes now—down on the table next to his and disappeared around the corner.

Diaz, having finished the song, returned to the couch.

"She is a kooky little peacock," said Mason, inclining his head down the hall after her.

Diaz nudged him with his elbow. "Yeah, well, that peacock wants the D."

Mason paused mid-sip. "Whaaat?"

"Dude, capital D. Can you really not tell?"

"Nah. Get outta here. I think she's just being . . . you know . . . the way she is."

"There's that, and there's this."

"I don't think—"

"Forget thinking. Haven't you ever just done something because you wanted to?"

"I guess, but . . . I don't even know what to say."

"What to say? I'm telling you, all you'd have to say is 'Wanna go get some fuckin' outta the way?'"

"No. C'mon, man. I don't wanna be"—he fumbled for the right word—"salacious about it."

Diaz stared at him for a beat. "Salacious?"

"Yeah," said Mason with the last sip of his drink. "Like, crude or, you know, inappropriate."

"Okay," said Diaz with a chuckle. "Well, you don't gotta be *salacious* about it. Here"—he pointed to her vodka cranberry—"bring her another and ask if she wants to go somewhere to talk."

Mason gave him an uncertain but not entirely unconvinced look.

"I'm tellin' you, it'll work. And frankly, you need this, homie." Diaz gave him a playful shove. "Go!"

He bit his lip and let out a long, protracted breath. "All right . . . here goes nothing."

"Well, don't say it like that."

A wide cartoon smile spread across his face. "Here goes nothing," said Mason in his highest falsetto.

"Better," said Diaz, pleased as fruit punch.

Mason went to the bar, fixed a vodka cranberry, and headed around the corner to wait for Sarah to come out of the bathroom. "Wanna go somewhere we can talk?" he said under his breath. "Hi. Wanna go somewhere we can talk?" he said again, shifting nervously from one foot to the other. "Hey, wanna go somewhere we can talk?"

The door opened behind him.

He froze. "Hey!" he practically barked at her.

"Howdy," said Sarah, surprised to see him standing right there. Surprised, but not disappointed.

"I noticed your drink was getting low. Wanna go somewhere we can—"

Before he could hand her the drink, she yanked him into the bathroom, spilling the contents onto the floor.

Once inside, they attacked each other, clawed at each other like a pair of lions lost to the mindless frenzy which had seized them both. She slammed him up against the door and shoved her tongue down his throat. He was instantly hard and grabbed her by the ass, lifting her onto himself as she wrapped her legs around him. He reached under her skirt and tore off the panties, hearing an audible *rip*, while she unzipped his pants.

"Ohhh . . ." she moaned as he pushed into her, finding a piercing he didn't know she had until now. He thrust as though he were trying to knock a hole through the wall behind her. She twisted and writhed, working him with her hips as much as he worked her.

"Oh, fuck yeah . . . *fuck yeah!*" she squealed through gritted teeth, and dug her black fingernails into the flesh of his buttocks, forcing him to pump harder. She stuck a finger in his mouth. He sucked on it, tasting cigarettes and cranberry. Then, much to Mason's shock, she pulled it out, snuck it downward, and her finger crept around the side of one cheek and went into his bum.

"Oh my god," he grunted, and pounded away even harder than before. She sank her teeth into his shoulder, muffling her squeals. He bared his teeth, grabbed a handful of her green hair, and pulled, craning her head back to see her face twisted in violent ecstasy. No love was made—that word doesn't factor into something so raw—just primal euphoric release.

He let her down, easy, both of them still panting.

"Well," Sarah panted, "that sure hit the spot." She turned around to wash her hands and gave him a wink in the reflection of the mirror. After drying them on the hand towel next to the sink, she left without another word.

Mason was out of breath, his heart thumping deliciously in his chest. He felt something he hadn't for a long time. Not something as cheap as intoxication, or as fleeting as joy, and certainly not as fickle as love.

He felt alive.

"Okay," he said to himself. "Definitely wasn't expecting *that*."

FORTY-THREE

After regaining his breath, Mason made fresh drinks. He noticed that there were fewer people now, most of the guests either gone or leaving, some of the team members as well. Grim had retired pretty much right after his song. Upon checking his phone, he saw that it was just after midnight.

Mason found Sarah sitting on top of the picnic table out the side door, gazing into the foggy night, two lit cigarettes dangling from her pierced lips. She traded him one for the vodka cranberry he brought for her. He sat down next to her and smoked.

Fog was not uncommon in Boston, but this had become thick and roiling like liquid pearl, all but blocking out the nearly full moon. Almost alive. It made great glowing orbs of the streetlamps, like giant dandelions in the night.

"Well, this is definitely one Halloween for the books," said Mason with a big dumb grin.

"Too bad you didn't get to go to Hellysium," said Sarah between drags.

Mason's lips lost their curl. "How did you . . . ?" He was pretty sure he hadn't said anything about it to her. And yet she knew, while he had all but completely forgotten. "Yeah. Too bad."

He would be there right now, crowded around bonfires with Julie and Dale, drinking shitty overpriced beer, slamming into the bodies of twenty thousand other head-bangers while the skull-crushing beats blared through towers of speakers. In short, having the time of his life. Another one of those good times you look back on even years later and say, "Now *that* was a blast!" Maybe in another life, that's just what had happened. He wondered if Rose would have let him go or not, if she would have been able to unclench just this once. She always got antsy when there was a field trip, never mind going all the way to Chicago.

He would have made it happen, though—snuck out and caught holy hell for it later, if that's what it took. It would have been worth it. They would have left yesterday, or possibly even the day before, skipped a whole day of school Friday to get a decent campsite lest they risk having to pitch their tent behind the outhouses. They would have stopped somewhere around Toledo to rest and refuel, had a quick nap and a bite to eat before the show started. Tonight, of course, would have been Metallica. And it was. It already happened. He just wasn't there.

Either way, it didn't matter now.

"So is this what happens every Halloween?"

"Pretty much," she said, exhaling a long plume of smoke. "No point in patrolling, and there's not much else to do. May as well unwind."

"What do you mean, 'no point'?"

"Because of the veil."

Mason stared at her blankly. "Yeah, I'm gonna need more than that."

"You never heard that Halloween is when the veil between the other side and this one is at its thinnest?"

"Oh. Yeah, actually I have. My grandma says—"

She doesn't say anything anymore, does she?

"... said that. She believed in all that stuff." Another thing he had never given any real credence before now.

" 'That stuff'?"

"Yeah, you know, astrology, mysticism, spiritual . . . stuff."

"You're talking to someone who believes in all that stuff."

"Well, sure, but you're a witch."

"Maybe *she* was a witch."

"I thought about it, but . . . I don't think so. Just a believer in every nutty thing you could imagine."

"You say that, but haven't you witnessed some pretty nutty things for yourself?"

"I think you're a little nutty," he said with a smirk. He didn't mean anything by it except to tease. Poke a little fun. It sounded better in his head.

"I know that." She pointed a slender finger at him, then directed it at her temple. "But if I *know* I'm nuts, doesn't that make me un-nuts?" She snapped her arm toward him as if dotting the question mark with the cherry of her lit cigarette.

Mason thought a moment. "Strangely, that makes sense."

"Guess that means *you're* nuts," she said, her quirk of a smile returned.

"That's what I get for hanging out with you."

"You're welcome." And stuck out her tongue at him.

The other side. Mason heard her words repeat in his head. As good a name for it as any. Like the wall before him, surrounding the compound. Him on one side, them on the other. Same place, but separate. All one need do was peek over it.

"That brings up a good question, actually," said Mason, breaking the brief silence.

She let out an exaggerated sigh. "Oh my god, you and your questions."

"What?" he said, shrugging his shoulders up to his ears. "I'm new to all this."

"Fine," she said, and spat off to the side.

No way around it now. Just ask her.

"What happened to your aunt Olivia?"

"Hmm. I figured you must have heard of her by now. As far as black sheep of the family go, Olivia don't get much blacker . . ." She trailed off, lost to thoughts far south of pleasant.

"Is . . . that it?"

Sarah took the longest drag of her cigarette he had ever seen someone take, shortening what was left almost down to the filter, and remained still and silent for a quiet moment, considering her response. "I'll tell you about it sometime. Just not now. Listen."

"What?"

"Just listen," said Sarah, stubbing out her cigarette, and closed her eyes, inhaling deep the cool, intoxicating splendor that was the night.

Mason kept his eyes open but breathed like her. They stayed like that for a perfect moment of hypnotic buoyancy. Two castaways adrift in a sea of mist.

He heard traffic. Distant voices. His pulse. Saw his inner self, an intricate network of light. This same essence in Sarah as well. Raw but contained, like a storm in a bottle. He felt the barrier around the chapterhouse too, the one which kept uninvited guests—alive, dead, and in between—from entering. He had felt it during meditation, but tonight it was thicker. Pressurized, as though he were inside a bubble beneath deep water. And when he pressed beyond the bubble, something else. A low surge of energy, like the current of a mighty ocean.

"Is . . . that singing?"

Sarah drew in a sharp breath as if intimately touched by invisible fingers. "The Song of the Dead."

Less like singing and more of a collective moan from countless throats. Faces appeared in the fog, wave after wave of them, swirling all around the walls of the compound and even high above. Disappearing the instant they passed through the light of the streetlamps, becoming clear again in the shadows. Mason finally realized that what he saw was no earthly fog, but an endless torrent of the dead. A sea of ghosts.

"My communion is the very air we breathe," said Sarah. "My church, the earth itself. And my god is truly almighty, for it is everywhere and everything. There's nothing supernatural about the dead. They're as much a part of nature as us."

He listened to them again. If a sigh could be sung, that would be the eerie chorus they made. But he wasn't afraid.

"They're happy."

"Wouldn't you be?" said Sarah. "Most of the time they wander aimlessly through a world they are no longer a part of yet can't leave. But tonight they have company. Tonight we share it, the beautiful mess, the weird bukkake funeral that is this world. Tonight it belongs to all of us."

After a few more minutes of listening, Sarah hoisted herself down off the picnic table. "I'm freezing my flaps off and I think that's enough exposition for one night. Let's go in."

"You paint with words." Mason dropped his long-dead cigarette butt in the can and they both headed toward the door. "Bukkake Funeral. Now there's a name for a band."

"Fuckin' right it is. Dibs!"

"Hey, I don't suppose you like Elvis?"

"Do I look like I like Elvis?"

"No, but you never—"

Everything went dark. The light above them, the streetlamps, the buildings around them, even the security building across the graveyard. All went out at once.

"Whoa!" said Mason. He had never seen a blackout before. Back in Stonehill, when there was a storm, sometimes the lights flickered, but they never went out . . . that was, not until a red-haired fiend came to town. "What the hell?"

"Haven't the foggiest," said Sarah.

Then the dogs started to bark.

Sarah put her hand on Mason's shoulder, meaning to guide him toward the side door. "I think we had better get in—"

A loud *pop!* sounded as something hit the other side of the building.

Then another.

Then the shattering of glass as a window broke not ten feet away.

Mason and Sarah had just enough time to duck under the picnic table as the rest of the assault came.

All around the perimeter round, pale objects were lobbed over the wall as if hurled by catapults. Bursting on impact. Raining sloppy guts and entrails down on them. Crashing against headstones in the graveyard. Littering every inch of the property while an ever-growing din filled the air. Had there been any light, the objects would have eclipsed it. If they hadn't smashed on the ground, Mason would have thought they were being pummeled by medicine balls. A hail of pale bits fell all around them, scattering clumps of stringy sinew. One hit the top of the picnic table hard. Both of them cried out. Then, as a fractured eye and part of a mouth rolled forward, bumping into his trembling hand, Mason felt cold flesh touch his own.

Hard and smooth on one side, soft and wet on the other. Not human, but something that had once been alive. As the smell of pumpkin filled his nostrils he realized that they were being attacked not with medicine balls, but with jack-o'-lanterns.

Mason looked up to see that one had landed a few feet in front of them, missing only the part of the face that had broken off and found him under the table. Though, unlike the others, this one was not empty. Even in the dark he could see the glint of a human eye and tiny corner of a mouth with teeth peeking out from behind the pumpkin around it.

All at once the onslaught stopped. Things were shouted from inside and dogs barked like crazy. Emergency lights around the perimeter came on, but nothing else. Mason was horrified to realize that there was a face inside the jack-o'-lantern. And he recognized it.

Held together with duct tape from having been cut in two. Behind him Sarah was shouting for him not to touch it, but he had to see what he had to see. Voraciously he tore at it until the two halves came apart.

The severed, rotting head of his grandmother fell out. Her skin gray and hanging off the skull. Hair matted to the scalp with orange bits of pumpkin. Only the eyes still held any hint of what had been. The one still in its socket, anyway.

His vision fluctuated between sharpness and a blur. He didn't yell or cry or anything. Just looked at it. Looked at *her*. Staring her dead woman's gaze at him.

> *Don't you touch my grandson, you filthy thing!*
> *. . . . . my grandson, you filthy thing!*
> *. . . . . you filthy thiiiiiing!*

Her words, though her mouth didn't move. There was something sticking out of it—a thin white line between shriveled lips.

Mason grabbed a corner of it and pulled out a crumpled polaroid. It showed Julie bound and gagged, a white hand holding today's paper over her shoulder. At the bottom, written in red ink, it said TRICK OR TREAT! in big block letters.

Once again Mason felt his mind break, as though he had been given a good hard shove out of reality and into a dark tunnel while staring into the face of his dead grandmother.

He felt himself being pulled away by strong arms. Protective. Soft whispering in his ear as the sight before him disappeared and was replaced with the inside of the chapterhouse. He knew the faces of the people trying to meet his gaze, but it didn't matter. They were saying his name and asking if he could hear them, but he may as well have been on the moon, for catatonic paralysis had grabbed him good and tight this time. There was nothing he could do to stop it.

Everything was going to be okay. He knew it. He knew because they said so, the people snapping fingers in front of his face, shining a penlight in his eyes. Words said but only half heard. The feeling of watching all this, sensing it going on around him but not in his own body. Near it.

Beside himself.

Ah, that's good, he thought through the fugue. *I'll be my own shoulder to cry on.*

Except he wasn't crying at all. He was laughing.

He knew he shouldn't. Of course he shouldn't. This wasn't funny . . .

Well, maybe a little. Right?

He'd wanted to see Rose and Julie again, wanted it desperately, and now he had. Wanted to leave Stonehill, and he had. Wanted to be something other than a gas-station nobody in the definition of shit-splat towns.

He got all of that and then some.

On second thought, why shouldn't he laugh? Who cared if the others stared? Who cared if he was scaring them while he cackled like a madman?

Because the old adage was true.

Be careful what you wish for . . . you just might get it.

And what was a wish, after all, if not a prayer addressed to whom it may concern? He hadn't gotten down on his knees and folded his hands. It was so much simpler than that. His very soul had ached for it, stretched a hand out toward the heavens, singing a silent hymn every time he thought about it. And when had he *not* thought about it? What waking hours were not filled with a yearning to be anywhere but where he was?

And sing hosanna, his prayers had been answered.

He vowed to never want anything again. For if this was how God answered prayers, he was better off dead. It was a joke. All of it. And he was the punchline.

At last the penny dropped, one falling from the top of a skyscraper that had to hit someone, it just happened to be him. He was not the star of this tragic little play. He was an extra. An understudy at best. There was no meaning or providence to his fate. He was a means to an end, a way to make sure the show went on. And when the curtain fell, he'd return to the background.

That's what must happen.

That was how this had to play out.

FORTY-FOUR

AT SOME POINT MASON HAD BEEN RETURNED TO HIS ROOM, everything in between a blur. There was a brief memory of shuffling down the hall as Rodriguez guided him, and then her face above his as he lay down on the bed.

She had a nice face. Strong and supple. And those eyes! God, what is it about the eyes that strikes us so? The one thing that doesn't change no matter how we age. For a second he saw himself through those eyes as he lay there, unresponsive.

He remained there now, staring at the ceiling. Cracks of the broken window sent spiderwebs of shadow spinning before him like a cheap phantasmagoria. Someone had come to check on him, driving a wedge of light through the shadow play, but since they did no more than crack open the door he could not say for sure who it was. But he knew who he hoped it was.

After an eon of immobility, Mason sat up. He'd been unaware that Bossy was curled up next to him, and his movement jolted her awake and off the bed. He looked out the fractured glass of the windowpane, amazed it was still intact.

Outside, the ghost fog still slowly roiled around the perimeter, as though he were in the eye of the calmest of hurricanes. He wondered what time it was and instinctively looked to the clock, but the red digits weren't there, indicating that the power must still be out. Though it seemed longer, he figured maybe an hour had passed.

The image of Rose's dead face burned into his mind's eye. Closing the other two did no good. *And Julie!* Christ, Julie was still alive and out there somewhere. Captive and helpless and who knew what else. A wave of nausea hit him at the very thought of what unspeakable things could have happened to her.

All this time.

Right now.

Mason stood and quickly made for the bathroom. He got two steps in before freezing on the spot. Unable to move.

A cold chill surrounded him, commanding every hair on his body to icy attention. Not a fresh cold. Not the fine gray cool of a rainy day. Not even the breath of winter which may fill one with a certain bracing vigor. A biting cold. Painful. Unfriendly. The kind that made you forget you were ever warm.

His panicked breaths were visible in the tufts of chilled air before him. The same fog he'd seen swirling around the perimeter earlier now felt as if it had shrouded his mind.

From the corner of his eye, Mason saw Bossy tense and her fur bristle as she reared up on her haunches, lowing and hissing at the presence she sensed. Her eyes darted to the window and whatever she saw there sent her running under the bed.

Good morning, starshine, the earth says hello. Flat. Joyless. Echoing in his head as if from the other end of a long tunnel.

He didn't want to look. Willed himself not to—(*oh god, oh god*)— yet found his head slowly turning toward the window.

There, like steam on a mirror, Rose's face appeared on the glass.

Pressed into the broken pane with startling clarity. Only it wasn't *her* face, at least not the one he had known. The eyes were milky white, neither living nor warm, their sockets sunken and dark. Every wrinkle etched deep enough to hold a shadow. She mouthed something he couldn't make out before the phantom breath that formed it dissipated. Then she was gone.

If he had to guess, it looked to him like she'd said "Home."

Mason approached and peeked out into the night. Even from a distance he recognized the ghostly figure he knew to be Rose across the road. Fog drifting through a long nightgown that Mason knew well. Her hair loose and free. At first she didn't move at all. Just stared back at him with a gaze he could feel even three floors up.

Slowly, she raised one hand and motioned for him to come, an action that made his bones prickle.

Come. Not "home." Come.

"Yeah fucking right!" he said out loud. Too loud. His head throbbed.

Without taking those dead eyes of hers off him, she raised the same arm and pointed away from them. Somewhere north, he couldn't tell where exactly.

I can show you, Mason, came Rose's voice, close, as if she were in the room with him. *I can take you to her. You can save her.*

It seemed he had no other choice. He would have to go to her.

But how? If he were seen they would surely try to stop him. Strolling casually out the front door was no good. Even if he wasn't seen inside, it was enough of a ways from the door to the gate for him to be spotted.

The side door? No, can't get out to the street from there. Plus, there was just an attack and security is definitely on alert, meaning there's sure to be increased patrols.

And right on cue, there was Lloyd, walking along the wall with a flashlight in one hand and the leash of one of the dogs in the other.

What about the tunnel from the garage? It goes underground and straight to the church, and I could easily make sure the coast is clear before leaving.

And if by chance he was seen by someone walking the perimeter, there was almost no distance from the church door to the gate. He could make a break for it before . . .

Wait a minute . . . the cameras!

There were security cameras all over the place. He would be seen as soon as he entered the hall, never mind the garage.

Well . . . shit.

Why not just tell Grim what was going on?

No, came Rose's voice. *They won't understand, Mason. They will want to wait until it's light out. You have to come now . . .*

How much longer could it be until dawn? Instinctively, he looked to the clock.

Oh yeah, still out.

Still out . . .

Sure enough, the surrounding buildings were absent of light as well. That meant the power hadn't been restored yet anywhere.

That meant no cameras.

"Oh, those devils," said Mason. "Those clever devils."

There was nothing for it. He gathered what he would need—his gun, the sword he had just been gifted a few hours ago, and his water bottle, which he filled to the top with holy water.

It occurred to him as he went about his business that he may well not make it out of this alive. In truth, he had always known this. But it didn't matter now. One way or another, this was happening.

Mason pushed the stubborn doubt from his mind and, as stealthily as he could, cracked open the door. With his head poked out into the hall, he cast his eyes upward to the security camera. Sure enough, no usual red light. Dead.

So heightened were his senses that he could actually feel the others throughout the building, points of heat of varying intensity, depending on where they were and how close. None were asleep. Understandable, given what had happened.

Mason tip-toed down the hall as quietly as possible.

Screw the elevator, he thought. *Too loud. The stairs it is.*

He even removed his shoes for good measure. There was no reason to think that even if he were seen it would arouse suspicion, but why take a chance?

"I'm going to the kitchen," that's all you have to say. And the reason you're fully armed? Hey, maybe that's not so unusual following an attack. Naturally they'll want to know how you are. And what would you tell them? What we all say when we're obviously not okay . . . *"I'm fine."*

When he reached the garage, Mason froze at the sight of another security camera. But this one too was missing its typical red eye.

So far, so good.

The door to the tunnel was locked, but luckily he had been given a key some time ago. He unlocked and guided the door quietly back into its frame with a *click.* The pitch dark of the tunnel awaited him. Were it not for the light on his phone, he'd have been suffocated by it.

"Okay, you can do this," he told himself. His chest flew apart like a swarm of bats in a cave.

He managed to guide himself through and past the door that led to the shooting range and holding cells. He hung a left where the tunnel turned sharply and continued on.

There was a very strange sense about being in a space this close, underground, in such utter darkness. Nearly a solid thing, it pressed against his skin. His breaths became faster. His pulse quicker. The smell of dust and concrete palpable, like being in a tomb. The only sound were his feet as they shuffled quickly across the gritty ground. It gave him the sense of being underwater. Drowning in darkness.

Mason felt a breath on his neck. He gasped and spun around.

"Hello? Is anyone there?"

But of course there wasn't. His senses told him so. What he felt was just a draft . . . but a draft from where? The thought didn't make his pulse any slower nor allow him to take a full dose of air into his lungs.

And suddenly he found meaning in Nietzsche's words. *When you gaze into the abyss, the abyss gazes into you.* We are warm in the knowledge of that which the light reveals. But the dark unnerves us so, not because of what is, but everything that could be. The mind abhors a vacuum, and so we fill it with one bizarre horror after another. Things we can't even imagine but fear nonetheless. It is because of this that we never truly stop being afraid of the dark. Not because of what it is, but what could be.

He realized that he had been holding his breath and continued forward to the end of the tunnel, unlocked the door, and hurried into the church basement.

Darkness there, too, but not nearly as total as the darkness he'd left, courtesy of the recently lit candles of the shrines nearby, shrinking down to a soft glow. Near and far, he felt their warmth, some stronger than others. A welcome contrast to the deathly chill of the tunnel. Hunched forms of the oddly arranged piles of covered junk rose up on all sides. The light from his phone did very little in a bigger space such as this, but it did the trick.

He clung to the wall, careful not to disturb any of the other shrines and altars as he circumvented the collection of relics. He couldn't help but think that someone might be waiting for him around every corner. Or worse, could lunge out at him from under the covers.

The outline of the stairs came into view, a wrinkle in the shadows. Relieved, Mason hurried up them as quickly as he could. With the darkness at your back it felt as if something were coming up out of it after you, to close its fingers around your ankle at the last second before you reached the door. It was the curse of all basements, it seemed, even that of a church.

Then he felt it. A presence right behind him.

"Where do you think you're going?"

Mason jumped. He slipped and nearly took a tumble back down the stairs as his heart pumped ice water. The heavily shadowed face of Miggs appeared at the base of the stairs behind him. He hadn't felt him nearby, nor had he heard any thoughts—likely due to the sheer volume of his own fears.

"Jesus fucking Christ, you scared the shit out of me!" Mason snapped.

"Don't you take the Lord's name in vain," said Miggs, raising his voice for the first time. "I asked you a question."

Mason stood, dusted himself off. "If you must know, I came here to pray." Mason continued up the stairs and through the back of the church.

"What a coincidence. Me too. I'll keep you company," said Miggs, following closely behind.

"No, thanks. I'd prefer to be alone," said Mason as they entered the church proper. He moved briskly past the altar and began down the aisle with purpose.

Miggs overtook him and blocked his path. "And I'd prefer you not lie to my face. For the last time, where are you going?"

Mason tried to dodge past him. "None of your business."

"Oh no?" said Miggs, holding a hand out. "I outrank you, soldier."

Mason stopped, pivoting from one foot to the next. "Oh, we're doing the soldier thing now?"

"We never stopped doing the soldier thing. Not now, not ever. Period," Miggs barked.

"Exclamation point!" Mason barked back.

"Cut the crap, kid. What's going on?"

"My grandmother! Okay?" Mason confessed. "She's waiting for me outside to take me to my friend Julie."

"Your grandmother's dead."

"I guess that would make her a ghost then."

"Yeah, nice try," said Miggs, his words dripping with skepticism.

"You don't have to take my word for it. C'mere, see for yourself."

Mason began heading through the pews, but Miggs didn't let him get more than a few feet. He peered through one of the windows on either side of St. Philip's shrine.

"There," said Mason, and pointed out across the street where, sure enough, Rose still waited.

Miggs sidled up next to him and looked out into the night. "Where?"

"What do you mean, where?" said Mason, eyes narrowed at him. "Right there!"

"There's nothing out there."

Mason stared at him in disbelief. "You mean . . . you can't see her?"

"See who? Look, I'm sure this has all been very stressful. I get it. But—" He took Mason by the arm, began leading him away, and was immediately thrown off. Miggs did not look amused.

"You get it, huh?" said Mason. "Do you get what it's like to see people you care about die before your eyes in the most horrible ways imaginable, so vivid that every time you close your eyes you see it again? Do you get what it's like to know that you, and you alone, could stop something horrible from happening to someone you care about, and if you don't then what happens to them is on you?"

Miggs leaned against one of the pews. "Yeah, I do."

Mason's blinked. "Which part?"

"All of it. Everything you just said, I know."

Silence passed through the church. Hollow. Lingering. The type that follows every awkward pause, lacking in sound but not resonance. As the two of them stood there, eyes locked on each other, a single common thread tethered them for the first time.

"Then let me go to her," said Mason, all but pleading now.

"Honestly," said Miggs, "nothing would please me more than to let you walk out of here. See, a chain's only as strong as its weakest link . . . and, Ram of God or not, that's you. With you gone, my sister and I could be free of this loco life for good. She's got a stubborn sense of faith in all this. Me? I could care less."

Go ahead, care less, Mason thought. He wanted to say it, was inches away from it, and had he not sobered up a bit he very well may have. *Not now, not when I'm so close.*

As he spoke, the shell around Miggs's mind wavered a little, letting things not even so cogent as thoughts through—stray emotions and impulses he had meant to keep guarded. And for the briefest of moments, Mason actually thought he was going to let it happen.

"But if I do, I'm putting a weapon in the hands of our enemies that will tip the scale in their favor and put us all in danger." Miggs stepped closer, got right up in his face. "*That* I can't allow."

Mason felt that little flutter of panic that accompanies anger, the kind you would do just about anything to unleash before it hits you.

"This may shock you," Mason said, "but you don't scare me. You don't impress me. You don't make me tremble or gasp. You make me yawn. I'm going whether you let me or not."

"Okay, playtime's over. Let's go." Miggs took him by the arm again, harder this time.

Mason didn't even realize what had happened at first. A flash of motion along with the tiniest spark of that white electric energy just before something hit the floor. He looked down to see Miggs in a crumpled heap at his feet. The feeling in his hand said that it had just connected with the face that was knocked out cold below him.

He had decked someone twice his size without even deciding to do it. It just happened. A simple muscle reflex, nothing more.

Mason stood there dumbfounded for a few seconds, replaying it in his head. Finally he snapped out of it and made for the entrance. As he placed his hand on the door's handle, there came the constant nag of pain. The same hand Angel had almost crushed.

He looked back at Miggs's unconscious form on the church floor and understood why he, as a sergeant and as a brother, did what he felt he had to do—understood a number of things about him now, actually. But there was something he couldn't deny.

Miggs was right.

This power, which he never should have had, didn't belong to him, and if Novak got his hands on it, it would spell disaster for everyone else. He was no soldier, no saint, no messiah. And he was certainly no savior to these people. Even if he wanted to be.

Mason returned to the spot where Miggs lay and with great difficulty sat him up on one of the pews. Slowly, he slipped off the chain he wore around his neck, letting it dangle in his hand as he looked at the cross resting in the dip of his palm. Both the cause of and the cure to his woes.

He knew what he must do.

Mason clasped it in both hands, kneeled next to the pew as he had seen Will Graves do, and repeated his words.

"Into my hands, I commit thy spirit."

A single rush of air like the flap of powerful wings. White light flashed between the cracks of his hands as an incalculable weight lifted from within him. His hands grew impossibly hot and he dropped the cross as if it were a fresh coal, clinking to the church floor beneath him.

His senses were suddenly snuffed. Stifled. Reaching no further than the immediate vicinity. He heard no voices, no distant sounds, now too far away to hear—nothing but the sound of his own breaths. All he could smell was the lingering tinge of slightly acrid cleaner that had recently been used to wipe down the pews. He saw only the low-lit walls and dark corners of the church and the candles around the altar, but he could not even guess at how many there were—something he would have known instantly less than a minute ago. He had no idea if anyone had been sitting nearby from leftover body heat. And the only thoughts he heard were his own.

Mason rose to his feet and returned to the door, this time without pause.

As soon as he stepped outside, there she was. A spectral form of his late grandmother, a husk of her former self, made up of a dark mist, hovering above the ground across the street from the church. There was no more sea of specters or song of the dead—at least not for him.

As he moved closer, Rose came clearer into view. The color had been drained from every part of her, from her skin to her clothes. The lines of her face were chasms of shadow. Hair loose and rippling in a breeze that didn't exist. Those dead milky-white eyes of hers watched as he approached, all traces of their once bright green now gone. She wore the exact same nightgown she had been wearing when she died.

In the center of her chest was a dry black hole where her heart should have been. No expression on her face at all, just a coldness he had never seen in her before, one which he felt inside and out.

"Take me," he said to her.

At first she didn't respond, making him wonder if he had been heard. Then she reached out her hand to him. Reluctantly, he put his in hers, finding it solid enough to hold despite its diaphanous appearance. She began walking him away from the church, down Newton, past cars and buses of people that saw only a boy wandering alone at night.

When they came to Columbus, she steered him toward downtown.

Office buildings and skyscrapers loomed in the distance, their many windows still lit. Clearly the blackout was not city-wide. At some point he was aware of passing over the Massachusetts Turnpike, the rush of traffic and occasional honk of a horn swirling around him.

He was familiar enough with Boston to have a general idea of where she was taking him, but not enough to know for sure. She led him around the corner of an apartment building and there was a giant crane towering above a construction site not far from the river. Mason passed Rose and approached the gated entrance, bound with chain-link fence and a sign warning away trespassers.

This final step filled him with distinct trepidation. After this, there was no going back. No mental exercises or trickery that could save him.

He turned back to Rose, but she was no longer anywhere to be seen.

He put one foot in front of the other, inadvertently clenching his teeth so hard that it hurt his face.

The fence he managed to climb easily, landing in an open lot of unpaved dirt. The hulking shapes of forklifts, bulldozers, and excavators were dispersed around the property like dinosaurs sleeping beneath the stars. It hardly could have been called a building, as it was still missing most of the exterior walls.

Each shadow, each corner, behind every machine he expected to see eyes piercing through the night and teeth rushing toward him. No sign of life among the dark, incomplete structure of steel and concrete. But he was not alone. Oh no. His senses may no longer be what they were, but they weren't so muted as to miss the feel of eyes on him. The prickle of danger as he drew nearer to *them*.

The only sounds were of traffic and the scrape of his feet on the loose, dry earth. He stopped just before entering the building. Took out the bottle, poured a wide circle of holy water around where he stood, and tossed it away.

Throw your weapons away as well, came Rose's voice from somewhere unseen. *Show them you're unarmed and submitting to them willfully.*

Even though he knew this was a bad idea, Mason did as suggested, throwing both the gun and sword away from him.

"Novak!" he shouted into the building. "You want me? Here I am. Let my friend go and I'm all yours."

No response.

He waited for any sign of movement at all.

Half a minute passed before he heard it—a muffled scream, so low that he almost couldn't make it out. His body tensed and he nearly put a foot outside the circle. *Not until she's safe, not until she's gone from here.* It was difficult, but he stood his ground.

He heard it again, only this time it was a voice he recognized.

Julie's voice. She was crying his name.

"No!" he shouted. "Let her go first, that's the deal."

Mason. You have to stop them.

He turned around to see Rose's ghost again, just outside the circle. The movement of her lips out of sync with her words, voice as vaporous as her form. Faraway no matter how close.

You have to save her. Save her like you couldn't save me.

He was back in Stonehill. On the floor. Staring into her face that had moments earlier been alive and furious and afraid.

Save her!

Mason cursed and sprang from the spot, leaving the protection of the circle. He gathered up the gun from where it had landed and dashed forward into the building, passing from one dark unfinished room to the next.

Oh god! Oh god! What the fuck am I doing? Just let me save her, God. That's all I ask. I don't care what happens to me. Just save her.

A sliver of light split the darkness and he made directly for it. It came from a space about thirty feet away, and there was Julie, bound and gagged to a steel girder, a bright orange tarp spread out across the floor in front of her.

Mason hurried toward her, giving no thought to his surroundings anymore.

He was close enough to see her eyes.

He sped up.

Almost there.

The minute he stepped on the tarp, the ground gave way beneath him, plummeting away into darkness, and he landed hard below.

Thanks for nothing, he thought, slipping out of consciousness.

A smiling white face beneath rusty hair appeared above him. The last thing he saw before he was swallowed by darkness.

FORTY-FIVE

Mason came to with a jolt. His vision slowly unclouded as his surroundings came into focus: a space several stories up from where he had quite literally fallen into the trap; buckets of paint next to a mound of crumbling drywall and broken concrete; wooden beams and PVC piping in scattered piles across the floor; a table saw and some other power tools near a portable floodlight projecting into one corner so as to brighten the room as little as possible. All of it old, forgotten. Much longer and it would start to look like a dump.

His head throbbed, swimmy with a heavy, persistent pain. Something thin and sharp cut into his wrists, which were bound behind the back of the chair he sat in. Miraculously nothing was broken, but his knees ached and his back was sore from the fall. He was also now more than a little aware that whatever effect had been working on him had ended. Spellbound—that was the only word for it. Compelling him, pushing him forward. Something that wore the face of his grandmother. Now he was back to his regular old self. A foolish fly in a web.

"Mason Cole."

The voice came from a darkened corner that Mason was sure had been empty moments before. A white face with empty eyes emerged from the shadows, as if a mask were surfacing from the depths of murky water. Fading *into* view. Unseen but there all along. Then the mask smiled and a sickening chill rippled through him.

He thought of every bit of Grim's advice. All his instructions, all his information and scientific diatribes—right now they made not one bit of difference. What use is trivia about the great white shark when one has you dead in its sights?

Then, suddenly, Novak stood before him. Only now did Mason realize just how much taller than him Novak was—a good three inches at least, probably more.

He hopped back, crouching upon the lumber pile, resting on the balls of his bare feet, perched like a greedy vulture. His serpentine face long and pointed. Thin red ribbons cracked the whites of his unblinking eyes. He smelled like an old bandage that needed to be changed. Bloodless skin with a few ugly blue veins winding beneath and a touch of freckles Mason hadn't noticed before. Any other body with such a pallor would surely be dead. The same disheveled hair, tossed about in a mess of rusted nails. Same studded leather jacket, worn and cracked as fish skin left out in the sun. The eyes were not solid black but rather impossibly thin gray irises that swallowed the contracting pupils in the light. However ethereal he had appeared moments ago, he was now solid and perfectly ghastly.

Every hair on Mason's body immediately pricked as if it were in close proximity to an ice sculpture. Terrified, but thankfully not lost. Even now his training surfaced, as Grim said it would, and with the inhale of a cautious breath, he tried to close his mind. His view of the city, hindered not by the mundanity of walls, dimmed all around. It was just the two of them now.

"At last," said Novak.

"You said that already," said Mason, gritting his teeth through the pain.

"So I did." A long white finger raised as if to signal that he was about to make a point. "And what does that tell you?"

"That you like to repeat yourself?"

"No, silly rabbit. That I gotcha again." He spoke calmly. Quietly. The way one does when trying not to alarm a trapped animal. "But we weren't formally introduced then, now were we?"

His hand dove inside his jacket and took out a small white rectangle. It left his fingers, hit Mason square in the face with a little prick from one of the corners, and fell into his lap.

A business card.

Novak T. Vampire

That was all it said.

"What does the *T* stand for?" Mason asked.

" 'The,' " he answered simply. "A pleasure to make your acquaintance."

"Well, congratulations, you've got me." said Mason, pulling against his bonds just enough to test them but not so much as to be seen. "Now let my friend go."

Novak sucked air through his fangs. "I'm afraid it's not that simple."

"Because she's dead, isn't she?"

Novak shrugged.

Mason sighed. "I was afraid of that. That's why before I came in here I sent a text to my team with the address to this place and—"

"No," said Novak, cutting him off.

"No?"

Novak shook his head very slowly. "You did no such thing."

Mason shrugged as much as his restraints would allow. "Okay, if you say so."

"Ikay, if yu meh-meh."

"Are you just repeating what I'm saying?"

"Are you shust ripidding weh-ehm-mehmeh? Your lips tell lies while your heartbeat, pupils, and facial tics, so small the human eye would have trouble seeing them, all betray you." Motionless, a statue of himself. His thin gray lips the only things moving. "Also, I have your phone." He held it up before him just long enough to crush it with a single squeeze. Bits of broken glass and plastic went dancing across the cement floor. "Is this it? Was this your whole plan?"

"What's *your* plan, huh?" Mason spat at him.

Novak began to chuckle at his outburst.

"No, really. Go on. Impress me. What could it be?"

"Oh yes!" he crowed. He sprang forward from his perch and opened his arms. "Oh joy! Callooh callay! I love me some good old fashioned banter! Are you ready to hear my diabolical plot? You better be, because it's a doozy." He leaned in close to Mason's ear, a wave of his foul breath assaulting every sense, and whispered, "Survival."

He pulled back, serious as could be. No malice nor mania in his face as he spoke. Mason saw now that what he mistook for freckles were actually speckles of dried blood.

"There's no plan. No evil scheme or plot for world domination. I'm just looking for a good time, and the holies you roll with are the biggest buzzkill there is. Simple and plain. To us, *you* are the vermin, pawns of an absent god whose flock has overrun this world. We are the silent cancer under their skin. I was chosen just as you were."

"I'm nothing like you," said Mason, low and serious.

Novak gave him a coy look of disbelief. "I don't think even you believe that. We are both of us burdened with a terrible gift. The only difference is that I've committed to mine."

"You know who always thinks he and the hero are not so different? The bad guy."

"But tell me . . ." Novak began pacing a circle around him. "Have you considered that maybe, just maybe, you are not the hero? That this isn't even your story at all?"

"Whose do you imagine it would be?"

"Mine."

Now it was Mason's turn to laugh.

Novak met his gaze. "You still don't get it, do you?"

"I get that you murder and torture and enjoy it."

"Congratulations, Señor Kettle. You just described humanity. You wish to fight true evil, squire? Look in the mirror.

"Despite whatever your pathetic band of rosary-rattlers has told you, we are both part of nature. And nature has no morals. It spares not the old or the young, the weak or the sick. It preys upon them. In so doing, the herd is the stronger for it. And your herd is greatly in need of culling. Frankly, you need us.

"Every creature on this planet is subject to the hierarchy in which they exist. They prey on those below them and are preyed upon by those above. Humans think they are at the top of that chain, but you couldn't be more blessedly unaware of your real place in this world. I'm no more the villain than a snake eating a mouse, or a wolf attacking a rival when threatened."

"Is that why you led us to Bartok?" Mason asked.

Novak paused. "Something like that."

"Something like that? Or just . . . that?"

"Let's just say he had it coming."

"Sounds like revenge to me. Doesn't get more human than that."

Novak wagged a finger at him, his smile a tiny crack in the alabaster. "Careful."

"If this was all a noble purpose you claim to pursue, you wouldn't take such pleasure in it."

"Oh, I don't deny that for a second. Killing is fun! My motto is, 'If you can't beat 'em, eat 'em!' The thrill of really taking your time, properly stalking your prey until that one pure and perfect moment of the kill . . . it sparks something so raw and juicy." He sucked air through his fangs again and, with a lick of his fingers, pinched his left nipple. "There really is nothing quite like it."

"You're sick," said Mason, a little creak coming from the joints of his chair as he squirmed. "Even for a vampire."

"And you're dim even for a human." Novak began picking between his fangs with the pointed fingernail of his pinky. "Go on now. Tell the truth for once. How did it really feel to kill the men I sent after you? Or sweet Angel? Pretty good, no?"

"No! As a matter of fact, it didn't. These aren't things common to everyone, you leech."

Novak's cheeky demeanor disappeared. A little twitch in the corner of his mouth, and for the first time he blinked. His thin lips became a wide, disquieting smile. Perversely content. He curled his index finger at Mason as if to say *Come closer, I have a secret to tell you*. The legs of Mason's chair dragged across the cement floor, drawing nearer to him with each noisy inch until they were nose to nose.

"Thank you," said Novak in that low, husky voice of his, rough and penetrating. "You just made this next part so much more yummy."

Mason gagged hard at the smell of his breath. A little hint of vomit surfaced at the back of his throat. "God, you need a mint."

"Ha!"

A wicked, grinning white face suddenly appeared right next to Novak's. He didn't even flinch. A pair of purple shades covering eyes so sharp that they pierced right through the dark lenses. Blood-red lips, a beauty mark near the right corner, curled to reveal fangs beneath. A frizzed mane of hair so blonde it was nearly white, the color of gold spun on a broken spindle. With her cheap patent-leather dress and knee-high boots, she looked like a common streetwalker with a call girl's polish. Grime and glow.

"He's a funny boy," she said with a sultry giggle. "I like him."

She moved forward on an invisible cloud and placed her hands in Mason's lap, slowly rubbing his thighs. It felt neither good nor arousing. Her hands went to his zipper. He felt a hand, cold as a dead fish, slip into the front of his pants.

"Want me to suck you, funny boy?" She let out a little moan. "Oh, you would love it! Come on, let me taste you."

"Get the hell off me!" Mason cried, and did his best to wriggle away from her.

She snickered to herself and took to Novak's side again, hanging off one shoulder.

"Allow me to introduce my worse half, Goldie," he said.

"Hiya, sailor," she said with a waggle of her fingers. "I see the witch's hex worked. How fun."

Witch's hex . . . which witch? Sarah's cousin?

Mason clenched his teeth together so hard that every bone in his face tightened. Though it cut into his wrists even more, he pressed them apart as much as he could and slowly began to move them away from his body little by little. "Would this witch be Sydney Vegesticka?"

"It would," said Novak.

"And would that mean she *gave* you the means to enter my home and murder my friends and grandmother?"

Novak's eyes narrowed skeptically. "I believe it was *you* who invited me in, so technically that would be your fault."

With one hard, painful motion the restrains snapped. Mason grabbed the chair, lunged at him like a runaway train, and brought it hammering down on him. Novak didn't move.

"You *bastard!*" Mason shouted, insults flying from him like bullets, as he landed one blow after another upon Novak. He may as well have been hitting him with a rubber chicken for all the good it did. The flesh his fists hit felt more like frozen meat than anything living. As his hands grew sore and his spirit tired, he fell to his knees, defeated.

He looked up at the vampire.

"That was our only chair," said Novak with a sigh, face hard as stone. "Let me give you some advice . . ."

The minor amount of distance between them disappeared in an instant.

"*DON'T INSULT ME!*" he shouted point blank in Mason's right ear. There was a *pop*, followed by a sharp pain, and the entire right hemisphere of his hearing muted, replaced with a high-pitched tone. With his good ear he heard dogs barking somewhere way off in the distance of the city he'd forgotten was even there.

Novak stood back up and strolled casually away from him. "Granny was stupid enough to make that mistake, and look what happened to her."

"You're going to pay," said Mason, fierce as a rabid dog. Blood rushed to his ears in a spike of red noise from his own raised voice. "*God* will make you pay! I really hope there is a Hell, so that you can burn in it!" He couldn't believe the words coming out of his mouth.

"Oh wow!" said Novak. "You've got your dick right in the peanut butter, don't cha?"

"I've seen things you could never know," said Mason. "Never understand. That makes a difference."

"Oh, let me guess." Novak stroked his chin. "A little something like . . . this?"

The padded cell of a psych ward. Fluorescent bulbs burning him away little by little. Not so much as a window to see the sun. Arms bound up in the folds and straps of a straightjacket. Staring into one of the four hard corners.

"Vell, Mason?"

He turned his head.

There sat Novak—or Dr. Novak, according to his nametag. White coat. Glasses. Hair parted to one side. The air of an all-knowing self-importance and invasive curiosity. Swung his chair around to face him as he clicked away at a ballpoint pen.

"Let'z ztart vith a few qvestions, shall ve?"

Doctor Novak flipped through his notes.

"Tell me . . ."

He floated off his chair, gliding toward Mason like a shark in water. Pointed teeth grazing the air as he neared. Slowly he slid his glasses down the slope of his nose.

"How many times have you faced DEATH?"

· · ·

Mason returned to reality, out of breath and reeling. Trading one cell for another.

"See? I can make you see what I want to. Just like they can."

Mason recoiled. "Who *are* you?"

"Like I said, I was chosen. Just. Like. You." Novak glared at him. Not angry, but absolutely serious.

No. It couldn't . . .

The thought got no further than that. Because the truth was that of course it could. None of this was supposed to be. But it was.

"Let me tell you something. God is neither loving nor kind. He doesn't want to see evil undone by good. He *created* evil. He is vengeful and spiteful and cruel. *He* did this to me. If you're looking for a creature made in His image, look no further.

"And ya know what? I'm not even mad." He stretched his arms out to either side like a crow slowly stretching its wings. "Now I no longer carry the burden of remorse. Now I'm free." He stayed like that for a few seconds, then turned smoothly on his heel and faced Mason.

"But!" said Novak with a flick of his finger. "We've strayed completely off the point, so the rest of this witty little diatribe will have to wait." He stood and began to pace, fingers locked behind his back. "As I said, it's not so simple to let your tasty little friend go, because you have gone and done something *very stupid, haven't you?*" he sang in a shrill little tune.

"Is she alive or not?"

"That all depends on you. You see, as you must have gathered, I've stood in the presence of the Ram of God before. I know the feel of that awesome power. It's like being near a lightning bolt . . . and you don't feel that way. Why is that?"

"I don't know what you mean."

Novak narrowed his eyes at him and knelt down again. Without even noticing that he was holding something, Mason heard a small *click* and felt the cool metal of a switchblade touch his Adam's apple.

"I want you to listen to me very carefully. I'm giving you a chance to tell the truth once and for all, because that's just the kinda guy I am. If you lie, trust me, you will be very, *very* sorry."

He's bluffing. He had to be. If Julie was alive, where was she? If a spell had been placed on him to get him here, how could he be sure he had even really seen her when he arrived? No, too much of this didn't add up, and there was too much at stake. Mason mustered his strength and made sure his mind was closed. Steps pulled up, trapdoor shut good and tight.

"Close your mind as much as you like. All that tells me is that you're hiding something." He lifted Mason's head upward with the edge of the blade.

"Go to Hell."

Had Novak's skin not been so cold, Mason would have thought he was fuming. Finger and thumb between his lips, he gave a sharp whistle. Grinning like a cheeky crocodile.

One may smile, and smile, and be a villain.

There was barely even the scuff of footsteps as someone entered. Vampire by the looks of him, wearing dungarees and sporting a pompadour. He carried someone. A girl . . . wearing a silver charm bracelet.

"Julie!" Mason shouted, and began scrambling to his feet. He would have succeeded had Goldie not caught him and looped her arms through his.

Handcuffed and gagged and barely conscious, but it was Julie, and she was alive. She wore exactly the same clothes he had last seen her in two months ago. Her skin achingly pale and dirty, hair hung in grimy strands over her face.

"Wait!" said Mason. "I'll tell you everything."

"Aha!" said Novak. "So now you wanna talk?" He lifted Julie easily, locking the chain of her cuffs into a winch attached to the ceiling, and left her hanging there like a pig in a butcher's shop while he disappeared behind Mason somewhere.

Mason opened his mind up completely so he'd know he was telling the truth and spilled it. He told them about the cross, where he left it, what exactly he had done and how. Everything. He hated himself for it. But as soon as he saw her, he couldn't help it.

Then came the sound of something heavy, something metal dragging across the concrete floor. When he returned, Novak carried two things—an old Sanyo ghetto blaster and a twenty-pound sledgehammer. "You mean to tell me that you just . . . gave it up? Were *able* to give it up and just chucked it away?" He let out a few nasal laughs as he approached Julie. "God has a real sick, twisted sense of humor."

"No, please don't! I'll do anything you want, just don't hurt her."

"Sorry, funny boy. No more talking."

And with that, Goldie clamped her cold hand down over his mouth so that barely a sound could escape it.

Novak placed the ghetto blaster down on the floor and pressed the Play button. "I think I'll sing."

Something about the way he smiled at Mason upset him more than anything he had seen so far. An impish flare of his narrowed eyes that said *You ain't seen nothin' yet, kid.*

A flourish of Japanese flute flew out of the speakers. Then another. Then trumpets and keyboards above a bassline. Novak began to sway and bob his head, twirling the sledgehammer with the ease of a baton. Dancing around and spinning like the jubilant fiend he was. All that was missing were a forked tail and horns.

"Hey, hey-ayyy," he sang, zooming in right up close to Mason's face.

He spun and pivoted around Julie in a ballet of hellish mirth, mouthing along to the words of Peter Gabriel's "Sledgehammer."

At the brief pause in the song, Novak swung. Stopping inches from her terrified face.

"I wanna be . . ."

He sang when the chorus returned and swung again. This time it hit. Julie's screams of pain were muffled by the duct tape over her mouth.

". . . your sledgehammer."

He swung again, this time hitting Julie in the leg, which broke with such a noise that it could be heard over the music.

Mason could barely even form words, just howled a hoarse bleat of insane torment. All he managed to choke out was "STOP!"

"You believe that God is on your side, yes? Then pray."

Novak hit her again. She didn't even scream this time. The flat slap of metal on meat only forced the breath from her lungs in a hard huff.

Mason tried to look away but felt Goldie's inhumanly strong hands tight on his face like the squeeze of a vise, forcing him to watch.

Julie wasn't even conscious anymore, blacked out from the pain.

"Pray for me to stop," said Novak.

"P-please!"

"Please what?"

"Please don't!"

"Don't ask me. Ask the man upstairs."

"Please stop!"

"Pray!"

"Puh-puh-please . . ."

"PRAY!"

"PLEASE, GOD! NO MORE!"

Novak hit her again. And again. And again. And again. He didn't slow or even seem to tire, the sledgehammer just a toy in his hands. Contusions from the blunt force now bloomed like angry purple flowers. Novak bore down on her, really putting his strength into it, eyes thrilled by the harm he inflicted. The preternatural force with which he swung his blows snapped bones right out of the skin.

Lost to maddened ravings, Mason screamed his throat into a tight, sharp knot. Each hit chipped away a little part of him, winnowing him down to bare nerves and cold tears. What came from his own voice was the most ghastly of cries he had ever heard. What life remained in Julie slowly slipped away. It was just a matter of time.

I've failed her now too.

Goldie loosened her viselike grip on his face and let his tear-filled vision drop to the floor.

I failed.

A pair of dirty bare feet painted with cerise nail polish came into view. Cold, bony fingers lifted his head from the chin. Those hollow eyes hooked into his with empty malice. Mason looked up, broken. Reduced to pitiful sobs. He heard the crinkle of plastic and tasted red cherry as Novak placed a lollipop in his mouth.

"Shhh. It's all right. God couldn't save her . . . but I can."

A glimmer of hope showed in Mason's eyes.

"She's not gone yet. I can heal her, bring her back from the brink of death. And in exchange, you will help me undo the damage you've done and bring that house of pretenders down upon itself from within . . . and return to me what should have been mine."

Mason couldn't even muster a voice anymore. Outside his body, watching this horrid little scene unfold, disconnected from the form still held tight and immobile by Goldie as his will bent to the sinister silkiness of her mate's words. Wondering against the odds, beyond all capacity for rational thought, at what they meant.

"Yes or no?"

For a moment there was a blink of a connection with his disembodied self as the muscles in his throat flexed just enough to choke out a word.

"Yes."

Novak moved back over to Julie's limp body and began tearing the clothes off of her, revealing every wound beneath, until she hung there naked as the day she was born. Sweat and tears molding dark streaks down her face. Her eyes were still closed when he raised a hand to eye level and slashed at his wrist with the other, opening a gash where appeared blood so dark it was nearly black, and, tilting her head back so that her face pointed upward, let his blood drip into Julie's mouth.

Oh god. "No! Not like that!"

"Too late." Novak didn't even look at him, focused intently on what he was doing.

Whether from terror, curiosity, shock, or some combination of them all, Mason couldn't speak.

At first there was nothing. She just hung there for five sickening minutes. Then . . .

A twitch.

"Look," said Novak, positively rapt. "It never ceases to amaze. Every cell, every drop of blood devoured, consumed from the inside out . . ."

Originating from nowhere in particular, Julie's muscles convulsed. It was slight, but enough to send her swaying at the end of the chain that held her like a tangled marionette. Then a spasm in her disjointed arm. Soon her whole body was vibrating as her eyes opened so wide it seemed they might pop out of their sockets. Her face contorted in a voiceless scream. What little human life was left in her beaten body was being eaten away. Bruises disappearing along with any remaining color in her skin. Her arm popped back into its socket. Broken bones snapped back into place. There was a faint scattering sound like a handful of rice dashed across the floor, and Mason saw her teeth fall to the floor beneath her. Her eyes closed again.

". . . and transformed." Novak swept his arms outward and took a bow. "Beautiful."

He removed the tape from her mouth and bonds from her wrists, unhooked her from the chain, and folded her into his arms.

"I'm going to see that she gets a proper meal. Take him to the farm for me, won't you, baby doll?"

"No problemo."

"Iggy, Devereaux." Novak snapped his fingers at the rockabilly vamp and another that had appeared, his skin dark as burnt wood. "Go with her."

"I can handle myself."

"I know you can, precious. But we want to be extra careful."

"Fine." She gave the side of Novak's face a quick little lick. "Go be naughty."

With that, hand clasped firmly around the back of his neck, Goldie marched Mason out of the room, followed closely by her two bodyguards. He looked back and had just enough time to see Novak give a short waggle of his fingers, bidding him adieu.

Without so much as breaking stride, Goldie threw her arm around Mason and dropped six stories down to the ground below. He didn't even have time to yell.

FORTY-SIX

THEY LANDED IN FRONT OF A WAITING PANEL VAN. HEADLIGHTS cut, exhaust chuffing from the muffler. The back doors opened, seemingly on their own. Mason was sat down between Iggy and Devereaux while Goldie sat across from him.

The van started to move, rocking back and forth over the uneven ground before leveling off once the tires found pavement.

The coppery tint that was the scent of vampires crept into Mason's nose. Blood in the cold air; wind-worn skin after the assault of a blizzard. The feel of their bodies pressed against his sent a sickening chill through him. It was as if he were sitting between marble sculptures. Hard and unyielding, yet flesh and blood. There were no windows, but soon traffic and the other sounds of the city were gone, replaced by the low hum of the engine.

Time escaped him. Lost all meaning in this limbo he found himself in, somewhere between awake and asleep. His captors didn't move or speak, still as mannequins. He could still feel the frostbite of Goldie's hand on his neck. She watched him every unbroken moment of the trip.

He tried closing his eyes but saw only Julie on the backs of his eyelids. Beaten, still, and then reanimated into one of these things. Unable to bear it, he picked a spot on the dirty floor of the van—the only place he had left—and stayed there.

But Goldie couldn't even let him have that. Her legs spread, trying to draw his eyes upward as the hem of her leather skirt slid back to reveal naked white thighs and the slit between.

Nothing? she said without speaking, tossing her hair to try and catch his eye. *Not even a peek?*

Mason felt his gaze slowly training upward . . .

"Stop!" he shouted.

The two vampires beside him chuckled quietly through their noses. Nothing from Goldie. He shook it off and resumed staring at his tiny empty spot on the floor. He didn't have to see the harsh look she was giving him. He could feel it touching every part of him.

Her shadow reached beside her and picked something up. The sound of steel sliding against wood was followed by a cold lick against his cheek as the tip of his sword caressed his face. Gently.

Goldie's face came into view . . . but it was the wrong way. Upside down, dangling her head from the seat, turning her mane of blonde hair into a crown, back pressed flat against the seat as her legs stretched upward along the wall, ankles crossed daintily over each other, pointing the tips of her high heels toward the ceiling.

"There's nowhere you can go, funny boy." Goldie slid the rim of her purple shades down, revealing her lidless eyes for the first time. Blue as sulfur fire. And then, holding the sword at either end, she bent it until the tip nearly touched the hilt. "You're mine."

He tried to block her out. Closed his eyes and breathed deep. Still, he saw her face in his head.

"Shhh," said Goldie with false pity, her red lips pressed together in a pout. "It's okay." She tossed the bent blade to the side. "I'll let you rest for now. You're going to need it." She winked at him deviously, seductively. Assuring him that she meant to make good on her advances.

His head and limbs fell heavily as if weighted down by tons of sand. He became a shadow frozen against the hard metal case around him. Trapped in every way. His eyes drooped and before long he entered a state of waking sleep. Eyes half closed. Mind half numb.

Something resembling sleep to crept in, and he dreamed of lips, a long forked tongue sliding out between them, revealing perfectly white, perfectly sharp fangs, and up the length of his erection, only to be bitten clean off. The blood that gushed from the stump was rubbed like lipstick until those lips were a bright shiny red.

Shoved hard back into the trap he was in. Then the whole thing would start again.

Much like *fornicate*, there's a certain connotation about the word *molest*. Plainly, it means to bother or harass someone in an aggressively persistent manner. But in common usage it implies a violation, specifically of the private parts. And that is just what was being violated now, his most private of parts. His mind.

After what felt like hours, the van slowed to a crawl before coming to a stop.

"What's the problem?" Goldie demanded.

"There's a bear carcass in the road," said a nervous human voice from the driver's seat. "Looks like it's been hit."

"And you're so useless that I have to *tell you* to go around?"

"It's...really big," he said, clearly trying and failing not to let the shiver in his voice show. "I think it has to be moved."

Goldie snapped her fingers at Iggy and Devereaux. They obeyed like the good dogs they were. Mason could hear their footsteps on the road around either side of the vehicle as they faded away.

Then silence.

An odd sensation overcame him—a charge in the air that clung to him like wet snow. A voiceless wave that rose and crashed. And he knew Goldie felt it as well. The feeling that something was about to happen.

"Oh shit!" shouted the driver, followed by the sound of pierced glass from the cab of the vehicle.

Goldie flew from where she was sitting and gathered Mason up like a bundle of rags. Back flat to the side opposite the doors, she positioned herself behind him and clasped her hand to his throat.

All went quiet again. No sound from outside.

"Whoever you are, *back off*, or I swear I'll cut his —"

A spear tore through the side of the van. Flew through the metal with the ease of a pencil through tissue paper, narrowly missing Mason's head.

She released him and he looked behind to see that the spear had caught Goldie in the throat, pinning her to the opposite side from which it had entered. She clawed at her neck, angry and panicked, dark blood spurting from the wound.

RUN!

He heard it in his mind but didn't know where it came from.

Finally free, Mason scrambled out of the van and started running.

He was in the middle of nowhere on a dark country road surrounded by nothing but trees. Not even the moon was out anymore—at least not that he could see. The distant glow of the sun was barely visible in the early-morning sky. He didn't care. He just knew he had to put as much distance between him and the truck as fast as possible. And so he ran.

Didn't think. Didn't look back.

He ran so hard that his legs were in danger of giving out, so hard that he felt that he might take off and leave the ground at any moment . . . when his feet kicked at nothing but air and he saw that that was exactly what had happened.

Carried away on desperate wings, it seemed, until he realized that he was held in limbs so strong they could only be made of solid rock. Into the trees he went, fabric rippling in the air, through leaves and branches as swiftly as the wind itself.

Had he died? Had his soul left his body, collected by a passing

reaper, spiriting away to the other side? Perhaps. But if so, a camouflage poncho and ski mask were strange attire for an angel of Death.

They dove head first to the ground, whizzing through foliage and
into the mouth of a small cave. Surrounded by stone, swallowed by a
disorienting darkness away from the trees, all at once. Mason stood
still now, on his own, and was told to remain so by the same disembodied voice that had told him to flee.

Damp and cold all around him, only a few feet underground but
enough to feel buried, immediately triggering his claustrophobia.

Through the opening of the cave he could see the tops of trees in
the distance, stretching toward the sky as the chilly autumn blue just
began warming to pink. No sound but the dawn chorus of robins
outside.

Good, thought Mason. *Let them sing.* Let him fall asleep listening
to their song and never wake. Let the next word he heard from the
shadows be *Rest.*

The robins stopped singing.

That was all it took for his heart to pump ice water and his whole
body to tremble.

Silent as the grave except for his rapid breaths. He put his hand
over his mouth to stop them.

A face appeared at the mouth of the cave from above like a bat
hanging from its perch. It was the one called Devereaux. Dark and
angry, a huge gash across one side of his face making the skin of his
cheek hang in a flap below the chin.

He swooped down from above and lumbered toward him. Not
the eerily graceful motions he had seen from vampires so far. Rigid.
Sluggish, even. Drained of blood and energy. He held an arrow in
one hand, wet with dark red dripping off the pointed end.

Mason backed away as he neared. The creature raised the arrow
up above his head, poised to strike.

A hooded figure appeared at the cave mouth, took aim with a
crossbow.

Devereaux heard the string tense and dodged just as the arrow flew. He lunged, still hindered by his injury, and clashed with his attacker.

A feral noise sounded through the cave, exploding against the rock wall in a concussive blast so strong he thought it might crack. Mason covered his ears, but it did little good against the sharp wail, his right ear already damaged enough to barely need protecting. If Hell had cats instead of hounds, they would sound like this.

The hooded one slammed the crossbow into his attacker's chest, stopping him from pouncing. Devereaux grabbed the crossbow and flung it away, out the cave mouth. They spat and hissed at each other, clawing with the merciless savagery of brawling panthers. Devereaux's exposed skin broke in one horrid gash after another. The camouflage clothes of Mason's guardian tore open one after another.

A powerful swipe landed on the slashed side of Devereaux's face, ripping the flap of skin that was his cheek clean off. He let out a guttural howl, made louder by the fact that his mouth had been widened by several inches.

Devereaux grabbed and threw the hooded one at the stone ceiling of the cave with all his might. The popping of bones sounded and as he fell toward the cave floor he was stopped by a knee into his chest.

Beaten, clothes torn in tatters, the hooded one lay motionless.

Devereaux crouched down and ripped what was left of the mask from his face and stood aghast.

"*You!*" he shouted.

He raised a foot, boot poised to hammer down on the exposed face. As it fell upon its mark, a hand flew up from below, grasping the arrow that had missed earlier, and pierced right through it.

Devereaux shrieked, eyes blazing, and fell to his knees.

The hooded one buried his hands between open jaws and pulled them apart with every ounce of strength he could muster. The face split in half, tendons snapping, until all that was left atop the neck was a mandible and two bottom fangs.

Mason sat motionless. Ears deafened, nerves frayed.

His guardian picked up both parts of the former vampire and

flung them out of the cave in different directions. The sun still had yet to show itself proper, but when it did the remains would be no more.

He turned toward Mason.

Mason had seen through the eyes that met his own, yet never laid them on the face they were part of.

The face of William Graves.

Same features, same long hair, same beard as when Mason had seen him knelt in prayer in an unexplored corner of a distant memory. Only now his skin was white beyond death, heavily burned and scarred. Pointed fangs marred each row of teeth. And if there was anything left of his kindly brown eyes, it was drowned in inky black pools of pupils swelled to full size in the darkness of the cave.

Whatever momentary amount of safety Mason had felt was suddenly gone.

They each said nothing, simply stood there regarding each other. Eerie how still he was. People can only be so still. There is always some movement—involuntary twitches, the chest rising with each breath, even just a blink. Will showed none of these. If he didn't know better, Mason would have thought time had stopped.

Until he spoke.

"Don't fall behind." Not menacing nor threatening, but deep and boundless as a hole in the earth. He pulled up his hood and began walking away.

And so Mason left the cave behind, along with everything he thought he knew up until now.

FORTY-SEVEN

The woods come alive when the sun rises. Birds chirp all around. Woodpeckers jackhammer holes into tree trunks. Leaves rustle as the wind blows through them and everything else it touches, sweeps them up and carries them away.

All of these were missing here. Instead, the woods were dead and bitter cold. Gray clouds clung to the sky, a frozen bed of ashes with only the tiniest bit of a glowing coal. Not so much as a puddle in which to cast even the shallow reflection of life.

They had been walking for not even ten minutes when Mason's foot came down with a dry crunch. A bundle of sticks, he assumed, until he looked down to see the gutted carcass of a cottontail rabbit. Little left but bone and fur, one eye closed to a half-moon cast upward at him. He wondered if they were out here too. The dead. Here, where no road was in sight and no voices to be heard.

Will halted. Raised a hand, signaling for him to stop. Mason stopped so abruptly that one foot dangled in the air halfway between steps before he placed it gently back down.

A wave of tension swept through him as the hairs on his arms pricked up. And not just in himself—he felt the same tension from

Will as well. Only his was more purposeful, pointing toward the stimulus.

Mason listened but heard nothing.

Before he could speak, Will had vanished before his eyes and the world fell away beneath him once again. Clasped tight in his arms, he was carried through the trees. Branches dashed dangerously close to his head, and more than once he felt the scratch of a twig against his face.

The trunk of a large oak came forth at break-neck speed, only to dart out of the way when Will changed direction. As they reached the edge of a clearing, he leapt, and for a second Mason was weightless. He thought his bones might continue on without him, but they caught up as they plummeted straight down toward the surface of a pond. Will braced Mason's head with his hand and they pierced the water together like an arrow through a pane of glass. Slicing through the water instead of crashing into it. Swift as could be. He barely had time to register the rush of water in his ears or the paralyzing cold before they sprang out at the other end of the pond.

"Are . . ." he choked—". . . you . . ."—out—". . . *crazy?*"—between coughs.

"*Quiet.*" Will commanded. Never had he heard a whisper so loud.

The wind from their speed bit at his cheeks worse than before now. It may have been bearable had he known where they were going or why.

They came to a small ravine. Will darted across it with no more effort than taking another step. Next thing Mason knew, they were surrounded by foliage and shadow, deep in a copse of pine trees covering the southern slope, his vision cluttered by the needles of their branches. What little he could see was of the escarpment on the other side, where they themselves had been mere seconds ago, branches still swaying on a bush they had sped past.

Fixed to the slanting ground like a tree stump, Will didn't so much as budge. Mason breathed a thankful sigh of relief and let his body rest against him.

All was quiet again except for the robins.

Then they too fell silent.

A cold whisper drifted into his head. *Do not . . . make . . . a sound. Not even a breath.*

His breath puffed out before him until he cupped his mouth with his hand. He heard no approach, none at all, but did exactly as he was told.

Through the trees on the escarpment he spied a most peculiar sight. A bear appeared in the clearing, moving as no bear could. It didn't lumber or plod the way any other member of its species would; instead, it moved with the gait and stance of a human. He knew that bears could stand on their hind legs but had never heard of them walking on them, nor moving with the swiftness of a panther. And certainly not carrying a spear.

It turned. With its underside now visible, he saw that it was no bear at all, but rather the skin of one worn like a suit. A woman's face where the chest should have been. Goldie's face.

She scanned the woods, head panning this way and that for any sign of life. The freshly cut hide made a cloak that hung loosely in thick folds of fur, protecting her from the all-seeing yellow eye of the sun. Blood smeared over every inch of exposed skin, making her once-pallid complexion a deep bronze. Her hair hung in patchy orange strands in front of her face. Even from a distance the gash in her throat was visible and crusted with dark dried blood as though a thick layer of rust had gathered on her neck.

Mason didn't have to be told not to breathe now.

Ehhh-hehsss . . . ehhh-hehsss . . .

The pit of his stomach became hollow and sick as he listened to the high-pitched rasp, the hiss of a fuming viper. She continued scanning her surroundings, sniffing the air. Senses overpowered by the wound in her throat and the animal carcass around her body, she grew visibly agitated when they revealed no secrets to her.

Mason tightened his hand over his mouth, unsure how much longer he could hold his breath. He didn't even dare wish her to go away lest she hear the stray thought. His heart hammered away in his chest, making Mason fear it would betray them.

. . . *ehhh-hehsss . . . ehhh-hehsss . . . ehhh-hehsss . . . ehhh-hehsss . . .*

Fear and cold. His body wanted to shake. It craved to. It needed to. But through sheer will, he grabbed his arms tight and made sure they didn't. He went inside himself. Deep in his head, picturing himself cowering in the bushes, as small as possible, and closed it all up. Tight.

So still and unyielding was Will, he might have been a shard of rock jutting up from a hidden bed of sediment.

. . . *ehhh-hehsss . . . ehhh-hehsss . . . ehhh—*

Satisfied that her prey was nowhere near, Goldie began to move off.

A rustle came from the ravine floor below, directly between her and them.

Goldie stopped and looked their way. With a steady pace she crouched and began stalking toward them. Each unwelcome step crunched leaves and snapped twigs. He imagined her high-heeled foot snapping his bones with the same ease.

The impulse to flee was so strong that had his limbs not been frozen stiff, he would have bolted right then.

She raised the spear, poised to strike.

Something ran for its life from the thicket as fast as it could, leaving a trail of shaking branches in its wake.

The spear flew and found its mark followed by a painful screech. Goldie disappeared from view, darting from her perch so fast that the bear skin fell to the ground. She fell upon her quarry, a raccoon by the sounds of it. The poor creature let out one tortured yip after another, all but pleading to be released from its misery.

She happily obliged.

The sun was beginning to climb higher into the sky, slowly winning its struggle with the clouds. The sounds of deep scratching and clawing at the ground could be heard as a cloud of dirt kicked up from the overgrowth where Goldie had gone. When the dust finally settled, all went quiet again.

After a few minutes, hushed but clear, Will said, "She sleeps."

He moved from his spot and out of the trees so deftly that the branches weren't even disturbed. A feat not even the breeze could achieve. Mason, however, was a lumbering moose by comparison, sliding and stumbling down the slope, as they moved steadily away from the ravine, due east through an open wilderness.

There was no mistaking that winter was not far off. The early fall morning chilled Mason to the bone. It didn't seem to phase Will at all. The sun, however, was another matter. Showing itself through the rapidly retreating darkness, splintering rays of light over the treeline. The trees provided much less cover now that their leaves had been shed. They kept to the shade as much as possible, but every now and then thin coils of smoke appeared where the light touched the wider tears in Will's poncho.

Mason followed several steps behind, stumbling over the rough, uneven terrain that didn't slow his fellow traveler in the slightest. Each breath danced in a curling plume before him. His feet mashed through the thick blanket of dead leaves, the early-morning frost giving a pulpy slog to his steps as it melted. Mason felt sluggish as a ship with drooping sails now that the numbing effects of alcohol were long gone. The embryo stages of a hangover growing with each step.

Not so with Will. Moving in an unbroken motion, he dipped and wove wherever the ground was uneven, each step taking him more than twice as far as they should have. Mason got the feeling that he was moving with only a fraction of the speed of which he was capable, that if he wanted to he could vanish from sight in the time between breaths. He had not spent this long in the presence of a vampire before, and each one had been trying to capture or torment him in some way. There was that same eerie sense of danger, of being prey within range of a predator; it pressed against his every nerve, making him want to cut loose and run. Only this was different somehow. Milder. Less chaotic.

There was something else, too, a connection he had felt with Will as they sped through the treetops; it was as if, for a moment, Mason had been the one carrying someone to safety with such ease. Seeing the branches rush past his face as though through his own eyes. It was how Mason knew that on his way to rescue him, Will had happened upon a pair of poachers, father and son, whom he had relieved of their blood, gear, and kill in the form of a rather large black bear. How he knew that the sun now caused an intolerable burning stink in his nostrils. And it was how he knew that, while Will could not help thirsting at the mere smell of a human so close to him, he was letting Mason know all this because he meant him no harm.

It was disturbing, thirsting for himself through the mind and senses of someone else. If *thirst* was the right word for it. An ache in both body and soul. Imagine the constant pangs of hunger, the despondent nausea of heartbreak, and the withdrawal from your drug of choice all at once, and it would but scratch the surface. He may have meant Mason no harm, but how long could this thirst last before it would need to be quenched?

After a few hours—one, maybe two, he couldn't be sure—they came to a clearing where a cheery brook innocently trickled away. The first sign of anything even vaguely resembling life since they began their trek through this desolate patch of forest.

Will stopped and crouched down.

"What is it?" said Mason nervously, crouching as well.

Will held up a finger, signaling for him to wait.

Nothing but the gentle flow of water.

Then the snap of twigs.

As if breathed into existence by the forest itself, a deer appeared. Completely unaware of their presence, she strolled calmly to the water, bowed her head, and drank. Mason had never seen a deer this close before, at least not for long. Usually it was just for a moment as they went bounding across the road.

Not very much older than a fawn, she stared back at Mason. Her big round eyes, dark and curious, sparkled in the sunlight.

Beautiful, but harmless.

Relieved, Mason stood.

With a single feline pounce, Will sprang from his crouched position and snatched her up. The animal bleated out in distress until her throat was caught by an iron grip. He stretched the neck and buried his face in it. Sleek velvet skin turned wet. Hooves beat frantically against the stones of the creek bed. When it had stopped moving, Will proceeded to lap up the matted blood like a cat licking a wound.

Something changed in Mason—a veil lifted from him, dropped at the very moment of the kill, exposing the true horrible essence of this sight. His emotions, calm, almost serene moments ago, now flared. A gentle ocean consumed by a full-blown storm.

Repulsed, Mason backed away. As he did, Will disappeared before his eyes again and the head of the deer fell limp to the ground.

Mason took another step backward and bumped into the trunk of a tree. He spun around to see that it was no tree at all, but Will. His face closer, clearer than it had been this whole time. Same eyes, same colorless skin. No sign of the fangs he knew were there, chin stained red, dripping off the beard that covered it.

"No, please!" Mason said. In that moment he was certain that his luck had finally run out.

Will raised a hand in front of his face, dragging his fingers down through the air, the motion leaving a ghostly trail behind them.

Sleep.

The word slid in one ear and flicked a switch in his brain. Mason's eyelids drooped and the hypnotic voice carried him off from the waking world.

Just like before, all light and color dimmed as the world dropped away into a black void. Peeking through a keyhole, he could see and hear but had no control over what took place on the other side of the door. He didn't recognize the faraway sights that were his surroundings, a haze of monochromatic shapes and silhouettes rushing lazily by.

And so it went, for how long he could not say.

Next thing he knew, the keyhole world had returned to full view, vibrance and motor functions along with it. The woods were gone, given way to the cement, metal, and glass of civilization.

FORTY-EIGHT

"Hello? . . . Hello?"

It took a moment for Mason's senses to return before realizing where he was. Sat on the curb of a parking lot, with a road ahead along with a few small buildings—a gas station and diner by the looks of it. He turned to see a payphone, the receiver resting patiently on top, beckoning him with its tinny voice.

A voice he recognized.

A woman appeared from around the corner, purse slung over one shoulder, poking at a handful of change with her finger as she closed in on the phone. She didn't even seem to notice him until Mason sprang to his feet and dashed ahead of her, scooping up the receiver just in time.

"Hello?" he said.

The woman's eyes went wide with alarm. She took a few nervous steps backward and disappeared back around the corner.

"Hello?"

"IQ?"

"Mason, is that you?"

"Hi, I'm here."

"Mason, are you okay?"

"I don't know. I . . . I think so."

"Where are you?"

"I don't know. Somewhere upstate, maybe. I'm not sure."

"What can you see around you?"

"Uh . . . a diner. Gas station." Mason turned left and spotted what he had not seen before. "There's a sign . . . says 'Warwick, three miles.' "

The tapping of computer keys came from the other end of the line.

"Okay, no problem. Just stay put. We'll send someone to come get you."

"Yeah . . . yeah, send someone."

"Are you sure you're not in danger?"

"Yeah . . . good. Send . . . someone. Good."

Mason dropped the receiver, the metallic rattle of its cord scraping along the side as it dangled like a hanging victim at the end of a noose. He raised his hands to his head and walked slowly away in a daze.

Of course it was all hitting now. It couldn't have been in the middle of the woods with no one around but the birds.

(And a vampire or two.)

He couldn't have been overwhelmed by waves of panic while surrounded by trees. No. It had to be now, in some parking lot, surrounded by cars and families and decent folk blissfully unaware of the things he had seen lurking wherever the light did not touch, beyond their convenient world of rest stops. Because that's what grief does. It waits. For the most inconvenient moment just to pour a little extra salt in the wound.

They all backed away, these decent folk, as he neared. Oh yes. If they were going into the diner, they hurried in. If they were coming out, they kept an eye on him while making their way to wherever they had parked. None bothered to ask if he was all right or needed help, only *Why does he have to be here? Why can't he take his troubles else-*

where? They didn't need to say it nor did he need to hear their thoughts.

Honestly, he couldn't blame them. He must have looked a fright, incoherently gibbering, wandering absently through the parking lot. Stinking of sweat, dirt, and whatever he had been drinking last night.

A car beeped at him as it passed, warning him to look where he was going.

Each shallow breath made him more dizzy, face flushed and chest numb, yet he continued forward. His heart didn't feel right, beating at a rapid, almost dangerous pace. A heart attack? No one his age should have any reason to fear such a thing, but that was what it felt like. And as the pins and needles spread from his chest, down his arms, he was filled with the overwhelming sensation that he was going to die. Eighteen years old, and how many times had he thought he was going to die?

Finally he slumped down against the outside wall of the diner and broke into a cold sweat.

He watched as the woman who had needed to use the payphone hung up the receiver at the end of her call and made her way back to her minivan. She slid the door aside, revealing a little girl, three or four years old, dancing a stuffed dog across the back of the seat in front of her. Not a care in the world. Now he felt bad. He had probably scared the hell out of her a minute ago. Even though he hadn't meant to, and approaching would likely just make things worse, he felt compelled to apologize.

Mason got to his feet and took one step off the curb.

"Mama," came a tiny voice from below.

He looked down to see he had stepped on something. A doll. Dirty and old, caked with dried mud. What had once been yellow hair and a green dress had both turned a filthy gray. Soft cloth now rough and gritty. Her happy, smiling face missing an eye.

He knelt and picked it up. It must have fallen out of a car that had stopped here ages ago, this thing that had been loved once. Some child's best friend, left behind.

He flipped her upside down to get a look under her dress for the tag. He took it between his fingers and found a name written in felt marker so everyone would know who she belonged to.

It was not just a name.

It was a sign.

"Mason," came a voice from beside him.

He had not even noticed footsteps as they approached.

Grim, somber and concerned and certainly not happy, had appeared next to the table he sat at. Outside the entire team gathered, all dressed in their civvies, weapons either covertly in hand or tucked somewhere easily accessible. Seeing them all here, a mixture of expressions on their faces—and Miggs sporting a swollen cheek—filled him with shame.

He couldn't remember actually entering the diner, but he did remember why. He had come in to get warm and sat in a booth by the window, nursing a cold coffee he couldn't pay for, holding the doll he'd found. He'd chosen a window seat so he would be seen by whoever came to collect him, but he hadn't expected that that meant everybody.

The place was thick with fresh-brewed coffee and frying batter of one kind or another. Silverware clinking on plates and the shuffling of chairs as customers either sat down or got up to leave. Somewhere in the parking lot outside, a truck fired up and drove away. The sun had been at his back when he sat down. It was now high in the sky and quickly moving west.

"Are you all right?" Grim didn't even look angry. Just worried. This was one of those times when he might expect to get a favorite adage of parents far and wide: *I'm not mad, I'm just disappointed.* Words he had never heard from Rose, even when he blew his savings on Patches. Then again, he had never given her any real reason to say them. Not like this.

"That's almost more of a philosophical question at this point," said Mason, slow and eerily calm.

"All right, well, let's get you home," said Grim. "We can talk about it on the way."

Mason looked down at the dirty doll he still held between his hands. "No."

"Beg pardon?"

Mason stayed seated. "We should talk about it now."

Grim gave him an incredulous look. It was asking a lot, he knew, but without so much as a sigh, Grim sat down across from him.

As soon as he did, the waitress returned. A squat, tired-looking woman in her fifties, hair tied back and a pair of glasses hanging on a chain around her neck. The nametag said her name was Peggy. Mason didn't remember it from before. Didn't even remember ordering his coffee.

"What'll it be?"

"Just tea for me, please," said Grim.

She left without another word. Once she returned with the tea and left the table again, Mason told him everything.

Rose's ghost. Miggs. Novak. Julie. And, last but not least, Will.

When he was finished, Grim remained quiet. Pensive. He reached into his inside coat pocket and took out the letter he had shown him before, addressed to Father Abbott but with Mason's name inside. He unfolded it and stared at the few words written on the page.

"It all makes sense now," he said with a slight break in his voice. "I wish that it didn't."

Mason barely heard his words, dwelling on the most particularly troubling part of it all. Thought about it long and hard. Sometimes we don't ask questions because we don't want the answer, even though deep down, where it matters most, we already know. And once again he found himself at a crossroads, only this time he saw no third option. To be, or not to be. He was damned either way.

"Who is Novak?"

The silence lingered until it was nice and uncomfortable. Awkward as it gets.

Grim took the deepest of breaths, one forced to breathe in the smoke of ruins he couldn't be rid of. "Novak was once Christopher Murphy. A normal person, just like you. Until one fateful day, also like you, tragedy befell him in the form of a car accident in which he was clinically dead for more than an hour. Fortunately, due to the cold weather, he was eventually revived. His parents, with whom he was traveling, however, were not so fortunate."

"Yep, good fortune all around," Mason said sarcastically.

Grim continued, unfazed. "With near-death experiences being something we keep an eye on, Will was sent to have a look at him. Lo and behold, he discovered that Nov—Christopher was distantly related to Saint Philip. Will had seen possession of the Holy Spirit claim the lives of his brothers, his father before him, his grandfather before that, and was desperate to avoid the same fate. It's why he became a missionary instead of a soldier. It's why he was convinced that Christopher, who very much wanted it, should have it instead of him.

"They grew close, the two of them. Praying together, asking that when the time came God bestow the Holy Spirit upon one rather than the other. But when the time came, it happened exactly as it always had.

"Christopher became distraught. Unstable. He returned to the chapterhouse constantly, insisting that they couldn't give up, until eventually he was told not to return."

"I'm going to guess he didn't like that."

"He did not. And to demonstrate his displeasure, he took a hostage at knife-point and demanded to see Will. One thing led to another and he was subdued, but the altercation resulted in him suffering a spinal injury which paralyzed him from the waist down."

"Okay. Starting to understand him a little bit."

Grim hung his head. "That's just what I was afraid of."

"How's that?"

"The truth? I didn't *want* you to understand him. I didn't want you to see his side of things or sympathize with him. My concern was that if you were looking for someone to blame for the series of misfortunes you've suffered, it may have been directed somewhere it didn't belong."

"*Sympathize?*" Mason raised his voice. "I'm just sorry no one had the balls to finish him off *before* he killed everyone I've ever cared about!"

His fists gripped the tablecloth, making two tight wrinkles on either side of him, as he caught the inquisitive glances of others in the diner.

Grim waited a moment before continuing. "Had we known then what we know now, we would have done differently. But that's just not how things work. Surely you can understand that."

Mason released his grip and straightened the tablecloth. "I suppose so," he said with a sip of cold coffee and an exceptional display of tact, the true purpose of which he kept hidden for now. "So how did he become a vampire?"

"We don't know. He was committed to Saint Jude's and then, one day just before Christmas, he escaped. Somehow, some time after that he became the glib, blood-thirsty fiend he is today."

"Do you have any idea how Will became one?"

"Until a few minutes ago I didn't even know he was still alive. If you could even call it that. No, I haven't a clue. And for the time being, I think it would be best if we kept that particular detail just between the two of us."

"Okay," Mason said, more than somewhat skeptical.

"Poor Will. This should not have happened to him. Or to you."

"You know, I think in all the cosmos, in all the infinite possibilities, somewhere there's a reality in which it didn't. One where he managed to stop the Quake from ever happening, and I went on to live a normal life with my parents and never knew anything about any of this."

He saw a future that would never come to be now. One in which he and Julie wound up together, got married, had kids, and, like many marriages, were simply not right for each other but stayed together anyway. She would eventually cheat on him, of course. He saw himself old and bald and overweight. Never having left Stonehill, never amounting to anything more than the manager of Gus's Gas & Garage. And eventually, a tombstone with his name on it, the line between the dates of birth and death as short and insignificant as the life it represented. All of that might have been bearable had his grave and Julie's been next to each other. But they weren't. She may have been a good friend, but she wasn't a good fit.

"I've thought about that so many times since all this happened," Mason said. "How I'd give anything to live in that world now. To be boring and normal. No different from anyone else. But we don't live in that world, do we?"

"No. I'm afraid not. And believe me when I say that if you strive for anything, let it be something other than normal."

Mason nodded slowly, methodically. "Then I finally know what I have to do."

"Does that mean what I think it means?"

"Yes." Mason held out his hand.

Grim reached into his breast pocket again—same one where he had kept the letter—produced a silver cross on a thin chain, and touched it to his open palm.

Mason held it for a moment, then clutched it tightly in his fist.

White fire burned up his vision.

Black explodes into white again.

An almighty eye. The sum of all existence and consciousness converging in a single blink. Watching him. Peering into him. Within its pupil every star to every speck of dust, its iris the eternal colored fibers of matter and energy feeding into the material plane around it. A supernova of color. Toxic red. Stone purple. Acid orange. Lovely strawberry yellow. The blue of a dead star. All burning white-hot enough to leave a sizzling brand on his retinas. And beyond, a sclera of emptiness that knows no bounds. In the crux of it all, strands of the aether collide. Left and right, top and bottom. And in this fraction of a fraction of an instant, the words are uttered . . .

"*Please. Save me.*"

Speed applies not to movement so sublime. Through dimension after dimension on a beam of light toward an imperfect piece of dirt orbiting an insignificant particle of light to the voice that pleads with its last breath.

Not looking at him, but rather he sees himself through it. The watched and the watcher. The crux not before him, but within. The words again.

"*Please. Save me.*"

Plunging through time and space. Only the form he enters this time is no longer that of a stranger, a dying boy long ago.

It is his own.

When Mason's vision returned to him, the startling clarity he had become accustomed to returned with it. He knew instantly that there were nine other people in the diner—five he could see, four he could not. Their minds jumbled together like scattered ripples on a pond. Immediately he commanded his senses to order and, without difficulty or interference, silenced them.

"Welcome back," said Grim, all but moved to tears.

"Good to be back," said Mason peacefully, slipping the cross over his head and around his neck where it belonged. That warm spot in his forehead was back too. Different this time. Comfortable. Cozy as a toasted marshmallow.

"Come. Let's get you home."

"We can't leave. We have to find Novak."

"Yes, we do. Let's get back to base so we can—"

"No. Now."

"Mason, this is hardly the time. We need to regroup. Just our

406

presence here this soon after an attack is a security risk. And you need to be checked out after what you've been through."

"I swear if I see the inside of that infirmary one more time . . ." For a moment, the table his hands rested on rattled. "It *has* to be now."

"We don't even know where to start looking."

Boarded-up windows of an old house. A barn with no sign of livestock. All surrounded by dead trees. Will must have left the image there, floating in his mind like a message in a bottle, before he left. "Ten miles, north-northwest of here. There's a farm. That's where we'll find Novak."

"How do you know?"

Mason turned over the letter Grim had placed on the table in front of him and held it up. "Because *he* does."

"Mason, I admire your zeal. But you're nowhere near ready for this yet."

At this he took the doll's tag between his fingers again and showed Grim the name it bore in thick black ink.

JULIE

"It's not hers, of course. That really would be a miracle. But I think I'm beginning to understand what you mean by God giving us signs."

"How so?"

"Well . . ." Mason looked at him quizzically. "Do you think this is a coincidence?"

Grim didn't have to think about it long. "No. I don't."

"Me neither. Had everything not happened exactly as it did, I would never have found it. I think it's a needle on a compass, pointing the way."

Grim pondered away, eyes down, turning the thought over and over like the doll he held. Or at least he made it look that way to disguise the fact that he had already made up his mind, but he still weighed the options between what is smart and what is right. For they are seldom the same.

"Grim," said Mason.

Their eyes met.

"You want me to be the messiah, yes? You want me to be the Ram of God? Then let me be."

And with that a smile creased Grim's face. "We had better get going then." He picked the letter up off the table, left some money for the coffee and tea, and got to his feet.

Mason, however, didn't get up. "One last thing."

Grim paused before he could get even a step away from the table.

"The full truth from now on. You keep nothing from me, I keep nothing from you. Agreed?"

Grim's face told him so much before he ever spoke. With his last word, Mason began scanning away, watching for any shift in his gaze, any change in his breathing. Listening for his pulse to quicken. But he found none.

"Agreed," said Grim, and made for the door.

And there it was. Faint, barely a whiff in the air as he passed, but unmistakable.

The burning smell of a lie.

FORTY-NINE

The farm was north of the town of Warwick, not far from the state line with New Hampshire, and surrounded by trees, most of which were bare. The frost which had gathered on them melted in the afternoon sun, dripping from the branches. It consisted of a single house with boarded-up windows—the universal sign of a place no one has lived in for ages—a barn that had seen better days, and a grain silo, but no sign of livestock. No vehicles parked. No one patrolling the grounds. It appeared to be abandoned.

So, of course, it was anything but.

"Looks like no one's home," said Mason as he handed the binoculars back to Grim.

"Yes, that *is* what it looks like," Grim said with an unconvinced furrow to his brow.

They hiked back to a dirt road at the outer perimeter of the property, a line of trees and an overgrown field between them. Mason could see the team donning Kevlar and readying weapons and gear as they approached. All except for Sarah, who wore a long gray coat and intently faced the direction of the house as if she were trying to move it with her mind.

Stepping into the truck, Mason first took two Motrin that Grim gave him for his hangover. Then he picked up a tactical vest and slipped it on. He found it surprisingly light. Gun and holster fastened to his side, he removed a blade from its sheath and examined it. A long, mean-looking tactical machete with serrated teeth. Functional, but ugly. Nowhere near the elegance of the katana he had been given mere hours ago. The image of Goldie bending it in half brought his blood to a boil. She may as well have wiped her ass with a van Gogh. With a harsh sigh at one more thing lost, he sheathed and strapped it around his chest.

Considering what they were about to do, he should have been overcome with nerves. But for the first time since this crazy ride began, he felt focused. Resolved. Still, that didn't make what lay ahead any easier.

Grim stepped over to Yen, who was sitting in the passenger's side of the truck's cab, focused on the pad controlling their surveillance drone.

"Thermals?"

Yen held up the display. It flickered with an infrared bird's-eye view of the house interspliced with shattered frames of static.

"Hmm."

"What is it?" asked Rodriguez.

Yen made a few quick signs.

"Some kind of interference," said Grim.

Rodriguez scoffed. "If that's not a sign that someone's home, I don't know what is."

Grim made his way to the back of the truck. The others followed.

"Okay, team. It seems we've got a vampire den on our hands. We'll likely find our friend Novak inside, probably a half dozen or so more. Sarah, any chance of hexes on the property?"

"Oh yeah." She hadn't taken her eyes off the place since they got there. "I can smell it from here."

"What does it smell like?" Mason asked.

She didn't answer for a few seconds, then whispered, "Fire."

"Well, that can't be good."

"In that case, you take point once the perimeter is secured," said Grim.

"Twenty-eight," she said with a salute, garnering blank stares from everyone.

"Then let us pray," said Grim, and they all joined hands.

"May I?" asked Mason.

Grim looked at him with surprise. "Please."

After a calm moment, Mason began to speak. "God, guide us in this, the task You have lain before us. Give us the courage and strength to brave the dangers we must face, and lead us safely home, wherever that may be. We fight for You. And each other. Amen."

"Amen," said the others.

"Amen indeed," said Grim. "Rodriguez, Miggs, Yen, secure the perimeter."

The three of them fanned out and made their way to the treeline as Mason watched through the binoculars. Yen went toward the barn while Rodriguez headed for the house. Miggs began walking around the whole property, stopping every few feet to look at the ground. A few minutes later, Grim's radio crackled to life and Rodriguez's voice came through it.

"Perimeter secure."

"Advance," said Grim.

With that, the team began walking across the field toward the house.

Rodriguez led the way, about twenty paces ahead, as they advanced down the long driveway of fine gray pebbles. Miggs and Yen were nowhere in sight. Not until she got closer to the house did they appear across the yard, an equal distance from each other, making up the three points of a triangle.

She began to move more slowly, almost sluggish. Finally stopping altogether.

"Hold positions." No hand signal.

"What is it, Lieutenant?"

There was no response at first. Then her knees buckled and her whole body convulsed. She dropped and let out a god-awful wail as if splashed with acid. From two separate spots at the other side of the property, the same horrible scream sounded from the other two points of the triangle.

Mason's muscles tensed, meaning to sprint forward and get to her. He had just shifted weight to his right foot, ready to lunge forward, when Sarah rushed past him.

A wisp of gray as her coat billowed out behind her was all he saw. She drew a dagger from her side, fell to her knees next to Rodriguez, and drove it into the ground with all her might.

A spark and a puff of smoke, just like in Stonehill, only instead of pure white it was a filthy black. The air became thick with the smell of burning rubber as a circle of scorched earth appeared around the property, reaching all the way to the far side of the barn.

Sarah helped Rodriguez to her feet, who offered a nod of thanks.

The team closed in around the house, and Mason got his first decent look at the place.

Two stories of weather-worn wood, barely showing any of the chipped white paint that had once covered it. The roof was crooked as an old man's back, slow and tired. Its chimney, crumbled to a jagged stump, stuck out like a broken horn. An angular porch with a swing stretched across the front before wrapping around the corner. All the windows were boarded up with rotted pieces of wood. If this had ever been a home, it was so long ago that even its ghosts had moved on.

The barn was in slightly better condition, but not by much. Red paint had faded to a pale brown and fallen leaves covered the roof. A length of heavy chain with a padlock hugged the ground door. The hay door, however, swayed open and shut in the breeze with a loud clatter. And above it, an iron weathervane jittered, more from the force of the strikes from the hay door than the strength of the wind.

Yen approached with a pair of bolt cutters, snapped the chain easily, and gave the door a good tug.

The barn was dark and filled with the scent of oil and grease and something else Mason couldn't quite put his finger on. A few breaks in the roof that would have been patched long ago had anyone lived here cast faint beams of light down through the gloom. Many of the livestock pens had been removed, and not deftly either. Whole paneled sides of stalls torn out, leaving jagged pieces of wood jutting out from the roof, and piled into a corner near the door.

Instead of cows and horses, the barn held vehicles.

A graveyard of old station wagons, pickup trucks, minivans, and even motorcycles had been jammed inside. Only one vehicle actually belonged—a beat-up old tractor entirely brown with rust and dirt toward the back. What little light there was glinted off their windshields, gave glimmers of life to their headlights. Bits of straw and hay covered their tops, no doubt drifting down from the loft above, which Mason kept a very steady eye on as Yen and Grim moved down the narrow path through the middle of the barn.

Grim climbed the ladder, knocking a few stray bits of straw down from above.

Yen backed up nearly to the door until he had a partial view of the loft, gun aimed up toward the piles of hay. Mason peeked around the doorframe from outside, watching intently. Once he was up, Grim drew his blade and began poking around the hay with it. He continued forward, disappearing from view.

Any minute Mason expected to hear a cry of pain or see a red-haired face pounce out from above. And with each passing moment that nothing happened, the more he dreaded it.

A minute later, Grim reappeared. "All clear," he said, sheathing his blade, and he began to climb back down. Yen holstered his gun and left the barn. Mason breathed a heavy sigh of relief.

With the barn out of the way, the team continued on to the house.

A sturdy tree, bare of its leaves so that it resembled a skeletal hand clawing at the sky, stood up next to the house through the dead grass that had grown tall from years of neglect. A frayed rope hung from the lowest bough. Too low for a noose, Mason figured it must have been a tire swing.

Rodriguez mounted the porch, passed the swing that had hadn't seen company in ages, and peeked in through the boards covering the windows, looking for any signs of movement. Miggs and Yen surrounded the house, moving clockwise and spraying holy water as they went. Thick patches of brown ivy wound their way up the front of the house, curling around the rickety balustrades of the railing.

Sarah went to the door and waved her hand over the tarnished doorknob while everyone else waited on the lawn.

"The door has a password," she said after about a minute. "I could try communing with the spirits guarding it, but it will take time. And there's no guarantee."

Grim let out a long sigh. "Better get started then."

Sarah sat cross-legged on the porch, closed her eyes, and placed her hands on her knees.

"Wait," said Mason.

Sarah opened her eyes. "Wait?"

"Let me try." Mason walked up the wooden steps to the porch and stood before the door.

He placed his hand on the doorknob, focused on its feel. Its shape. Its material. Every little detail about it. Forming a picture of it in his mind, searching for the spot where the molecules of it had absorbed and held its memories and the emotions that went with them. Both lock and key. And to find the right one, he drew on his own memories.

First, happiness. He thought of his last day in Stonehill, driving to pick up concert tickets with his friends.

A family once lived here. Flannel, bell-bottoms, and sideburns. John Denver singing about the Rocky Mountains on the radio. The children all had the same flaxen hair that fell on the wind as they played on the tire swing hanging from the nearby tree.

Sadness. There was almost too much to choose from. Every face he'd never see again.

The same family again. Older now. Bank foreclosure sign on the lawn. Belongings packed into their station wagon as they closed the door to their home for the last time and drove away.

Anger. This took no effort at all, stemming easily from the previous attempt. The sharp face and red hair of the one who had caused it.

The farmer flinging the door open with one hand, shotgun in the other, as he shouted at the taxman (who looked conspicuously like a younger and only slightly less husky Wayland LaVey) to get off his property before he filled him so full of lead he'd be shittin' shrapnel.

More specific, maybe?

Lust. Rodriguez's hands on his waist, the smell of her close to him.

Nothing . . . but let's come back to that later.

Guilt. Every time he'd thought Dale was an idiot for believing in nonsense; every time he hadn't answered the phone when Rose called.

The farmer scolding his boy for shooting one of their chickens with a BB gun as he led him inside, removing his belt as he did.

Pride. He thought of this. Right now. This moment. Doing something that had, before, seemed impossible, inconceivable.

Whispers tickled Mason's ears, voices that were not human.

A girl with muddy brown hair cut off into bangs pricked her thumb with an ornate blade very like the one Sarah carried, letting a fat drop of blood bloom through the cut. She smeared it across her palm in an arcane symbol, made a tight fist while reciting an incantation she prayed to the Horned One that she remembered correctly, and grasped the doorknob. And lo, a swell of pride when the appropriate charge of energy rose and passed from her to the threshold at which she stood. Someone appeared to her right—rusty hair and hollow gray eyes that appeared to see all. She told him to speak. His lip curled above his pointed teeth and he said the words that would guard this door.

Not a word. Words.

Mason loosened his grip on the doorknob.

"Well?" said Grim. "Did you get it?"

He turned his head to find Grim standing where Novak had stood in his vision.

His lip curled in a wicked smile. "Wouldn't you like to know."

Grim was taken aback by this. Surprised and, if Mason didn't know better, a little annoyed. Just before he was about to say something, an audible *click* came from the door. He stepped up to it, cautiously put his hand on the doorknob again, and gave it a little twist.

"How droll," said Grim wryly.

"I'm starting to like this guy," said Diaz.

"You're kidding, right?" said Mason. "Novak?"

"Oh, he still gotta die though."

Grim opened the door slowly but easily, careful not to let it creak. It did anyway.

Mason felt a shudder move through him as Grim instinctively froze. Nothing more than wood and nails, no threat to anyone. But it plucked at his nerves all the same. Then, in a single rapid movement, Grim pushed it the rest of the way open, this time with less complaint from the hinges.

Mason took the gun from its holster, clicked on the light attached to the barrel, and followed them in. All except for Yen, who stood guard outside, filed through the front door and into the house.

There was barely any light inside on account of the boarded windows. Although it was only midafternoon, it seemed like dusk. Narrow blades of light cut through the shadows, illuminating lazy motes of dust drifting through the air. The few pieces of furniture were draped with sheets grayed from the drifts of dust that had collected upon them like snow. It smelled of wet wood and mold. In the fireplace a small pile of broken bricks had been gathered, topped with leaves and twigs that had blown down the chimney. Inside it the squeak of nesting bats could be heard. From what he could see, the light fixtures had no bulbs in them. The corpses of rats littered the place—none drained of blood, all appearing to have been stomped into the floor.

Every surface—windowsill, countertop, even the steps of the staircases—held melted candles, their wax dripped and hardened below them like the mineral deposits of some untouched cave. At this, Grim and Rodriguez looked to each other and nodded. Mason didn't have to wonder what that meant.

This was the place. Here there be dragons.

Grim made a circular motion with his free hand, and with that Rodriguez and Miggs headed off to survey the rooms to their right while he went left. They moved quietly, no more than the odd creak in the floorboards.

Mason, Diaz, and Sarah waited by the door.

"See," said Diaz quietly, leaning close to Mason's ear, "if someone asks what the password is, you can say 'Wouldn't you like to know' and no one would know."

"Yeah, I got it," Mason whispered, shoulders shaking as he stifled a stubborn chuckle in his chest. "How dare you make me laugh now."

"Now's the best time, yo."

Something small and dark skittered across the floor in front of them. Mason took in a sharp breath from the suddenness of the motion, flinching out of the way as a rat the size of a kitten ran across the length of the hall.

Sarah had been gazing up the stairs since they entered, much like she had been at the house from a distance.

"What's up?" said Mason.

"Wanna see something cool?" she asked without taking her eyes off the space they were fixed on.

"Uh . . . sure?"

She took two steps toward the stairs and began to climb them, motioning for him to follow.

"Wait!" Mason whispered loudly. "I thought we were supposed to stay here."

"Fine, stay there," she whispered back.

"Sarah?" he choked out. It was no use.

Mason looked to Diaz.

"Don't look at me," he said.

He deliberated for a few moments, but finally curiosity got the better of him and he went after her just as she disappeared from view. He climbed the stairs as quietly as possible, each one groaning like arthritic joints, and stopped when he could just see over the top step.

Sarah stood at the door of a room directly across from him. She opened the door and crept slowly inside, drawing her dagger as she did.

Sparsely furnished with only a polished full-length mirror hung on one wall and an old oak wardrobe at the other across from the door. Somehow he couldn't see it leading to Narnia.

Sarah stood in the middle of the room, motionless, staring that fixed stare of hers on the wardrobe, then turned back to him with a mischievous look. A wicked smile like that of a little girl dangling a lit match too close to the drapes. He saw her grip tighten on her dagger, holding it carefully at her side, tip pointed toward the floor.

She crept toward the wardrobe, slow as could be.

"*Come owwwt, come owwwwt, wherehhhhver you are,*" she sang, channeling Glinda the Good Witch.

In one rapid motion, she spun ninety degrees and hurled the dagger at the mirror.

Mason didn't even have time to jump before the blade crashed into it, shattering the glass into a million pieces. As did the frame. As did every single piece of what had formerly appeared to be a simple mirror but, as the shards danced through the air, coalescing into their true form, revealed itself to be a person. An actual living person that hit the floor with a cry and a loud thud.

Sarah's dagger stuck out from her shoulder, a swell of red staining the knitted sweater she wore. Her muddy brown hair, cut into bangs just above angry eyes, hung loose beneath a woolen hat that clung to her ruddy cheeks. She tried to scramble to her feet, stopping as soon as the dagger, which had seconds ago been stuck in her shoulder, was held by an invisible force to her throat.

"Hi, Dolly," said Sarah in a cheery tone. She rose her hand, and the dagger hovering in the air rose with it, which in turn rose the throat it touched until the two stood eye to eye.

"Hi, Tuna," said the girl, her voice high and nasal.

Footsteps thundered up the stairs and soon the rest of the team was standing behind them on alert, weapons all pointing inside the room.

Sarah shook her head. For half a second, Mason thought she was going to slit the girl's throat right then and there.

"Auntie Kath's gonna be pissed," she said, and began leading her from the room.

Mason studied her face as she passed. Not alike, but somewhere between the eyes and the mouth Mason saw the resemblance between them. Dismal, deep-set eyes, blazing with such hatred through the round pair of glasses perched high on her snub nose. Not at him. At Grim.

Things moved in slow motion. The bottom of his stomach dropped away as she disappeared from view down the stairs.

That was her, the person responsible for Rose's death. The one who hexed me. Did god knows what with Rose's body in order to conjure and twist her immortal soul into an ugly shadow of itself to lure me into a trap. Probably cut off her head herself.

And she's just walking away . . .

Mind soaked in bloody thoughts, Mason felt his hand drop to the grip of the gun at his side. The spark of a reflex flashed in his brain, one that would lead to the muscles of his arm contracting, raising the hand that held his weapon, aiming it at the back of her head, telling the finger to squeeze the trigger while his vocal chords vibrated with a madman's howl, drowned out by each deafening report from the barrel.

But he didn't draw the weapon. And then she was gone.

"Are you all right?" said Grim.

He wasn't. Not by a long shot. His hangover was in full swing, his shoulders were tight, and there was a stiffness in his jaw upon realizing that he had been clenching it all this time.

"Please stop asking me that," he said, and took his hand off the gun.

FIFTY

THE TEAM SWEPT THE UPPER FLOOR, FINDING ONLY TWO MORE
bedrooms—one had twin beds with bare, yellowed mattresses, the
other a collapsed four-poster frame—and more rats. But no one else
hiding.

When they returned to the main floor, Yen silently announced
that whatever had been causing interference in the thermal feed had
cleared up. Mason didn't have to think too hard to realize why. Yen
zoomed in, past the cluster of orange silhouettes that were the team,
to five blue ones scattered across the floor below.

The kitchen was just as squalid as the rest of the place. Mason,
being the last one in, got a noseful of it. Everywhere else was old and
almost chipper with a potpourri of wet wood, mold, and dead leaves.
All around him he could smell adrenaline on the rest of the team,
sour like battery acid but in an oddly pleasant way. But the kitchen
outright stank of rot. Grim opened the back door, letting what little
light there was in and the smell out.

Mason looked around for the source of the odor, but what his
eyes couldn't see his nose had tracked to the fridge. Instinctively, he
reached out for the handle.

"Do *not* open that," Miggs commanded.

Mason froze and without a word backed away from it sheepishly.

Directly across from the back door was another which led to a cellar by the looks of it. Grim tried the doorknob. It didn't move.

"Silas," he said quietly to Diaz.

"On it," said Diaz, and took a kit from the side pocket of his vest. Inside were a variety of metal tools, all differently shaped. He knelt down to eye level with the lock, which looked much newer than the door and indeed anything else in this relic of a house, and went to work. Less than half a minute later, it opened with ease.

"Nicely done," said Mason, impressed.

Diaz blew on his knuckles as he placed the tools back in the kit. "You know it."

Rodriguez holstered her gun, drew the blade strapped to her back, choked up on it like a baseball bat, and took up a position next to the door.

Grim signaled for everyone else to step back and placed his hand back on the doorknob, ready to open. Diaz and Miggs took at least one good step back, rose their weapons, and trained them on the door. Mason did the same, his pulse so fast he could feel it pumping in every vein he had. His mouth became dry with each breath, pulling in more and more dust.

Grim took a deep breath to steady himself. Slowly, he turned the knob and, once it was as far as it could go, flung the door open and jumped back all at once.

An axe snapped down from above.

Mason flinched. His finger squeezed the trigger of his gun but it didn't fire. He wasn't sure which he was more thankful for—that the safety had been on, or that no one had noticed.

Grim reached up and removed the axe from its place with a hard tug and the audible clicking of gears. Rusty and old, it didn't look very sharp, but with that kind of force it wouldn't have mattered. Had he not moved when he did, his face would have been split in two. He set it down, leaning it against the wall.

Gun still at the ready, Grim cautiously angled it down into the cellar, the light attached to the barrel doing what little it could.

Mason came up next to him. Nothing but darkness. The light from outside illuminated what little it touched. The others clicked on the body lights attached to their vests. Mason looked down to see that he had one too and did the same.

Not much could be seen except for one important detail—no stairs. Torn out like the animal pens in the barn, a few remaining jagged bits stuck out just beyond their toes, dropping away to the floor below. Just one big patch of exposed earth throughout.

"Well," said Grim with a thoughtful rub of his chin, "it's not that far down, but getting back up will be tricky."

Rodriguez looked at Mason. "Cadet, go back to the truck and get the rope. That should do the trick."

He didn't move, keeping his gaze fixed below.

"That means you, chico," said Rodriguez with a nudge of her elbow.

He held up a finger as he scanned the ground with his light. "Something's not right."

"How so?" she asked.

Mason waved the light over the ground. "See the footprints?"

Rodriguez strained her eyes. "Oh . . . yeah. Barely."

"They're everywhere, all over the place." He dragged the circle of light toward where they stood and stopped about ten feet away, where a partially buried piece of scrap wood lay on the ground. "Until right here." With the light he traced a path to the nearest wall in a straight line where it fell upon a single cinder block.

He gestured to the axe still resting next to Grim. "May I?"

Grim picked up the axe and handed it to him. It must have weighed a good six pounds. He just hoped that would be enough.

Mason aimed it at the ground directly beneath the stairs and, with a good hard downward motion, threw it.

The axe impacted with the ground, sinking the entire surrounding area by several inches. One corner of a dirt covered-canvas came loose and folded in revealing a pit below. Dirt began falling away, dragging the axe with it as it slipped away into nowhere. When it hit the bottom the axe made a light splash.

"Hmm," said Grim, peering over the edge into the pit. "That's vexing."

"Forget the rope," said Rodriguez. "We need a ladder."

"The one from the barn should do," said Grim.

Diaz holstered his gun. "I'll give ya a hand."

"Good job, cadet." Rodriguez gave him a subtle smile.

Mason and Diaz headed out the front door. Yen stood silently on guard, keeping a watchful eye on the surroundings.

Seeing as how it was the first day of November, the sky had grown visibly darker. Only an hour of daylight left, two at the most. Out of nowhere, a chill went down Mason's spine. Not just the regular chill of early winter. An ethereal chill. A death chill. The ghostly fog he had seen last night had returned with his gift, but now it was thick again.

In the field beyond the farmhouse, figures appeared where they hadn't been before. Languidly drifting about the property as if through water, emerging from a deep watery murk to less-forgiving shallows.

Men and women. Some teenagers and children. Visible from the waist up, bones of arms and rib cages showing beneath their spectral skin.

For the most part they were just aimless wanderers. Lonely, but not alone. Then one, a woman, stopped and looked directly at him. Her eyes white and vacant. No life. No luster. Like Rose's had been.

"What's up?" said Diaz.

Mason didn't answer at first, stunned. "You don't see them?"

Diaz cast his gaze about the property, seeing only empty land. "See who?"

"Never mind," Mason said as the ghost carried on to a destination she would never reach.

They quickly retrieved the ladder from the barn and brought it inside. Extended it out over the hole beneath them, thankfully touching down on the other side of the hole with room to spare. One by one, the team climbed down. Despite being wooden and a bit on the rickety side, the ladder held.

"Maybe you should wait here," said Grim, holstering his sidearm. "Just until we have a look around."

Mason agreed. Grim disappeared down into the cellar, leaving him with Yen, who waited just outside the kitchen now. He peered out at the field beyond. Not a living soul ahead. No one to see or hear or have any idea of what went on here. Just the gentle sway of leafless tree branches and a ripple of wind that made waves through the overgrown grass.

A minute later Grim reappeared, signaling him to come down.

This is it, Mason thought with a deep, dreadful breath. One wasn't enough, and he took another. The moment of truth. From this there was no going back. If there ever really had been.

FIFTY-ONE

After an uncomfortable and nerve-racking climb over the pit below, Mason entered the cellar. Completely devoid of furniture and as thick with cobwebs as it was shadows. Laid out across the earthen ground he saw nine plywood boards, three by three. From the tension he felt in the rest of the team and basic common sense as they poured rings of holy water around each one, Mason deduced what lay beneath. Very slowly the boards were removed from their place.

Mason saw an image in his mind of fanged grins above clutched teddy bears, dreaming whatever sweet little nightmares vampires would dream.

Instead there were pale, still, sleeping figures. Not atop beds of taffeta with satin pillows, but piles upon piles of clothes. Those of their victims, Mason guessed. Padding their putrid little nests with the shed skins of those whose ghosts wandered the property. Hands— no teddy bears in sight—folded over their chests, which neither rose nor fell.

Though he felt the prickle of danger from being in their presence, it was not the same as before. Now it was muted in their slumber. No thoughts or images swirling about their heads. For all intents and purposes, they were dead to the world.

The very first one Mason recognized, a male with mutton chops in a simple jacket and blue jeans who had been with Novak in Stonehill. The two grave-beds next to him were vacant, as were the two directly behind them. The first of the second row, however, was occupied by one of the twin female vampires that had chased after Grim and Mason as they made their escape. Her sister slept in the grave below her. The bed next to hers held a doll-faced young woman with a pair of Minnie Mouse ears who he had never seen before. And in the final grave . . .

Please let it be him, Mason willed to no one in particular. *For the love of all that is good and holy, let me see red hair, closed eyes, and a throat begging to be cut.*

"Captain?" said Rodriguez, eyes fixed on whatever she saw beneath.

Grim immediately looked up at her from where he stood, hunched over the top row of graves.

"You wanted to know when we found Julie Walsh." She met Grim's gaze. "Found her."

Mason's face fell into his palms and he stepped over to where she was without so much as looking up.

And there she was. Julie Walsh. Formerly his best friend. The girl who had rescued him from his own coffin of metal in the form of a locker. Who he had so wanted to be more than friends with, to kiss and hold and say sweet, stupid things to and have them said to him in return.

She was somehow cleaner than the last time he had seen her, strung up naked while a hammer beat the life from her body. Wearing clothes that weren't hers, and didn't really fit—the sleeves of the denim jacket she wore were too long, covering most of her hands so that only the tips stuck out. No shirt underneath. From the waist down just a pair of red-sequined hotpants. He wondered if she had slapped together this ensemble from the bed of clothes she slept upon or taken it from her first victim. Her honey-colored hair appeared almost black in the gloom. Skin smooth as porcelain. Cheeks of her round face flush and full of blood, still retaining a hint of the humanity that was fading away with each passing moment. Her chin stained pink with streaks of dried blood, like a rape victim left out in some forgotten field still bearing the stain of her violation. Cold and deader than dead, for it was no longer really her. She looked almost peaceful.

As if he were staring straight down from a dangerous height, he was hit by a wave of sickening vertigo. This was why he had to come, to release her from this curse of living death. It may not have been his fault, but now it was certainly his responsibility. That didn't make it any easier though.

Grim said, discretely as possible, "If this is too much for you, I understand."

The term "too much" just didn't seem to mean anything anymore. "Five of them, five of us."

"But if you want to take another one instead . . ."

"No." His mouth became a thin, hard line. "No, it should be me." She had been dragged into all of this because of him, had been turned because of him, and now she should be released from it by him.

"God be with you," said Grim. "Remember, go for the neck, not the heart. It makes the next step easier."

"What next step?"

"Removing the head."

"Oh," said Mason. *Swell.*

The team unsheathed their blades and took positions, straddling one grave or another. Grim took Mutton Chops at the front, Rodriguez and Miggs each took a twin, and Diaz the one wearing mouse ears. Hilts clasped in both hands, tips pointed down toward their mark.

"On five," Grim said softly, and, as the conductor of this morbid orchestra, raised his blade in the air.

"One . . ."

Grim touched the hilt of his sword to his forehead. The others did the same.

"Two . . ."

Lowered his clasped hands down to his chest. The others did the same.

"Three . . ."

Touched the hilt to his right shoulder. The others did the same.

"Four . . ."

Touched the hilt to his left shoulder, then immediately brought his hands up over his head.

Mason took one last look at that cherubic face of hers. The blade dangled, practically salivating. Savoring every ounce of this moment.

And on "Five," Grim thrust down into the grave beneath him, followed by the others.

Julie came alive. There it was, the adrenal buzzsaw.

His own hands flew up into his face, driving a hard punch into his nose, forcing him to lose his footing and fall backward onto the hard, unforgiving ground. A warm gush slid down his top lip as the taste of blood found its way into his mouth.

Furious, Julie spat and clawed at him, unable to reach from her resting place that had become a cage around her.

Rodriguez, already done with her kill one grave over, drew her gun and took aim.

"Holster that sidearm, Lieutenant," Grim commanded, not quite yelling but certainly louder than Mason had ever heard him before now.

She did as ordered.

Mason got to his feet, clutching his blade, seething with the rage to swing it. But it wasn't enough. It was still her face. Her eyes. Her mouth.

Her mouth . . .

"Julie!" Mason shouted.

She stopped and looked at him, eyes wild but focused. Waiting for any part of him to come near enough to grab. Wondering what he tasted like.

"Did you really blow Eric Riley?"

Her lips curled into a wicked smile, exposing a brand-new set of fangs, and hissed. "You bet I did!"

He sprang forth and swung, swift and true. Saw blood before he even felt the cut. Something hit the ceiling and landed on the ground in front of him, rolling on its axis like the cleft half of a cantaloupe. Her head, slashed in two just below the nose, fell down into the grave with the rest of her.

The moment hung in the air like the stench of death.

And like the crack of thunder that follows lightning, the team erupted in a triumphant cheer, clapping him on the back and rubbing his shaved head. Even Miggs offered a meagre but undeniably impressed slow clap.

"I'm proud of you, son," Grim said, placing a hand on his shoulder.

Mason offered a simple "Thanks" in return. "So what happens now? Is there a cleanup crew or something?"

"Yeah, you're looking at it," said Diaz.

"Ah."

"Well, since you've technically . . . taken care of the next step, why don't you take five? We'll need someone back upstairs to haul them out."

"I can do that."

He couldn't be sure, but just then Mason thought he caught a dirty sideward look from Miggs. Instead of looking away, he faced him head on.

Miggs did the same. And with the slightest of nods, he said, "Not bad."

Those two words the closest thing to a compliment Mason had yet received from him.

He got up nice and close—not uncomfortably so, but just enough to be personal—the bruise on his face now good and dark, swelling the cross tattoo below his eye. "But messiah or not, sucker punch me again and it's on."

He had him there. "Fair enough."

Grim took the radio from his belt and spoke into it. "Sarah, is our guest secure?"

Dead air for a few seconds before it crackled. *"She's not going anywhere."*

"Good. You can bring the truck around now. And we'll need the bags."

"Ten-four." Some static and then it cut out.

"Ohhh," Mason said with realization.

"Beg pardon?" Grim asked.

"Oh . . . nothing. I just got something."

Mason climbed back out of the cellar as the rest of the team got to work. He heard the crunch of gravel and whine of brakes, followed by the slamming of the truck door.

Sarah approached, a cigarette dangling from her lips, carrying two large black bags in both hands.

"Twenty-eight," said Mason. "I got it."

She dropped the bags at his feet. "You *just* got that?"

"Hey, better late than never."

"Disappointing, Kiwi," said Sarah, exhaling a larger-than-usual cloud of smoke. "So? How was it?" She handed him a cigarette which lit seemingly on its own once he put it to his lips.

He breathed in its lovely poison, exhaled, and chuckled to himself.

"What?"

The opening words to an Alice Cooper song floated through his head and softly out his lips. *"Welcome to my nightmare. I think you're gonna like it . . ."*

"See? This life agrees with you." She scanned him head to toe. "I can see it."

"Think so?"

"For sure. You're an autumn child. You're meant to have a touch of woe. You don't feel right without it."

"I . . . can't argue with that."

"Don't. Go with it. You have dragon's blood running through your veins."

"Yeah," Mason scoffed. "I wish."

"No, really, you do."

"Say what now?"

". . . Pfft! I'm just messing with you. Dragons aren't real."

"I didn't think so."

"Unicorns are, though," she said with a long drag of her cigarette, and then she began unfurling the body bags.

He and Sarah stood side by side, watching as the rest of the team went in pairs—Grim with Diaz, Miggs with Rodriguez—to each grave and set about their work. Cautiously, one would reach into the hole and lift the body up by the head while the other chopped it off. It took more than one chop in most cases, making Mason's single strike all the more remarkable.

It took a good twenty minutes to get the bodies and heads bagged and out of the cellar. The heads were easy enough to toss up. The bodies were another matter, needing to be pulled up with the ladder one by one. Once they were all out, the team followed. They carried the bodies to the truck, where Mason saw Sydney unconscious in the passenger seat, head leaning against the window. His finger still itched to hook its way around the trigger; he felt it drawing near the gun at his side as he stared at her. But no, there were answers he needed in that head, and to stop himself from doing something rash, he walked away.

He stopped at the barn door, leaning on its frame. Soon after he heard footsteps approach behind him.

"Why wasn't he here?" said Mason, tight-lipped with a shake of his head, peering hard into the barn as if it would make his quarry suddenly appear.

Grim, sharing his frustration but trying not to let it show, pushed his glasses up his nose and stared out the barn. "When we do find him—and we will—you can ask him yourself."

Mason kicked the cut padlock, left discarded until now, clear across the barn. It went skipping away, straight down the narrow path through the vehicles, and then under the old tractor, where it made a *thonk*. It was wrong—both the sound and the shape it made. Hollow and cylindrical.

He and Grim looked at each other curiously and began moving toward it. Mason crouched down, squinting through the tight space beneath the tractor to see what he could see.

"There's something under here."

He tried pushing the tractor, hoping it might roll away like a car with a flat tire, but he may as well have been trying to move a boulder from where it had spent the last million years.

"Try moving it with your mind," said Grim as he took a step back.

Mason considered this a moment, then gave him a nod and lowered a hand toward it.

Standing a few feet away, Mason reached out toward the broken machine before him. He could feel the cold, hard metal, the rough shape and rusted texture of the side nearest to him, as if his hand were pressed against it.

It budged—not much, but just enough to say that it had.

"Close your eyes," said Grim. "Breathe."

Mason closed his eyes and breathed deeper than he had ever breathed in his life. The world around him disappeared but remained, imprinted upon his inner vision almost immediately, as if carved out of amber. Grim's spirit—a core of nebulous light in his skull, humming and effervescent with particles extending throughout his body in intricate pathways—stood next to him. His own surged through him, a current of powerful electricity that was his to command.

Your hand is the focus, the physical counterpart to guide the mental, like a crystal or a cross. The stronger your connection with it, the stronger you are. Reach out toward it.

That gave him an idea. Without opening his eyes, Mason took the cross from around his neck and wrapped the chain between his fingers. It all coalesced into a single moment of lucid coherence. His hand rose before him, and again he felt the shape of the tractor. Energy weaving between every part, inside and out.

Good. Now breathe in and grip it.

With another breath, he heard a series of metallic creaks as his inner hand held it in a way he never could have physically.

Now breathe out . . . and push.

The tractor whined in protest, wheels scraping heavily across the barn floor. The sound almost broke his concentration, but he held fast until the tractor was pushed far enough to nudge a nearby car.

Mason opened his eyes. A thick cloud of dust hovered around the tractor, which had been moved a few feet away from where it had been. "I did it!"

"You did it," said Grim, hands clasped, practically crying hallelujah.

In the space where the tractor had been lay a hatch in the barn floor.

Grim knelt down and opened it.

A grated metal staircase led diagonally down from the top of the hatch into a pit of pure black. Just then Mason heard something, so quiet it was barely even a sound. He listened for it again. Even with one ear deafened, there was no mistaking it.

A whimper.

"Did you hear that?" said Mason. "Someone's down there."

Grim radioed for the rest of the team, all of whom rushed into the barn.

"I'll go first," he said to Mason, and started down the steps. "Wait for my signal."

Down Grim went into the space below, a good twenty feet at least. When he reached the bottom, he drew his gun and clicked on the light attached to the barrel, panning back and forth with it a few times before disappearing from view entirely.

Nearly two minutes passed, every second of which Mason spent staring into a black hole of worry, ready to piss his pants. Some strange metallic sounds came from inside that he couldn't place, like someone attempting to move an oil drum. The bright little light returned, and with it Captain Grimshaw, gesturing for him to come down.

"Vaya con dios," said Rodriguez.

"Uh-huh," Mason replied nervously, and went down through the hatch.

It felt very like the tunnel under the chapterhouse. Close. Oppressive. The same sense of suffocation, descending into a blinding darkness. But this time he wasn't afraid of it. This time he wasn't alone.

When he reached the bottom, Mason looked up to see all their faces looking down at them from above. Grim had clicked on his body light, etching the features of his face in the black around them. The beam of light moved over every surface it touched, blessing it for an instant with a wash of white.

At the opposite end from the ladder, down a narrow space of concrete, was a steel door built into the wall. A rectangle with rounded corners and a handwheel in the middle, as one might find attached to a missile silo.

"It's too tight," said Grim as he gripped the handwheel with both hands. "I need your help."

Mason grabbed hold of it. "Clockwise or counter?"

"Clockwise. On three."

Grim counted them down, and at the same time they twisted it with all their might. It groaned stubbornly, but they didn't give up. After a few seconds of gritted teeth and elbow grease, the door gave way.

It must have been airtight, because as it opened a waft of soft, dry air escaped. The smell it carried, however, was anything but soft. So strong it was nearly a solid thing, hitting them both like a punch in the face, robbing them of every ounce of breath. A sinister odor with a fermented sweetness overpowered his senses, bringing an immediate sickening sadness.

The stench of death.

Beyond, a cement chamber with more thick steel doors, dimly lit with flickering lightbulbs. Mason heard no whimper now. Nothing but the sound of their breath. It was difficult to tell with the assault on his senses, but beyond the doors came a faint bit of shuffling. Footsteps.

"Do you hear that?" Mason whispered.

Grim nodded. He approached one of the doors and knocked three times.

All went quiet as a held breath. Whatever he heard stopped, and the term *silent as the grave* came to mind.

Grim knocked three more times.

Hands hammered the door. And the one next to it. Then the one across. Soon the noise overtook the chamber. Shouts and cries for help so loud his ears rang. So loud that neither he nor Grim heard one of the doors open behind them.

Mason turned to flee, freezing the instant he saw Novak in front of him holding a girl by the throat.

Bent low, cowering behind the girl so that little of him was exposed except for those vacant eyes behind loose strands of red hair. Younger than Mason, but not by a lot—fourteen, maybe fifteen years old, with choppy black hair, her chubby face caked with dirt and sweat. Confused eyes brimming with tears and scared for her life. The same face he had seen on Julie when Novak held *her* hostage.

"Well, well," hissed Novak. "If it isn't Grimsy and the Funny Boy. My favorite duo." He gave a wag of his finger. "Don't you know it's rude to interrupt a man in the middle of breakfast?"

"Sorry to disturb you," said Grim.

"Sorry meh-mehmeh-meh," Novak mimicked. "I'm going to take a wild stab and say I have one William Graves to thank for this little intrusion."

"Wouldn't you like to know," said Mason, mirroring the cadence of his voice as he had heard it when the password to the farmhouse had been made.

"Okay, that was pretty good," said Novak pleasantly.

"Let the girl go," said Grim.

"Ugh! Worst banter ever. Next you'll be telling me I don't have to do this."

"You don't have to do this."

"C'mon, make it your own, for Chrissake."

"This isn't a fucking game!" Mason shouted.

"Yes, it is," Novak growled through bared teeth, the volume in his voice making Mason nervous for his good ear. "That's all any of it is. One big sick fucking game. And I don't intend to lose."

"Well, this *is* all pretty sick, not gonna lie."

"Hmm . . . wish I could take all the credit, but that'd make me a liar. Anywho, du'y calls"—he switched to his cheesy British accent again—"so if you would kine'ly remove ya'selves, I'll be on me merry way."

Grim stretched his arms so that the gun was locked on him. "We can't let you leave."

Novak shrugged. "Then I can't let her live. Cheerio!"

For a second Mason saw a streak of red appear where Novak had held her. The girl's eyes went wide as she dropped to the floor in a heap.

Novak pounced at them.

Grim held up his fist, the one bearing the signet ring. Novak stopped dead, as if he had hit a wall. Shrieking. Covering his face. A shot fired just as he sped away in a blur of shadow.

While Grim gave chase, followed by many scattered cracks of gunfire from above, Mason rushed to the girl's side and rolled her over. Blood spilled from her neck and onto the floor. Her throat had been cut, but not wide open. Rather, thin and precise, the type of cut a fingernail might make if it were razor-sharp. She clutched at her throat with a horrible gurgle as Mason tore off his Kevlar and then his shirt.

"Please no, no, no."

He shouted for help. Screamed for it. Desperately, hoarsely, red in the face. Pressed the wadded-up shirt to the girl's neck, keeping as much pressure on it as he could. Adrenaline so high he was afraid he might crush the neck he was trying to save before she bled out or choked on her own blood.

Her eyes began to flutter.

"*No!*" he shouted, watching as life slipped from the girl's face, racked with sadness and fear. "Please," he begged to anyone who was listening. "Don't let her die. Don't let her die! Because I won't. I won't let her die!"

Time slowed, stretched out in all directions, spread flat across a single moment until it stopped.

Another pair of hands came into view. Made of a brilliant spectral light, they slid over Mason's with a warm glow, guiding them into place. Two pairs as one. The hands removed the blood-soaked shirt and pressed a thumb to the middle of the wound. At the touch of skin, a heavenly warmth radiated from the point. His other hand was moved to the side of her neck and pressed firmly.

The girl began to breathe again.

There was a gust of air and the whispered patter of silken wings. Mason slowly inclined his head upward. A single golden feather drifted down to the floor, fading as it fell before vanishing altogether.

The gunfire and shouting above had ceased. Footsteps hurried into the room behind Mason as Rodriguez fell to her knees and frantically unzipped a medkit.

"What happened?" she said, out of breath.

"Her throat was cut," Mason answered, still stunned by what he had just witnessed.

"How long?" Rodriguez took out a roll of tape and a bottle of anti-septic and placed them beside her.

"I dunno . . . a minute. Maybe less."

"Let me see," she said, unraveling a generous length of gauze.

Mason slowly removed his hands from the girl's bloody neck and closed his eyes, wincing.

It was met with stunned silence.

"That's impossible," said Rodriguez.

He shot one eye open, and then the other, making sure he really saw what he saw.

Instead of an open gash, the wound had been reduced to a thin line of raised skin.

Rodriguez fumbled for words as she stared at him. "How?" A touch of reverence in her voice.

Mason looked at his hands, still wet with blood. "I prayed."

He got to his feet to see Grim walking toward him down the darkened passage leading to the chamber. Sweaty and tired. The shadow of defeat hanging heavily on his face, avoiding Mason's gaze.

"He got away, didn't he?"

Grim finally met his eyes and nodded regretfully.

Mason breathed a heavy sigh and began walking away.

"Where are you going?" Grim asked.

"I need a minute," he said softly. This time it wasn't a request.

Mason left the chamber. The banging of hands and cries for help had resumed from behind all the steel doors. He heard something about needing backup before it was replaced with the *pong* of his steps on the stairs, and up through the hatch he went.

Back in the barn, the others were resting, shaken and out of breath, on the hoods of cars. Diaz said something to him as he passed. He didn't hear it and kept walking, dreamlike, until he was outside.

It had begun to snow. Drifting down from the darkened sky above like soft white ash, each flake giving his skin a cold little peck. Oblivious to the fact that he was naked from the waist up, he continued forward until he reached the treeline.

Once he was sure he was alone, Mason dropped to his knees. With as much snow as he could gather, he rubbed his hands clean of all the blood and clutched them together. Not for warmth, but to be close to his chest.

"Thank you," said Mason. Head tilted upward, face fallen to quiet reflection as the snowflakes that touched the side of his face were joined by a tear. "Thank you."

I so wanted to go to him, whisper in his ear and tell him everything he would need to know right then and there. But it wasn't time.

Not yet.

FIFTY-TWO

WITH THE SUN NOW SAFELY BELOW THE HORIZON, NOVAK moved through the woods. His hip and shoulder sang with exquisite pain from the bullets that had hit him. Slowing to a frustrating pace, he lurched through the trees like the typical shambling undead. He reached into the hole the gunshot had made in the leather, stuck a finger into the wound, gritting his fangs as he did, and dug out the bullet.

"Damn!" he said, tossing the tiny bit of metal aside. "I liked this jacket."

He did the same with the shot in his hip, and already he could feel the pain subsiding.

His ears pricked up as they caught what they sought. Somewhere in this cold winter's night, due south, Goldie was rising from her bed in the earth. Still weak, but healed. And she was thirsty.

"Now Daddy's pissed . . ." he fumed, raking his fingernails across the naked trees, clawing deep swaths in them as he passed. *They'll pay for this. Do you hear me, God? I will slaughter your Ram, and the one after him, and the one after that, until none are left alive and you*

441

have no choice but to hand me the Holy Spirit yourself and beg—BEG!
—my forgiveness. And until then, I will make him wish he was dead.
Oh yes. I swear it to the Devil himself. He will be sorry.

"I'm coming, precious," he said, too quietly for human ears but
loud enough for hers, and quickened his pace. "I'm coming."

FIFTY-THREE

THE FIRST THING HE FELT WAS THE SUN. WARM BUT NOT altogether there, hiding just behind the backyard fence. Long, fresh grass tickling his shins below the picnic table. Smell of leaves from the towering maple, casting a rich shade over him. And everywhere, cats. In the garden. The branches above. Weaving in and out between his feet. Peeking out from one of the nearby shrubs, Bossy waved at him with her plump white paw. He waved back.

Julie and Dale sat with him at the picnic table, one on either side. Odd smiles spread across their faces, the kind people made when something was wrong but they were trying to hide it. Dale turned his head—what was left of it, at least. Julie's smile grew wider and he saw a set of fangs.

The back door swung open and out came Rose with a tray of pink lemonade. A gaping bloody hole in her chest he could see straight through.

"Drink up, sugar."

She placed the tray down on the table before taking a seat across from them. Julie and Dale reached for a glass. Mason took the one that remained, topped with a floral paper umbrella. He rose the straw to his lips and took a good long sip.

It tasted wrong. Very wrong.

Mason pulled the glass back and saw where the rosy pink color came from. A chilled eyeball floating among the ice cubes. Optic nerves dangled long and bloody below it.

He looked at both Julie and Dale, voraciously gulping theirs down. Dale's had a nice bloody ear. Julie's had a tongue. They finished and slammed their glasses down on the table.

"Sweet daddy long-legs, that's good," said Dale, the whole left side of his head crushed in.

"I'll say," said Julie. The word UNSAFE was now scrawled messily across her chest with what looked like a finger of soot and bacon grease.

"Too much pulp for me." Mason set the glass down on the table. "So what happens now?"

"Now," said Rose, "you let us go."

Mason felt hands on each shoulder, looked behind him, and saw his parents. Filthy. Covered with dust and ash. Eyes closed as though they were sleepwalking. But they were smiling, so their dreams must have been nice, at least.

"Do I have a choice?"

Rose handed him a shard of sharp glass. The piece of mirror he had almost cut himself with. He let it drop, slipping between the boards of the table and out of sight.

"We'll be waiting." Rose took his hands in hers. "Right here."

FIFTY-FOUR

When Mason woke it was dark. His clock flashed 12:00 from the power outage on Halloween, but a touch of pink glowed from the window. There was something about pink in the sky that said *morning* to him. Bossy dozed at the foot of his bed, stirring and stretching, as he rose and went to the window.

For the first time since he could remember, he hadn't kept a light on. Not intentionally—he had just been too tired to think of it. Which meant it didn't matter anymore. He hadn't even noticed that the curtains were open.

It had continued to snow through the night, dusting the city with a soft layer of white. Everything was quieter for it. Calm and silent. A solid slate of gray hung in the sky, broken only by the bright eye of the sun spreading eyelashes of light out from the horizon.

And though he was nowhere near it, the smell of death still permeated his nostrils.

"Mrrrow?"

Mason turned to see Bossy, fully awake now, sitting up and looking at him. He emptied a tin of food into the dish and gave her a scratch behind the ears.

The rest of the chapterhouse was still asleep. All except for Grim, who was sitting at a table in the kitchen. When they'd returned to Boston, he had received a call from Bishop Strauss to set a debrief for tomorrow morning, bright and early. That was now today. Nothing about the call itself made Mason uneasy, but given the reason for it, he felt it in the pit of his stomach.

Figuring he had a little while to spare, he went to join his captain. He found him sipping a cup of tea, glasses off his face, looking out the window toward dawn. Here, but a million miles away, offering a half smile as Mason approached.

"Sleep well?" Grim inquired.

Mason returned the other half of the smile. He hesitated for a moment, considering the dream he had. But also, he realized, because he still could not hear properly.

"I feel like I've slept for days." Mason rubbed at his bad ear with the palm of his hand, hoping it might *pop* back to life.

"How is your ear?"

The half smile became none at all. "If it were a tire, it would be flat."

"Hmm. I was afraid of that. Given enough time and treatment you might see some improvement, but I'm afraid you will likely have some permanent hearing loss."

"What's one more scar, right?" said Mason, knowing it wouldn't be the last. That thought triggered a memory. "Wait!" he barked with alarm. "Where's the girl?"

Grim raised a hand to calm him. "She's all right."

"Really?"

"Well, as all right as one in her position can be," Grim admitted. "She will be scarred and carry the memory of that day forever, but she's alive."

Mason's face darkened at his next question. "Where's Sydney?"

Grim took plenty of time answering. "For the moment she's here, but she will be moved to another facility shortly."

"May I see her?"

He looked at Mason gravely for a moment. "I don't think that would be wise."

It was the answer he'd expected. More or less. "Because I might do something . . . rash?"

"Best not to complicate things," said Grim with a small gesture of acknowledgment. Trying to be diplomatic, perhaps, but instead it just came off as evasive. But he was also not wrong.

"I don't mean to harm her," Mason lied.

Grim gave him an unconvinced look. "I think we both know that that's not true."

However he had tempered his impulses yesterday, he knew that if he saw Sydney today, he would kill her. Answers be damned. And he meant to. He didn't know how or when, but one day he would take her life. Just as he would Novak. And Goldie. And anyone else who had a hand in the death of his family and friends. He knew this just as he knew that beneath his skin were blood and bone.

Mason hung his head. "Can you blame me?"

"No. I can't."

"She's still with me, you know. Rose. Not in a philosophical, Maya Angelou sort of way. I can feel her . . . like I've got a second shadow. Watching over my shoulder." He wished that had been hyperbole, but he now felt the telltale chill in the space next to his good ear.

"I was afraid of that too. That hex . . . lessened now without Sydney to puppet her, I'm sure, but to be rid of it altogether you'll need to undergo a ritual purge."

"Like an exorcism?"

"In a way. It's one thing to be haunted naturally, but intentionally, with the helping hand of the family demon—that's a bit more complicated."

Earl's orange eyes and rotten black teeth flashed in his mind, forcing a nervous swallow. "Is that going to be a problem?"

"Fortunately, Sarah can help you with that."

"Okay." Mason chose his next words very carefully. "Look, I just need to see her. I need to look Sydney in the eye and tell her what she's done to me and ask her why. I don't know if that will do any good, but I just . . . need to."

"If I allow this," Grim started, also choosing his words carefully, "you must promise me two things. One, that you will make no attempt to harm her. That's not how we do things here and I just can't allow it."

Mason gave the weakest of nods. "And the second?"

Grim gently turned the teacup around in its saucer. "I'm going to tell Bishop Strauss a slightly different version of events today. If asked, all you need do is concur with what I've said. Understood?"

Momentarily taken aback, Mason replied, "Deal."

He heard the others begin to stir—getting out of bed, brushing their teeth, using the toilet, and a dozen other things that comprise our morning routines. "I'd better get ready," said Mason, and went to leave, stopping with a hand on the doorframe. "Oh, one more thing. Will's sword . . . I'm afraid I lost it."

Grim, his gaze having returned to the world outside, didn't say anything. Then, finally, with a short breath of regret, he said, "That's a shame," as he placed his glasses back on his face and took a sip of his tea. "But you found *him*."

More like he found me. Mason was about to ask if he thought they would see Will again, but deep down he already knew the answer and left Grim to his tea and whatever thoughts he had to think.

Everyone made their way to St. Augustine's by way of the underground tunnel. They entered the same meeting room in which Mason had first met them the day after arriving in Boston. Everyone was arranged around the long table very much as they had been before, with Father Coffey and Bishop Strauss at the far end.

No cup of coffee for Strauss this time. He didn't look at Mason as he entered, not directly. Instead his eyes passed over him for the briefest of moments before darting away, cued by nothing more than the motion Mason had made upon entering the room.

Again Mason took the nearest empty seat by the door.

Grim gave a rundown of what had happened. First the incident on Halloween, which had made the news with reports of jack-o'-lanterns swiped from every neighborhood in a ten-block radius by a person or persons unknown. Then Mason's disappearance, fully and truthfully, which surprised him, as this was the detail he expected Grim would alter.

"Cadet Cole managed to escape when the vehicle in which his captors held him was involved in a collision, causing a rupture to his eardrum and partial hearing loss as a result. Fortunately he was able to get to a telephone and contact us."

There it was, the detail he had omitted: Will's involvement.

Mason's pulse quickened, and his breaths grew heavy. He did his best to hide it, shifting in his seat to place a fist in front of his mouth while he studied the very (un)interesting patterns in the woodgrain of the table. He didn't dare look at Strauss, fearing that if he did it would give him away. But he could feel his stare.

The Bishop was focused intently on Grim, listening to the events that occurred on the farm—a "blood farm," Grim called it, implying that such things were known to them—pausing occasionally to allow for comments where he thought one might arise.

It was met with eerily collected patience from Strauss, hands clasped in front of him with that big violet ring of his on full display. He didn't say one word during. Not one.

Grim closed the file in front of him, bringing an end to his report.

Strauss took in a long breath and cleared his throat. "That's all very amusing, Captain Grimshaw," he said, laying both hands out on the table.

Amusing? Mason's jaw clenched so tight he thought it might pop out of its socket.

Strauss glowered at Mason. "But what your report failed to

explain is *why* exactly Cadet Cole decided to leave the chapterhouse with threats abound."

Clearly not expecting this, Grim said with a slow nod, "As I said, Your Eminence, he was coerced to leave and help his friend who was being held hostage."

"Alone?" said Strauss. Less of a question, more of a spotlight on just how idiotic that was. A detail which Mason could not disagree with.

"Yes," said Grim. "I realize this is a breach of protocol, but—"

"That it is," said Strauss, chopping his answer in half. "And, as it turns out, a very serious one, since it put our greatest weapon in the hands of our enemies."

Mason hated people talking about him when he was sitting right in front of them. What's more, he hated being referred to as a weapon, as if he were no better than a piece of furniture in the room.

During his report Grim had left out the part about Miggs trying to stop him for this very same reason—which meant he also left out the part where Mason assaulted a team member and subsequently relinquished that "weapon" before leaving. A fact which likely would have caused the Bishop to cream in his cassock. Thankfully, Miggs did not speak up, and Mason sensed that he had likely been ordered not to.

"Briefly," said Grim, nodding. "Very briefly."

"However brief, this cannot go unaddressed."

"Yer Eminence," spoke Father Coffey for the first time. "Innocent lives were saved thanks te the boy. That's no small thing."

"It is not. Neither is the matter at hand. And how exactly is it that the location of this"—he waved a wrinkled hand in the air, trying to stir words out of it—"blood farm came to be known?"

Grim thought fast and looked imploringly at him. "It was mentioned by his captors. Isn't that right, Mason?"

"Yeah," Mason said, in barely a whisper, with a nervous nod. "They said it was just north of the town."

Grim looked back at the Bishop for a response.

"Gentlemen," Strauss said with the thinnest show of a smile Mason had ever seen on him, "I may not possess your mental abilities"—he looked first at Grim, then at Father Coffey—"but I've heard many a confession in my time, so I know a lie when I hear one."

"No, really, it's true," said Rodriguez.

Sarah piped up next to Mason. "Once I had the direction, I tried scrying for the farm and found it. No sweat."

"That's how I remember it going down," said Diaz.

The next thing Mason knew, everyone had joined the chorus. All clamoring for attention, assuring the Bishop that what was said was the truth.

"Enough!" Strauss barked. "Every member of this order must learn the discipline to resist any and all methods of coercion. If Cadet Cole is not receiving said discipline here, then he must report to Saint Petersburg to undergo proper training. That is all." He rose from his seat and began marching past the others seated around the table.

"You're sending me to Florida?" said Mason, dumbfounded.

Diaz leaned in. "That's Saint Petersburg, *Russia.*"

"What?!" Mason barked back.

"Your Eminence, please," said Grim as he stood. "I realize the situation is unorthodox, but he is far better off here than halfway around the world."

Strauss stopped at the door. "I disagree, Captain Grimshaw. And as Overseer of this chapter, this is a decision well within my purview to make."

"Sir, if you would just—"

"The matter is closed, captain," said Strauss, not even bothering to slow down.

Grim stood silent and defeated. "Then it seems I have no choice . . ."

The Bishop reached the door.

"I invoke Imperatu Supersede."

Strauss halted, as if the words had locked his limbs in place, and returned to the conference room. Totally silent, Strauss stood face to face with Grim. If looks could kill, Grim would have dropped dead on the spot.

"I believe," Grim said, not altering his gaze, "the charter of Militia Dei still includes this amendment, yes?"

"A dogmatic proviso if ever there was one."

"And thus one I imagine Your Eminence will appreciate."

Sarah spun around in her chair, away from the two men standing by the door next to her, eyes wide with shock, and mouthed, *Ohhh SHIT!*

Strauss puffed up with a long inhale, his stare hard and unbroken. For a moment Mason thought he was going to shout right in Grim's face. From the unusual way he fumed—without turning red in the face, without a vein bulging in the forehead, without even a blink —he almost wished that he had.

"Very well," said Strauss. He turned heel and left without another word.

Mason felt like offering a round of applause, but as everyone else merely regarded their captain in stunned silence, he guessed this would have been inappropriate. Grim made his way back to where he had been sitting, gathered up the file.

"I don't know what just happened," said Mason. "But thank you."

Grim adjusted his glasses and looked at him. "You don't need to thank me, Mason. I would have done the same for anyone under this roof. We're a team."

Mason looked at the faces around him and knew it was true. Like Rose's collection of figurines that had been broken and glued back together, for better, worse, and everything in between, he belonged here with them.

"If there's nothing else, we've got a full day ahead of us." Grim shifted his gaze to Rodriguez. "And you have a flight to catch, don't you, lieutenant?"

"A flight?" said Mason.

"Yeah," said Rodriguez. "Got a case in Phoenix for a couple weeks, maybe more. Which reminds me, I left a little something for you in your room, since I probably won't be around for the thirtieth."

"What's the thirtieth? Oh," said Mason, feeling silly. "Well, that's very nice of you. You didn't have to do that."

"No big deal." And with a rub off his shaved head, she continued toward the door, spinning around for a minute to add something else. "Don't let this cabrón push you around, huh?"

Mason looked behind him and saw that she was pointing to Miggs, who passed by, saying something to her in Spanish Mason didn't quite catch.

Father Coffey had just walked up to the altar when a sudden need arose in Mason.

"Excuse me, Father?" he said quietly.

Coffey spun around, surprised, capping the lid of his flask and swallowing the sip he had taken from it. "Yes, lad?"

"I was wondering if I might have a word with you?"

"But of course. What's on yer mind?"

"Well . . . I was actually hoping we might . . ." He looked to the confessional.

"Step into my office?"

"Exactly."

Coffey smiled. "Right this way."

Mason followed him to the finely carved booth to the left of the altar. Coffey stepped into the center compartment as Mason entered the latticed opening to the right of it.

Coffins are less cramped.

"There's . . . nowhere for me to sit."

"That's because yer meant te kneel."

"Oh." Mason dropped his knees to the floor, barely able to see through the prayer window.

Father Coffey looked at him awkwardly for a moment. "Actually, yer supposed t'kneel on that li'l step just there."

Mason looked down and saw where he was pointing. He brought his knees up onto the step. "That's rather uncomfortable."

"That's rather the point," said Coffey, his face crisscrossed with the pattern woven into the little window. "First we make the Sign of the Cross." He touched the four points, as did Mason. "Tell me yer sins, my son."

"Oh wait, I know this one. Forgive me, Father, for I have sinned. Right?" The words felt strange on his tongue. Foreign. He fidgeted with the cross he wore around his neck, sliding it back and forth on the thin little chain. "I . . . have never confessed before."

"There's a first time for everythin'."

"I'm not even sure if what I have to tell you is a sin, but on the other hand, how could it not be?"

"I'm listening," said Father Coffey intently.

"When I was first given this gift, it was not one I wanted to receive, because it was not my choice. But the second time, it was. I was free of the burden—the miracle and the sin, as you put it. And yet I chose it again."

"And ye feel this is somehow a transgression?"

"I chose it not because I wanted to do good. I mean, I do want to do good, of course. But in truth, I have little interest in being a savior or a hero. I just don't want to be a *nobody*. I chose it because it felt good. To be powerful instead of powerless. And because I met a devil. *The* Devil, as far as I'm concerned. He had red hair and cruel eyes. Told me things, said he could heal someone I cared about . . . someone I loved . . . if I agreed to aid him. And I did. I agreed. Not just to do what he asked . . . but with the things he said. About us. How savage we are. Made me question who the real monsters are. And in doing so, I fear some of his wickedness has imprinted onto me."

"Go on."

"I condemned her soul. Julie, my . . . friend. Intentionally or not, her fate is on me. So I took it upon myself to end it. It was difficult, took some . . . regrettable methods, but I did it. I keep thinking, was that me? Did I really do that? Or was it this thing inside me? And when I killed her, I thought I would feel terrible. But I didn't . . . I was glad."

The words poured out uncontrollably now, like blood spilling deep from a fresh cut. Hot and messy.

"Glad she wouldn't have to suffer such an existence, but also glad to be rid of her. Just like my grandmother. I loved my grandmother, I really did. But if it weren't for her, I *know* that I would never have left Stonehill. I would never have wished for what happened to her. Never. But regardless of how it happened, I'm relieved. Relieved that . . ."

He sat there in stunned silence at his own words.

"Oh god. I don't even know what I'm saying anymore."

"The path te righteousness is not always a straight one," said Father Coffey. "I dare say it seldom is. It does not make ye wicked nor a sinner te have conflicted feelings."

"Then what *does* it make me?"

"Human."

"I just want to know that she's safe. My friend. That she's not in pain and will go somewhere good. She deserves no less."

"Then keep the faith, my son. Pray fer her. Pray harder than ye ever have in yer life. And hope the Heavenly Father sees fit te cleanse and redeem her soul. Three Hail Marys and four Our Fathers."

"That's all?"

A moment of silence as Coffey thought. "Make it five Our Fathers."

"Does that really work?"

"It will certainly help te learn yer prayers. And as an act of penance, I implore ye te go forth and be the very thing ye fear te be. Do good. Right wrongs. Smite evil. Entrust yer fate into the hands of the Lord and let Him lead ye. For no matter how crooked the path, He knows the way. Make certain the choices ye've made, whatever the reason, are not in vain."

"Yes, Father."

"I absolve you in the name of the Father, the Saint, and the Holy

Spirit. Amen." Father Coffey made the sign of the cross, tapping his fingers to a different part at each of the four points. "By the way, do ye know what 'amen' means?"

"I . . ." Mason's mouth hung open. "No. I don't."

"It's a Hebrew word for 'so be it.' An affirmation that the words attached to it be the truth."

"In that case . . ." said Mason, clutching the cross around his neck. "Amen."

He returned to the chapterhouse, opting to walk outside rather than plod through the dank little tunnel between it and the church. He had seen enough underground darkness recently and wanted to feel the crisp winter air. It didn't chill or sadden him; it invigorated him as he happily breathed in lungfuls of it, watching every outward breath dance in front of him, feeling each crunch of snow underfoot.

If asked not so long ago, Mason would have said that he would rather have a mind opened by wonder than one closed by belief. But, in a twist of fate he never could have predicted, he found himself somewhere between the two. A mind opened by belief.

He was committed now. That much was certain. He had had an experience. A revelation. An awakening. And he couldn't go back to sleep now.

"Okay, God. I'm listening."

You're going to regret this, he thought. *You know that, right? This will not be easy. It will be hard and grueling. You're going to be sorry you ever even considered this path you're about to walk. You're going to want to give up and turn back and run as fast as you can. You're going to be afraid. And you know what? Good! Accept it, and get out there and do something about it. Because you're not the Jerusalem Boy anymore. You're a soldier now. Quitting is not an option.*

Not until the job is done.

FIFTY-FIVE

Upon returning to his room, Mason found Bossy curled up on his bed next to a small package—a simple packing envelope lined with bubble wrap on the inside. The return address was from Durham, UK. A piece of cream-colored card stock folded in two had been placed over the shipping address with tape. From the feel, shape, size, and weight he easily deduced that what lay within was a book.

And sure enough it was.

He tore it open and found a copy of *Hamlet* inside. Not just any edition—the same he'd owned and lost somewhere between Gus's Gas & Garage and the Boston chapterhouse of the Holy Order of Militia Dei. For a moment he thought that it was the very same copy, but it did not have the same boxing to the corners, the smear of print along the edges of each page from being thumbed through time and again, or the stamp on the inner cover that said PROPERTY OF MASON COLE. This one was new and crisp, as if it had been printed yesterday. He flipped through its pages, breathing in the familiar smell of paper and ink, varnish and adhesive, and with it a rush of endorphins.

How did she do that? he wondered. She had never seen it, and there was no way she could have known. Unless . . .

Of course. He had been lamenting its loss that night in St. Augustine's after Irish's funeral. Which meant she had felt the weight of everything he had lost, just as he had felt hers. She had looked into his mind, just as he had looked into hers. And she had gone to the effort of finding this exact same edition.

He took the card off of the front of the envelope and flipped it open.

Lost and found.
—Gabriella

That was all it said, and all it needed to say.

Warmed to his core by such an incredible gift, he slid it into its rightful place between *As You Like It* and *Twelfth Night*, and felt whole again.

Heavy combat boots came clomping down the hall toward his door.

"Yo," said Sarah, poking her head around the corner. "C'mon, let's do this thing."

Mason searched his brain. "What thing?"

"The purge. To get Rose's spirit out of you."

"Oh. Right."

"And bring the feline." Sarah pointed a bony finger at Bossy.

"What for?"

"I don't have time to explain every little thing today." A spike of exasperation in her voice. "Just bring her."

Mason scooped Bossy up and carried her to Sarah's room down the hall, where he already could see the flickering glow of candles. Dozens had been lit and placed around the room, giving it the dim ambiance of a murky lake. Igor basked in the red light of his heat lamp nearby, causing Bossy to stretch her head forward, twitching her nose at him curiously.

Sarah sat down on the floor. Mason followed.

"All right, so the good news is that Rose is already here and with you. That's usually the hard part. The bad news is that she's holding on pretty tight."

"Is that normal?" Mason asked as he held Bossy in his lap.

"Can be, if a spirit feels they have unfinished business. So here's what's gonna happen." She reached out for Bossy. After a moment's hesitation, Mason handed her over. "I'm going to channel her into me while you convince her to cross over."

"Okay," said Mason, waiting for her to say more. "How do I do that?"

"You'll have to talk to her. Find out what she wants."

"Alrighty then," he said, uncertain of how to do that other than to ask. *Maybe that's all it will take.*

"Ready, Eddie?"

Mason nodded. "As I'll ever be."

Sarah closed her eyes. *In the name of the Goddess, our Mother.* She spoke with her inner voice, loud and clear enough that Mason could hear it. *By the powers of the earth, by all that is and was and will be, I call to thee, Rose, daughter of . . .*

"What was Rose's mother's name?"

"Um . . ."

"You don't know?"

"Hold on . . . started with an E." *Edith? Esther? Edna? Eglantine?*

"Evelyn!" he said. "It was Evelyn."

Rose, daughter of Evelyn. Come unto me.

A few moments passed. The candles fluttered, even though there was no draft. Sarah drew in a perforated breath. And when she opened her eyes, they were no longer Sarah's mismatched blue and hazel, but Rose's long-lost green.

"Hiya, sugar." Sarah's voice, Sarah's face, Sarah's body, but from the tiny trace of Georgia softening her Rs, the way she looked at him, the way she held and rubbed Bossy under the chin, he knew it was her.

"Hi, Rose." He gave her the saddest smile you ever did see. "How about some eggs and grits?"

She smiled. "Coming right up."

The poor excuse for a smile faded from his face as tears appeared. "I'm so sorry."

"For what?"

For every time he could have gone in for a hug and didn't. For secretly being angry with her whenever she would avoid talking about plans for his future though he understood why. For letting each silence fester into resentment. For . . .

"This. For everything."

"Listen to me, Mason. You didn't do anything wrong. Ya hear? Not a damn thing. I always knew you were special. I'm so proud of you. You're going to be just fine."

He hadn't enough tears for hearing this from her one last time. "You'll cross over then?"

She clutched Bossy close to her chest. "I can't."

"Why not?"

"He won't let me."

"Who?" said Mason. "Who won't let you?"

"The one with the red eyes. Eyes that burn. That twist. That scream with the pain of a thousand tortured souls . . ." She stopped speaking suddenly. A shadow moved across her face before Bossy scrambled out of her lap. "He's here."

The last word had barely escaped her lips before they were wrenched apart in a voiceless howl. Face overtaken by untold rapture, eyes fluttering faster than a racing heart.

And then, as suddenly as it began, it ended. Her head hung limp.

"Rose?"

He had time to take in a single harrowed breath before she spoke.

"*Rose . . .*" another voice slithered out between her teeth, "*is with us now.*"

When she looked up, her face had turned dark with gray skin and rotten teeth. The reek of sulfur and wet sickness. Eyes polar negatives, whites turned to black, irises red, pupils points of a harsh burning light he could feel on his face. A droning sound emanated from the intensity of her gaze like the sound of bees buzzing in a distant hive. It was not her voice anymore but something deep and ugly, like the mouth of Hell itself and with a heat to match.

The droning filled his ears. In the points of fire that were her stare, he saw various horrifying scenarios in tiny but hellish clarity. Rose, cycling over and over from decrepitly old to as young as an infant, being used in all manner of violent perversions. When it was done, her body reddened and crushed from the sheer force of it all, scores of other foul souls took their turn. One after the other. Two at a time. Three at a time. Four. Five. Six! Defilement without end.

"*And that's just the beginning,*" she growled with a lick of worm-ridden lips, many voices speaking as one now. "*Once her soul is sufficiently twisted by the unique pain only we can inflict, she'll be our minion. Our pet. Help us hunt down and corrupt other lost souls to add to our collection. Just say the word and you'll be free . . . and she'll be ours.*"

"No!" Mason pulled the cross from his neck, lunged, and decked her in the face with it as hard as he could. He fell upon her, pressed it to her forehead. A shrieking wail let out from the triad of mouths beneath, faces twisted in the throes of agony in the presence of holy light.

"I cast you out! Do you hear me?" Mason commanded, a tenor to his voice he had never known before. "You will not take her! You will not harm her!"

Papers blew around the room. Glass rattled. The flames of each candle sputtered, clinging to their wicks. The demon's whole face gaped so wide he thought it might split.

"I . . . cast . . . you . . . OUT!"

And as suddenly as it had begun, it ended.

A calm settled in the room, aside from the menagerie of reptiles stirring in their tanks. No sign of Bossy. Papers fluttered slowly in zig-zag patterns as they landed. Smoke billowed from the snuffed candles. The wailing thing beneath had returned to one he recognized. Eyes returned to normal as she panted desperately for air.

"That was either the bravest . . . or the stupidest thing I've ever seen," said Sarah, trying to catch her breath.

"I guess we'll find out." His gaze moved over her, studied her, looking for signs of anyone else lingering in her face. "Is Earl gone?"

"Oh, that . . . wasn't Earl," said Sarah. "That was something much . . . much older."

Not someone. Some*thing*. "Well . . . fuck! That didn't go as planned."

"No monkey-loving shit, it didn't."

Mason rubbed his knuckles, wondering what to do now. "Sorry I hit you."

"No sweat," she said, rubbing her jaw. "I like it rough." Her gaze then flattened and her mouth pinched shut. "But not that rough." With a flail of bony arms and a streak of green hair, Sarah clambered to her feet and into the bathroom, slamming the door behind her, followed by the distinctive wretch of vomiting.

Bossy had just appeared from under the bed, no more than a nose and half an eye below the seam of the blanket above her. Mason went to pat her on the head. She hissed and ran out of the room.

Somewhere between sanity and delirium, he stood and went to the window. Looking through it. Beyond it. In the polished glass appeared a face next to his. Rose's face. Only this time it wasn't on the other side of the glass, but rather in the empty space behind him. Her dead eyes locked with his.

It's okay, he thought. *It's going to be fine. I am not alone. We are not alone.*

And he believed that. But with the cold touch of her hand on his shoulder, deep in his core where it mattered most, he wasn't so sure.

AFTERWORD AND ACKNOWLEDGMENTS

This book almost didn't happen.

For one thing it took a long time to write. Years, actually which is longer than some say it should take to write anything worth reading. (not that I care one whit about such things, just acknowledging that such schools of thought exist).

My confidence was shaken not just once but multiple times all throughout. In the story, in my approach, in my decisions, in myself as a writer, in myself as a person.

There were no shortage of very real obstacles in the very real world; many of which so serious that more than once I truly did lose hope. I suffered losses during the writing of this book; personally, professionally, familially, romantically, mentally, emotionally and more ways that cannot be easily categorized nor divulged in detail here. I lost a little piece of myself during. And at times it was quite honestly all I had keeping me going.

If one cared to see through this particular lens, you could say that it seemed God was working equally hard to obstruct me. Like poor Job. To dishearten me to such a point that he make sure this story never saw the light of day.

So I was faced with a choice—give up and discard it, or do it anyway and consequences be damned. Since you hold proof of my choice in your hands, I can tell you that in the end the reason was a simple one: I don't give up.

I worked and bled and sweated and fought and cried and paid for every word of it. I thought about it every single day and whittled away at it between the cracks of my daily routine. It was a struggle, but I did it. And if I had to name just one, that would very much be the core moral of the story. Perseverance. So you see, no matter what I could not simply let this go. It was not up to me. It was, in and of itself, an exercise in the very thing it stood for.

And you know what? I'd do it all again.

I also gained a lot. The little piece I lost is gone for good, but I found something else in the process. Something stranger. Purposeful. Deviously sanguine. A way to mold misfortune into meaning. There is and continues to be a light at the other end of the tunnel. It's not always an easy path, but I believe that it is worth it. I have to. Where that leads and what is waiting for me there, well, that still remains to be seen.

I have kept the faith, I have fought the good fight...and I will continue to.

Thanks especially to my friends and family.

To my father for always encouraging me to follow my heart, even when it leads down a dark little corridor like this one. To Tyler, my best friend, my brother and partner in crime, who listens to everything I have to say with a smile on his face and a free-range chicken ready to fook. To Elizabeth for being an unparalleled superhuman paragon of love, kindness, and generosity the likes of which is far too rare in this world. Could you *be* anymore amazing? To Paul and Mari for each having hearts bigger than my own, letting me rant and rave from whatever ledge I frequently found myself on, and then talking me down from it. To Chloe for providing translation and telling me that I was already a writer when I didn't see myself as one. Merci beaucoup, mon ami! Maintenant et toujours. To Katilin for being one of my earliest editors and the type of lovely, twisted nut who will laugh with me at things we really shouldn't. To Ken and Dan whose individual influences off the page very much inspired things on them. To Fazal, Rob, Mike, Aunt Becky, and Gloria for being the first ones to buy a copy. And of course to my friends Suzanne and Mugsy, my cat Pearl, and my grandmother Carol. I miss you all.

Thanks to my editor Spencer Hamilton for riding this roller-coaster with me. To Jay Alexander for welcoming me into the Blood Rites family and giving this book a home. To Kirk Shannon and Kealan Burke for making true works of art out of my coffee-stained napkin scribblings. To Annalise de Palma for taking time away from the timberwolves of Kananaskis to help make my ugly mug look good.

To my Tabby, you've been my writer's caddy, number one *fayunnnn*, co-host of the Haus, and this book means what it does to me because of you. Thank you!

And last but certainly not least, to you, dear reader. May our paths cross again. Remember, for true horror one need only look to reality.

-MH-

November 8, 2020 (and again: April 24, 2022)

ABOUT THE AUTHOR

 Marcus Hawke primarily writes horror and dark fiction, some fantasy and sci-fi, and a few things that defy categorization. He was born in Toronto and moved around quite a bit during the dreaded formative years before finally settling in Calgary where he studied at the Alberta College of Art and Design. He lives with his feline overlord in an apartment building haunted by the type of neighbors that make a person wish a ghost would come to visit.

Visit www.marcushawke.com for more.

facebook.com/MarcusHawkeAuthor

twitter.com/hawkehaus

instagram.com/marcushawke

Made in the USA
Coppell, TX
04 September 2022

82521693R00265